ASIANS AND PACIFIC ISLANDERS

ASIANS AND PACIFIC ISLANDERS IN THE UNITED STATES

Herbert R. Barringer

Robert W. Gardner

Michael J. Levin

for the
National Committee for Research
on the 1980 Census

RUSSELL SAGE FOUNDATION / NEW YORK

Library of Congress Cataloging-in-Publication Data

Barringer, Herbert R.
    Asians and Pacific Islanders in the United States / Herbert R.
Barringer, Robert W. Gardner, Michael J. Levin.
      p. cm.—(The Population of the United States in the 1980s)
    Includes bibliographical references and index.
    ISBN 0-87154-095-9
    1. Asian Americans. 2. Oceanian Americans. I. Gardner, Robert
W. II. Levin, Michael J., 1947– . III. Title. IV. Series.
E184.06B37 1993
973'.0495—dc20   92-4867
                                                     CIP

RUSSELL SAGE FOUNDATION
112 East 64th Street, New York, New York 10021

10 9 8 7 6 5 4 3 2 1

88432

Preface

This volume is one of a series of monographs commissioned by the Social Science Research Council's National Committee for Research on the 1980 Census, and also supported by the Russell Sage Foundation and the Alfred P. Sloan Foundation.

The subjects of this monograph, Asian Americans and Pacific Islander Americans, are distinct and quite different entities. Consequently, they are treated completely separately. Chapters 2 through 8 are about Asian Americans; Chapter 9 deals with Pacific Islanders.

Each of the chapters in this book can be read independently, but we recommend that Chapter 2 be read first, since it deals with the history of Asian immigration and sets the stage for much of what follows. Chapters 2, 3, 4, and 5 give basic demographic and social profiles of Asian Americans. Chapters 6, 7, and 8 hang together, all treating the subject of socioeconomic conditions.

For purposes of correspondence, we should point out that Chapters 2, 3, and 4 were the primary responsibility of Robert Gardner. Michael Levin produced Chapter 9, while Chapters 5, 6, 7, and 8 were the obligation of Herbert Barringer. Because we read and criticized each other's drafts, we assume joint responsibility for the volume as a whole. Nevertheless, for further clarification or information, please contact the relevant author.

Acknowledgments

In any project like this, it is difficult to know where to start in acknowledging support, patience, and hard work. We should start by thanking the Social Science Research Council's National Committee for Research on the 1980 Census and the Russell Sage Foundation and the Alfred P. Sloan Foundation for financial support. Lisa Nachtigall, director of Publications, has been most patient and helpful.

The initial suggestion that this volume become a part of the SSRC–Russell Sage Ethnicity Monograph Series from the 1980 Census was from William Wetzel of the Census Bureau, who got in touch with Charles Westoff of the National Committee. Westoff in turn contacted Lee-Jay Cho, director of the East-West Population Institute. That institute, by the way, gave generously of time, money, and administrative support for the project. The Center for Korean Studies, University of Hawaii, provided funds for computer time.

We are especially grateful to Professor William Liu, former director of the Pacific/Asian American Mental Health Research Center, for a copy of the specially prepared Public Use Samples (PUMS) "A" data tape on Asian Americans. Marie Pees and Diana Smith, Population Division, Bureau of the Census, assisted Michael Levin in providing special tabulations on Asian Americans and Pacific Islanders.

Dr. William H. Sewell provided us with invaluable suggestions as our good shepherd, and Professor Charles Westoff, director of Princeton University's Office of Population Research, showed unfailing patience in overseeing the project. Among others, Won-Moo Hurh, David Takeuchi, Kiyoshi Ikeda, Hagen Koo and Alvin Y. So have read manuscripts and provided a wealth of good advice. Of course, they are not responsible for what became of it.

Shanta Danaraj acted as principal research assistant throughout the long course of this project. She set up computer files, conducted much of the computer analysis, and generally kept things together. At various stages, Macrina Abenoja, Quang Liu, Gerald Plett, Ruth Sahara, Shawn

Uesugi, and Su-Yong Yi in Hawaii and Emily Lennon in Washington helped immensely with research assistance.

Finally, colleagues at the East-West Population Institute, including Fred Arnold, James Fawcett, and Peter Xenos, contributed much thoughtful advice.

Some parts of this manuscript have in one form or another appeared in the following publications:

Robert W. Gardner, Bryant Robey, and Peter C. Smith, "Asian Americans: Growth, Change and Diversity," *Bulletin of the Population Reference Bureau* 40:4 (October 1985).

Herbert Barringer and Gene Kassebaum, "Asian Indians in the United States," *Sociological Perspectives* (January 1990).

Herbert R. Barringer, David T. Takeuchi, and Peter Xenos, "Education, Occupational Prestige and Income of Asian Americans," *Sociology of Education* 63 (January 1990).

Herbert R. Barringer and Sung-Nam Cho, *Koreans in the United States: A Fact Book, Papers,* Center for Korean Studies, University of Hawaii, #15 (December 1989).

Finally, we wish to apologize for the late appearance of this volume. For the most part, we plead circumstances beyond our control.

Contents

List of Tables

List of Figures

1

INTRODUCTION

The superior man goes through his life without any one precon-
ceived course of action or any taboo. He merely decides for the moment
what is the right thing to do.

—K'ung, Fu tze

The Aphorisms
Translated by Lin, Yutang

F LEXIBILITY was a trait greatly admired by the ancient Chinese. Few
Asian Americans read Confucius these days, and many have no
reason to do so. Nevertheless, their many modes of adaptation to
American society might very well have pleased the great teacher. Asian
Americans come from extremely diverse societies, and from all social
classes. They are to be found in America in all walks of life, as doctors,
teachers, businessmen, and laborers. Correctly or not, they have ac-
quired the image of highly successful immigrants—the "model minorities." Whatever one may think of that cliché, it must be admitted that
it is a far cry from the "yellow peril" of not so many years ago.

The United States has looked traditionally to Europe for its roots,
most especially to England. It has developed, through racial suppression
and intolerance, an image of a "white" America. But gradually it is becoming clear to even the most insulated that America is a multiracial
society, with non-whites outnumbering Caucasians in many metropo-
lises, and perhaps, eventually, throughout the land. Immigration to the
United States has shifted radically since the immigration reform acts of
1965, from Europe to Central and South America and Asia. Asian Americans and Pacific Islanders numbered only 7,273,662 persons in 1990 (2.9
percent of the total American population), but these figures represent
more than a 100 percent increase of the 3.5 million counted in 1980.[1]

[1] Asian Indians and Koreans increased by 125 percent; Vietnamese, by 134 percent.

Moreover, their influence is felt far beyond their numbers. In this volume we hope to bring understanding to the remarkable adaptation of people of Asian and Pacific ancestry to American society, and also to give some idea of its costs and limitations. Before we can begin this undertaking, however, we must examine what is meant by "Asian Americans," or "Asian and Pacific Islander Americans."

Who Are the Asian Americans?

It is easier to define "Asia" than it is to define "Asian Americans." For our purposes, Asia begins with Pakistan on the west and includes all countries lying east of Pakistan, including the countries of South Asia, Southeast Asia, and East Asia, but not including Mongolia or the Soviet Union. An Asian American, then, is someone living in the United States having some sort of "roots" in Asia. Included are immigrants, native-born Americans of Asian descent, students, refugees, and other citizens of foreign countries residing in the United States on Census Day. Excluded are visitors, businessmen, and others temporarily visiting the United States (1980 Census of the Population. PC80-1-C13, p. c2).[2]

Practically or theoretically, it makes little sense to lump together Americans of Asian origin, much less those of Asian and Pacific origin. Peoples from the various societies of Melanesia, Polynesia, South Asia, Southeast Asia, and East Asia have no more in common than those from Africa, Northern Europe, or Central America. Yet social scientists often refer to "Asian Americans" as if they were a single entity. Furthermore, the Census Bureau treats "Asian and Pacific Islander Americans" as a single category for some purposes.[3] No doubt this is because of the traditional orientation of the United States toward the West, particularly Europe, and to the relatively recent immigration of Asian and Pacific Island peoples to the United States.

In any case, we have chosen to examine each of the larger Asian American groups separately in each substantive chapter, and to relegate the Pacific Islanders to a chapter of their own. We believe that questions addressed to misleading categories, such as "How do Asian Americans adapt to the United States?," will inevitably result in misleading answers.

---

[2]However, "permanent" businessmen, such as factory managers and the like, are included in the count.

[3]Even Asian Americans often feel obliged to refer to themselves as a single category, either to counter misinformation or to respond to minority programs, which usually lump all Asian Americans together. There is also some interest in political organization, which some feel can be best realized in larger numbers.

Quite apart from the question of national origin, the identification of various Asian ethnic groups within the United States can be difficult because of U.S. Census conventions and definitions. In this volume, we focus primarily upon Asian groups listed separately on the "race"[4] item of the 1980 Decennial Census. The Asian groups included Japanese, Chinese, Filipino, Korean, Asian Indian, and Vietnamese. Asian Indians and Vietnamese appeared for the first time in 1980. Koreans appeared for the first time in sufficient numbers for analysis in that year.[5]

The number of Asian categories provided for on the census form and tabulated by the Census Bureau has changed over the years. Thus, in 1970, published data on Asian Americans were restricted to Chinese, Filipinos, Japanese, and Koreans. In earlier years, there were fewer categories. Asian Indians in 1970 were included in the "white" category, while Southeast Asians were placed in the "other" group.

Asian Americans in 1980 numbered about 3½ million, concentrated in 6 major groups: Chinese (812,000), Filipino (782,000), Japanese (716,000), Asian Indian (387,000), Korean (357,000), and Vietnamese (245,000). Twenty-two smaller Asian groups were reported in 1980, the largest of these being Laotian (47,700), Thai (45,300), Cambodian (Kampuchean) (16,000), and Pakistani (15,800). Table 1.1 compares figures for 1980, upon which our analyses are based, with those for 1990.

Race, Ancestry, Language, and Birthplace

The census provides information pertaining to ethnicity other than race. Table 1.2 shows race, ancestry, language, and birthplace responses for selected groups. The Census Bureau tabulated the data on the basis of correspondence to the race responses. For example, Japanese was the only acceptable language for a matching to the Japanese race response. The code allows correspondence with several Indian languages—Sanskrit, Hindi, Bengali, Panjabi, Marathi, Gujarthi, Bihari, and so on.

Ancestry and race items differ from other sociodemographic queries because responses may be more subjective or "incorrect" as compared to questions about age and income. Although we cannot determine the accuracy of a reported ancestry or race, we can study those factors which

---

[4]The Census Bureau's use of the term "race" stems from a question on the long form (⅙ sample) that asks respondents, "Is this person ———?" This is followed by a list of names of ethnic groups, or by writing in another response identifiable as Asian. The procedure does not allow for mixed-race responses. This of course has no necessary relation to biological race, and might better be termed "ethnicity."

[5]Two other Asian groups—Laotians (47,683 persons) and Thais (45,279 persons)—had more than 45,000 responses in 1980, but they are not analyzed here. They and other groups will be in larger numbers in the 1990 Dicennial Census.

TABLE 1.1

Race and Origin for the United States: 1980 and 1990

Race and Origin	1980 Census		1990 Census		Percent Change 1980–1990
	Number	Percent	Number	Percent	
All Persons	226,545,805	100.0	248,709,873	100.0	9.8
Asian or Pacific Islanders	3,500,439	1.5	7,273,662	2.9	107.8
Japanese	700,974	0.3	847,562	0.3	20.9
Chinese	806,040	0.4	1,645,472	0.7	104.1
Korean	354,593	0.2	798,849	0.3	125.3
Filipino	774,652	0.3	1,406,770	0.6	81.6
Asian Indian	361,531	0.2	815,447	0.3	125.6
Vietnamese	261,729	0.1	614,547	0.2	134.8
Hawaiian	166,814	0.1	211,014	0.1	26.5
Samoan	41,948	0.0	62,964	0.0	50.1
Guamanian	32,158	0.0	49,345	0.0	53.4
Other	*	*	821,692	0.3	*
Hispanic origin	14,608,673	6.4	22,354,059	9.0	53.0
Black	26,495,025	11.7	29,986,060	12.1	13.2
White	188,371,622	83.1	199,686,070	80.3	6.0

SOURCE: U.S. Department of Commerce *News*, CB91-125, 12 June, 1991, Table 1.
* N/A.

relate to the choice of an ancestry. We can look at race, language, and own birthplace from the 1980 Census. (From the 1979 Current Population Survey researchers were able to examine birthplace, mother's birthplace, father's birthplace, mother tongue, and current language, with interesting results [Levin and Farley 1982]).

The Census Bureau collected language data continuously over the last century. Birthplace data also have remained consistent over time except when political boundaries changed or countries reformed into other entities because of war or independence movements. Both race and ancestry responses have other problems.

Race, for example, reflects self-identification by respondents in the census, and does not denote any clear-cut scientific definition of biological stock.[6] Also, for persons who could not provide a single response to the race question in 1980, the Census Bureau used the race of that person's mother. If respondents did not provide a single response for the person's mother, the bureau used the *first* race the person reported. This is a change from the practice in 1970, when the person's father's race was used.

[6]There exists no such thing as a clear-cut scientific definition of biological race with which more than one scientist agrees.

4

The bureau directly tabulated the six groups listed in Table 1.2 which appeared on the questionnaire. Staff also coded Thais, Laotians, and other write-in entries. Finally, the bureau classified persons who did not place themselves in one of the designated categories by a specific set of rules. For example, Nipponese and Japanese Americans were classified as Japanese, and entries of Taiwanese, Cantonese, or Hong Kongese as Chinese.

In 1980, respondents were asked the direct ethnic question, "What is———'s ancestry?" Hence, respondents were self-identified. Some individuals in the census reported a single ancestry group; others reported more than one group. Staff coded all single- and double-ancestry responses, and seventeen frequently reported triple-origin ancestries. The bureau coded only the first two reported ancestries for all other responses of three or more ancestries. Persons reporting multiple ancestries appeared in more than one group, so the sum of the ancestries reported was more than the total population. The bureau tabulated persons reporting "Chinese-Hawaiian," for example, in both the Chinese and Hawaiian categories. None of the 17 triple responses included an Asian or Pacific Islander group. A person reporting "Chinese-Filipino-Hawaiian" would appear only in the Chinese and Filipino categories.[7]

Ancestry refers to a person's nationality group, lineage, or the country in which the person's parents or ancestors were born. Thus, persons are classified by ancestry group regardless of the number of generations removed from their countries of origin. This means that we cannot distinguish recent immigrants from even fourth- or fifth-generation Asian Americans.[8] Responses to the ancestry question reflect only the groups with which people identify, not the strengths of their identifications.

The "Total" row in Table 1.2 includes all Asian-coded responses. We excluded Pacific Islander responses unless they appeared as part of a multiple response along with an Asian ancestry. The lack of a complete total resulted from the creation of separate files for Asians and Pacific Islanders from the complete sample-detailed file. We could not combine the two files for tabulation since households with Asian–Pacific Islander marriages would appear twice.

Altogether, 3,482,178 persons reported an Asian race compared to 3,627,759 persons reporting one or more Asian ancestry responses, a difference of 4.2 percent. Persons who responded with multiple race re-

---

[7]It would appear that the "race" and "ancestry" items differ mostly in the way responses were coded. Race can have only one response; ancestry can have two or (perhaps) three. Both are really self-identification items, and either might better be called "ethnicity."

[8]Nor can we distinguish true immigrants to the United States from seasonal workers, such as those from Mexico, or from workers in foreign firms located in the United States. Managers of Japanese firms are almost always rotated back to Japan, but they will appear in our analyses as "Japanese" or "Japanese Americans."

TABLE 1.2

Asian.Population by Race, Ancestry, Birthplace, and Language: 1980

Identifier	Total	Ethnicity					
		Japanese	Chinese	Filipino	Korean	Asian Indian	Vietnamese
Race	3,482,178	716,331	812,178	781,894	357,393	387,223	245,025
Ancestry	3,687,759	791,275	894,453	795,255	376,676	311,786	215,184
Race or ancestry	3,966,125	847,402	973,387	907,134	403,180	438,513	263,046
Race and ancestry	3,143,812	660,204	733,244	670,015	330,889	260,496	197,163
Single ancestry	3,126,164	666,839	757,243	630,188	343,705	280,253	201,319
Multiple ancestry	501,117	124,436	137,210	165,067	32,971	31,533	11,165
Non-Asian	429,224	97,950	94,461	137,918	25,427	27,236	7,534
Language	2,397,735	336,318	630,806	474,150	266,280	243,402	194,588
Birthplace	2,254,783	221,794	369,459	501,440	289,885	206,087	231,120

SOURCE: Unpublished tabulations, U.S. Bureau of the Census.

sponses would have lost the second and subsequent entries in coding and tabulation. Also, persons responding with multiple ancestries would have lost the third and subsequent responses. The larger number of ancestry responses, then, reflect in part the additional responses allowed in the coding for the ancestry item.

An Asian response appeared in both the race and ancestry categories in 3,143,812 cases (90.3 percent of all Asian race responses and 86.7 percent of all Asian ancestry responses). There were 3,966,125 cases of an Asian response in either the race or ancestry categories (but not necessarily both), equaling 113.9 percent of the Asian race response and 109.3 percent of the Asian ancestry responses. The data showed essential consistency for the race and ancestry responses for the Asian groups overall.

Each of the selected groups also showed about the same consistency. For example, for Chinese, the largest group by race and ancestry, the ancestry responses were 110.1 percent of the race responses, 122.0 percent of the combined race and ancestry responses, and 91.9 percent of the race or ancestry responses.

Table 1.2 also shows the correspondence of birthplace and language with race and ancestry. Lieberson and Santi (1983) assessed the use of nativity data to estimate ethnic characteristics and patterns for selected groups. For our data, in every case except birthplace, the numbers reporting corresponding language and birthplace were smaller than those reporting correspondence between race and ancestry. It is likely that the Vietnam by birthplace total was larger than Vietnam by ancestry total because persons of other races, notably Chinese, were born in Vietnam but were not identified as Vietnamese by ancestry.

A relationship appeared to exist between speakers of a language and persons born in the corresponding place according to periods of peak migration. Some groups, such as Japanese, who had peak periods of migration to the United States in the earlier decades of this century, showed a smaller proportion of persons born in the corresponding area and speaking the language of the area. On the other hand, groups like the Vietnamese had large proportions speaking the language and having been born in the corresponding language area. By the same token, Japanese were older as a group than the Vietnamese.[9]

In summary, numbers of Asians and Pacific Islanders, whether defined by race or ancestry, were similar. Language and birthplace showed more variation than race and ancestry because of selection by age and by recency of peak immigration to the United States.

[9]The proportion of recent immigrants is in fact least among Japanese, and greatest among Vietnamese. Other groups contain mostly immigrants as opposed to native-born Americans, but this varies considerably among groups.

Subsequent chapters of this text will use the census "race" definition for the larger Asian American groups, namely, Japanese, Chinese, Filipinos, Koreans, Asian Indians, and Vietnamese. Of course, some of the differences discussed above will be obscured, but at this point the reader will understand that continued analysis with the complex interrelationships of different census definitions of ethnicity would produce ungainly and overly complex explanations. We shall, instead, proceed with other variables, such as recency of immigration, which should lead us to about the same understandings. It is unfortunate that small numbers preclude examination of smaller ethnic groups, such as Laotians, Thais, Pakistanis, and others. Likewise, census data do not allow examination of some important distinctions *within* groups, such as the Taiwanese, People's Republic of China, and Hong Kong contingents of Chinese.

The Research Problems

Between the decennial censuses of 1970 and 1980, the United States population as a whole grew about 11 percent. By way of contrast, the Asian American population grew 141 percent during that same period. This unprecedented growth of a theretofore minuscule part of the American population caught many social scientists by surprise. It also caught the fancy, and has held the attention of, the mass media (examples include Lindsey 1982, McBee 1984, Doerner 1985, and Bell 1985; images are widely reported in Asian sources as well, e.g., *Newsweek*, Asia/Pacific Edition, 1987).

The unprecedented growth of Asian Americans, as described in Chapter 2, was mostly due to changes in U. S. immigration law, enacted in 1965, and to the flood of refugees from Vietnam, Laos, and Cambodia following the fall of South Vietnam in 1975. Asians in very small numbers entered the United States as early as the late eighteenth century. During the late nineteenth and early twentieth centuries, fair numbers of Chinese, Japanese, Korean, and then Filipino farm laborers were brought to California and Hawaii, so a very small Asian American minority was visible. The experiences of these early immigrants are summarized well in Cheng and Bonacich (1984). Briefly, the early Asian Americans were mostly farm laborers, and were from pre-industrial, rural backgrounds. Most had no preparation for English language or other aspects of American society. Many suffered fierce discrimination, notably the Chinese in the gold-rush period of the West, and later, the Japanese in 1941. Although the experiences of each Asian group varied somewhat, their adaptation to American society appeared somewhat tenuous, especially considering the experience of Japanese Americans in the early days of World War II.

Some studies seemed to show that Asian Americans achieved reasonable socioeconomic status during the decade between 1960 and 1970, but there was little consensus concerning their status *vis-à-vis* white Americans (see Chapter 8). Furthermore, the continuing lack of improvement in the status of resident black, Hispanic, and American Indian minorities gave rise to fundamental questions about the relationship of minorities to dominant white American society. The optimism of Civil Rights movements in the 1960s gave way to a pessimistic, structuralist, and often neo-Marxist view of minority relations in the United States, including many students of Asian Americans.

In the meantime, the newer influx of Asian immigrants between 1970 and 1980 gave rise to questions about the changing demographic and socioeconomic conditions of the newcomers and their impact upon Asian minorities already resident in the United States. In the face of a continuing deterioration of the situations of blacks and Hispanics, Asian Americans began to appear to the popular media, and to some social scientists, as "success" stories. As discussed subsequently, many Asian Americans protested this image, for various reasons.

The census data for 1980 provided us with rich data for further examination of the situation of various Asian American groups. Vietnamese and Asian Indians appeared in the census tables for the first time, and sufficient numbers of Koreans allowed us to expand the range of Asian Americans studied. Also, nearly all the newer influx of Asian immigrants had entered the United States after 1970, so the 1980 data allowed us to examine these newcomers for the first time, and to study their impact upon the existent Asian American groups.

This study is, simply, about how some of the larger Asian American ethnic groups are faring in American society. Or, to put it in the terms of Morrison Wong (1980, 1982), how they are "making it" in America. In the present study, Asian American groups are compared on a number of demographic and socioeconomic dimensions with white, black, and Hispanic Americans. Many previous studies of such phenomena have concentrated on either demography (which seems inexorably intertwined with census data in many minds), or upon social-status attainment alone. We believe that it is a serious mistake to divorce demographic and socioeconomic analyses. Quite often, seemingly perplexing sociostructural phenomena are at least partially explained by demographic underpinnings. For example, as we shall show, Koreans appear to fare less well than Chinese or Filipinos on some socioeconomic measures. A very large part of the explanation for this rests with demographic characteristics of Korean Americans: more recent immigrants, a younger population, and a significant gender imbalance (Barringer and Cho 1990). The same logic of course applies to comparisons of Asian groups with white Americans.

The present study may be properly called a "census study," since we rely heavily upon data from the U.S. Census Bureau. However, we have drawn upon many other data sources and studies of minorities in the United States. Our analyses focus upon the 1980 Census data, but we have employed comparisons with earlier censuses when applicable. We have also included some recent data from the 1989 and 1990 editions of the Current Population Survey, though these samples are not broken down into specific Asian groups.

Theoretical Considerations

The question posed above, how the various groups of Asian Americans are adapting to the United States, is of considerable value in its own right. The answer has profound implications for Asian Americans, obviously, but also for U.S. government policies and, most important, for America itself. After all, the United States has been built historically by successive waves of immigrants, of whom Asians are the most recent. Given these questions, we do not pretend that this is primarily a "theoretical" study; but we cannot begin to face the issue of Asian Americans without encountering the social-scientific theoretical questions associated with adaptation of immigrants to a host society. We believe that this volume has important implications for some ongoing debates.

Assimilation

During the late nineteenth and early twentieth centuries, observers of American society coined the phrase "melting pot," to describe the phenomenon of adaptation and apparent assimilation of successive waves of European immigrants to the United States (blacks, Hispanics, and Asians were usually ignored). In the 1930s, Robert E. Park (1950) and his colleagues at the University of Chicago formulated a specific assimilation theory, in which immigrants were thought to become increasingly assimilated in irreversible stages, the last of which was "amalgamation," or racial mixing. Various modifications and criticisms of Park (see, for example, Lind 1967) led to a rather complex modification by Milton

Gordon (1964), which remains the classic statement of assimilation in American sociology. The assimilation viewpoint initiated considerable research on Asian Americans, reviewed in Chapters 6, 7, and 8. We wish to point out here only that most of the research on Asian Americans has questioned some or all of the assumptions of assimilation theory.

On the other hand, certain aspects of assimilation cannot be ignored. As immigrant groups remain in the United States, they usually do take on some of the demographic characteristics of the host society such as age, gender, and health, as well as acculturation and structural assimilation (i.e., language and occupations). They may also take on other characteristics of the host society, such as single householding or divorce.

In our view, the question of assimilation is one of *relative* assimilation. It is not necessary to assume (and certainly not to advocate) complete homogenization with the host society in order to ask the research question of how much and what kinds of assimilation are taking place, or if they are taking place at all. Nor is it necessary to assume that assimilation takes place by some Horatio-Alger-like acquisition of the culture of individualism and free enterprise.

In any case, each of the succeeding chapters either explicitly or implicitly addresses the assimilation question by the very nature of our method: we systematically compare various Asian and Pacific Islander groups with whites, blacks and Hispanics. At the same time, we wish to make clear that this is *not* primarily an assimilation study. Among other reasons, census data are not especially good for that purpose.

Structural Pluralism

The failure of the Civil Rights movement to go much beyond legal discrimination, combined with the apparent ineffectiveness of "The Great Society" in dealing with racial inequality, led to a reexamination of the melting pot ideal, both among some American minority members and among some social scientists. Writers such as Lieberson (1980), Steinberg (1981), and Cheng and Bonacich (1984) turned to structural explanations for continued inequality and nonassimilation of American minorities. In the case of Asian Americans, Cheng and Bonacich argued that structural inequalities in the international system led to the importation of Asian labor to the American economic periphery, continuing ethnic inequality.

Furthermore, structuralists pointed out that one of the supposed routes to social mobility by immigrants, education, was not used by first-generation Europeans in the nineteenth century, nor by Asians in the early twentieth century. Rather, by entering economic "niches" in the host society, immigrants gained economic security first, and then used education for their childrens' mobility. The failure of educational institutions to accommodate to the needs of racial minorities has been one of the chief criticisms of the structuralists (see Chapter 6).

The structuralist position emphasizes exploitation and continued segregation of ethnic and racial minorities, hence ethnic pluralism, rather than assimilation. Consequently, we are in the position of looking for evidence of such inequality, either in terms of geographical segregation, fertility, and mortality, or in household and socioeconomic characteristics. Census data do not provide direct evidence of exploitation nor of unequal treatment, but our comparisons with whites, blacks, and Hispanics will give much room for thought.

There has been a tendency for assimilation and structural theorists in the social sciences to caricature each other's positions much in the same way as Chinese once used sacrificial straw dogs. We shall avoid the horns of that controversy and simply try to bring to light evidence to support or contradict either position. On the face of it, both assimilation and pluralism do appear to exist side by side in America. Our question is, how do Asian Americans fit?

The "Model Minority" Controversy

Although this is not a theoretical issue in the strict sense, there is a corollary to the assimilation-pluralism debate which has appeared consistently on literature concerning Asian Americans. Harry Kitano (1976), after reviewing the existing research on Asian Americans (mostly Japanese Americans, in fact), noted the high levels of education, professional occupations, and high incomes attained by Asians in the United States. These accomplishments were accompanied by relatively stable families and comparatively low rates of crime and deviance. Such evidence led Kitano to coin the phrase "model minorities" in reference to their successful adaptation to American life, by American standards. About the same time, other researchers and the popular press began to trumpet the "success" aspect of Asian immigrants to the United States (see Chapters 6, 7, and 8 for a review of this literature).

There was an immediate reaction to this, mostly from Asian Americans themselves. Bob Suzuki (1977) and Kim and Hurh (1983), among others, attacked the success image, pointing out that controlled comparisons of Asian Americans and whites demonstrated relative disadvantages of Asian Americans. The President's Commission on Civil Rights (1978), using census data, demonstrated the advantages of whites with such controlled comparisons. Nevertheless, the popular image of the "model minority" continued to stir controversy.

Some of the reasons for dissatisfaction with the "success" image of Asian Americans do not lend themselves to argument on the basis of evidence. There is an emotional component to this debate which we understand our data cannot resolve. Nevertheless, we urge readers to note the theme of heterogeneity that will emerge over and over in the following chapters. It is clear to us that variations within and between each of the Asian American ethnic groups preclude any easy generalizations about the "success" of Asian Americans.[10]

Genetics

Social scientists are quite unified in skepticism about claims of genetic determinism applied to such matters as education, income attainment, and household composition. However, the case is not so clear-cut when we examine such factors as mortality, health, and, perhaps, fecundity. Consequently, Chapter 3 does address the issue in reviewing studies, but without any conclusions (except for mortality). Given the genetic diversity of Asian Americans and other complications raised in Chapters 2 and 3, we see no particular reason to pursue the subject. Again, the heterogeneity of Asian Americans precludes any easy generalizations, even if genetic links were established with demographic factors. It also should go without saying that relevant genetic factors have no simple correspondence with popular conceptions of "race."[11]

Data and Methods

Most of the data used in this volume are from the 1980 U.S. Census. Other sources were used concerning, for example, mortality and health. In such cases, of course, data sources are cited.

No data source that we know of is completely free from defects, and that includes U.S. Census figures. The principal concern most scholars express regarding census data regards the enumeration itself: the error introduced in producing a list of household addresses for the population

---

[10]Since none of the present writers are of Asian descent, there are some aspects to the debate about which we may not be qualified to comment.

[11]We bring this up only because of the pervasive racial consciousness in some segments of American society. We doubt if the question would even be raised if we were looking at European immigrants.

in the first place, and then securing cooperation from the public in completing questionnaires. There has always been some concern that minorities are especially underrepresented, including Asian Americans (E. Y. Yu 1982a). Furthermore, any survey, including the census, may contain misinformation through carelessness, ignorance, or deliberate falsification in responses. We acknowledge all these problems, and have attempted to signal the reader about data which may be less than completely valid.

When all this is said, however, the U.S. Census remains the only national survey with large enough numbers of smaller minority groups to allow the kind of analysis we undertake here. Some kinds of data collected yearly by the National Opinion Research Center of the University of Chicago are better, but sample numbers are far too small for any serious study of Asian Americans. Sometimes community surveys, many of whom we cite, contain far richer data on particular subjects than does the census. But in all cases we know of, sampling problems[12] produce biases which appear more serious than those of the census. Furthermore, the United States conducts a census every 10 years, so data are available for many purposes over time.

The Census Bureau uses two questionnaires. The first, a "short form," consists of a small number of enumeration questions required for a basic count of the population and households. Every sixth household receives a "long form," which includes many items on socioeconomic status and housing. Most of the data we use here are based upon that ⅙ sample (sometimes erroneously referred to as the "20 percent" sample) or from sub-samples of it. Note that one-sixth of the population is a *large* sample, so we can usually ignore concerns about sampling error with those materials.

Our data on Asian Americans from the 1980 Census came from two major sources: first, a set of crosstab tables from the ⅙ sample prepared especially for this project by one of the authors, Michael Levin;[13] second, a special tape from the 5 percent Public Use Sample (5 percent PUMS "A"). This tape was prepared from all households in the 5 percent sample with at least one Asian member. It was provided for our use by the Pacific/Asian American Health Research Center. The special tables are referred to in some of the text as the "ENS" (Early National

[12]Nearly all community surveys by necessity use household sampling based upon very incomplete lists of minority households. The incomplete lists are probably much less reliable than those used by the Census Bureau, simply because there are no complete lists of persons or households by ethnic group available in the United States. Household sampling always appears to introduce a middle-class bias, and snowball sampling brings with it a Pandora's box of unknown biases.

[13]Most of these tables are now available in a Census Publication: Bureau of the Census, *Asian and Pacific Islander Population of the United States: 1980.* PC80-2-1E.

Sample Tables). The tape is ordinarily cited in the text as the "5 percent PUMS 'A' Tape." Other data were taken from Bureau of the Census publications.

Our tape sources included data on whites, blacks and Hispanics drawn from the 1 percent Public Use Sample (A and B samples combined). Hispanics by census definition do not constitute a "race" and are tabulated differently. We drew our Hispanic samples in such a way that there was no overlap with Asian Americans (e.g., Koreans of Mexican origin will not appear as Hispanics if they designated themselves Koreans). The tape samples of whites, blacks and Hispanics are fairly small (5,000 each).

Please note that all data provided in Bureau of the Census tables and publications are reported out as population numbers (the ⅙ sample was readjusted to population values). However, when we report data from the Public Use Sample tapes, we *do not* readjust to population values. The numbers shown are sample, not population, figures.

In addition to other Bureau of the Census publications, we were provided with special tabulations of the 1989 Current Population Survey. These data were aggregated for Asians and Pacific Islanders combined, so we were unable to identify particular ethnic groups.

Chapters 5, 7, and 8 contain multiple-regression predictions of income and occupation. These were conducted with the PUMS tape data described above. Multiple Classification Analysis was used for regression because many of the predicting variables were categorical, and some could not reasonably be reduced to dummy variables. The prediction solutions for each of the nine ethnic groups were somewhat different. Those interaction effects which were statistically significant were small and were different for each equation, so the task of reporting them out became next to impossible. Consequently, they have been ignored.

The Plan of the Book

The following seven chapters are devoted to Asian Americans. Chapters 2, 3, and 4 are, broadly speaking, demographic, and Chapters 5, 6, 7, and 8 concentrate on socioeconomic factors. Chapter 9 is devoted exclusively to Pacific Islander Americans, including approximately the same subjects as the chapters preceding it. Specifically, contents of the chapters are as follows:

Chapter 2: Immigration, Size and Growth, Nativity, and Citizenship

This chapter contains a brief history of Asian immigration to the United States, followed by a detailed examination of recent immigration patterns of each of the major groups. The consequent size and growth of Asian American ethnic groups are examined, followed by a study of nativity and citizenship.

Chapter 3: Fertility, Mortality, and Age and Sex Composition

Material in this chapter is basic demography, including a detailed analysis of fertility, mortality, and age and sex composition of each Asian group. Included are comparisons with host societies as well as with other American groups.

Chapter 4: Geography: Residence and Migration

This chapter examines initial residence patterns of Asian immigrants, and subsequent geographical mobility. Of special interest here are patterns which might suggest differentiation and possible segregation from other groups in the society.

Chapter 5: Family and Households

Household and family composition are examined here, with special attention to marriage, divorce, and other patterns supposedly related to family stability. Household income, poverty, and housing quality are explored.

Chapter 6: Educational Attainment

Given the popular belief in Asian American emphasis on education, this chapter looks at educational levels of various groups, with special attention to nativity, gender, and length of residence. Accusations of blockages to Asian education are examined.

Chapter 7: Employment and Occupations

This chapter begins by reviewing employment, unemployment, and underemployment of Asian Americans, especially by gender, length of residence, and geographical location. This is followed by a study of occupational attainment, and determinants of occupation.

Chapter 8: Incomes: The Question of Parity

Chapter 8 continues the themes of Chapters 6 and 7, asking what effects education and occupation have on Asian personal and household incomes (among other determinants). Special attention is given to comparisons with whites, blacks and Hispanics.

Chapter 9: Pacific Islanders in the United States

This chapter recapitulates most of the preceding analyses of Asian Americans, but on Pacific Islanders. There is a review of who the Pacific Islanders are, where they originated, and their migration patterns. Their geographical distribution in the United States is examined, followed by a description of their demographic characteristics. Household and family, education, occupation, and incomes are also explored.

Some Common Threads

This volume has been long in inception. Prior to the actual manuscript preparation, the authors met many times to discuss research findings. In addition, drafts of various chapters have been in circulation among us for some time. Consequently, we have become acutely aware of certain themes that run through the book. They are essential to our approach, and we would like to sensitize the reader to them.

Heterogeneity

On every dimension we have studied, Asian Americans vary as much as or more than the total American population. This is true of their demographic characteristics, geographical distribution, migration history, and socioeconomic characteristics. Of course, they vary as individuals, but the characteristics of each of the major Asian ethnic groups are so different from each other, that it becomes impossible to make intelligent (or intelligible) generalizations about Asian Americans as a whole. Consequently, they are analyzed separately throughout the chapters. The same may be said about Pacific Islanders, and certainly we shall avoid the temptation to say anything about Asian *and* Pacific Islander Americans in the same breath.

Comparisons

Assertions about the various Asian American ethnic groups are vacuous without some specific comparative reference. Consequently, we have systematically compared them with white, black, and Hispanic Americans, the largest American ethnic groups. This leads to some exceedingly large and cumbersome tables. We beg the reader's (and editor's) indulgence in this. We do believe that this is the only way to proceed.

Other Differentiations

Asian Americans differ not only by ethnicity, but also by gender, age, social class, length of residence in the United States, and by nativity.[14] There are many differences between native-born Asian Americans and immigrants, but sometimes even greater differences exist between recent immigrants and longtime residents. Asian American women are not free from sexual discrimination, but even that varies from group to group.

We shall be returning to these themes in the final thoughts of this volume. With them in mind, we shall turn the reader over to Chapter 2, and the history of Asian immigration to the United States.

[14]Some confusion may occur with terminology concerning "native" Americans. When capitalized, "Native" Americans refers to American Indians. Without capitalization, "native" Americans refers to persons born in the United States, regardless of ethnicity.

IMMIGRATION, SIZE AND GROWTH, NATIVITY, AND CITIZENSHIP

Introduction

I N THIS chapter and the next we look at the demography of Asian Americans: the size of the population, the factors contributing to its growth (immigration, emigration, births, deaths), and some basic demographic characteristics (age and sex composition). Knowledge of these demographic factors is essential to a broader understanding of the socio-economic situation of Asian Americans today.

Immigration[1]

Of all the factors affecting the size, growth, composition, and distribution of the Asian American population over the years, immigration has undoubtedly been the most important. From the first unrecorded

[1]In the small space available here we cannot hope to do justice to the complex phenomenon that has been and is immigration from Asia. For the interested reader an extensive annotated bibliography is available that lists many works on immigration (Kim 1989). Especially interesting perspectives are provided by Cheng and Bonacich (1984) and Hune (1977).

trickles of Asians to these shores, to the sudden rush of Chinese to California in the middle of the nineteenth century, to the days of the Depression when more Asians left than arrived, to today, with large numbers of Asians arriving annually, immigration has dominated the demography of Asian Americans.

There have been significant impacts on the U.S. population and American society from recent high levels of immigration from Asia subsequent to the 1965 changes in immigration law. Between the censuses of 1970 and 1980, a decade in which the total U.S. population grew by only 11 percent, the Asian American population soared by 141 percent, and some Asian groups grew much faster. The corresponding figures for the 1980–1990 decade were 10 percent and 99 percent. This dramatic development, which took many people by surprise,[2] was the direct result of two factors: (1) changes in U.S. immigration law enacted in 1965 and fully operational by 1968, and (2) the influx of refugees from Vietnam, Laos, and Cambodia following the fall of Saigon in April 1975.

The past few years have seen much debate and many changes in immigration law, as we shall see below, but the changes seem not likely to affect Asian immigration substantially and will almost certainly not result in any diminution of immigration from Asia.

Before 1882, anyone from anywhere was free to move to this country, although there *were* laws affecting immigrants differentially. The Naturalization Act of 1790 provided for citizenship by naturalization for any free white person of good moral character who had resided in this country for at least 2 years. The Naturalization Act of 1870 extended this privilege to aliens of African birth and persons of African descent; nothing was said about allowing naturalization to individuals neither white nor black. In subsequent years, a number of Asians applied for naturalization and a few succeeded, only to have their citizenship later declared null. It was not until 1952 that the racial basis of exclusion from naturalization was removed from the books.[3]

---

[2]In 1964, in testimony before a House subcommittee, the Attorney General of the United States, Robert Kennedy, said, "I would say [the number of immigrants to be expected] for the Asia-Pacific triangle . . . would be approximately 5,000, Mr. Chairman, after which immigration from that source would virtually disappear; 5,000 immigrants could come in the first year, but we do not expect that there would be any great influx after that." Quoted in Glazer 1985, p. 7, from Reimers, David M., "Recent Immigration Policy—An Analysis," p. 35 in Barry R. Chiswick, ed., *The Gateway: U.S. Immigration Issues and Policies,* Washington, D.C.: American Enterprise Institute, 1982.

[3]Anyone *born* in this country has always automatically been a citizen, so the U.S.-born children of Asian immigrants were U.S. citizens. This did not mean, of course, that they were always provided the full protection of the Constitution and the laws of the land, as events during World War II made abundantly clear to native-born citizens of Japanese descent.

The earliest Asians to come to the territory of what was to become the United States were probably "Filipino sailors who jumped ship and fled into [a] cypress swamp" near "the Spanish provincial capital of New Orleans" in 1763 (Bartlett 1977, quoted in Espina 1988). The collection of United States immigration statistics began in 1820, and these statistics show 13,100 Chinese admitted in 1853, but only 198 Asians, including 88 Chinese, admitted before then.[4] The pre-1853 estimates are undoubtedly low, but it is certainly true that it was only after the discovery of gold in California in 1848 that the first great flow of Asians to the United States began. The combination of opportunities to make money on the one hand, and the need to escape civil unrest and a set of disasters and poor situations in China (a famine in Canton, a depression in southern China, and a flood on the Yellow River) on the other, resulted in large numbers of Chinese laborers migrating to the United States, mostly from the province of Guangdong in southern China.[5]

"The pull was the developing need for contract laborers in California, men to undertake the hard and menial work of a frontier region . . ." (Wilson and Hosokawa 1980, p. 102). "The bulk of Chinese immigrants . . . became a source of cheap labor to work the railroads, mines, fisheries, farms, orchards, canneries, garment industries, manufacturing of cigars, boots, etc." (Asian and Pacific American Federal Employees Council 1984, p. 1).

Chinese, mostly male laborers, dominated Asian immigration to this

---

[4]There is much doubt as to the reliability of immigration statistics throughout the nineteenth century and into the twentieth. For example, land border points of entry were first established on the Mexican and Canadian borders in 1904. No Japanese were recorded as arriving through Pacific ports from 1871 until 1882. Before 1906, all alien arrivals were counted as immigrants, even if only returning from a short stay abroad. In some years, cabin class passengers on arriving ships were not counted as immigrants; only steerage passengers were so counted (Historical Statistics, p. 98). Over the years, statistics changed from "country from which immigrant came" to "country of last permanent residence" to "country of birth." All in all, the record shown by immigration statistics is flawed in many ways. Nevertheless, it is just about all we have, and there is little doubt that the broad outlines of the history of immigration to the United States are portrayed adequately.

[5]We are limited by space considerations from presenting a more thorough discussion of many aspects of Asian immigration to the United States, including the issue of why Asians, as opposed to immigrants from Europe or Mexico, came to California in such numbers in the decades following 1850. A thorough examination of Asian immigration, based on an analysis of modes of production and the development of capitalism, is found in Cheng and Bonacich (1984). A chapter by Bonacich (1984) presents the following view of the source areas of Asian immigration: "In general, imperialist activity in Asia helps explain why this area became a major source of cheap labor in the western United States. This was not an isolated phenomenon. In the second half of the nineteenth century Asian labor was moving, or being moved, to many parts of the colonial world . . . Asian immigration to the United States and Hawaii was part of a more widespread trend" (pp. 160–161).

country for more than 3 decades (Figure 2.1, Table 2.1). Virtually no immigrants from elsewhere in Asia arrived at all. The Chinese laborers were valued by their employers (mainly mining, agriculture, and the railroads) for their industry and their willingness to accept low wages.[6]

The white labor force and small producers, however, were not so favorably inclined toward the immigration of Chinese. The immigrants were seen by such "anticapitalist" groups as docile tools of capital (Bonacich 1984). Anti-Chinese agitation and violence throughout the West resulted in pressure on Congress and the eventual passage of the Chinese Exclusion Act in 1882. This legislation excluded Chinese laborers (and later their wives, an important point) but not teachers, students, merchants, or tourists; the act also excluded foreign-born Chinese from naturalization.[7] Chinese immigration was never again substantial until recent decades.

With Chinese excluded, but with cheap labor still needed by the "dependent capitalist" sector of the economy, especially the plantations in Hawaii (which we include in this discussion, although Hawaii was not annexed by the United States until 1898),[8] the first significant immigration of Japanese began. A few Japanese had come to this country before 1880, but they made little impact. As with Chinese, Japanese immigrants were mostly males, laborers from areas of Japan where agriculture was suffering hard times (Wilson and Hosokawa 1980, p. 48). Like the Chinese, they did not come intending to stay in this country, but rather saw themselves as sojourners, here to achieve personal gain and then to return home.

Many of the Japanese immigrants worked in agriculture, because there was a large need for unskilled farm labor. But the Japanese immigrants were never content to remain as hired laborers or even to lease land, and they began to buy land which they farmed successfully, concentrating on crops requiring high inputs of labor and little input of cash (Knoll 1982, p. 61–62).

The reaction to the Japanese in the western United States was much the same as it had been decades earlier to the Chinese: agitation and

---

[6]Certain features of the U.S. and California economies made it imperative that the "dependent capitalist" sector in which most Chinese were employed be able to pay extremely low wages. Bonacich (1984) cites the ineligibility of Chinese (and later Asian) immigrants for U.S. citizenship as having "staggering" implications in terms of control over their selection, treatment, wages, and expulsion when undesirable (pp. 162–165).

[7]This was 4 years *before* the dedication of the Statue of Liberty in New York Harbor, lifting her lamp beside the golden door.

[8]See various chapters of Cheng and Bonacich (1984) for details about Asian immigration to Hawaii.

22

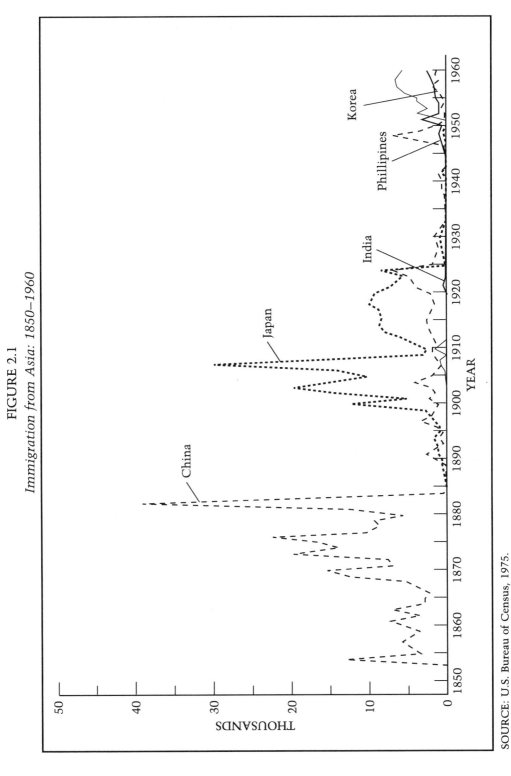

FIGURE 2.1

Immigration from Asia: 1850–1960

YEAR

THOUSANDS

SOURCE: U.S. Bureau of Census, 1975.

TABLE 2.1
Immigration to the United States from Asia: 1820–1990

Date[a]	Total U.S.	Total Asia[e]	China[b]	Taiwan	Hong Kong	Japan[c]	Philippines[f]	Korea	India[d]	Vietnam	Kampuchea	Laos	Thailand	Pakistan
					Country from Which Immigrant Came									
1820–1825	48,888	5	2	—	—	—	—	—	3	—	—	—	—	—
1826–1830	102,936	7	1	—	—	—	—	—	6	—	—	—	—	—
1831–1835	252,494	30	8	—	—	—	—	—	22	—	—	—	—	—
1836–1840	346,631	17	0	—	—	—	—	—	17	—	—	—	—	—
1841–1845	430,336	24	18	—	—	—	—	—	6	—	—	—	—	—
1846–1850	1,282,915	47	17	—	—	—	—	—	30	—	—	—	—	—
1851–1855	1,748,424	16,685	16,668	—	—	—	—	—	17	—	—	—	—	—
1856–1860	849,790	24,755	24,729	—	—	—	—	—	26	—	—	—	—	—
1861–1865	801,723	24,306	24,282	—	—	1	—	—	23	—	—	—	—	—
1866–1870	1,513,101	40,250	40,019	—	—	185	—	—	46	—	—	—	—	—
1871–1875	1,726,796	65,633	65,428	—	—	128	—	—	77	—	—	—	—	—
1876–1880	1,085,295	57,880	57,773	—	—	21	—	—	86	—	—	—	—	—
1881–1885	2,975,683	60,011	59,801	—	—	112	—	—	98	—	—	—	—	—
1886–1890	2,270,930	4,239	1,910	—	—	2,158	—	—	171	—	—	—	—	—
1891–1895	2,123,879[g]	10,656	5,017	—	—	5,597	—	—	42	—	—	—	—	—
1896–1900	1,563,685	30,153	9,782	—	—	20,345	—	—	26	—	—	—	—	—
1901–1905	3,833,076	77,554	12,792	—	—	64,102	—	—	660	—	—	—	—	—
					Country of Last Permanent Residence									
1906–1910	4,962,310	77,561	7,813	—	—	65,695	(3,554)[h]	—	4,053	—	—	—	—	—
1911–1915	4,459,831	48,209	10,492	—	—	36,457	(15,248)[h]	—	1,260	—	—	—	—	—
1916–1920	1,275,980	58,988	10,786	—	—	47,380	(14,441)[h]	—	822	—	—	—	—	—
1921–1925	2,638,913	53,633	22,330	—	—	29,927	(39,051)[h]	—	1,376	—	—	—	—	—
1926–1930	1,468,296	11,622	7,577	—	—	3,535	(38,873)[h]	—	510	—	—	—	—	—
1931–1935	220,209	4,206	2,464	—	—	1,428	(7,388)[h]	—	314	—	—	—	—	—
1936–1940	308,222	3,694	2,464	—	—	520	528	—	182	—	—	—	—	—
1941–1945	170,952	2,323	1,368	—	—	358	252	—	345	—	—	—	—	—
1946–1950	864,087	22,500	15,341	—	—	1,197	4,439	107	1,416	—	—	—	—	—
1951–1955	1,087,638	26,176	1,948	—	—	14,660	8,313	581	674	—	—	—	—	—
1956–1960	1,427,841	57,242	7,709	—	—	31,590	10,994	5,650	1,299	—	—	—	—	—
					Country of Birth									
1956	321,625	14,318	4,456	—	418	5,713	1,873	703	328	34	1	2	26	118
1957	326,867	19,128	5,432	—	546	6,554	1,996	648	355	27	0	2	41	110

TABLE 2.1 (continued)

Immigration to the United States from Asia: 1820–1990

Date[a]	Total U.S.	Total Asia[e]	China[b]	Taiwan	Hong Kong	Japan[c]	Philippines[f]	Korea	India[d]	Vietnam	Kampuchea	Laos	Thailand	Pakistan
1958	253,265	15,525	3,214	—	342	6,753	2,236	1,604	519	45	0	2	38	152
1959	260,686	19,214	5,718	—	844	6,159	2,633	1,720	513	51	2	1	76	172
1960	265,398	20,111	3,681	—	475	5,843	2,854	1,507	391	56	1	0	133	154
1956–1960	1,427,841	88,296	22,501	—	2,625	31,022	11,592	6,182	2,106	213	4	7	314	706
1961	271,344	17,790	3,213	—	625	4,684	2,738	1,534	421	83	4	2	126	142
1962	283,763	18,301	4,017	—	652	4,268	3,437	1,538	545	105	1	1	137	169
1963	306,260	20,823	4,658	—	712	4,390	3,618	2,580	1,173	140	4	4	137	193
1964	292,248	17,236	5,009	—	639	4,142	3,006	2,362	634	219	13	4	170	155
1965	296,697	16,062	4,057	—	712	3,858	3,130	2,165	582	226	9	9	214	187
1961–1965	1,450,312	90,212	20,954	—	3,340	21,342	15,929	10,179	3,355	773	31	20	784	846
1966	323,040	34,433	13,736	—	3,872	3,868	6,093	2,492	2,458	275	8	10	230	347
1967	361,972	51,755	19,741	—	5,355	4,315	10,865	3,956	4,642	490	8	8	409	646
1968	454,448	49,284	12,738	—	3,696	4,142	16,731	3,811	4,682	590	23	14	645	673
1969	358,579	63,209	15,440	—	5,453	4,478	20,744	6,045	5,963	983	27	15	1,250	851
1970	373,326	80,897	14,093	—	3,863	5,108	31,203	9,314	10,114	1,450	22	30	1,826	1,528
1966–1970	1,871,365	279,578	75,748	—	22,209	21,911	85,636	25,618	27,859	3,788	88	77	4,360	4,045
1971	370,478	89,690	14,417	—	3,204	5,326	28,471	14,297	14,310	2,038	21	24	2,915	2,125
1972	384,685	105,065	17,339	—	4,391	5,777	29,376	18,876	16,926	3,412	39	35	4,102	2,480
1973	400,063	108,795	17,297	—	4,359	5,676	30,799	22,930	13,124	4,569	66	46	4,941	2,525
1974	394,861	114,330	18,056	—	4,629	4,917	32,857	28,028	12,779	3,192	40	61	4,956	2,570
1975	386,194	116,521	18,536	—	4,891	4,293	31,751	28,362	15,773	3,039	98	96	4,217	2,620
1971–1975	1,936,281	534,401	86,645	—	21,474	25,989	153,254	112,493	72,912	15,250	264	262	21,131	12,320
1976	398,613	130,700	18,824	—	5,766	4,275	37,281	30,803	17,500	3,048	103	137	6,923	2,888
1976TQ[i]	103,676	31,991	5,034	—	1,493	1,142	9,738	6,887	4,572	1,182	23	26	1,173	748
1977	462,315	134,387	19,765	—	5,632	4,192	39,111	30,917	18,636	4,629	126	237	3,945	3,183
1978	601,442	226,118	21,331	—	5,158	4,028	37,216	29,288	20,772	88,543	3,677	4,369	3,574	3,876
1979	460,348	160,604	24,272	—	4,118	4,063	41,300	29,248	19,717	22,546	1,432	3,565	3,194	3,967
1980	530,639	206,244	27,651	—	3,860	4,225	42,316	32,316	22,607	43,483	2,801	13,970	4,115	4,265
1976–1980	2,557,033	890,044	116,877	—	26,027	21,925	206,962	159,463	103,804	163,431	8,162	22,304	22,924	18,927
1981	596,600	231,136	25,803	—	4,055	3,896	43,772	32,663	21,522	55,631	12,749	15,805	4,799	5,288
1982	594,131	282,009	27,100	9,884	4,971	3,903	45,102	31,724	21,738	72,553	13,438	36,528	5,568	4,536
1983	559,763	247,409	25,777	16,698	5,948	4,092	41,546	33,339	25,451	37,560	18,120	23,662	5,875	4,807
1984	543,903	222,693	23,363	12,478	5,465	4,043	42,768	33,043	24,964	37,236	11,856	12,279	4,885	5,509
1985	570,009	229,477	24,787	14,895	5,171	4,086	47,978	35,253	26,026	31,895	13,563	9,133	5,239	5,744

25

TABLE 2.1 (continued)

Immigration to the United States from Asia: 1820–1990

Date[a]	Total U.S.	Total Asia[e]	China[b]	Taiwan	Hong Kong	Japan[c]	Philippines[f]	Korea	India[d]	Vietnam	Kampuchea	Laos	Thailand	Pakistan
							Country of Birth							
1981–1985	2,864,406	1,212,724	126,830	53,955	25,610	20,020	221,166	166,021	119,701	234,875	69,726	97,137	26,366	25,884
1986	601,708	231,247	25,106	13,424	5,021	3,959	52,558	35,776	26,227	29,993	13,501	7,842	6,204	5,994
1987	601,516	222,894	25,841	11,931	4,706	4,174	50,060	35,849	27,803	24,231	12,460	6,828	6,733	6,319
1988	643,025	227,370	28,717	9,670	8,546	4,512	50,697	34,703	26,268	25,789	9,629	10,667	6,888	5,438
1989	1,090,924	264,629	32,272	13,974	9,740	4,849	57,034	34,222	31,175	37,739	6,076	12,524	9,332	8,000
1990	1,563,483	287,397	31,815	15,151	9,393	5,734	63,756	32,301	30,667	48,792	5,179	10,446	8,914	9,729
1986-1990	4,500,656	733,637	143,751	64,150	37,406	23,228	273,805	172,851	142,140	166,544	46,845	48,307	38,071	35,480

SOURCES: 1820–1960: U.S. Bureau of the Census, 1975, Series C89-119. 1956–1989: published and unpublished data from the Immigration and Naturalization Service.

NOTE: Refugees physically enter the United States long before they become eligible to change status from refugee to immigrant. It is only when they change status that the Immigration and Naturalization Service counts them as immigrants. Thus, although large numbers of refugees arrived from Vietnam in 1975, they only start appearing as immigrants in 1978. See Table 2.3 for data on actual arrivals from Vietnam, Laos, and Cambodia.

[a] 1820–1831, 1844–1849: year ending September 30. 1833–1842, 1851–1867: year ending December 31. 1869–1976: year ending June 30. 1977–present: year ending September 30. Other: 15 months ending December 31, 1832; 9 months ending December 31, 1843; 15 months ending December 31, 1850; 6 months ending June 30, 1868.

[b] Includes Taiwan beginning 1957, ending 1981.

[c] No record of immigration from Japan until 1867.

[d] Includes present-day Pakistan and Bangladesh until 1947.

[e] Includes only those countries listed through 1956–1960. Historical statistics of the United States include in "Asia" countries of Southwestern Asia, including Saudi Arabia, Jordan, etc. Our definition of Asia includes only those countries to the east of Afghanistan, i.e., Pakistan and east, not including the Soviet Union in Asia or Mongolia. The figures in this column are thus slight underestimates of the total Asian immigration, since some countries (but not the major sources) are missing. Beginning with the single-year data for 1956, Asia totals are for all countries included in our definition of Asia, not just those listed.

[f] From 1898 until 1934, the Philippines was a territory of the U.S., and thus Filipinos did not "immigrate" to the U.S., since they were already there. In 1934, the Philippines became a Commonwealth, and immigration officially could occur. There is thus no record of the number of Filipinos who came to the current Unites States before 1935. This column does contain some records for Hawaii before that date.

[g] Data for Asia not available separately for 1892.

[h] Figures for Filipinos arriving in Hawaii are from data from the Hawaii Sugar Planters Association, found in Nordyke, 1977, Table 12. Not included in totals for Asia.

[i] Transition Quarter July–September 1976.

discrimination.[9] In 1900 the Japanese government (which watched over its citizens in a way that the weak government in China never had), alarmed over the treatment of Japanese in the United States, ordered prefectural governors to stop issuing passports to the U.S. mainland. Passports to Hawaii were still issued, however, and since Hawaii was now a territory of the United States, Japanese immigrants simply landed in Hawaii first.

Increased pressures and many anti-Japanese incidents finally led to the Gentlemen's Agreement of 1907–1908, in which the Japanese government agreed to regulate the issuance of passports to laborers to the mainland United States and to Hawaii.[10] This did not end Japanese immigration in the same way that the Chinese Exclusion Act had virtually ended Chinese immigration, because under the agreement the wives and family members of Japanese already in the United States could continue to receive passports. The predominantly male Japanese community began to marry "picture brides"[11] who then immigrated; the result was not only continued Japanese immigration in large numbers, but the establishment of a much more viable Japanese American community, since substantial numbers of both sexes were now present. This was in contrast to the situation of the previous Chinese immigration, which was always dominated by males, precluding the establishment of an ongoing Chinese community.

Continued Japanese immigration, competition, and success resulted in the passage of alien land laws in many states, the first being California in 1913. These laws prohibited "aliens ineligible for citizenship" (i.e., all non-white, non-black aliens) from owning property or, eventu-

[9]Anticipating what follows in our discussion, we quote Bonacich (1984): "Each Asian group [Chinese, Japanese, Koreans, Indians, Filipinos] came to face hostile reactions of multiple kinds from the surrounding population, including riots, anti-Asian legislation, and ultimately, exclusion laws or efforts to prohibit further immigration. These came in sequence, with each group arriving and then facing mounting hostility and, finally, exclusion" (pp. 173–174).

[10]Since Korea was under Japanese rule at this time (Japan formally annexed Korea in 1910), the actions of the Japanese government applied to Koreans as well. Immigration statistics do not list any Koreans by country until 1948, but census tables by race show Koreans beginning to arrive in 1910, and list as many as 2000 arriving before 1950. It was not until the 1965 changes in immigration law that Koreans immigrated to the United States in substantial numbers.

[11]"[A] Japanese man residing in this country can marry a Japanese woman residing in Japan by personally affixing his seal to the document to be presented before the registrar in Japan." (Ichihashi 1932, p. 246, quoted in Wilson and Hosokawa 1980, p. 55). Marriages could thus be concluded in Japan, without the presence of the husband, and the new wives could immigrate to the United States. "No reliable figures are available on the number of picture-brides, but at most they were only a handful, nowhere close to the hordes portrayed by the anti-Orientalists . . . the total was roughly 5,000 [out of the] approximately 20,000 Japanese women [who] emigrated to the United States between the turn of the century and the end of the picture-bride era two decades later" (Wilson and Hosokawa 1980, p. 56).

ally, even leasing it. Japanese often found ways around these laws (e.g., buying land in the names of their U.S.–born citizen children).

In the United States, however, interest in immigrants and in immigration was not limited to or even focused on immigrants from Asia. In fact, the prime thrust of the major restrictive immigration legislation passed in the years 1917 through 1929, culminating in the National Origins Act, was to regulate the composition of European immigration, which was becoming decidedly too Southern and Eastern European for the tastes of many. Eventually (1929), quotas based on national origins were set up, limiting immigration in proportions equal to those of the 1920 U.S. population distribution by birth or descent (LeMay 1987, pp. 87, 91; Bernard 1982, pp. 97–98). North and West Europe could send about 83 percent of the total 150,000 allowable immigrants; South and East Europe, 15 percent; and the rest of the world, 2 percent. Asians did not share in the 2 percent, however, since another provision of the act barred from immigration all aliens ineligible for citizenship.

Thus, by the late 1920s immigration from almost all of Asia was effectively prohibited, except for small numbers of exempted wives of U.S. citizens, young students, ministers, and professors. For example, during 1921–1925, almost 30,000 Japanese immigrated; for 1926–1930 the figure was about 3,500, and for the next 5 years, barely more than 500. Total immigration from Asia, which had reached nearly 60,000 during 1916–1920, fell to lows of 3,700 in 1936–1940 and 2,300 in 1941–1945. *Net* immigration was actually negative in some periods (Table 2.2).[12]

One group of Asians, however, was not immediately affected by the National Origins Act: the Filipinos. The Philippines had been annexed by the United States at the turn of the century, and Filipinos were therefore U.S. nationals, able to enter the country without "immigrating," without restrictions, and without being counted. As Japanese filled the gap left by the exclusion of Chinese, so did Filipinos fill the gap left by the exclusion of Japanese. The Filipino population of the country rose rapidly, from just under 3,000 in 1910 to more than 26,000 in 1920 and almost 110,000 in 1930. As with their predecessors, a high proportion of the Filipino immigrants were males.

[12]Seldom mentioned in discussions of immigration is the fact that numerous individuals *emigrate* from the United States. Ordinarily the number of emigrants from the United States of a particular ethnic group are outnumbered by the corresponding immigrants, but this is not always the case. The United States does not currently keep records of emigration, but it did for the years 1908–1957, although data are spotty for the 1930s. In Table 2.2 we have summarized information from the annual reports of the Immigration and Naturalization Service on immigration, emigration, and net international migration for the five Asian ethnic groups for which we could find data. The data clearly show that emigration was substantial for some groups, especially Chinese, in some time periods, and that net emigration actually occurred. The data ordinarily presented on immigration alone obscure this fact.

TABLE 2.2

Asian Immigration, Emigration, and Net Migration,
by Race: 1908–1957

Period	Immigrant Aliens Admitted				
	Chinese	Indians	Japanese	Koreans	Filipinos
1908–1920	24,137	5,391	106,229	1,105	—
1921–1930	24,345	1,177	31,999	598	—
1931–1950	9,925	290	1,632	116	3,626
1951–1957	18,276	1,259	27,378	1,715	9,362
1908–1957	76,683	8,117	167,238	3,534	12,988
	Emigrant Aliens Departed				
1908–1920	32,420	1,658	30,232	857	—
1921–1930	40,376	1,098	20,178	379	—
1931–1950	12,338	1,589	5,617	208	10,000
1951–1957	3,411	3,659	4,552	428	4,282
1908–1957	88,545	8,004	60,579	1,872	14,282
	Net Immigration				
1908–1920	−8,283	3,733	75,997	248	—
1921–1930	16,031	79	11,821	219	—
1931–1950	−2,413	−1,299	−3,985	−92	−6,374
1951–1957	14,865	−2,400	22,826	1,287	5,080
1908–1957	11,862	113	106,659	1,662	−1,294

SOURCES: Annual Reports of the Immigration and Naturalization Service, especially 1926, 1931, and 1944.

NOTES: No data available for 1932–1938. Data for Filipinos begin in 1939.

According to the Historical Statistics volume (U.S. Bureau of The Census, 1975, p. 98), the reliability of net figures for immigration is impaired because while immigrants were admitted for permanent residence, they could depart prior to residence of one year, in which case they were counted as immigrants on arrival and nonemigrants on departure. Persons coming in temporarily, however, as nonimmigrants who left after one year would have been called emigrants on departure.

These figures are by race of individual and thus the immigration figures differ from those of Table 2.1, where the tabulation is by country of last permanent residence.

By now the story should be familiar: a Filipino "invasion" was feared, and restrictionists sought to have Filipinos excluded from entering the country. This would have violated the terms of annexation, however, so another approach was used. In 1934 the Tydings-McDuffie Act was passed, guaranteeing independence to the Philippines in 10 years. In the interim, the Philippines was given the status of commonwealth, which meant that immigration from there could be limited. And it was, to 50 a year. All Philippine-born Filipinos were declared aliens. Another panel of the golden door had swung shut, and by 1940 the Filipino population of the country was smaller than it had been 10 years earlier.

With the golden door shut, the size of the Asian American population of the United States stayed almost constant during the decade of the 1930s, and really only began to grow again after the end of World War II. In 1943 the Chinese Exclusion Act was repealed (by then, China and the United States were allies), but China was given only a token immigration quota of 105. Foreign-born Chinese were declared eligible for citizenship.

In the years following World War II, other barriers to Asian immigration and citizenship began to crumble, but it was not until 1952 that any really significant changes occurred. Before 1952, the number of immigrants from Asia had been increasing, but these were mostly special cases, such as war brides from Japan and China and former members of the U.S. armed forces.

In 1952 Congress passed, over President Truman's veto, a new Immigration and Naturalization Act (the "McCarran-Walter Act").[13] The act abolished the category of aliens ineligible for citizenship, meaning that every immigrant now had the right to apply for citizenship, including those who had resided in the United States for decades. Another provision of the act established quotas for Asian countries,[14] but the quotas were still laughably low: 185 for Japan, 105 for China, and 100 each for countries of the "Asia-Pacific Triangle."[15]

The 1952 act also established the principle of preference categories, with high priority given to skilled immigrants and to family reunification. A non-quota "exempt" classification allowed in without restrictions the immediate relatives of citizens. It was these family-oriented provisions that helped set the stage for the eventual great increases in the number of Asian immigrants. The immediate result of the act, however, as far as Asian immigration was concerned, was a gradual rise in

[13]Truman objected not only to the changes in the immigration provisions but also to the internal security measures contained in the act, which was enacted at the height of the "Red scare." Truman's veto message can be found in Herman 1974, pp. 110–114.

[14]Actually, the quotas for Asians were based on *race*, not country of origin, so that a Japanese born in Brazil would be counted against the Japanese quota. This was not the case for European countries, where place of birth was the criterion. Thus the act still contained elements of racial discrimination.

[15]First established in 1917, the "Asiatic Barred Zone" covered most of China, India, Indochina, parts of Afghanistan and Arabia, Burma, Siam (Thailand), the Malay States, Asiatic Russia, most of the Polynesian and all the East Indian Islands. In 1917, only laborers from these areas were excluded.

the number of immigrants to a level of around 20,000 per year for the years before 1965.[16]

The real change in the situation, however, occurred in 1965. The Hart-Cellar Act, which took full effect in 1968, finally abolished the quota system, which discriminated on the base of origin or race. In its place was established a limit to immigration of 290,000 per year (except for exempt immigrants: spouses, unmarried minor children, and parents of U.S. citizens), with a limit for each country of the Eastern Hemisphere of 20,000. Western Hemisphere countries were given no limits or preference system but operated on the first-come-first-served principle. (Later changes brought the system for the Western Hemisphere into line with that for the Eastern Hemisphere.) Family reunification was given higher priority than in the 1952 act.

With these changes, the door stood almost wide open for the first time since 1882.[17] Asian immigration rose rapidly, from 16,000 in 1965 to over 100,000 annually by 1972 to more than one-quarter million in 1989 (Figure 2.2). Prominent among the new arrivals were Filipinos, Chinese (from China, Taiwan, and Hong Kong), Asian Indians, Koreans, and Vietnamese (Figure 2.3). Japanese in large numbers were conspicuous by their absence; the lack of a "push" for migration from Japan, much more prosperous than other Asian countries, has meant that in recent years immigration from Japan has averaged only about 4,000, far fewer than the numbers from some other Asian countries.

Many of the early immigrants who came in under the new law utilized the occupational preferences, especially the third preference favoring professionals and scientists. The result was an immigration stream more highly qualified and trained than any other in our history. As these immigrants became established, they brought in members of their families under the family reunification categories. Since not all these more recent immigrants were so highly trained, the overall qualification level of recent Asian immigration has fallen slightly below that immediately following the passage of the new law. Even so, it remains true that the bulk of immigration from Asia today is composed of highly selected and trained individuals, representatives of the best their countries have to offer. As we note later in this volume, this has meant different patterns

---

[16]This figure is based on Asia defined as Pakistan and east, while the earlier figure for 1850–1955 uses Asia defined as the Immigration and Naturalization Service defines it, i.e., to include West and Southwest Asia, except Turkey in Asia. In this monograph we prefer the former usage, but for earlier periods only the latter is available.

[17]Of course, "wide open" is still a relative term. Numbers of immigrants from each country are still limited (except for the exempt category), and the preference category emphasis on family reunification and qualifications still means that only certain citizens of sending countries are eligible to emigrate to the United States. LeMay (1987) therefore calls it a "Dutch door," not an open door.

FIGURE 2.2

Immigration from Asia: 1960–1989

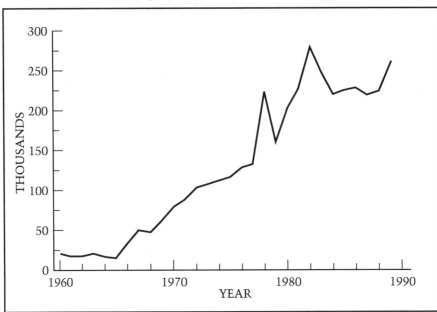

SOURCE: U.S.I.N.S. Annual Reports.

of adaptation, adjustment, and success than have been the case with any previous group of immigrants.

There is one group, however, that does not quite fit this mold—the refugee-immigrants from the countries of Vietnam, Cambodia (Kampuchea), and Laos. Since 1975 a large number of refugees from these countries have arrived in the United States. The pattern of arrival for these refugees has not been at all smooth, but numbers have been concentrated in just a few years, with a different sequence for each group (Table 2.3). Vietnamese first peaked in 1975, with 125,000 refugees arriving that year. These individuals were highly trained and well placed in their old society and thus represented something of an elite, much as did the early post-1965 immigrants of other Asian countries.

A second "wave" of Vietnamese refugees peaked in 1980, representing the flow of "boat people" fleeing the country by whatever means available to them. In contrast to the first wave, they brought with them relatively few possessions and little training. These refugees arrived almost entirely after the 1980 census, so that our 1980 data on Vietnam-

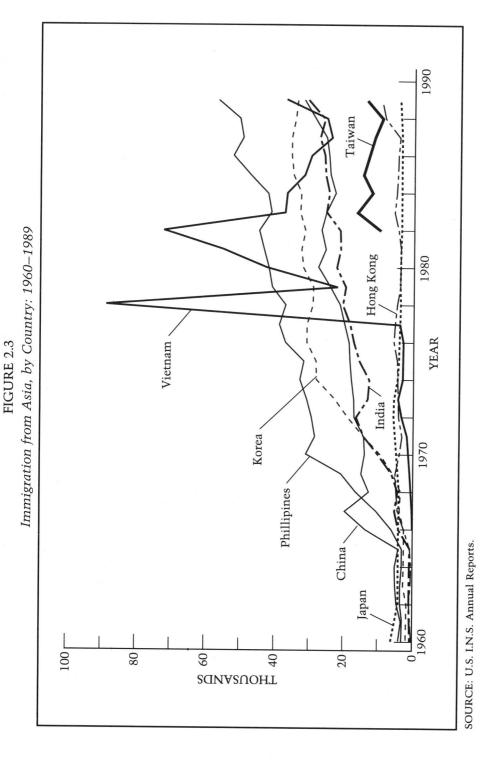

FIGURE 2.3

Immigration from Asia, by Country: 1960–1989

SOURCE: U.S. I.N.S. Annual Reports.

NOTE: Taiwan Included with China before 1982.

TABLE 2.3
Refugees and Immigrants from Southeast Asia: 1975–1990

Fiscal Year	Total Arrivals from				Refugees as Percentage of Total Arrivals from			
	Cambodia	Laos	Vietnam	Total	Cambodia	Laos	Vietnam	Total
1990	2,720	8,921	53,700	65,341	86.3	97.2	48.5	56.7
1989	2,450	13,017	37,116	52,583	86.1	98.2	58.9	69.9
1988	3,135	14,769	21,548	39,452	89.4	98.6	81.8	88.7
1987	1,981	15,691	25,400	43,072	89.4	98.8	87.5	91.7
1986	9,266	11,328	26,335	46,929	98.6	98.3	79.1	87.5
1985	19,300	5,400	30,100	54,900	99.2	97.3	84.5	91.0
1984	20,100	7,300	29,800	57,200	99.2	97.8	83.6	90.0
1983	13,300	3,000	25,800	42,100	99.1	96.4	89.2	92.8
1982	20,200	9,500	45,100	74,800	99.7	99.2	94.6	96.5
1981	27,200	19,300	87,800	134,300	99.7	99.8	98.0	98.6
1980	16,100	55,600	99,300	171,000	99.3	99.8	95.9	97.5
1979	6,200	30,300	50,900	87,400	97.4	99.6	87.5	92.4
1978	1,400	8,100	13,000	22,500	94.8	98.5	85.5	90.7
1977	400	600	6,500	7,500	70.4	62.8	29.1	34.2
1976[a]	1,200	10,400	7,400	19,000	89.7	98.4	43.1	76.2
1975	4,700	900	128,000	133,600	97.9	89.3	97.6	97.6
Total	149,700	214,100	687,800	1,051,700	98.1	98.9	86.0	90.4

SOURCES: 1975–1985: calculated from Gordon, 1987, Table 7.2. 1986–1990: U.S. Immigration and Naturalization Service annual yearbooks and unpublished data.

NOTES: 1975–1985: refugee arrival figures compiled from mostly unpublished records maintained by the State Department, the Immigration and Naturalization Service, the Office of Refugee Resettlement, and its predecessor, the Indochina Refugee Assistance Program. Figures for refugee arrivals in source table were rounded to nearest hundred, so percentages in this part of the table are not exact.

In this table, "arrivals" in any year are composed of refugee arrivals and new arrival immigrants; that is, arrivals are individuals physically arriving in this country. The usual INS data on "immigrants" for a given year include not only new arrival immigrants but also adjustments of status from refugee (or other nonimmigrant status) to immigrant (permanent resident alien) status. Such figures do *not* encompass nonimmigrant arrivals, which include refugees. In an attempt to capture the actual numbers physically entering the United States, this table estimates arrivals rather than immigrants. For 1975–1977 the figures include a (probably very small) number of adjustments from nonrefugee status.

[a] Includes Transition Quarter of July–September 1976.

ese presented a very selected picture of the Vietnamese currently in this country.

The greatest year for the arrival of refugees from Laos and Cambodia was 1980, when more than 55,000 and 27,000, respectively, arrived. By the end of fiscal year 1990, more than 586,000 Vietnamese refugees had arrived in the United States, following the 68,000 Vietnamese who had been admitted directly as immigrants in the previous 30 years. Refugees from Laos totaled about 309,000; only about 2,200 regular Laotian immigrants had entered the United States earlier. Cambodian refugees totaled about 146,000; only 2,300 immigrants from Cambodia had arrived earlier.

Legislation passed in the autumn of 1986 by Congress was aimed mainly at problems associated with illegal immigration. It has affected Asian immigration relatively little. Although there are some Asians in this country illegally (i.e., visa overstayers), their numbers or proportions are nowhere near those for some other groups, particularly those from Latin America.[18]

In 1986 Congress also passed legislation aimed at ending the practice of aliens marrying U.S. citizens solely to become citizens themselves. The new regulations established a waiting period of 2 years after the alien's admission to the United States before granting of permanent residency. If the marriage was not found to be fraudulent, then the process of becoming a permanent resident alien and eventually a citizen could proceed.[19]

In the autumn of 1990 Congress enacted numerous changes in immigration law affecting legal immigration. As a compromise between those who wished to retain family reunification as a central principle of immigration law and those who sought more emphasis on qualifications of immigrants, the new law retained essentially the same family preference system, but added provisions for substantially more "new seed" immigrants, those who would qualify for admission without having family already in the United States. A brief summary of the provisions of the new law is found in Figure 2.4.

It is unlikely that the new law will result in any diminution of immigration from Asia. The country limit is actually several thousand higher, so countries such as the Philippines, which have reached their quotas each year, may be able to send more immigrants. The category of immediate relatives (the exempt category) is basically unchanged. Asian

[18]In fiscal year 1990, Asians granted "amnesty" under the 1986 law included 8,849 Filipinos, 3,609 Mainland Chinese, 2,184 Pakistanis, 2,753 Koreans, 1,988 Asian Indians, 1,733 Thais, and 1,312 Taiwan Chinese (USINS 1990 Statistical Yearbook, p. 67).
[19]The two-year conditional status period will count toward the period of lawful permanent residence required under naturalization procedures (U.S. Senate 1986, p. 7).

FIGURE 2.4

Outline of the 1990 Immigration Act

Overall Limit: 700,000 (reduced to 675,000 beginning in FY 1995); *this does not include refugees* and can be "pierced" if the number of immediate relatives rises beyond 239,000.

Family-Based Immigrants (Immediate relatives and family-sponsored immigrants): limited to **480,000** per year (465,000 for FY 1992, 1993, and 1994).
    Exempt from numerical limitations: **Immediate Relatives** (spouses, unmarried children, and parents of U.S. citizens).

Three Classes of Numerically Limited Immigrants:
    Family-sponsored (alloted 245,000)
        Unmarried adult sons and daughters of citizens **(23,400)**

        Spouses and minor children of permanent resident aliens (minimum of about 87,900 visas); unmarried adult sons and daughters of permanent resident aliens (about 26,300) (total of **114,200**)

        Married sons and daughters of U.S. citizens **(23,400)**

        Brothers and sisters of adult U.S. citizens **(65,000)**

    Employment-based (140,000)
        Priority workers: persons of extraordinary ability: outstanding professors and researchers, certain multinational managers and executives, athletes, artists, scientists **(40,000)**

        Professionals (advanced degrees) and workers of exceptional ability **(40,000)**

        Skilled workers (2 years' experience), professionals (B.A. degree), and other workers (not-skilled limited to 10,000) **(40,000)**

        Certain special immigrants (U.S. government employees, former international organization workers, religious workers) **(10,000,** of which religious maximum is 5,000)

        Employment-creating immigrants (agreeing to invest in a new business with $1,000,000 in capital that will employ at least 10 people **(10,000)**

    Diversity (55,000 per year)
        Mostly from low-admission states in low-admission regions, some from low-admission states in high-admission regions. Restricted to high-school graduates or those with 2 years' work experience.

Source: Gardner, 1992.

countries will, however, generally not profit from the "diversity" category, since it is reserved primarily for immigrants from countries that have not sent numerous immigrants in recent years.

We have dealt so far mainly with the immigrant flows. We now turn to data on the resulting populations of Asian Americans in the United States over the years.

Size and Growth of the Asian American Population

Data on the size of the Asian American population at the national level are found almost exclusively in the decennial censuses, beginning with their first appearance in the census of 1860. Coverage of the different groups has not been consistent over the years. In particular, the censuses of 1950, 1960, and 1970 did not have quite the same detail on Asian Americans that earlier and later censuses did. Since the censuses were our only source of data on the numbers of Asian Americans, we were forced to live with the occasional gaps and inconsistencies. The numbers presented in Table 2.4 on total number of Asian Americans for census years before 1980 are thus simply the sum of the groups listed individually by the census; there was no easy way of knowing how many Asian Americans were not included, but the number of such omissions in any case had to be small.[20]

In 1860 the only Asian American group of any significance in the United States was the Chinese. Their numbers grew rapidly until 1880, after which the Chinese Exclusion Act cut off most immigration from China. The number of Chinese in the country diminished steadily until 1920 (except, of course, that the addition of Hawaii in 1897 added a large number of Chinese and Japanese to the total; to incorporate the change, we present figures for 1900 both with and without Hawaii and Alaska). There was some growth in the numbers of Chinese between 1920 and 1930, then essentially none until during and after World War II, when numbers began to rise again. Following the 1965 changes in the immigration laws, growth skyrocketed, and today there are well over 1.6 million Chinese Americans. The intercensal growth rate of 6.2 percent annually for Chinese between 1970 and 1980 was the highest recorded for this group during their entire history in this country, and yet it was exceeded by the 1980–1990 rate of 7.1 percent. Chinese have been the

---

[20]The Census Bureau does not always publish all the data it collects; furthermore, data on Asian Americans for early years are found scattered in different volumes, rather than in one volume, as has been done more recently.

largest of all Asian American groups enumerated in the past two censuses (1980 and 1990).

Japanese were the second group of Asian Americans to appear in the census, but their numbers outside Hawaii were smaller than those of the Chinese for many years. Between 1900 and 1910, however, the positions were reversed, and through 1970 Japanese were the largest group of Asian Americans and in fact represented over half of the total Asian American population from 1910 through 1960 (Table 2.5). Low recent rates of growth have meant that Japanese now stand third among Asian American groups for the first time ever and will likely surrender even that position soon.

The third group to arrive on the scene was the Filipinos, coming primarily to work on the plantations of Hawaii. The number of Filipinos grew rapidly at first, to more than 108,000 in 1930, then fluctuated as did the other groups until after 1965, when numbers rose rapidly. The 1970–1980 annual growth rate of 8.2 percent enabled Filipinos to move into second place among all Asian Americans in terms of numbers, a position they had held only once before, in 1930.

Until the 1965 law changed, other Asian American groups had been present only in small numbers in this country. A few thousand Asian Indians appeared in census reports from time to time, but Indian growth really began around 1970. Asian Indians in the United States are now the fourth largest group of Asian Americans.

Koreans were found in census reports in small numbers since 1910 (except 1960, when they were not tabulated separately). By 1970 there were almost 70,000, and since 1970 the growth of the Korean American population has been rapid. Koreans are now the fifth largest Asian American group and are growing more rapidly than Asian Indians.

A third group of recent arrivals was the Vietnamese, whose numbers began to rise only in the mid-1970s, after the fall of Saigon and the beginning of the refugee flows. Of the six large groups we focus on, the Vietnamese have shown the fastest recent (1980–1990) growth. Several other smaller, predominantly refugee, Indochinese groups (Laotians and especially Cambodians) have shown even faster growth rates.

Although Asian Americans have now been part of the American scene for more than 135 years, until recently their numbers have been quite small in relation to the total U.S. population. In 1860, Chinese made up barely one-tenth of 1 percent of the total population. By 1950 Asian Americans still accounted for less than one-half of one percent of the population. Rapid recent growth, however, in the presence of much slower growth of the total population, has led to an increase in the Asian American share of the total. By 1980 Asian Americans were over 1.5 percent of the total population, and by 1990 the figure was 2.8 percent.

TABLE 2.4A

Population of the United States, by Race, Each Census Year: 1850–1990

Date	United States[a]	White	Black	American Indian[b]	Total[c]	Asian American Chinese	Japanese	Filipino[d]	Korean	Asian Indian	Vietnamese	Other
6/1/1850	23,191,876	19,553,068	3,638,808	—	—	—	—	—	—	—	—	—
6/1/1860	31,443,321	26,922,537	4,441,830	44,021	34,933	34,933	—	—	—	—	—	—
6/1/1870	38,558,371[e]	33,589,377[e]	4,880,009	25,731	63,254	63,199	55	—	—	—	—	—
6/1/1880	50,155,783	43,402,970	6,580,793	66,407	105,613	105,465	148	—	—	—	—	—
6/1/1890	62,947,714	55,101,258	7,488,676	248,253	107,527	107,488	2,039	—	—	—	—	—
6/1/1900[f]	75,994,575	66,809,196	8,833,994	237,196	114,189	89,863	24,326	—	—	—	—	—
6/1/1900[g]	76,212,168	66,868,508	8,834,395	237,196	204,462	118,746	85,716	—	—	—	—	—
4/15/1910[h]	92,228,531	81,812,405	9,828,667	276,927[i]	257,480	94,414	152,745	2,767	5,008	2,546	—	—
1/1/1920	106,021,568	94,903,540	10,463,607	244,437	341,121	85,202	220,596	26,634	6,181	2,495	—	23
4/1/1930[i]	123,202,660	110,395,753	11,891,842	343,352[j]	500,902	102,159	278,743	108,424	8,332	3,130	—	114
4/1/1940[j]	132,165,129	118,357,831	12,865,914	345,252	500,957	106,334	285,115	98,535	8,568	2,405	—	—
4/1/1950	151,325,798	135,149,629	15,044,937	357,499	606,121	150,005	326,379	122,707	7,030[k]	—	—	—
4/1/1960	179,323,175	158,831,732	18,871,831	523,591	877,934	237,292	464,332	176,310	—	—	—	—
4/1/1970	203,211,926	177,748,975	22,580,289	792,730	1,439,562	436,062	591,290	343,060	69,150[l]	—	—	—
4/1/1980	226,545,805	188,371,622	26,495,025	1,364,033	3,466,421[m]	812,178	716,331	781,894	357,393	387,223	245,025	166,377
4/1/1990	248,709,873	199,686,070	29,986,060	1,878,285	6,908,638[n]	1,645,472	847,562	1,406,770	798,849	815,447	614,547	779,991

TABLE 2.4B

Growth Rates of the Population of the United States, by Race: 1850–1860 to 1980–1990

Date	United States[a]	White	Black	American Indian[b]	Asian American							
					Total[c]	Chinese	Japanese	Filipino[d]	Korean	Asian Indian	Vietnamese	Other
1850–1860	3.0	3.2	2.0	—	—	—	—	—	—	—	—	—
1860–1870	2.0	2.2	0.9	-5.4	5.9	5.9	—	—	—	—	—	—
1870–1880	2.6	2.6	3.0	4.1	5.1	5.1	9.9	—	—	—	—	—
1880–1890	2.3	2.4	1.3	13.2	0.2	0.2	26.2	—	—	—	—	—
1890–1900	1.9	1.9	1.7	-0.5	0.6	-1.8	24.8	—	—	—	—	—
1900–1910	1.9	2.0	1.1	1.6	2.3	-2.3	5.9	—	—	—	—	—
1910–1920	1.4	1.5	0.6	-1.3	2.9	-1.1	3.8	23.3	—	—	—	—
1920–1930	1.5	1.5	1.2	3.3	3.7	1.8	2.3	13.7	—	—	—	—
1930–1940	0.7	0.7	0.8	0.1	0.0	0.4	0.2	-1.0	2.2	-0.2	—	—
1940–1950	1.4	1.3	1.6	0.3	1.9	3.4	1.4	2.2	2.9	2.2	—	—
1950–1960	1.7	1.6	2.3	3.8	3.7	4.6	3.5	3.6	0.3	-2.6	—	—
1960–1970	1.3	1.1	1.8	4.1	4.9	6.1	2.4	6.7	—	—	—	—
1970–1980	1.1	0.6	1.6	5.4	8.8	6.2	1.9	8.2	16.4	—	—	—
1980–1990	0.9	0.6	1.2	3.2	6.9	7.1	1.7	5.9	8.0	7.4	9.2	15.5

SOURCES: *1850–1900:* U.S. Bureau of the Census, 1975, Series A 1-5, 91-104, and 119-134. *Twentieth Century:* Most of the twentieth century data are from the Bureau of the Census, 1980 Census of Population, PC80-1-B1, Table 40, with the following exceptions:
1990: "Census Bureau Releases 1990 Census Counts on Specific Racial Groups," U.S. Department of Commerce News, Release Wednesday, June 12, 1991, Table 3A.
1980: 1980 Census of Population: PC80-S1-12 and PC80-1-C1, Tables 74, 75, 77, 161, and 167;
1970 data for Koreans are from 1970 Census of Population: PC(1)-D1, Table 270;
1950 data for Koreans are from 1950 Census of Population: PC(2)-C52, Table A;
1940 date for Koreans are from 1940 Census of Population: Nonwhite Population, text table, p. 2., and Population Characteristics, Second Series, text table, p. 1, and Table A;
1930 data for Koreans are from the 1930 Census of Population: Chapter 2, Table 8, footnote 2; Chapter 3, Table 1; Chapter 10, Table 15, and Outlying Territories and Possessions, Hawaii, Tables 3 and 4, and Alaska, Table 2, footnote 1;
1920 data for Koreans are from the 1920 Census of Population: PC(3), text table, p. 11, and PC(3), Hawaii, Tables 2 and 11;
1910 data on Koreans are from the 1920 Census of Population: PC(2), Chapter II, Table 1 and the 1910 Census of Population, PC(3), Hawaii, Tables 6 and 10 and Alaska, Table 5, footnote 3.
Early data on Asian Indians are from the 1930 Census of Population: II, General Report, Table 20, and the 1940 Census of Population, 2nd Series, US Summary, Table 22.

TABLE 2.4B (continued)

NOTES: 1970 figures for Chinese, Japanese, and Filipino are different from those in Table 4.4, due to different samples in the underlying census data.

— indicates 0 or unavailable.

[a] Excludes Hawaii and Alaska up to 1900; includes Hawaii and Alaska beginning in 1900.

[b] First distinguished in 1860; excludes Indians in Indian Territory and on Indian reservations, 1860–1880.

[c] Represents the sum of the listed groups only, except beginning in 1980.

[d] Included with "Other" for the United States in 1900 and for Alaska in 1920 and 1950.

[e] Unadjusted for underenumeration in Southern states. Adjusted totals are 39,818,449 and 34,337,292, respectively.

[f] Excludes Hawaii and Alaska.

[g] Includes Hawaii and Alaska.

[h] In Alaska, the census was taken on December 31, 1909.

[i] Special efforts were made in these years to secure a complete enumeration of persons with any amount of Indian ancestry.

[j] In Alaska, the census was taken on October 1 of the preceding year.

[k] Data are for Hawaii only.

[l] Excludes Koreans in Alaska.

[m] Includes 166,377 Other Asian Americans. 1980 data on Asian Americans in this table are from a sample, and do not agree exactly with the 100 percent tabulations found in 1980 Census of Population: PC80-1-B1. Figures from the 100 percent tabulations are as follows: Japanese, 700,794; Chinese: 806,040; Filipino: 774,652; Korean: 354,593; Asian Indian: 361,531; and Vietnamese: 261,729. See discussion in 1980 Census of Population: PC80-S1-12, Page 1.

[n] Includes 779,991 Other Asian Americans: Cambodian: 147,411; Hmong: 90,082; Laotian: 149,014; Thai: 91,275; Bangladeshi: 11,838; Burmese: 6,177; Indonesian: 29,252; Malayan: 12,243; Okinawan: 2,247; Pakistani: 81,371; Sri Lankan: 10,970; All other Asian: 148,111.

41

TABLE 2.5

Percentage Distribution of the Asian American Population of the United States Each Census Year: 1900–1990

	1900[a]	1910	1920	1930	1940	1950	1960	1970	1980	1990
ASIAN AMERICAN	100.0	100.0	100.0	100.0	100.0	100.0	100.0	100.0	100.0	100.0
Japanese	41.9	59.3	64.7	55.6	56.9	53.8	52.9	41.1	20.7	12.3
Chinese	58.1	36.7	25.0	20.4	21.2	24.7	27.0	30.3	23.4	23.8
Filipino	—	1.1	7.8	21.6	19.7	20.2	20.1	23.8	22.6	20.4
Korean	—	1.9	1.8	1.7	1.7	1.2[b]	—	4.8	10.3	11.6
Asian Indian	—	1.0	0.7	0.6	0.5	—	—	—	11.2	11.8
Vietnamese	—	—	—	—	—	—	—	—	7.1	8.9
Other	—	—	—	—	—	—	—	—	4.8	11.8
ASIAN AMERICANS AS A PERCENTAGE OF TOTAL U.S.	0.3	0.3	0.3	0.4	0.4	0.4	0.5	0.7	1.5	2.8

SOURCE: Table 2.4.

NOTES: Total may not equal 100.0 percent because of rounding. Total includes only those groups listed, with the exception of 1980 and 1990, when many more Asian American groups were tabulated.

— indicates unavailable or less than 0.05 percent.

[a]Includes Hawaii and Alaska.

[b]Includes Koreans in Hawaii only.

Although Asian American growth in numbers accounted for only 2.2 percent of national growth for the first 8 decades of this century, it was more than 8 percent of 1970–1980 growth and over 15 percent of 1980–1990 growth. Asian Americans are still a small percentage of the total population, of course, but this percentage is likely to continue to grow rapidly in the coming years.

Foreign-Born among Asian Americans over the Years

The percentage of foreign-born among the total U.S. population has varied over the years, never reaching 15 percent since at least 1860 and falling to less than 5 percent in 1970, just as changes in immigration law began to take effect. By 1980 the percentage of foreign-born had risen to over 6 percent, and the figure has likely risen since then. The recent rise has been centered in the non-white section of the population. The percentage of foreign-born among whites, which stood at a century low in 1980 in spite of the influx of many foreign-born Hispanics who are usually counted racially as white, will also rise if Hispanic immigration continues at high levels and because large numbers of undocumented Hispanic aliens obtained amnesty under the 1986 amendments to the Immigration and Naturalization Act.

For all the Asian American groups for which we have data, the time patterns of percentage of foreign-born have had similar U shapes. (Data on Filipinos are missing until 1950, as the Philippines was a part of the United States and Filipinos were not considered foreign-born.) The recent rises have been occasioned, of course, by the recent increases in immigration from Asia. Even Japanese, who have not immigrated recently in large numbers, still showed in 1980 the highest percentage of foreign-born since 1940.

If present immigration trends continue, we can probably expect to see a rise in the percentage of foreign-born among Asian Americans for at least a few years more. However, unless immigrant numbers rise substantially, the percentage of foreign-born among the various groups must begin to fall, since the number of native-born Asian Americans will rise as children are born to the immigrants. The *number* of foreign-born, however, will continue to rise for some years into the future, until deaths of immigrants outnumber the number of new immigrants.

Nativity, Recency of Immigration, and Citizenship in 1980

One theme that runs throughout this monograph is that of heterogeneity: Asian American groups are not alike. We have identified four major dimensions of this heterogeneity: nativity,[21] age, gender, and economic level. Within any of the Asian American groups, for many characteristics there are important differences, sometimes striking, between the foreign-born and the native-born. There are further differences among the foreign-born according to period of immigration, and differences as well according to whether the immigrant has become a naturalized citizen or not.

In this section we focus on the nativity and citizenship status of Asian Americans in 1980. Data on nativity are shown in Table 2-6. In 1980, the percentage of foreign-born among Asian Americans ranged from 28 percent to over 90 percent. For all this diversity, however, Asian American populations could still be characterized as having relatively high proportions of foreign-born individuals compared to the other groups listed.

The single exception was the Japanese, whose percentage of foreign-born was roughly equal to that of Hispanics.[22] Japanese were the only group of Asians, among the six largest groups, who did not participate in the post-1965 increases in immigration. Fewer than a third (28 percent) of all Japanese Americans in 1980 were foreign-born, and among these, an exceptionally large percent were pre-1960 arrivals. Only whites, with a far smaller proportion of foreign-born (6.2 percent), had a higher proportion of early arrivals among immigrants in 1980.

Table 2.6 documents the fact that several of the large Asian American groups established themselves in the United States only recently. More than 70 percent of Asian Indians, Koreans, and Vietnamese were foreign-born in 1980, and fewer than 4 percent of these foreign-born had come to the United States before 1960. The extreme case, of course, was that of the Vietnamese, with more than 90 percent foreign-born in 1980

---

[21]Nativity refers to the place of birth of Asian Americans: in the United States or in a foreign country. Data on nativity come in two forms in the census. In some tables we have data on race and on whether native-born or foreign-born, and we must often infer that a Chinese, for example, who was born abroad was born in China. In other tables we have data on country of birth, and must often infer that a person born in China is Chinese. Neither of these inferences is always accurate, but they are probably not far off and must be lived with.

[22]Illegal immigrants, who are assuredly present in higher proportions among Hispanics than among other groups, must be essentially all foreign-born and are probably undercounted by the census.

TABLE 2.6

Population of the United States, by Race, Nativity, and Year of Immigration: 1980

Group	Total Population	Foreign-Born Population	Percentage of all Foreign-Born	Percentage Foreign-Born	Percentage of Foreign-Born by Year of Immigration			
					1975–1980	1970–1974	1960–1969	Before 1960
TOTAL U.S.	226,545,805	14,079,906	100.0	6.2	23.7	15.8	12.8	47.7
White	189,035,012	9,323,946	66.2	4.9	—26.8—		—73.2—	
Black	26,482,349	815,720	5.8	3.1	—55.4—		—44.6—	
Hispanic[a]	14,603,683	4,172,851	29.6	28.6	—52.7—		—47.3—	
All Asians[b]	3,300,244	2,010,070	14.3	60.9	45.9	24.3	18.6	11.3
Chinese	812,178	514,389	3.7	63.3	37.5	22.9	24.8	14.8
Filipino	781,894	505,504	3.6	64.7	34.9	29.3	22.4	13.5
Japanese	716,331	203,338	1.4	28.4	34.1	13.4	20.8	31.6
Asian Indian	387,223	272,617	1.9	70.4	46.3	32.2	17.8	3.7
Korean	357,393	292,573	2.1	81.9	52.9	31.7	12.7	2.7
Vietnamese	245,025	221,649	1.6	90.5	91.5	6.6	1.8	0.1

SOURCES: Bureau of the Census, unpublished tabulations; 1980 Census of Population: PC80-1-C1, Tables 77, 99, 161, 167; PC80-1-D1-B, Table 313.

NOTES: The foreign-born of a particular race are not necessarily all born in the nation of the same name. For example, 66 percent of foreign-born Chinese were born in China, 95 percent of foreign-born Filipinos in the Philippines, 91 percent of foreign-born Japanese in Japan, 70 percent of foreign-born Asian Indians in India, 95 percent of foreign-born Koreans in Korea, and 92 percent of foreign-born Vietnamese in Vietnam.

[a]Hispanic may be of any race.

[b]Includes only the 6 groups listed separately.

45

and with more than 90 percent of these having arrived in the previous 5 years.

One can distinguish several different patterns among the Asian American groups with regard to nativity and recency of immigration. The first pattern belongs to Japanese alone, who came early and are coming in small numbers now in comparison with other groups, with earlier Japanese immigration, and with the total Japanese American community. A second pattern is shown by Chinese and Filipinos, who, along with Japanese, were well established in this country prior to the 1965 law changes, with more than one-third of the 1980 foreign-born having arrived before 1970.[23] Filipinos and Chinese continued to immigrate in considerable numbers, in contrast to Japanese. In fact, Filipinos topped all Asians in numbers of immigrants in recent years.

A third pattern is shown by Asian Indians and Koreans, whose populations grew rapidly through immigration from previously small populations. Vietnamese make up an extreme fourth case, with more than 91 percent of the 1980 population having arrived in the period 1975–1980. Vietnamese immigration, of course, did not come about as "spontaneously" as a result of the changes in the immigration law, but rather because of the sudden changes in the political situation in Vietnam.

Immigrants to the United States have the option of remaining "permanent resident aliens" or of becoming naturalized citizens. Asians generally naturalize to a greater extent and faster than immigrants from other parts of the world. Of all 1970–1979 immigrants to the United States, 55.4 percent of those from Asia had naturalized by the end of fiscal year 1988, compared to 42.7 percent of those from Africa, the next ranking group (USINS 1988 Yearbook, p. xi). Among all those naturalizing in selected years, the shortest time elapsed since entering has consistently been shown by Asians and Africans (op. cit., p. xxxiii).

The percentage of immigrants who have naturalized varies greatly by group (Table 2.7). Over 40 percent of Chinese and Filipino and 33 percent or more of Koreans and Japanese immigrants, in contrast to under 11 percent of Vietnamese immigrants, have become citizens.

The percentage of immigrants becoming citizens is, of course, at least partially dependent upon how long the immigrants had been in the United States. For example, Vietnamese were mostly very recent arrivals, and one would not expect high proportions to have become citizens already. The relative propensities to naturalize are seen better by examining immigration "cohorts"—groups who all arrived during the same period.

Among Asian immigrants who arrived during the 5 years preceding

[23]The changes in immigration legislation were passed by Congress and signed into law in 1965, but became fully implemented only in 1968.

TABLE 2.7
Asian Americans, by Nativity and Citizenship: 1980

	Asian Americans[a]	Chinese	Filipino	Japanese	Korean	Asian Indian	Viet-namese
TOTAL	3,300,044	812,178	781,894	716,331	357,393	387,223	245,025
Native-born citizens	1,289,974	297,789	276,390	512,993	64,820	114,606	23,376
Foreign-born	2,010,070	514,389	505,504	203,338	292,573	272,617	221,649
Percentage of total	60.9	63.3	64.7	28.4	81.9	70.4	90.5
Naturalized citizens	694,847	211,065	222,045	75,218	97,455	65,676	23,388
Percentage of foreign-born							
All foreign-born	34.6	41.9	43.9	37.0	33.3	24.1	10.6
1975–1980	7.4	5.5	9.8	4.4	10.3	6.4	6.5
1970–1974	39.7	38.7	45.6	20.0	47.2	27.8	49.2
1960–1969	67.1	70.2	71.4	51.0	82.5	50.9	69.8
Before 1960	80.5	85.7	83.0	70.1	89.7	83.7	76.4
Foreign-born not citizens	1,315,223	303,324	283,459	128,120	195,118	206,941	198,261
Percentage of total	39.9	37.3	36.3	17.9	54.6	53.4	80.9

SOURCE: Unpublished tabulations of Asian Americans by Census Bureau.

[a]Includes groups listed only. Total Asian Americans in 1980 = 3,466,421. The groups in this table form 95.2 percent of all Asian Americans.

the 1980 census, between 4 and 11 percent of the 6 groups had become citizens by the census date.[24] For immigrants during the previous 5 years, 1970–1974, the range was from 20 percent for Japanese to almost 50 percent for Vietnamese. The low figures for Japanese and, to a lesser extent, Asian Indians, stood out; more than 38 percent of the 1970–1974 immigrants of the other 4 groups had become citizens by 1980.

The pattern was similar for 1960–1969 immigrants: high proportions of citizens among Koreans (especially), Filipinos, Chinese, and the few Vietnamese, with low proportions among Japanese and Asian Indians. For pre-1960 immigrants, the Japanese once again stood out as having the lowest proportion of citizens; even so, over 70 percent of Japanese immigrants in the United States over 20 years had become naturalized citizens.

The set of figures for percentage of population who were not citizens (i.e., neither native-born nor naturalized) fits in very nicely with the four patterns of immigration described above. Although Japanese immigrants did not naturalize as much as other groups, the fact that such a high proportion of all Japanese immigrants were long-term residents resulted in the fact that only 18 percent of Japanese Americans in 1980 were not citizens. Between 36 and 38 percent of Chinese and Filipino Americans were not citizens; about 54 percent of Koreans and Asian Indian Americans—the more recently established groups—were not citizens; and almost 81 percent of Vietnamese Americans were not citizens.

It is not surprising that with longer residence the proportion of Asian immigrants becoming citizens increased, nor that a very large percentage of Asian immigrants to the United States eventually became citizens. On the other hand, there were substantial numbers who did not take out citizenship and apparently never will, and the proportion of these was consistently highest among Japanese. This may have been because of a higher identification with the home country among Japanese than among other Asian groups, in some sense a lesser degree of "assimilation" to their new home. Another factor at work may have been that citizenship is a necessary prerequisite for sponsoring immediate relatives as immigrants. Alone among the six major Asian American groups, Japanese currently are not moving to the United States in great numbers. Thus, petitioning immediate relatives may not have been an important reason for Japanese immigrants to naturalize.

[24]An immigrant must reside continuously in the United States for 5 years as one of the requirements for becoming a citizen. There are exceptions, such as some spouses of American citizens, for whom the requirement is only 3 years. High rates of naturalization among groups that include many wives of U.S. citizens are partly explained by the shorter required wait. About 85 percent of all naturalizing individuals have waited the full 5 years (INS 1987, pp. xxxii–xxxiii).

As we proceed in our discussion of the demographic, social, and economic characteristics of Asian Americans, we shall frequently have occasion to look at differences by nativity. Although differences among immigrants by period of arrival and citizenship are also of importance, we shall spend less time on them, partly because data are less readily available.

Projections

The Asian American population is the product of more than 140 years of immigration. Today there are more Asian Americans than ever before, some 6 million-plus. Although still a small proportion of the total U.S. population, the Asian American population is growing rapidly, which portends a growing influence and impact on American society. Currently composed predominantly of immigrants, the Asian American population will of necessity come to be dominated by the native-born, as projected fairly constant levels of immigration feed into a growing native-born base.

We have not attempted any new projections of the Asian American population in this volume for two reasons: such projections would quickly become outdated once more recent figures are available on the total Asian American population, and, in any case, immigration law reform might have an effect on Asian immigration that would throw off any projections. We will, however, briefly present a set of projections made well before the 1990 census (Table 2.8).[25] These projections show a total of

[25]In making projections, assumptions must be made about future levels of fertility, mortality, and immigration and, if separate projections are desired for each group, these assumptions must be group-specific as well. In this monograph one of our continuing themes is the heterogeneity of Asian Americans, and it is clear that no one set of assumptions can apply to all groups. Fertility and mortality levels differ (see the next chapter), and levels of immigration differ even more.

Bouvier and Agresta (1987) prepared projections of the Asian American population to the year 2030, 50 years beyond the base year of 1980. The assumptions of the Bouvier-Agresta projections include the following:

First, a value for life expectancy at birth for *all* groups that begins at 69 years for males and 76 for females in 1980 and rises to 76 for males and 82 for females by 2010. This assumption in essence is that the mortality of Asian Americans is not significantly different from that of the total U.S. population, which of course is not true and which can be viewed as only approximate in the light of our discussion in the next chapter.

Second, fertility (measured by the Total Fertility Rate) for those Asian Americans in the United States in 1980 is set at 3.0 births per woman for Vietnamese and other Indochinese in 1980, 1.6 for Japanese, 1.8 for Koreans, Chinese, Filipinos, and Asian Indians. Fertility for post-1980 immigrants is set slightly higher, but converging with that of already-present groups to 1.8 births per woman in 2010.

Finally, immigration of Asian Americans is set at 240,000 annually, close to the

TABLE 2.8

Projections of the Asian American Population, by Ethnicity: 1980–2030

Ethnicity	1980	1990	2000	2010	2020	2030
Chinese	812,178	1,259,038	1,683,537	2,084,509	2,457,046	2,779,127
	(23.4)	(19.3)	(17.1)	(15.8)	(14.8)	(13.9)
Filipino	781,894	1,405,146	2,070,571	2,717,330	3,353,990	3,963,710
	(22.6)	(21.5)	(21.0)	(20.5)	(20.2)	(20.0)
Indian	387,223	684,339	1,006,305	1,331,762	1,634,601	1,919,163
	(11.2)	(10.4)	(10.2)	(10.1)	(9.8)	(9.6)
Japanese	716,331	804,535	856,619	893,135	929,914	945,534
	(20.6)	(12.4)	(8.7)	(6.8)	(5.6)	(4.7)
Kampuchean	16,044	185,301	386,673	603,874	833,415	1,073,111
	(0.5)	(2.9)	(3.9)	(4.6)	(5.0)	(5.4)
Korean	357,393	814,495	1,320,759	1,853,003	2,394,602	2,946,986
	(10.3)	(12.4)	(13.4)	(14.0)	(14.4)	(14.8)
Laotian	52,887	259,674	502,599	762,398	1,035,273	1,317,353
	(1.5)	(4.0)	(5.1)	(5.8)	(6.2)	(6.6)
Vietnamese	245,025	859,638	1,574,385	2,331,827	3,122,591	3,934,661
	(7.1)	(13.1)	(16.0)	(17.6)	(18.8)	(19.7)
Other	98,873	261,442	448,919	645,656	849,434	1,055,168
	(2.8)	(4.0)	(4.6)	(4.8)	(5.2)	(5.3)
Total	3,466,421	6,533,608	9,850,364	13,223,494	16,610,866	19,934,813
	(100.0)	(100.0)	(100.0)	(100.0)	(100.0)	(100.0)

SOURCE: Bouvier and Agresta 1987, p. 292.

6.5 million Asian Americans in 1990 (compared to a census count of 6.9 million), rising to almost 10 million in the next decade and to almost 20 million by the year 2030. Of course, the farther into the future we peer, the cloudier the picture, but based on the 1990 data, these figures will almost certainly be exceeded.

It seems certain that the Asian American population of the United States will be considerably larger in the years to come. It also seems likely that the relative sizes of the various components of the Asian American population will change. For example, in 1980, Chinese ac-

---

annual average for 1980–1984, divided among the various groups about as was the case in 1980–1984. These assumptions are perhaps the most problematic in the whole procedure, for there is no strong reason to suppose that 1980–1984 immigration patterns will be typical for years to come. Changes in immigration laws may radically alter the patterns. For example, a lowering of family reunification quotas might well cut Asian immigration to levels well below those experienced recently. On the other hand, political and economic trends in Asian countries might result in greater pressures to emigrate to the United States. High levels of refugee movements from Indochina will probably not continue. However, if diplomatic relations with the countries of Indochina are resumed, then the refugee flow might be replaced by a heavy flow of regular immigrants; the situation is still uncertain.

counted for more than 23 percent of the total Asian American population; the projections show their share at less than 14 percent by the year 2030. Japanese are also projected to lose in their share of the total, from over 20 percent to less than 5 percent. The big gainers are projected to be the Vietnamese, but this is probably the large group where lies the most uncertainty, since the high levels of recent immigration have been fueled by refugee movements, and when these diminish, as they must, unless normal immigration fills the gap the growth of the Vietnamese community will be restricted mostly to natural increase.

In any case, the growth of the Asian American population is assured, but its composition will depend upon immigration, which we have discussed in this chapter, and on fertility and mortality, which are discussed in Chapter 3.

THE DEMOGRAPHY
OF ASIAN AMERICANS:
FERTILITY, MORTALITY,
AND AGE AND SEX COMPOSITION

Introduction

ALTHOUGH immigration has clearly caused much of the recent growth of the Asian American population, fertility and mortality have also affected the size, growth, and character of the population. In this section and the next we examine these two factors, then conclude the chapter with a discussion of the age and sex composition of Asian Americans.

The United States has excellent vital statistics. They do not allow us, however, to calculate estimates of current or recent fertility or mortality for Asian Americans of a level of quality comparable to estimates for blacks, Hispanics, and whites.

Birth rates and death rates require data both on events and on the population experiencing those events. In the United States these data come from two separate statistical systems. The National Center for Health Statistics (NCHS) collects data on events, while the Bureau of the Census collects data on population. These systems define race in different ways: for births, NCHS employs certain rules to decide the race of a child from the race of the parents; for deaths, the reports of parents or other individuals are used to decide race; and individuals (or a household member) report their own race and those of their children on the census.

Even *within* the vital statistics system, reporting of race of parents and child can cause problems. In 1980, for example, 11 percent more Asian American births occurred than there were Asian American mothers (because births of mixed marriages can be of a race different from their mothers'; see Taffel 1984). An Asian American birth rate calculated from such statistics would be biased upward.

Such problems also plague fertility data from the census on the ratio of young children to women of childbearing age (the Child-Woman Ratio). (In the census, as with vital statistics, the child's race need not necessarily match that of the mother.) One source of information on the fertility of Asian Americans, however, had no such problems: census data on children ever born (CEB), or cumulative fertility. In each census a sample of female respondents was asked a question on number of children ever born. Children of these women were automatically assigned the race of the mother. We will use the responses from this question to examine Asian American fertility.

The study of mortality is also hindered by difficulties in relating vital statistics numerator data on deaths to relevant census denominator populations at risk (i.e., the race of a mixed-race individual is often reported differently on the census than on the death certificate). This has become a problem of increasing importance because the census has several times changed its rules for assigning ethnicity over the years. This problem of comparability of numerator and denominator data is of greater potential importance, according to the proportion of mixed-race individuals. A newly arrived immigrant group with very few marriages outside the group would probably show relatively few differences between the ethnicity listed on the census and that on the vital statistics forms. On the other hand, established groups with long histories of outmarriages would have much greater problems of ethnic identification. In 1980, only 59 percent of Japanese wives had Japanese husbands (33 percent had white husbands). Comparable figures were 68 percent for Filipino wives and 83 percent for Chinese. Among Japanese husbands, 81 percent had Japanese wives; Filipinos had 78 percent and Chinese 87 percent wives of the same ethnicity (U.S. Bureau of the Census, 1980 Census of Population, PC80-2-4C, Marital Characteristics, Table 11, p. 175, 1985).

For fertility analysis there are census data on children ever born. There are, however, no comparable data from the census on mortality. Furthermore, Asian American groups are still so small that national sample surveys of mortality or disease cannot collect statistically reliable information on them. To look at Asian American mortality levels, then, we are forced to rely heavily on studies of particular groups and diseases—studies which are not necessarily generalizable to the national level—or else accept vital statistics data but treat them with caution. We shall do both below.

Fertility

The children of a woman can have been born at any time since she reached childbearing age. Information on the number of CEB to women of ages 15–49 refers to a period of some 35 years' duration before the date of the census. Data on CEB are thus not precisely "current" or "recent." We can mitigate this defect to some extent by focusing on the CEB only of relatively young women, say 25–34, whose children must have been born in the previous 15–20 years. We will therefore look at two measures of fertility: CEB to all women aged 15–44, taking into account the age structures of the different populations, and CEB to women aged 25–34, to capture more recent levels and differentials.

The recent fertility of Asian Americans was not high by current American standards (Table 3.1, line 1). The average number of CEB per 1000 women aged 15–44 in the United States in 1980 was 1,429 (after controlling for age differences between the total female population and the Asian American female population). In contrast, Asian American women had an average of only 1,164 children per 1000 women, more than 18 percent lower. The figure for Asians was lower than that for whites (1,358) and far lower than the figures for blacks (1,806) and Hispanics (1,817).

One Asian group clearly stood out as having higher fertility than the others: Vietnamese. One possible reason was that Vietnamese were the Asian Americans who arrived most recently in the United States; therefore, a high proportion of their children must have been born outside this country and under different fertility-influencing conditions. (As we shall see below, of all the groups, Vietnamese show the largest fertility differentials between foreign-born and native-born women.)

After accounting for age differences, the second highest fertility group among Asian Americans was Asian Indians, followed closely by Filipinos and Koreans. Chinese had the second lowest fertility, and Japanese had the lowest of all groups considered. The 912 Japanese children ever born per 1000 women aged 15–44 was the only figure less than 1000. (Japanese could still be replacing themselves, since the average woman aged 15–44 is considerably younger than 44 and not yet near the end of her reproductive years.)

TABLE 3.1

Children Ever Born per 1,000 Women, by Race, Nativity, Urban/Rural Residence, and Education: United States: 1980

	Total	White	Black	His-panic[a]	Asian Amer-ican[b]	Chi-nese	Fili-pino	Japa-nese	Korean	Asian Indian	Viet-namese
Children Ever Born per 1,000 Women 15–44[c]											
TOTAL	1,429	1,358	1,806	1,817	1,164	1,020	1,217	912	1,139	1,224	1,785
Children Ever Born per 1,000 Women 25–34											
TOTAL	1,476	1,404	1,859	1,922	1,201	939	1,270	908	1,244	1,336	1,775
Nativity											
Native-born	1,470	NC	NC	NC	951	669	1,520	768	996	1,343	1,608
Foreign-born	1,562	NC	NC	NC	1,268	1,024	1,227	1,104	1,252	1,336	1,777
Residence											
Urban	1,391	1,293	1,816	1,984	1,181	930	1,237	884	1,239	1,320	1,760
Rural	1,740	1,700	2,179	2,223	1,526	1,190	1,739	1,239	1,314	1,597	1,997
Years of schooling											
<9	2,348	2,201	2,676	2,638	2,030	1,766	1,839	1,119	1,246	2,233	2,543
9–12	1,764	1,699	2,098	1,929	1,509	1,318	1,723	1,342	1,288	1,574	1,834
13–16	1,106	1,076	1,351	1,199	992	763	1,144	807	1,186	1,293	1,033
17+	620	596	805	813	726	537	801	466	903	1,055	847

SOURCE: 1980 Census of Population: PC80-1-D1-A, Tables 255, 271; PC80-1-C1, Tables 84, 131; and unpublished tabulations by the Bureau of the Census. NC: not calculated.

[a]Hispanics may be of any race.

[b]Includes all Asian Americans, and not just those listed separately.

[c]Standardized on the age structure of all Asian American females.

When we restrict ourselves to recent fertility, looking at women 25–34 (Table 3.1, line 2), essentially the same picture emerges.[1] Asian American numbers of CEB per 1000 women aged 25–34 (1,201) were below those for the total population (1,476), whites (1,404), blacks (1,859), and Hispanics (1,922). Again, Vietnamese showed the highest fertility among Asian Americans: 1,775 children ever born per 1000 women. Asian Indians (1,336) were next highest, followed by Filipinos (1,270) and Koreans (1,244). Chinese (939) and Japanese (908) showed the lowest fertility among the selected groups. Inferential data on the birth order and median ages of mothers of Asian American children from vital statistics in 1980 support this observation of the low fertility among Japanese and Chinese (Taffel 1984).

Factors in Asian American Fertility Levels

We now look at three factors generally known to affect fertility, but before presenting these data, two warnings are in order (cf. Burch 1979). First, the 1980 Census collected information on CEB only from a sample of the population. In some cases that follow, the differences in CEB figures are very small (as small as 0.1 child per woman for Japanese birthplace differences). Small differences from sample data may not be statistically significant; a good guide, of course, is that the larger the difference, the more likely it is to be real and not a statistical artifact.

Second, looking at the fertility of any group without considering where its members were born ignores the fact, already mentioned, that nativity (place of birth) affects fertility. For example, we would generally expect the fertility levels of native-born Asian Americans to be closer to national levels than those of foreign-born Asian Americans. We might also expect recent immigrants, especially adults, to exhibit fertility close to that of their home country. Preferences for large families exist in the origin countries of some Asian immigrants to the United States, such as the Philippines and Vietnam (see the discussion in Rumbaut and Weeks 1985). Other origin countries, however, such as Japan, have exceptionally low fertility. For example, Table 3.2 gives the range of Total Fertil-

---

[1] Even restricting ourselves to women aged 25–34 does not provide us with unequivocal comparisons. There is still the possibility of confounding the factors of *quantity* (number of children ultimately born to a cohort of women) and *timing* (when in their childbearing years the women have their children). It is quite possible that later timing of childbearing affects comparisons of fertility among women aged 25–34 of groups that will eventually have the same completed fertility. Rindfuss and Sweet (1977) found, for earlier periods, slightly lower proportions of completed fertility achieved by age 35 for Japanese and Chinese Americans compared to most other groups they looked at (Table 6.9, page 142).

TABLE 3.2

*Total Fertility Rates of the United States and
Selected Populations of Asia: 1980*

Area	TFR
U.S.	1.8
Laos	6.2
Kampuchea	4.7
Vietnam	5.8
Philippines	5.0
Republic of Korea	3.2
Taiwan	3.1
China	2.3
Hong Kong	2.6
Japan	1.8

SOURCE: Population Reference Bureau, 1980.

NOTE: Data are most recent from the period 1975–1980. For areas without complete registration data, best estimates are used.

ity Rates (TFRs)[2] for the United States and for the Asian populations from which large numbers of immigrants come to the United States. The rankings generally parallel those of Table 3.1.

There are differences in fertility levels by nativity partly because the immigrant females lived much of their reported childbearing years in the origin country. This effect is especially true for very recent arrivals, such as refugees from Indochina. Furthermore, length of residence in the United States interacts with age at arrival. That is, even if 2 women have lived in the United States for 20 years, they might have different fertility because one immigrated at age 5 and one at age 25.

The expected direction of the birthplace fertility differential depends on the fertility level in the origin country. Even knowing that, however, it is still difficult to predict immigrant fertility. "Selection" is undoubtedly at work in the home countries for at least some immigrants: migrants generally have different fertility than those left behind because, for instance, the migrants may be primarily urban and well educated. Other groups, in particular the "second-wave" refugees from Indochina, were probably not selected for fertility levels (but "first-wave" Vietnamese refugees probably were; Rumbaut and Weeks 1985, p. 7).

Data in Table 3.1 show there were indeed fertility differences by nativity among Asian Americans. Foreign-born Asian American women

[2]The Total Fertility Rate is the number of children an average woman would have if she had lived to the end of the childbearing years and had children during her lifetime at the age-specific birth rates of a certain year.

aged 25–34 had an average of 1,268 children per 1000 women in 1980, compared to 951 for those who were native-born. The differential was in the same direction for all the major Asian American groups except one: Filipinos, where native-born, at 1,520 children per 1000 women aged 25–34, were higher than foreign-born at 1,227. A possible factor in this is that the parents of native-born Filipinos generally had rural and traditional backgrounds, whereas recent immigrants had predominantly urban modern backgrounds.

Changes over time in immigrants' region of origin within their home country and in home-country levels of fertility may help explain another observation: for all six groups we examined, cumulative fertility for women aged 25–34 was lower, the more recent the period of immigration (data not shown; education level was controlled for and did not affect the results). We expected to find the opposite: that the more recent arrivals had higher levels of children ever born, because of having spent more time in their home countries.

Regardless of place of birth, however, in 1980 Chinese and Japanese Americans had lower cumulative fertility than other Asian Americans. Vietnamese Americans had the highest.

There were also urban/rural residence differentials in fertility. For the total United States, rural fertility for women aged 25–34 in 1980 was almost a third of a child higher than urban fertility (1,740 vs. 1,391, respectively). The differential was in the same direction for whites, blacks, Hispanics, and for Asian Americans as a group as well as for each separate group. Rural background as well as current rural residence affected fertility, and past rural residence probably played an important role in the high numbers of children ever born of immigrants now living in urban areas (see the discussion in Rumbaut and Weeks 1985).

With regard to educational attainment, there was a common pattern: fertility was lower for women with higher levels of education. Education takes time, changes values, and provides training and opportunities for alternate uses of time and sources of satisfaction. The bottom panel of Table 3.1 shows that strong educational differentials in numbers of children ever born were present for the United States in 1980. Women aged 25–34 with fewer than 9 years of education in the country had an average of 2,348 children per 1000 women. For women with more than 4 years of college, the figure was only 620.

Rindfuss and Sweet, using data from the 1970 census, found a similar general inverse relationship between education and fertility for the groups they studied, including Japanese and Chinese Americans (1977, p. 133).

Whites, blacks, Hispanics, and all Asian Americans had similarly strong differentials. Among the Asian Americans, only Japanese and Koreans, at lower levels of education, showed any deviation from the strict negative relationship between education and fertility. Interestingly, at higher levels of education (more than high school), Vietnamese do not show the highest fertility; Asian Indians hold that distinction. Some of the high fertility of Vietnamese, then, comes from the predominance in that population of individuals with low education. Controlling for education, however, does not change the observation that Chinese and Japanese had the lowest numbers of children ever born.

We reached essentially the same conclusions when we looked at educational differentials in fertility for foreign-born women, taking into account the year of immigration (data not shown). Almost without exception, fertility was lower for the better-educated women, no matter when they immigrated.

We did not examine differentials with regard to income, but using 1970 data, Rindfuss and Sweet found a positive relationship for Chinese and Japanese Americans: the higher the income, in general, the higher the level of fertility (1977, p. 149). (The same was true for urban whites, but not for Southern rural blacks, Hispanics in the Southwest, and American Indians.)

Own Children Analysis

Another way to estimate fertility is to use the own-children method. Earlier publications have described this method in detail (see especially Cho et al. 1986), so we review it only briefly here. The method is a reverse-survival technique[3] for estimating age-specific birth rates for years previous to a census or household survey. Children are matched to their mothers within households on the basis of responses to questions on age, sex, marital status, relationship to householder, and, in the present application, number of children ever born. (As with CEB, children are assigned the race of their mothers.) The matched (that is, "own") children, classified by own age and mother's age, are reverse-survived to estimate numbers of births by age of mother in previous years. Reverse-survival is also used to estimate numbers of women by age in previous years. With estimates of both births and women for previous years, we can calculate both age-specific birth rates and Total Fertility Rates (TFRs) for those years.

In the present application we have grouped calendar years into three periods: 1965–1969, 1970–1974, and 1975–1979. Since the census oc-

---

[3]"Reverse-survival" means that we take the number of people alive at a certain point in time, e.g., the census date, and use survival rates from mortality tables to calculate how many people must have been alive at an earlier date to produce this many survivors.

curred on April 1, these periods run from April 1 to March 31. For example, 1975–1979 means April 1, 1975, to March 31, 1980. We summed age-specific birth rates to Total Fertility Rates and report only the latter here.[4]

Table 3.3 shows estimated trends in TFRs for Asians by nativity and year of immigration. Also shown are comparative figures for the United States and the major racial groups of whites, blacks, and American Indians. Total fertility for the total United States fell from 2,601 to 1,810 children per 1000 women between 1965–1969 and 1975–1979. The TFR fell from 2,488 to 1,714 for whites, from 3,182 to 2,115 for blacks, and from 3,398 to 2,409 for American Indians.

In general, the data showed fertility that was lower than white fertility for Japanese and Chinese Americans, somewhat higher fertility than whites for Filipinos, Koreans, and Asian Indians, and quite high fertility for Vietnamese. All Asian groups showed falling fertility over time.

Nativity was an important factor affecting these comparisons. Because they could not control for nativity, Rindfuss and Sweet (1977) chose not to examine Filipino fertility; the nativity composition of the Filipino population in the years preceding the 1970 census had been changing too rapidly. Similar changes had been occurring to all Asian American populations before the 1980 census, so disaggregation by nativity was extremely important.

Among *native-born* Asian Americans in 1980, recent fertility among most groups was lower than that of whites; earlier fertility was higher for Filipinos and, especially, Vietnamese. Fertility for the native-born of all groups declined over the periods shown.

Among the *foreign-born*, as we have already discussed, several factors need to be kept in mind, even if they cannot be attended to statistically. *Some* past fertility may have occurred in the country of origin, not in the United States. "Disruption" of fertility may have occurred during the period of time surrounding the actual move. And length of time in the United States is a measure of how long assimilation effects can have been in operation.

The fertility of foreign-born Asians declined over the three periods, except among Asian Indians, whose fertility increased slightly. The fertility of the foreign-born was higher than the fertility of native-born, as expected, except for Filipinos and Japanese during 1965–1969. Native-born Chinese and Japanese achieved an extremely low level of fertility of 1.2 children per woman by 1975–1979.

---

[4]Retherford and Cho (1978) showed that own-children estimates of TFRs for the United States agree closely with corresponding estimates derived from vital statistics. Methodological details about our application here of the own-children method appear in Retherford and Levin (1989).

TABLE 3.3

Trends in Total Fertility Rate, by Race and Nativity

Group and Time Period	Total	Native-Born	Foreign-Born		
				Year of Immigration	
			Total	1965–1980	Pre-1965
ASIANS					
1965–1969	2,399	2,196	2,484	2,574	2,677
1970–1974	2,179	1,576	2,335	2,490	1,787
1975–1979	1,948	1,345	2,133	2,207	1,595
Chinese					
1965–1969	2,331	2,093	2,384	2,335	2,646
1970–1974	1,869	1,306	2,005	2,098	1,706
1975–1979	1,597	1,161	1,737	1,800	1,415
Japanese					
1965–1969	1,880	1,987	1,787	1,860	2,090
1970–1974	1,651	1,426	1,929	2,181	1,429
1975–1979	1,409	1,209	1,761	1,831	1,432
Filipino					
1965–1969	2,574	2,910	2,523	2,376	3,601
1970–1974	2,319	2,112	2,323	2,388	2,252
1975–1979	2,148	1,788	2,177	2,228	1,843
Korean					
1965–1969	2,404	1,834	2,412	2,427	2,637
1970–1974	2,391	1,765	2,408	2,473	1,845
1975–1979	2,183	1,519	2,216	2,238	1,695
Asian Indian					
1965–1969	2,155	2,172	2,216	2,209	2,536
1970–1974	2,115	1,803	2,176	2,204	1,899
1975–1979	2,239	1,478	2,302	2,343	1,322
Vietnamese					
1965–1969	5,435	3,739	5,473	5,513	3,154
1970–1974	4,395	3,638	4,408	4,440	1,642
1975–1979	2,671	1,812	2,687	2,699	1,256
UNITED STATES					
1965–1969	2,601	NC	NC	NC	NC
1970–1974	2,070	NC	NC	NC	NC
1975–1979	1,810	NC	NC	NC	NC
White					
1965–1969	2,488	NC	NC	NC	NC
1970–1974	1,959	NC	NC	NC	NC
1975–1979	1,714	NC	NC	NC	NC
Black					
1965–1969	3,182	NC	NC	NC	NC
1970–1974	2,487	NC	NC	NC	NC
1975–1979	2,115	NC	NC	NC	NC
American Indian					
1965–1969	3,398	NC	NC	NC	NC
1970–1974	2,722	NC	NC	NC	NC
1975–1979	2,409	NC	NC	NC	NC

SOURCE: Retherford and Levin 1989.

NOTE: for similar data on Chinese and Japanese Americans for the period 1955–1969, see Rindfuss and Sweet 1977. NC: not calculated.

Discussion

For many years, sociologists have sought to explain the observed fertility levels of ethnic minorities in the United States.[5] Interest and study of Asian Americans in this regard are relatively recent; earlier attention focused primarily on groups of European descent.

Until recently, the "characteristics," "compositional," or "assimilation" approach was the dominant explanation for minority differential fertility. That is, differentials in the social, economic, and demographic characteristics of the various groups were assumed to cause fertility differentials. If the characteristics for a minority group become more and more like the characteristics of the total population, or more properly of the majority white population, the group becomes "assimilated" and its fertility will converge on white fertility. If this explanation is correct, then as Asian Americans acquire "the social, demographic, and economic characteristics of the majority, [their] fertility behavior will tend to resemble that of the majority group" (Rindfuss and Sweet 1977, p. 112).

A second approach sees fertility differentials as the product of *minority group status* (Goldscheider and Uhlenberg 1969; Kennedy 1973; Halli 1989). "Membership in a minority group can exert an influence on fertility independent of the social, economic, and demographic characteristics of that group. This minority group effect may operate either to lower or to elevate the fertility of the minority group in relation to the fertility of the dominant group. Whether or not the effect is to depress or to elevate fertility depends on a variety of intervening factors." (Rindfuss and Sweet 1977, p. 113).

A third approach is the cultural or "particularized ideology" approach, which posits that values and norms unique to different groups (and not simply status as a minority group) cause fertility differentials; socioeconomic characteristics are not as important (Beaujot, Krotki, and Krishnan 1977). Minority status might be associated with high fertility, not low, for example, if the group has high-fertility norms and ideals.[6] It is also clear that norms and ideals can change as "assimilation" occurs.

The results of the "Value of Children" project confirm this perspec-

---

[5]There has also been interest in explaining the varying levels and patterns of mortality of minority groups. Some of the points made in the discussion of minority fertility are also applied later to mortality differentials.

[6]Halli (1989) distinguishes between structural effects and normative (or cultural) effects of minority status on fertility. The structural are discussed in this volume under the minority status hypothesis, while the normative are discussed under the particularized ideology hypothesis.

tive. "Evidently culture can have a considerable influence on the satisfactions associated with having children . . . Children mean different things to different people. They serve different functions in different cultures, ethnic groups, and SES groups" (Arnold and Fawcett 1975, pp. 41, 133).

This perspective might partially explain fertility differences between the native-born and the foreign-born of a particular ethnic group: the native-born have moved closer to the dominant values and norms. In the Value of Children study, for example, urban Filipinos in Hawaii showed values for children intermediate between those of rural Hawaii Filipinos, who hold traditional values, and urban Japanese and Caucasians, who are more "modern" (Arnold and Fawcett, op. cit.).

Tests of the various theories yield no clear winner because all factors operate simultaneously. Controlling for social, economic, and demographic characteristics washes out some but not all observed fertility differentials (Gurak 1978, 1980), which means that the compositional approach is not sufficient. Whereas some studies support the particularized ideology hypothesis (Beaujot, Krotki, and Krishnan 1977), others support the minority group hypothesis (Johnson and Nishida 1980). Rindfuss and Sweet find "confirmatory evidence" for different perspectives, using 1970 data (1977, p. 114).

A study of 1980 census by Kahn (1988) sought further to explore the factors affecting *immigrant* fertility. (Because this study focused on immigrants, it did not deal with native-born descendants of immigrants.) Kahn hypothesized that fertility differentials among immigrant groups (from high-fertility developing countries) were related to the following factors:

1. fertility levels in the countries of origin (immigrants from higher-fertility countries will tend to have higher fertility . . . a particularized ideology perspective);

2. life-cycle stage when immigrating (immigration as an adult means fertility levels closer to those of the origin country, while immigration as a child means more opportunity to socialize to the host-country norms and behaviors . . . combines particularized ideology and assimilationist approaches);

3. selectivity in the country of origin (better-educated immigrants will assimilate more quickly and will have had nonaverage fertility values in the country of origin . . . partly an assimilationist approach); and

4. degree of assimilation in the United States (the more like the host population in many ways, for example, in language spoken, the closer the fertility to that of the host population . . . an assimilationist approach).

Kahn looked at the nine largest U.S. immigrant groups from the developing world, including immigrants from China (Hong Kong, Taiwan, and the People's Republic of China), India, Korea, and the Philippines, and tested her hypotheses in a multivariate approach. Her results (which did not examine the minority group hypothesis) in general supported all her hypotheses.

We conclude that culture, selection, composition, assimilation, and minority group status all affect the fertility of immigrants and of Asian Americans.

Further research will tell us more about the sources of these fertility differentials. In the meantime we can speculate briefly about future trends in Asian American fertility. An assimilation approach would predict that, if Asian Americans become more like other Americans in their demographic, social, and economic characteristics, their fertility will become more and more like that of other Americans as well. Such reasoning underlies the fertility assumptions in a set of projections by Bouvier and Agresta (1987). The projections assume that by "the year 2010, all immigrants and their descendants will exhibit the same fertility as that of the" total population (p. 289). A recent study of Indochinese refugees found that fertility was lower when socioeconomic adaptation was greater. Refugees with the highest family income had the lowest fertility since arriving in the United States, and vice versa (Rumbaut and Weeks 1985, p. 18).

It is interesting to note that controlling for education does not eliminate fertility differentials between Asian Americans and whites. Vietnamese stand out as having high fertility regardless of education, but other groups, most notably Filipinos and Asian Indians, have higher fertility than whites within three of the four education levels shown. Similarity in education alone, then, between Asian Americans and whites does not result in similar fertility.[7]

The minority group perspective would predict that Asian American fertility will remain low (for Japanese and Chinese, especially) or become low (for Filipinos and Vietnamese) if group members perceive low fertility as a route for upward mobility. Again, if thorough assimilation of these groups occurs, then the groups may lose their sense of a "group" striving for mobility, and Asian American fertility will become more like that of the rest of the nation.

The particularized ideology approach also rests on whether assimilation, especially cultural assimilation, occurs. If ethnic groups do not

---

[7]We must note, however, that this is a treatment of education *without* taking age structure or other factors into account.

"melt" into the overall "pot," then fertility norms and values and behavior may not converge toward those of the total nation. The low fertility of some Asian American groups may remain low, and others may remain high.

Such reasoning might predict that, for example, if Vietnamese do not readily assimilate, their fertility could remain at exceptionally high levels. Although Vietnamese fertility is far higher than that of any other Asian American group, it is not as high as the fertility of blacks or Hispanics, who are long established in this country. However, Vietnamese fertility will probably fall rapidly as the group becomes more established, with immigrants making up a smaller proportion of the Vietnamese population. Data from the Rumbaut and Weeks study (1985) show that some fall in fertility has already taken place.

In the light of the above considerations, we expect Asian American fertility levels to come closer to national levels but to continue to exhibit some differences, whether rooted in social and economic characteristics, culture, or continued perception of minority status and striving for upward mobility and success.

Mortality[8]

Recent publications state that "[t]he health status of Asian Americans as a group is remarkably good" (USODPHP 1987, p. 18-1) and that "[t]he Asian/Pacific Island minority, in aggregate, is healthier than all [other] racial/ethnic groups in the United States" (USDHHS 1985, p. 81). Nevertheless, we find it difficult to come to any firm conclusions about the precise current levels of mortality and health of Asian Americans in general or of specific Asian American groups in particular. This is because of the same problems of data comparability that confound the study of Asian American fertility.

The information we have on the mortality of Asian Americans can be divided into several types. There are national-level and state-level studies. There are studies which focus on one particular age group, principally studies of infant mortality and the analysis of health status at birth. There are also works focusing on causes of death, such as cancer and heart disease. Some of the studies we look at do not deal with matching problems, while others try to take them into account.

---

[8]An expanded version of the material in this section can be found in Gardner (forthcoming).

TABLE 3.4

Crude Death Rates: 1940–1980, and Age-Standardized
Death Rates: 1970–1980, by Race

	Crude Death Rates					Age-Standardized Death Rates	
	1940	1950	1960	1970	1980	1970	1980
TOTAL	10.8	9.6	9.5	9.5	8.8	7.1	5.9
White	10.4	9.5	9.5	9.5	9.1	6.8	5.6
Black	13.9	11.3	10.4	10.0	8.6	10.0	8.6
Chinese	15.3	9.0	6.8	4.7	3.7	4.9	3.5
Japanese	6.7	6.1	5.1	4.2	4.0	3.3	2.9
Filipino	—	—	—	—	2.4	—	2.5

SOURCE: 1940–1960: NCHD, Vital Statistics, 1960, Volume II, Section A, 1970, 1980: Yu et al. 1984.

NOTES: Deaths per 1,000 population. Standardized on the 1940 age distribution.

National-Level Studies

The most basic measure of the mortality of a population is the crude death rate: the number of deaths in a given year divided by the midyear population of the group at risk. Published crude death rates (CDRs) for Asian Americans suffer from at least two shortcomings. First, in common with all crude death rates, they are affected by the age compositions of the populations: a "young" population will have a lower CDR, all else equal, than an "old" population, because a higher proportion of the population is at ages where death rates are low. Second, the published CDRs suffer from the familiar problems of matching.

Keeping the above in mind, we present the CDRs for U.S. whites, blacks, American Indians, Chinese, and Japanese since 1940 in Table 3.4. The picture from these data is one of very low Asian American mortality, higher white mortality, and quite high black mortality. The comparisons are made more valid for the last 2 census years by the calculation of age-standardized death rates, thus removing the effects of the differing age structures on the rates. If we accept these figures at face value, we must conclude that Asian American mortality levels, at least for the groups for which data are available, are substantially below those for the country as a whole and even those of the majority white population.[9] However, the low rates for Asian Americans are suspect because

[9]As we shall see below, other figures for 1979–1981 give the same picture (Table 3.9).

of possible mismatch of numerators and denominators. There is no quick and easy way to correct for this problem, but the study discussed next went to some effort to deal with it.

The best early national study of mortality which included data on Asian Americans was the classic work on differential mortality by Kitagawa and Hauser (1973). This work matched records for some 340,000 deaths that occurred from May through August 1960, to 1960 census records in order to obtain kinds of information about the decedents which are not ordinarily available (such as income, which does not appear on the death certificate). The matching process enabled adjustment of ethnic death rates by examination of discrepant reporting of ethnicity between the death certificates and the census schedule. The resulting adjustments revealed that uncorrected 1960 data for whites, blacks, and Japanese were reasonably accurate, but that data on Chinese were somewhat flawed by mismatch problems.

According to the authors, "[p]erhaps the most striking finding is the very low mortality of the Japanese." (p. 101). Mortality indexes for Japanese for infants, children under 5 years of age, and individuals over 5 years were all about one-third below the rates for whites. Further, "Japanese mortality for each sex was well below the White level in each of the (geographic) regions for which sufficient numbers of Japanese made calculations possible" (p. 126).

For Chinese males the corrected mortality index for ages 5 and over was 10 percent above that for whites, but for females it was about 9 percent lower. (Chinese numbers in 1960 were so small and data problems so important that other comparisons could not be made.)

Kitagawa and Hauser (1973) also calculated life tables from *uncorrected* age-specific death rates for whites, blacks, and Japanese (those groups for which their correction procedures had little or no effect). Life expectancy for Japanese males was estimated to be 74.4 years, while that for Japanese females was 80.4 years. Comparable figures for whites were 67.5 and 74.7 years, respectively (Table 3.5). These figures are close to those from a California study by Hechter and Borhani (1965) for the same time period.

A study of 1979 data by the National Center for Health Statistics (NCHS) added evidence to the picture of relatively low levels of Japanese American and Chinese American mortality (1980, pp. 16-17), but neither this study nor those discussed immediately below made any adjustments or attempts to correct for numerator-denominator mismatch. (The NCHS authors caution that "observed rates . . . may contain a large error component" [p. 33].) At all levels these groups showed age-specific death rates lower than those for whites, with Japanese rates lower than those of Chinese at most ages.

TABLE 3.5

Estimated Life Expectancy at Birth, Combined Sexes, by Ethnic Group, Hawaii:
1920–1980, and California and United States: 1960 and 1979–1981

Year	White	Chinese	Japanese	Filipino	Hawaiian, Part/Hawaiian	Total
			HAWAII			
1920	56.5	53.8	50.5	28.1	33.6	45.7
1930	61.9	60.1	60.1	46.1	41.9	54.0
1940	64.0	65.3	66.3	56.9	51.8	62.0
1950	69.2	69.7	72.6	69.1	62.5	69.5
1960	72.8	74.1	75.7	71.5	64.6	72.4
1970	73.2	76.1	77.4	72.6	67.6	74.1
1980	76.4	80.2	79.7	78.8	74.0	78.0
			CALIFORNIA			
1960[a]	71.3	72.9	77.9	—	—	—
1979–1981	74.9	82.5[b]		—	—	74.8
			UNITED STATES[a]			
1960	71.2	—	77.4	—	—	—
1979–1981	74.5	81.9[c]				73.9

SOURCES: Hawaii: Gardner 1984; California, 1960: Hechter and Borhani 1965; California, 1979–1981: California Center for Health Statistics, 1983; United States, 1960: Kitagawa and Hauser 1973; United States, 1979–1981, Asian and Pacific Islander: Duke University Center for Demographic Studies, 1984; White and Total: U.S. National Center for Health Statistics, 1985.

[a] Simple average of male and female life expectancies.

[b] Combined Chinese and Japanese.

[c] Asian and Pacific Islander.

A National Institutes of Health Task Force on Black and Minority Health looked at data on the health and mortality of minority groups for 1979–1981. Life tables prepared for this effort (again uncorrected for matching problems) showed Asian Americans (here grouped with Pacific Islanders, who formed about 7 percent of the Asian-Pacific Islander total in 1980) with the lowest mortality of any group listed (Table 3.5).

Another study undertaken as part of the work of the Task Force on Black and Minority Health represented a major effort to summarize the recent mortality experience of Asian Americans (Yu et al. 1984). The authors of this study used unpublished data from the National Center for Health Statistics to calculate a number of measures of Asian American health and comparable figures for the U.S. white population for 1980. The data were restricted to Chinese, Japanese, and Filipinos, and the authors were not able to deal with what Kitagawa and Hauser termed "discrepancies in the reporting of race on death certificates and census records" (1973, p. 101), so we have no way of knowing how well the data portrayed the actual situation. We will look at the results of this study when we discuss causes of death.

State-Level Studies

The state of Hawaii is a natural "laboratory" for studies of ethnic mortality differences, since so many ethnic groups are present in relatively large numbers. In Hawaii the Department of Health annually conducts a Health Surveillance Survey that provides sample estimates of the population by age, sex, and ethnicity. The ethnic estimates of the population from this survey are usually accepted as better denominators for calculating birth and death rates than are data from the census, because the definitions used are closer to those used for vital statistics. Data from this source have been used to produce life tables for the major ethnic groups of the state in recent years; in earlier years census data were appropriate as denominators. We thus have a series of estimates of life expectancy by ethnicity for Hawaii dating back to 1920, estimates that are less affected by data problems than are most of the national data.

The Hawaii data show large mortality differentials among the ethnic groups in 1920, narrowing as time passes (Table 3.5). Early in this century white life expectancy was the highest of any group's, but Japanese life expectancy passed that of whites between 1930 and 1940, followed by Chinese some 10 years later. In 1980, Chinese life expectancy in Hawaii was the highest of any group for which we have reliable data, with Japanese, Filipino, and white trailing and with the descendants of the original residents of the islands, Hawaiians and part-Hawaiians, showing the lowest life expectancy.

The factors behind these differentials and patterns can never be completely untangled. However, newly arrived immigrant groups in Hawaii generally started off at the bottom of both the economic and mortality ladders (Gardner and Schmitt 1978).[10] In the last years of the nineteenth century, the mortality of the recently arrived Japanese in Honolulu may have been as much as twice as high as white mortality, while the

---

[10]For the country as a whole, it was reported that in 1921 the Chinese American crude death rate was twice that of the white population (Winslow and Hoh 1924, cited in Liu 1986). These were *not* newly arrived immigrants, to be sure, but they were still near the bottom of the economic scale. However, the crude death rate is badly affected by the age structure of a population, and since the Chinese population in 1921 was composed principally of the aging survivors of earlier immigrants, this comparison is not as convincing as it might have been otherwise.

mortality of Chinese, who were long established in Hawaii, was only slightly higher than that of whites (Schmidt 1967). Over the years, as the economic conditions of immigrant groups improved, so did their absolute and relative mortality.

The economic situation of a group is undoubtedly important in determining its level of mortality, but it certainly cannot be the only factor, since the ranking of life expectancy in Hawaii in 1980 did not exactly parallel the ranking of incomes for the various groups. Nevertheless, we can surmise that newly arrived immigrant groups may be at something of a disadvantage, in terms of health and mortality, especially if they are relatively poor as well. In the United States today we might expect to find relatively high mortality among the Vietnamese, who arrived recently and whose incomes, according to data shown later in the volume, are quite low compared to those of other groups (we discuss infant mortality among Vietnamese below). On the other hand, we would expect to find relatively low mortality among Japanese, whose per capita income is high and whose population is composed mostly of native-born individuals.

Hechter and Borhani looked at mortality in California (1965). Their study, which did not show whether any attempt was made to deal with mismatch of numerator and denominator, found that Japanese in California during 1959–1961 had a much higher life expectancy (74.5 years for males, 81.2 years for females) than did Chinese (68.5 and 77.3, respectively), whites (67.8 and 74.8), and blacks (64.4 and 70.0). The age-specific death rates upon which the life tables were based showed lower Japanese than white or black mortality at every age (age data for Chinese were not shown). These death rates were also found to be close to those of Japanese in Hawaii at the same period.

Infant Mortality

Of all aspects of mortality, infant mortality has traditionally received the largest share of attention. Data on infant mortality rates (IMR) show levels that were very low for Asian Americans (Figure 3.1). The IMR for Chinese in 1987 was 5.0 infant deaths per 1000 births; for Japanese, the rate was 4.6 and for Filipinos, 4.4. These compared to the white level of 8.6 deaths per 1000 births and the national level of 10.1; the figure for blacks was 17.9. Data on IMRs back to 1950 indicate similar differentials have existed for at least several decades.

Several studies have found that babies of mixed ethnicity tended to be classified more often as white at death than at birth (e.g., Frost and Shy 1980), which would bias white IMRs upward and other IMRs down-

FIGURE 3.1

Infant Mortality Rates, by Race, U.S.: 1950–1987

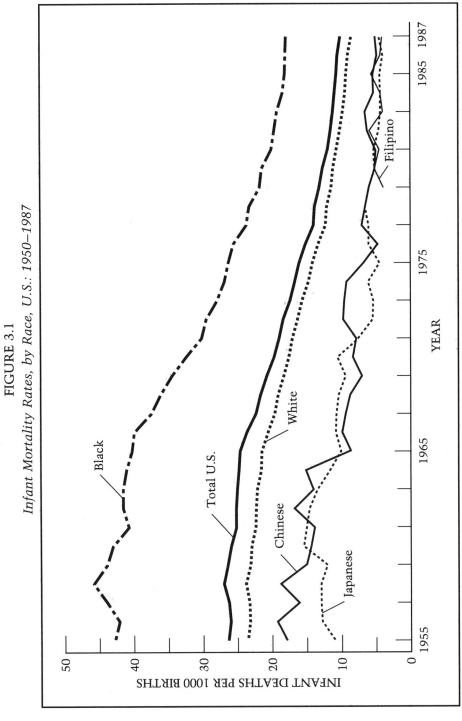

SOURCES: Vital Statistics of the United States, Volume II (Mortality), Part A, Section 2; for the given years, and unpublished NCHS data.

ward. In California, after adjusting for such classification error, 1965–1967 Japanese infant mortality rates (at 22.0 deaths per 1000 births) were 62 percent higher than before adjustment and were actually higher than those for whites in California (19.3 per 1000) (Norris and Shipley 1971). Chinese rates, on the other hand, which were 13.6 infant deaths per 1000 births before adjustment, rose 25 percent after adjustment but were still the lowest for any racial group. (After adjustment, American Indian IMRs had risen by 109 percent, "others" rose by 134 percent, whites fell by 3 percent, and blacks barely changed.) In Hawaii, ethnically the most heterogeneous state in the country, fully 8.4 percent of infant death certificates for the years 1978–1981 showed a different race from that coded for the infant at birth (Burch 1983). (However, only 12 percent of the deceased infants were classified as white when their birth certificates had showed non-white races.)

Such studies demonstrate that, unless births and deaths are "matched," we must use a great deal of caution in looking at all infant mortality rates for subgroups of a population.

Elena Yu (1982) sought explanations for the extremely low reported levels of mortality among Chinese infants. She looked for possible explanations among such candidates as underreporting of infant deaths and misreporting of race on the birth and death certificates. She concluded that none of these provided a sufficient explanation for low Chinese infant mortality. Turning to matched birth and death records for California, Yu found that "the best available data suggest that the true infant mortality rate for Chinese Americans may be lower than that found for White Americans" (p. 263).

Yu was "tempted to posit that perhaps [the Chinese advantage was because] the Chinese American women who gave births [sic] during 1973–77, being 86% foreign-born (non-U.S. residents excluded)—compared to about 8% foreign-born in the White population—may have retained a traditional set of sociocultural health habits or lifestyles which contribute to their advantage in fetal survival [including] herbal medicine and dietary preferences" (p. 263).

Yu did not mention Japanese infant mortality more than in passing, but her data showed that it, too, although higher than Chinese, was substantially below white and national levels.

A more recent matching study from San Diego County, California, for the period 1978–1985 (Rumbaut and Weeks 1989) focused on Indochinese refugees but collected data on other ethnic groups as well. Table 3.6 presents data from that study. These data clearly showed that, at least in one part of California, Asian American levels of infant mortality were generally below those of other major ethnic groups. The data also indicated that there are differences among the separate Asian American

TABLE 3.6

*Infant Mortality Rates, by Ethnic Group, San Diego
County: 1978–1985*

Ethnic Group	Infant Mortality Rate
All Indochinese	6.6
Hmong	9.1
Lao	7.2
Vietnamese	5.5
Khmer	5.8
Filipino	7.2
Chinese	6.9
Japanese	6.2
Black	16.3
White (non-Hispanic)	8.0
Hispanic	7.3
Total	8.5

SOURCE: Rumbaut and Weeks 1989, Table 2.

NOTE: Calculated from linked records.

groups and that, although the predominantly refugee groups compared favorably with non-Asian groups, some refugee groups, in particular the Hmong, had relatively high infant mortality rates (although still only marginally higher than the rate for white non-Hispanics).

The above data on Vietnamese and other Indochinese groups are among the few pieces of information we have so far on mortality of Asian American groups other than Japanese, Chinese, and, to a lesser extent, Filipinos. The low rates are especially remarkable, according to the authors of the study

(1) because they reflect a very rapid reduction in infant death levels from those of their sending environments and their own prior experiences, and thus a positive adjustment to the receiving environment in the United States; (2) because their currently observable patterns of infant mortality, especially among the Hmong and Lao, involve greater than average proportions of post-early neonatal deaths which may in principle be preventable, thus leaving open the likelihood that their IMRs can be reduced further still; and (3) because this major epidemiological transition has taken place in the context of their extraordinarily stressful migration and resettlement experiences, and *despite* the fact that these refugees generally . . . reflect high-risk socioeconomic profiles overall (p. 189).

The National Center for Health Statistics recently produced publicly available computer tapes of matched birth and death certificates, allowing researchers the opportunity of examining infant mortality at the national level without having to worry about problems of matching. The ethnicity used in such studies is that of the mother.

The first studies using this rich new data source are now beginning to appear. Kleinman (1990), looking at data on infant mortality for the years 1983–1984, noted that

> [f]or whites and blacks, the race coding on the birth certificate differed from that on the corresponding death certificate in <2% of the linked files; however, 25%–40% of infant deaths among births coded as American Indian/Alaskan Native or Asian on the birth certificate were coded to a different race on the death certificate (p. 32).

Kleinman found that Asian infant mortality (8.6 deaths per 1000 births) was below that of whites (9.1), and within Asian groups, Japanese rates were lowest (6.0), followed by Chinese (8.3), Filipino (8.5), and "Other Asian (9.0)."

Information on infant mortality for the slightly longer period 1983–1985, again using the linked data, is found in "Health United States, 1990" (USNCHS 1991). Japanese, Chinese, and Filipino infant mortality rates, in that order, were found to be below those of whites and most other groups studied.

Matched Hawaii data for 10 ethnic groupings for a longer period, 1979–1988, showed Chinese had the lowest IMRs, followed in order by Japanese, Samoans, Caucasians, Hispanics, Filipinos, Koreans, others, Hawaiians and part-Hawaiians, and blacks (Park and Horiuchi 1991). Standardizing by birthweight resulted in some rearrangement: Japanese levels were lowest, followed in order by Chinese and Filipinos, Koreans, Hispanics, blacks, Caucasians, Hawaiians and part-Hawaiians, and Samoans.

A second perspective on infant health and survival is provided from birthweight records. Weight at birth is known to be significantly associated with infant survival; a birthweight of less than 2500 grams is considered low. In the United States in 1988, 6.9 percent of all births were below 2500 grams in weight (Table 3.7). The percentages for some Asian American groups, however, were lower: 4.7 percent for Chinese and 6.2 percent for Japanese. The Japanese percentage of low-birthweight infants was above that for whites (5.6 percent) but below that for the only other Asian American group tabulated, Filipinos, whose figure was 7.1 percent.

Taffel (1984) notes that a major factor involved with low birth-

TABLE 3.7

Percentage of Births of Low Weight, by Ethnicity: 1970–1988

Group	1970	1975	1980	1981	1982	1983	1984	1985	1986	1987	1988
TOTAL U.S.	7.9	7.4	6.8	6.8	6.8	6.8	6.7	6.8	6.8	6.9	6.9
White	6.8	6.3	5.7	5.7	5.6	5.7	5.6	5.6	5.6	5.7	5.6
Black	13.8	13.1	12.5	12.5	12.4	12.6	12.4	12.4	12.5	12.7	13.0
Asian and											
Pacific Islander	8.4	7.0	6.6	6.6	6.6	6.5	6.5	6.1	6.4	6.4	6.3
Chinese	6.8	5.3	4.9	5.6	5.3	5.0	5.1	5.0	4.9	5.0	4.7
Japanese	8.6	7.2	6.2	6.1	6.2	5.8	6.1	5.9	5.6	6.3	6.2
Filipino	9.4	8.0	7.4	7.3	6.9	7.3	7.7	6.9	7.3	7.3	7.1

SOURCE: USNCHS, 1991, Table 7.

NOTES: Percentage of births with weight less than 2,500 grams (5 pounds, 8 ounces). For comparison, 1980 figures for California are, from top to bottom: 6.0, 5.3, 11.7, —, 4.7, 6.3, and 7.3 (California Center for Health Statistics, 1984).

weights is the educational status of the mother. Asian American women are known to be relatively well educated, but controlling for this factor statistically does not account for all the observed differences in birthweights. Taffel suggests that other factors, such as the low percentage of out-of-wedlock and teenage Asian American births, may be responsible for the observed ethnic differences in the percentage of low birthweights.

Birth-record data thus indicate that Chinese infants have the best chance for survival, followed by Japanese and then Filipinos. These rankings are in substantial agreement with the data on infant mortality rates and also with the overall mortality data from Hawaii. An earlier review of minority health by the National Center for Health Statistics (1980) showed essentially the same results.

Causes of Death: National Level

None of the studies of causes of death which we could locate included corrections or adjustments for numerator-denominator problems. Nevertheless, the results are worth reporting.

A USDHHS report included 1979–1981 data on several major causes of death and presented figures for whites, blacks, Native Americans, and Asian/Pacific Islanders without further breakdown. For almost every cause of death, the death rates for Asian/Pacific Islanders were the lowest of the four groups (Table 3.8).

More detailed information on Asian American death rates for specific causes is presented in Figure 3.2. The columns represent the ratios of the Asian American age-standardized death rates to the white age-standardized rate, and once more show the advantage that Asian Americans have over whites, according to the data.

Also interesting are the rankings of the diseases for each group. As Yu et al. (1984) note, "Insofar as the first 4 leading causes of death are concerned, all four groups have identical rankings" (p. 21). That is, heart disease, cancer, cerebrovascular disease, and accidents are the most important causes of death for Asian Americans and for whites as well. Together these account for just over 70 percent of the deaths of all these groups.

A major study by the National Cancer Institute (1986, cited in USODPHP 1987) produced age-standardized site-specific cancer incidence and death rates for three Asian American groups—Chinese, Japanese, and Filipinos—as well as whites and native Hawaiians. Results showed that Asian American cancer incidence and mortality rates for the period 1978–1981 were well below those of whites, Hawaiians, or

TABLE 3.8

Age-adjusted Death Rates and Death Rates from Specific Causes: 1979–1981

Rate per 100,000

Cause of Death	White		Black		Native American		Asian/Pacific Islander	
	Male	Female	Male	Female	Male	Female	Male	Female
ALL CAUSES	736.0	405.0	1,084.6	611.7	740.0	408.1	449.8	244.4
Cancer	159.2	106.9	227.9	127.3	80.7	59.3	106.0	67.1
Heart disease	274.4	131.9	319.4	194.4	177.8	93.3	146.2	62.2
Stroke	41.2	34.7	76.0	60.2	32.6	24.5	34.4	26.7
Homicide	10.9	3.2	73.4	14.4	24.6	8.4	8.0	3.3

SOURCE: USDHHS, 1985, pp. 65, 90, 108, 111, and 158.

FIGURE 3.2

Ratios of Age-Standardized Cause-Specific Death Rates of Asian Americans to Those of Whites: 1980

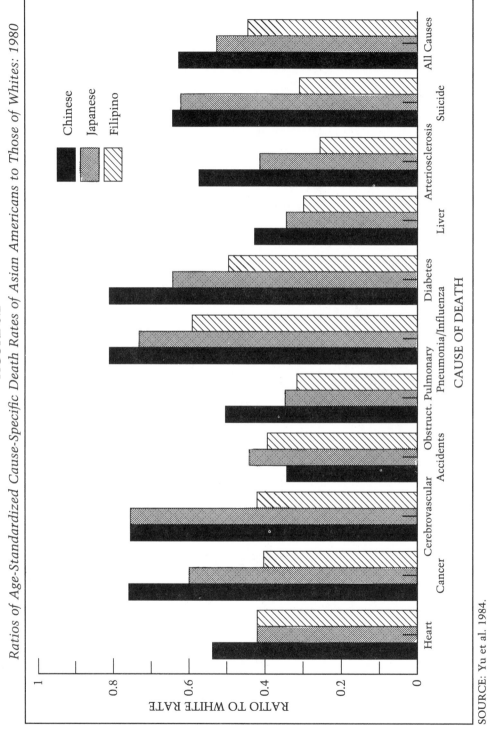

SOURCE: Yu et al. 1984.

Native Americans. For all sites combined, the death rate for Hawaiians was 200.5 per 100,000, whereas for whites it was 163.6 per 100,000 (p. 18-10). Chinese rates were 131.5 per 100,000, Japanese were 104.2 per 100,000, and Filipino rates were lowest, at 69.7 per 100,000. For specific sites, there were only rare instances where an Asian American rate was higher than that of whites. The most prominent example was for cancer of the stomach, where the Japanese rate (17.5 per 100,000) was more than three times the white rate.[11]

Sparse data on non-disease causes of death reflected the same patterns of low Asian American mortality. Death rates from unintentional injury, suicide, and homicide among Asian Americans for the period 1977–1979 were below those reported for whites, blacks, and Native Americans (Baker et al. 1984, cited in USODPHP 1987, p. 18-12).

Causes of Death: Group-Specific Studies

A number of important studies look at causes of disease and death for specific Asian American groups. A study of a single ethnic group avoids criticisms directed at the practice of looking at Asian Americans as a homogeneous group (e.g., Table 3.8). As we have seen, Asian Americans are a very mixed group with respect to health status and mortality. "[H]ealth status in fact differs widely in this population, and both mortality and morbidity rates often vary considerably among different ethnic groups" (Lin-Fu 1988, p. 21).[12]

The two most important diseases studied within ethnic groups have been cancer and heart disease, and the ethnic groups most studied have been the Japanese and the Chinese. The studies are especially interest-

[11]A quote from USDHHS 1985 (p. 96), provides some detail regarding specific cancer sites for Asian Americans:

> Stomach cancer incidence is 2.5 times higher for Japanese males and 3.8 times higher for females than for nonminority males and females. Esophageal cancer is also 2.5 times higher in Japanese males compared with nonminorities. Migratory studies of Japanese point to dietary practices as a cause in three major cancer sites: stomach, breast, and colon. . . . Chinese Americans have an increased incidence of about 17 percent over nonminorities of multiple myeloma. Incidence of esophageal cancer is higher for Chinese males and females than for nonminorities. Most studies on the causes of esophageal cancer suggest that the major risk factors are smoking and alcohol consumption, with the combined use having a synergistic effect. Consumption of hot beverages also has been implicated in esophageal cancer. Pancreatic cancer incidence is about 20 percent higher among Chinese females than among nonminorities, and an upward trend in incidence exists for Chinese of both sexes. Excess risk for pancreatic cancer has been found among cigarette smokers.

[12]Lin-Fu goes on to note that there are also differences within the different ethnic groups, as between the foreign-born and the U.S.-born. This is discussed below.

ing because they have looked at the mortality of Asians in Asia, of Asian immigrants in the United States, and of native-born Asian Americans. A common question running through many of these studies is whether or not there is a "gradient" for the death rates of the various groups. The existence of a gradient could be interpreted as showing that environmental factors are important, and that as the environment changes from the home country to the new country, so too will death rates. A gradient might also be interpreted as indicating that health-related behaviors change as individuals move from one country to another and as succeeding generations appear.

Haenszel and Kurihara (1968) commented that there was no single pattern relating disease levels for origin and destination in Japanese populations, but that for certain diseases interesting patterns were present. For example, cancers of different body sites showed different patterns. Breast cancer among Japanese in the United States remained at the relatively low levels characteristic of several "Mongolian" groups, while stomach cancer for Japanese immigrants showed an "incomplete transition" from high death rates in Japan to the relatively low rates characteristic of U. S. whites (King and Haenszel 1973, p. 641). The authors expected further changes to take place among the second-generation Japanese, since "stomach cancer mortality (among immigrants generally) relates more to country of origin than to country of destination" (Haenszel and Kurihara 1968, p. 522). (A similar pattern was found for Chinese: King and Haenszel 1973, p. 640.) For colon cancer, on the other hand, a "rather complete transition had occurred from the low risks in Japan to the characteristic high risks of U.S. whites. "[F]or colon, migrants (typically) gravitate to the experience of the host population" (Haenszel and Kurihara 1968, p. 53).

King and Haenszel (1973) looked at cancer among Chinese Americans in much the same way. The data were more sketchy, since Chinese in the United States were not as numerous as Japanese in 1960. Overall mortality levels for Chinese were close to those of U.S. whites and higher than Japanese American levels. King and Haenszel found relatively high risks for cancer of the nasopharynx, liver, and esophagus for Chinese, and relatively low risks for cancer of the prostate and of the female breast. These differences followed the general pattern for Chinese in Asia; the authors concluded that migration to the United States may have diluted risks for these sites but had caused no fundamental change (p. 643).

King and Locke (1987), on the other hand, found evidence of a "convergence of . . . cancer mortality" among Chinatown Chinese and Chinese in the United States more generally, and stated that the Chinese experience was "compatible with the transition experience noted for the U.S. Japanese migrant population" (p. 571). They suggested that it would seem advisable "to look into . . . the degree of acculturation among different segments of Chinese population to Western dietary habits in reference to such cancer sites as esophagus, stomach, colon-rectum, liver, pancreas, gallbladder, lung, urinary bladder, kidneys, breast, endometrium, ovary and cervix" (op. cit.).

Colorectal cancer was the topic of a recent study by Chinese and American researchers (Whittemore et al. 1990). Comparing Chinese Americans in western North America with Chinese in the People's Republic of China, the study found that colorectal cancer was significantly associated with saturated fat consumption (the only dietary association) and with sedentary occupations. Among immigrants, the risk of colorectal cancer increased with the number of years lived in North America. Thus, both dietary and life-style factors were seen to influence this particular cancer. The levels of colorectal cancer among Chinese American men were comparable to those of white American men; the rates among Chinese American women were intermediate between those of Chinese women in China and white American women. (The different relationships for males and females were explained by longer average residence by males in North America.)

Turning from cancer to cerebrovascular accidents (CVA), Haenszel and Kurihara (1968) found that death rates for Japanese in Japan were much higher than those for whites in the United States; Japanese Americans (native and immigrant combined) showed rates close to the U.S. white levels, a relatively "complete transition."

For coronary heart disease (CHD), by way of contrast, U.S. white levels were much higher than rates in Japan; Japanese American rates were intermediate, with Japanese immigrants showing a rise from the low levels in Japan. More change in an upward direction was expected among second-generation Japanese. Filipino immigrants also showed an "upward displacement" in a Hawaii study (Hackenberg et al. n.d.).

Haenszel and Kurihara concluded that "much of (the overall Japanese) advantage can be ascribed to the carry-over from Japan of the low risks of heart disease, coupled with a sharp reduction in mortality from vascular lesions of the central nervous system (CVA)" (p. 46).

King and Locke (1987) looked at levels of ischemic heart disease among Chinese immigrants, Chinese in major origin areas (Foshan and Hong Kong), and U.S. whites. They found that immigrant mortality far exceeded that of origin Chinese, but "remained significantly below that of the host white population" (p. 567).

A smaller study of Filipinos in Hawaii by Gerber (1980) similarly found that Filipino immigrants in Hawaii had higher rates of mortality from CHD than prevailed in the Philippines but lower rates than for the total United States.

It thus appears that for some diseases and causes of death there does exist a gradient in mortality from the origin country to the United States, with first-generation (i.e., immigrant) groups showing intermediate rates and native-born members showing a mortality level closer to that of the U.S. white population. The exceptions to this pattern are many, however, and Haenszel and Kurihara warn that, for cancers, not all types "present an orderly, uninterrupted sequence from home-to-host populations" (p. 56).

Age Patterns of Asian American Mortality

The age patterns of mortality for whites, Chinese, Japanese, and Filipinos for 1980 are portrayed in Figure 3.3 (these are data uncorrected for definitional problems). All the curves followed a commonly observed J-pattern, with high rates at the extreme young and old ages (the curves would be higher for the youngest ages if age 0 were distinguished from ages 1–4). The curve for whites was higher at every age than the curves for any of the Asian American groups. At all ages except the oldest, Chinese rates were next highest, followed by Japanese and then Filipinos. Filipinos thus showed the lowest mortality of any of the groups shown, a finding in agreement with the ranking of age-standardized death rates from the same study (Yu et al. 1984).

The ratios of the death rates for Asian Americans to those for whites at each age are shown in Figure 3.4. Here the information shown in Figure 3.3 was made more dramatic: Asian American mortality at all ages was well below that of whites for 1980. In all but one case, Filipino age-specific death rates ranked as the lowest of the groups shown, with Japanese usually second and Chinese highest.

Sex Ratios for Mortality among Asian Americans

As is generally true today, no matter what population is being examined, the death rates for Asian American males are higher than those for Asian American females at almost every age (the only exception noted in Yu et al. is for Chinese ages 5–14 years). A similar situation is observable for death rates for the major causes of death: males die at higher rates almost without exception. These specific differences between males and females are summarized in the life-table values for all Asian and Pacific Islanders, where the female value for e_0 is 8.5 years higher than that for males.

FIGURE 3.3

Age-Specific Death Rates for Whites and Asian Americans: 1980

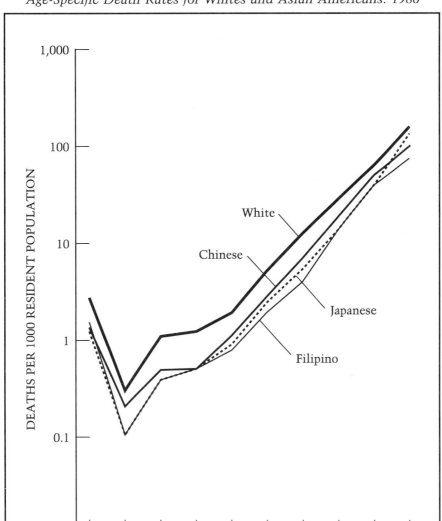

SOURCE: Yu et al. 1984, Table 12.

FIGURE 3.4

Ratios of Asian American Death Rates, by Age, to Those of Whites: 1980

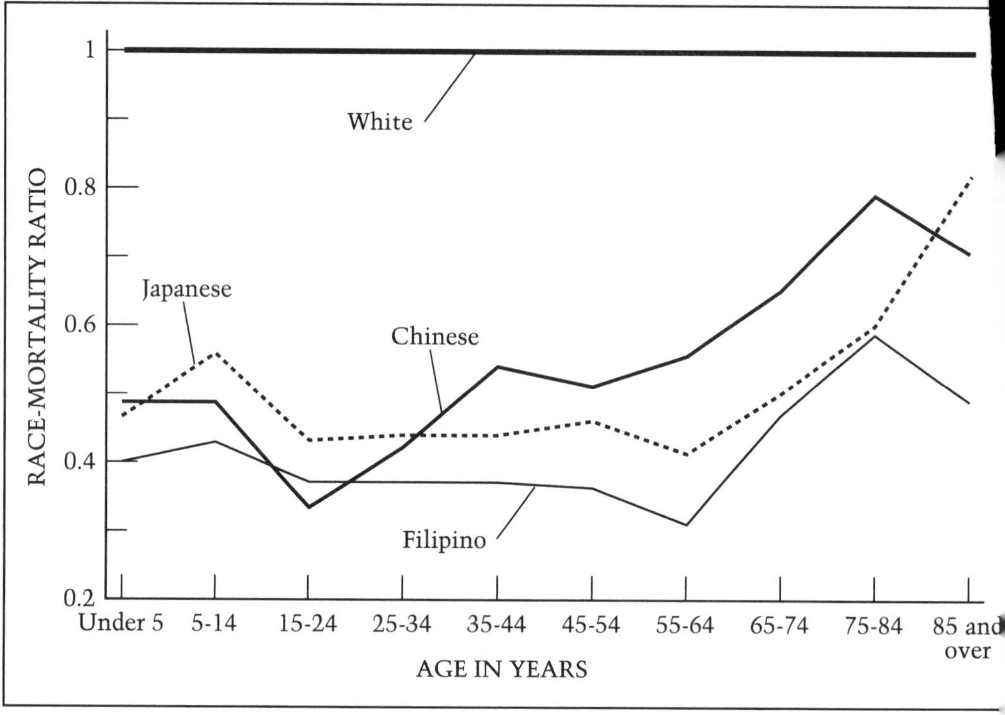

SOURCE: Yu et al. 1984, Table 12.

Nativity as a Factor in Asian American Mortality

A final factor that Yu and her coauthors investigated was nativity: U.S.-born or foreign-born. Their data showed that both crude and age-adjusted mortality rates for Asians born abroad were higher in 1980 than the comparable rates for native-born Asian Americans. "For every one of the 10 leading causes of death, the mortality rates for foreign-born exceeded the native-born—on average—by a ratio of at least 2.0, if not larger" (p. 31). Insofar as a population of Asian Americans is composed primarily of native-born (such as Japanese) or foreign-born (the prime example being Vietnamese), we would expect its mortality levels to be correspondingly influenced downward or upward.

Comment

The fact that many of the above findings are based on vital statistics data unadjusted for comparability with census data, coupled with the fact that Kitagawa and Hauser and others have noted some discrepancies during matching procedures, leads us to suggest extreme care in interpretation. For example, whereas Kitagawa and Hauser found that Japanese death rates tended to be about one-third lower than white rates, Yu et al. found ratios more of the order of 50 percent, varying by age and cause of death. Kitagawa and Hauser did not even attempt to calculate certain measures for Chinese, so important were the mismatch problems.

A second reason for some skepticism is the fact that Filipinos are shown to have the lowest mortality among all the groups studied by Yu and her coresearchers. If we look at the various factors presumed to affect mortality (see the discussion below), we would not expect such low mortality levels for Filipinos. We might expect a ranking for Filipinos similar to that found in Hawaii in 1980 (Table 3.5), but standardized death rates less than half those of whites seem a bit low.

Mortality levels for Asian Americans indicated by the *unadjusted* vital statistics data are probably lower than the actual levels because of data comparability problems. These problems may be greater for some groups than for others; as noted above, Filipinos and Japanese tend to marry out more than Chinese, so the potential numbers of mixed-race children and eventual adults are greater, and therefore so is the potential for death rates, which may be too low.

Some of this effect may also be at work in the nativity differentials. The foreign-born of all groups were found to have higher death rates than the native-born. Assuming that the foreign-born are less likely to give discrepant information about their ethnicity, it makes sense that their mortality is better captured by the use of vital statistics data than is the mortality of individuals of mixed ethnicity. While not arguing that the foreign-born would otherwise have lower mortality than the native-born, we suggest that a part of the nativity differential may be due to the mismatch effect's being greater among the native-born.

There is no reason to suppose, however, that Asian American mortality levels, especially those of Chinese and Japanese, are higher than those of whites. There is too much evidence in the opposite direction. Rather, we would simply caution against placing too much reliance on the size of the Asian-white differentials reported above.

Factors Affecting Mortality Levels of Asian Americans

We now come to the question of what factors affect the observed levels and patterns of mortality among Asian Americans. A discussion of the determinants of Asian American mortality levels and why these levels differ from those of whites and others in the country parallels to some extent our discussion of fertility differentials. A "characteristics" approach would seek to attribute differences in mortality to differences in income, education, and the like. From this perspective, if the characteristics of two groups are the same, then mortality would be the same. A "particularized ideology" or cultural perspective would assume that behavioral differences, such as in diet, are at least partially responsible for mortality levels and, if dietary differences persist, so too will mortality differences.

A third perspective is that of selection: immigrants are probably "positively" selected on the basis of health. A fourth perspective is one not found with regard to fertility, the genetic perspective. There is some evidence, as we shall mention below, for a genetic basis for differences in at least some causes of death.

Kitagawa and Hauser took an essentially assimilationist approach and mentioned a number of factors that have been influential regarding mortality levels and their decline over the years in the United States and elsewhere. These include "increased productivity, higher standards of living, decreased internecine warfare, environmental sanitation, personal hygiene, public health measures, and modern medicine climaxed by the advent of the pesticides and chemotherapy" (p. 151). There have been many attempts to disentangle the importance of these various factors in mortality declines (e.g., the classic McKeown and Brown study 1962), but that is not our task here. Rather, we hope simply to look at the available skimpy evidence to come to some observations about the sources of the observed mortality differentials among whites and Asian Americans.

Chief among these sources are probably socioeconomic factors. Kitagawa and Hauser noted that "the race differentials, in general, are consistent with the inverse relationship between mortality and socioeconomic status" they had observed earlier in their volume (p. 102). However, apart from Hauser and Kitagawa's study, the data linking mortality levels among Asian Americans to their socioeconomic status are all inferential: there are no direct data on mortality levels by economic status (cf. Yu et al. 1984, p. 18).

In any case, socioeconomic status cannot be the only factor involved, and in fact one observer feels that "[s]ocial class differences have not lent themselves as convincing explanation in the mortality statistics and morbidity data" [used in an Alameda, California, study by Breslow and Klein 1971] (Liu 1986, p. 164.).

Genetic factors are mentioned in the literature as being involved in ethnic differentials in mortality. For example, the extremely high levels of nasopharyngeal cancer observed among Chinese, especially those from certain high-risk areas of China, have been attributed to genetic causes (mentioned by King and Haenszel 1973, and by Hu and White 1979; Yu et al. 1984, cite Ho 1979, as well). Haenszel and Kurihara say that "persistence of low breast-cancer rates among the second-generation Nisei (Japanese) suggests a role for genetic factors" (p. 57).

Not everyone agrees that genetic factors are at work, or at least that they are of much importance. For example, Liu states that the evidence "has failed to suggest that differences in mortality and health care are due to genetic (racial) differences, as Asians have achieved both high and low mortality rates relative to the U.S. general population" (1986, p. 164).

Diet is a commonly mentioned behavioral factor. Immigrants coming to this country may seek to retain their origin diets, but eventually they or their descendants probably come to have a diet closer to that of the rest of the nation. Insofar as diet is linked to disease, convergence of the mortality rates of immigrants and their descendants to the levels and patterns of the host country would be expected to follow convergence of diet. For example, the Japanese diet, traditionally high in sodium, has been implicated in the high levels of CVA found in that country. Japanese American levels of CVA are lower than those of Japan, if still higher than those of U.S. whites, indicating the impact of a possible change in diet away from extremely high levels of sodium.

A second set of behavioral factors has to do with smoking and drinking. Yu, in her (1982) examination of infant mortality and Yu et al. (1984) in their look at Asian-white mortality differentials emphasize the fact that apparent low Asian American levels of smoking and alcohol consumption may lie behind the observed low Asian American perinatal death rates and low adult death rates for certain causes of death for which tobacco or alcohol has been shown to be a major risk factor.

The behavioral factors of level of exercise and diet have been cited as affecting colon cancer in Chinese. The traditional Chinese life-style is seen as healthier, and as noted earlier, Chinese in the United States who adopt the Western life-style are at greater risk of colon cancer (Whittemore et al. 1990).

This leads to consideration of a more general and elusive factor, "acculturation" and life-style. Diet is one facet of acculturation or assimilation, of course, but there are many others. As with the presumed resulting disease and death rates, there is probably a behavior continuum from first-generation Asian Americans, reared at least partly in the origin country, and second and later generation Asian Americans, brought up in the United States. Marmot and Syme (1976) looked at cultural factors possibly affecting heart disease among Japanese American males, including use of language, ethnicity of associates, and religion. Citing the steep gradient in CHD mortality rates from low in Japan through intermediate for Japanese in Hawaii to high for Japanese in California found by other researchers (Gordon 1957 and 1967; Kagan et al. 1974; and Marmot et al. 1975), they studied Japanese American males in eight San Francisco Bay Area counties. Using measures of culture that distinguished traditional from nontraditional, Marmot and Syme (1976) found that traditional Japanese males in the United States tended to have low levels of CHD, while nontraditional Japanese males had high levels. The most traditional group has a prevalence rate for CHD only one-fifth the rate of the group most acculturated to the United States, which tended to be characterized by relative lack of stability and accent on the individual rather than the group (p. 246). "(T)his study supported the suggestion that a stable society whose members enjoy the support of their fellows in closely knit groups may protect against the forms of social stress that may lead to CHD" (p. 245).[13] The results of this study are especially important because the authors took into account possible confounding factors such as diet, age, smoking, high blood pressure, serum triglyceride, weight, and levels of serum cholesterol.

The importance of culture is also emphasized by Liu (1986). He states that "[t]he changes of mortality rates over time can only be explained by changes of life styles, environment, and the way people take care—or fail to take care—of their health" (p. 164). This includes not only diet but also use of traditional versus modern medicines and seeking medical help, especially from a nonethnic source, if at all. Also important may be the existence of a personal support system (Berkman and Syme 1979, and Roberts and Lee 1980, both cited in Liu 1986). The important factor may not so much be something specific to a particular culture as the existence of a support system, whatever the culture. For example, the coronary heart disease mortality differentials observed among Japanese in Japan, in Hawaii (a mixture of Japanese and American cultures), and in the mainland United States can be traced at least in part to viewing "Japanese society [as] the most cohesive and familistic of the three, and

---

[13]Another effect of support was cited by Rumbaut and Weeks (1989) in their study of infant mortality. They suggest that certain types of family structures and community supports may shape "positive *adaptation* outcomes," which in turn are reflected by surprisingly low (in the light of socioeconomic situations) infant mortality rates (p. 190).

the United States the least integrative (between the individual and his group) and the most individualistic" (Liu 1986, p. 168).

Rumbaut and Weeks (1989) also place emphasis on the importance of culture, finding that groups with poor economic status nevertheless can achieve quite low infant mortality rates. They suggest that "the low rate of infant mortality within this seemingly high-risk population is at least partly due to such sociocultural factors as a generally nutritious diet in socially supportive familial and co-ethnic contexts, combined with virtual non-use of drugs, alcohol and tobacco by Indochinese women" (p. 191).

Research into the mortality of Asian Americans so far, then, has shown that there are differentials and that these differentials can be traced to differences in many factors, including socioeconomic status, diet, genetic inheritance, and life-style and cultural factors. Nowhere near enough research into the situation has been conducted, however, and with the recent rise to numerical prominence of Korean, Asian Indian, and Vietnamese groups, all bringing with them still different constellations of traits and behaviors, it is clear that researchers in the field of ethnic differentials in mortality still have much to study and much to learn.

Summary

Crude death rates and life tables unadjusted for numerator-denominator match problems show extremely low current mortality levels for Asian Americans. Age adjustment diminishes the advantage of these groups but does not erase it, nor do attempts to take into account the important definitional and data problems. Although completely reliable data on the mortality of Asian Americans are simply not available, it seems safe to conclude that at least Japanese and Chinese Americans enjoy low levels of mortality and associated good health. It is commonly assumed that the relatively high socioeconomic standing of these two groups is an extremely important factor in determining their mortality levels.

Mortality levels of other Asian American groups are more problematic. Filipino mortality may be higher than that of Japanese and Chinese but not necessarily higher than the U.S. white mortality level. Mortality levels of Koreans, Asian Indians, and Vietnamese have not yet been calculated at the national scale, so little can be said about them now. One smaller group of refugees from Southeast Asia, the Hmong, have been plagued by the sudden unexplained deaths of a number of males; the lack of a biological or medical explanation for these deaths suggests a cultural influence that is harder to examine. The Hmong, of all recent immigrant groups, are the least like the general U.S. population in terms of culture, so their efforts at and problems relating to assimilation are undoubtedly the greatest of any group.

What of the future of Asian American mortality? Some researchers assume that in the absence of strong evidence to the contrary, Asian American mortality, if not already very close to that of the total U.S. population, will soon be essentially equal to national levels and stay that way (e.g., Bouvier and Agresta 1985). Such an assumption is implicitly based on the belief that the factors affecting mortality will be at about the same levels for Asian Americans as for the total population. Thus, insofar as Asian Americans are "assimilated" and come to have incomes, occupations, educations, and behaviors similar to those of the total population, so too will they share the mortality levels. If Asian Americans differ from the overall population in one or more important characteristics or behaviors that affect mortality, then their mortality might be expected to be higher or lower than the average. Predicting their mortality, then, means predicting their socioeconomic status in society and their health-related behaviors. Genetic predispositions to certain diseases, of course, are less susceptible to change, but must be taken into account if and when they are found to exist.

We might thus predict that the mortality levels of Asian Americans will eventually approach national levels. First-generation Asian Americans, of course, will continue to bring with them their different backgrounds and behaviors and will undoubtedly continue to exhibit somewhat different mortality patterns than their native-born counterparts.

Possibly the most important factor is economic. If Asian American groups are successful economically, their mortality levels will be low. If they are not successful, their mortality levels will be higher. We need only look to the situation of blacks to see that this is indeed the case regardless of length of a group's residence in this country. Black socioeconomic status has never been equal to that of whites, nor have their mortality levels. The economic success of Asian Americans, then, will go a long way toward determining their mortality levels.

Age and Sex Composition

The age and sex composition of a population, like its growth rates, is completely a product of that population's history of births, deaths, and migration. In turn, the age and sex composition has many implications for the present and future demographic and socioeconomic situations of the population. A careful look at the age and sex structures of

TABLE 3.9

Median Ages of Total U.S., White, Black, Hispanic, and Asian American Populations: 1980

Population	Median Age		
	Total	Male	Female
TOTAL UNITED STATES	30.0	28.8	31.2
White	31.3	30.0	32.5
Black	24.9	23.5	26.1
Hispanic	23.2	22.6	23.8
Japanese	33.6	31.4	36.2
Chinese	29.6	29.4	29.8
Filipino	28.6	27.9	29.1
Korean	26.1	23.3	27.1
Asian Indian	29.2	29.7	28.6
Vietnamese	21.2	20.3	22.3

SOURCES: PC80-1-B1, Tables 41, 47.

NOTES: These data are from complete-count tabulations. Data from the sample are generally quite similar, except for Asian Indian females, whose median age is calculated to be 30.1 and for whom the data are suspect. The Census Bureau suggests using full-count data whenever possible.

Asian American populations is especially interesting, since these populations have experienced varied and turbulent demographic histories.

In this section we will look in some detail at the age and sex composition in 1980 and will then turn briefly to historical data.

Age Structure in 1980

The age structure of a population is often summarized by the median age.[14] Data on median ages for Asian American groups illustrate their great heterogeneity. In 1980 Japanese Americans had a median age of 33.6 years, much higher than the figure of 30.0 years for the total population (Table 3.9). Asian Indians and Chinese had median ages close to the national figure, while Filipinos, Koreans, and especially Vietnamese had medians lower than for the country as a whole.

As well as being different for the different groups, the median ages differed by sex within the groups. We usually expect the median age of

[14]The median age divides the population into halves, 50 percent older than that age, 50 percent younger.

females in a population to be higher than that of males because females live longer, thus having a higher proportion of their populations at older ages. Among Asian Americans in 1980, the female median age was higher for all groups except Asian Indians (and as we note below, there seem to have been some problems with age and sex data on Asian Indians in the census). The median age for Japanese females was almost 5 years higher than for Japanese males. Superficially, then, the median ages of the Asian American populations seem to reflect "normal" situations.

However, although similar median ages *may* reflect similarities in age and sex structure, they may also conceal major differences. To help us in looking into this, in Figure 3.5 we present population pyramids for the six largest Asian American populations for 1980 and the pyramid for the total U.S. population as well. Although the total U.S., Chinese, and Asian Indian populations in 1980 had quite similar median ages, their age-sex pyramids were not at all similar, being the products of quite different histories. While the U.S. pyramid had been influenced primarily by the numbers and trends of births in the past 7 or 8 decades and not so much by migration, the Chinese and Asian Indian pyramids, and those of the other Asian American groups as well, had been strongly affected by immigration trends (and, no doubt, by emigration as well; we usually use "immigration" to cover both phenomena).

Immigration, as is true of migration more generally, tends to be strongly age-selective: young adults are usually more mobile than those of other ages. Similarly, immigration is often sex-selective, but the direction of the sex selection varies from time to time and place to place. The effects of both age- and sex-selection can be seen in the population pyramids.

The pyramids of Asian Americans are all different. The reason for this becomes clearer when we divide the populations into native-born and foreign-born and divide the latter into those who arrived in this country between 1970 and the 1980 census and those who arrived before 1970—essentially those who came before the 1965 changes in immigration law.

Let us look first at the native-born, the inner parts of the pyramids. These are the children both of foreign-born and of native-born individuals.[15] In populations with little or no immigration, a regular history of births and deaths in the past would lead to a regular, or smoothly tapering, pyramid. Even in a population with significant immigration, a regular history of births will produce a regular pyramid of native-born, as is true for Filipinos and Koreans.

The Japanese native-born population, however, and to a lesser de-

[15]With 1980 census data there is no way of distinguishing the generations, as there was with previous censuses when a question on place of birth of one's parents was asked.

gree the Chinese native-born population are made up of the children of two waves of immigration. Each has notable native-born populations at older ages—the children of early immigrants. The younger native-born populations are the children of postwar immigrants or the grandchildren (or even great-grandchildren) of earlier immigrants.

Chinese and Japanese differ in their recent immigration histories, however, with only Chinese arriving in large numbers since 1965. This has resulted in a rising number of Chinese births but a falling number of Japanese births, reflected in the tucked-in base of the Japanese pyramid.

Filipinos and Koreans have also come to the United States in two waves, but they do not show significant bulges of native-born at the older ages. This is because, for the Filipinos, most of the early immigrants were unaccompanied males who never married (note the bulge in the Filipino pyramid representing pre-1970 immigrants), and for Koreans, the earlier immigrants were quite few in number.

Asian Indian and Vietnamese native-born populations are distributed as we might expect for groups that had only small populations before the recent heavy immigration (the median age of native-born Vietnamese in 1980 was under 5 years).[16]

Turning our attention to the foreign-born population, we see more directly the population consequences of immigration. Japanese show the highest proportions of early immigrants among the total foreign-born, clustered at the older ages. The most prominent feature is the overwhelming proportions of females in the adult ages. These are the aging cohorts of Japanese women who married American servicemen in the years after World War II.

Chinese and Filipinos show the effects of long histories of immigration with much more evidence of recent immigration, including immigration of children as parts of whole families (immigration data confirm this). Asian Indians and Koreans show aging groups of earlier immigrants, probably mostly 1960–1969 arrivals. These are heavily male in the case of Indians (perhaps professional and working males preceding their families), heavily female in the case of Koreans (many of them brides of U.S. servicemen).

Vietnamese, unsurprisingly, show almost no immigrants from the pre-1970 period. Recent immigrants dominate the Vietnamese population more than they do any other group, although Koreans and Indians also show high proportions of recent immigrants. It will be a long time before the population structures of these three groups will be free of the effects of the heavy waves of recent immigration.

[16]We cannot explain the large numbers of very old native-born Asian Indians except as a data problem and not reflective of the actual situation.

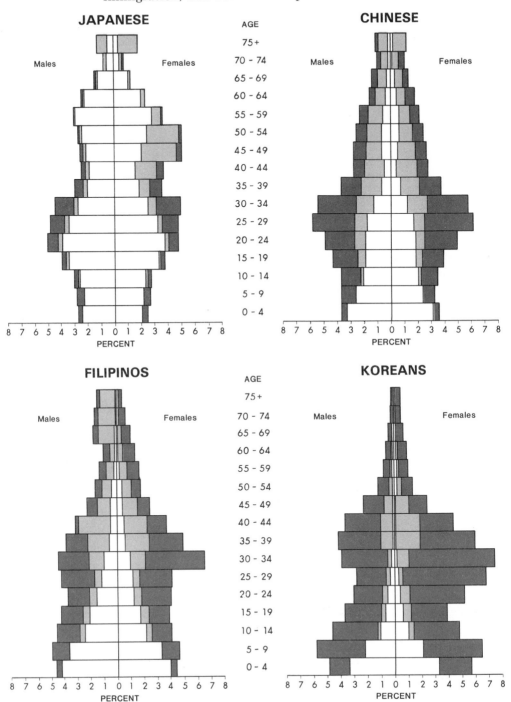

FIGURE 3.5

Age-Sex Composition of the Six Major Asian American Groups, by Period of Immigration, and Total U.S. Population: 1980

SOURCES: Bureau of the Census. *1980 Census of Population*, PC80-1-B1. *General Population Characteristics.* Table 45, and special unpublished tabulations of the Asian American population.

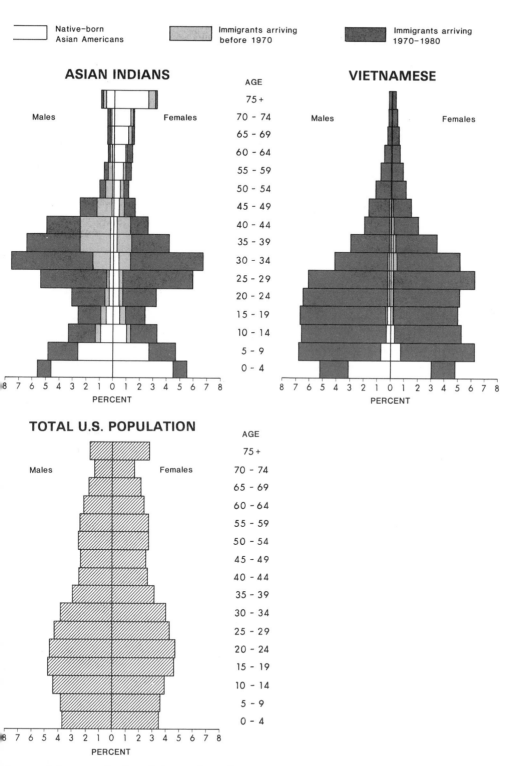

Source of diagrams: Gardner, Robey, and Smith, *Asian Americans: Growth, Change, and Diversity.* Used with permission of the Population Reference Bureau, Inc. 1985, 14–15.

Filipino and Chinese pyramids combine heavy recent immigration with large proportions of native-born and earlier immigrants, and we might well expect the pyramids of Vietnamese, Koreans, and Indians to grow to resemble those of Filipinos and Chinese as the years go by. Even if immigration continues at current high levels for these groups, eventually there will be a much larger base of prior immigrants and native-born in the populations.

Differences in median ages by sex also reflect the history of immigration. For example, among Filipinos who arrived before 1970, the male median age in 1980 was about 45.5 years, while for females it was 40.7, reflecting the male dominance of earlier immigration. Figure 3.5 shows these males at the oldest ages, balanced by very few older females. Recent Filipino immigration, however, has been heavily female, so the overall age differential is reversed.

One of the major consequences of the age composition of a population is economic "dependency": how many nonworking people there are for each working person. Simple data on the age structure do not, of course, tell us who is working and who is not, but they do tell us the basic dimensions of dependency.

Dependent populations are usually divided into two groups, the young (usually chosen as those under 15) and the old (those 65 and over). Added together, these comprise the total dependent population. A *dependency ratio* is the ratio of one of these three groups to the potential working population, those 15–64.

In 1980 the dependency ratios of Asian Americans varied considerably (Figure 3.6). Vietnamese and Koreans, followed by Asian Indians and Filipinos, showed relatively high youth dependency ratios. In the case of Vietnamese, there were 56 people under 15 years of age for each 100 persons of working age. At the other extreme, the low-fertility Japanese had only 21 youth per 100 workers.

Old-age dependency patterns were somewhat the reverse, but all at lower levels. Vietnamese and Koreans had only 3 and 4 older persons, respectively, for each 100 workers. Filipinos, Chinese, and Japanese showed relatively high values, with Filipinos highest at 11 aged per 100 workers.

Together, these figures added up to a substantial burden of dependency for Vietnamese, Koreans, and Filipinos, slightly less for Asian Indians, and much lower for Chinese and especially Japanese. An average Japanese American of working age was supporting, in a sense, only about one-third of an additional person, while the figure for Vietnamese was almost twice that. The implications for use of income, even if incomes were equal for the two groups, are obvious.

FIGURE 3.6
Asian American Dependency Ratios: 1980

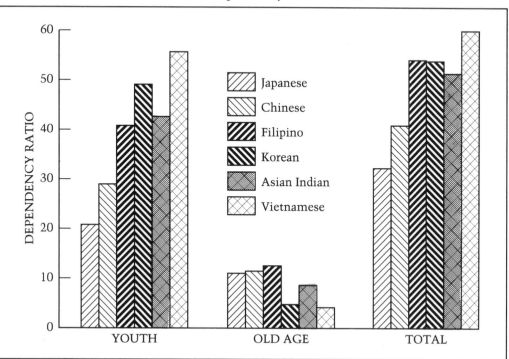

SOURCE: PC80-1-B1, Table 47.

NOTE: These data are from the 100 percent tabulations and may vary from the sample figures.

Sex Composition in 1980

In a population not strongly affected by sex-selective migration, the sex ratio (the number of males per 100 females) shows a regular pattern. At birth there are about 105 to 107 males per 100 females. The sex ratio falls slowly and smoothly to the oldest ages, the result of higher male mortality.

For the United States as a whole in 1980 the sex ratio was 94.5 males per 100 females. Whites (94.8), blacks (89.6),[17] Hispanics (99.3), and American Indians (97.5) all showed values near that of the total national population.

[17]This is perhaps low because of some differential underenumeration of black males.

TABLE 3.10
Sex Ratios, by Ethnicity and Nativity/Year of Immigration: 1980

| | | | Foreign-Born | | | |
| | | | | Year of Immigration | | |
Group	Total	Native-Born	Total	1970–1980	1960–1969	Before 1960
Chinese	102.3	105.5	100.8	95.9	92.6	131.5
Japanese	84.5	101.6	55.2	84.0	30.2	32.9
Filipino	93.4	106.3	86.7	72.3	83.3	227.3
Korean	71.5	103.3	66.7	68.8	53.5	68.4
Asian Indian	107.2[a]	64.3[a]	119.9	111.0	178.9	93.7
Vietnamese	107.6	104.2	108.9	110.8	39.6	108.3[b]

SOURCE: Total: PC80-1-B1, Table 47. Others: unpublished sample tabulations of the Asian American population.

NOTES: Data by nativity not available from the 100 percent tabulations. Except for the total, data are based on a sample and do not agree exactly with the full-count figures. Sample figures for the "total" column are, respectively, 102.4, 84.8, 93.2, 72.3, 99.8[a], and 108.5.

[a] The discrepancy between full-count and sample figures for Asian Indians is due to an apparent large number of native-born Indians, especially females, at the older ages in the sample. The sample data for older Asian Indian females are probably wrong.

[b] There were very few Vietnamese in the United States before 1960; this figure is therefore based on a very small sample and unreliable.

Two Asian American populations, however, showed sex ratios above 100: Vietnamese (107.6), and Asian Indians (107.2) (Table 3-10).[18] Relatively high sex ratios can be the result of two factors: (1) male-dominant immigration, and (2) an especially young population, with a consequent predominance of the young ages where there are more males than females.[19] For Asian Indians and Vietnamese, the data indicate that at

[18] These are data from the complete count tabulations. Data from the sample tabulations are very close except in the case of Asian Indians, who show a sex ratio of 99.8 for the sample; the Census Bureau recommends using the full-count data when available. Sample data on Asian Indians, especially native-born, seem suspect in other ways as well; witness the strange bulge at the top of the Asian Indian population pyramid in Figure 3.5. There seems to be no way there could actually be so many native-born Asian Indian females, given the history of Asian Indian immigration to the United States. A large number of females mistakenly classified in the sample as Asian Indian native-born would also mean a large number of extra females classified as Asian Indians, thus deflating the sample sex ratio for this group. The impossibly low sex ratio for native-born Indians (64.3) corroborates this reasoning.

[19] Another factor can be differential mortality that favors males, i.e., higher death rates for females than for males. Such a situation has been observed occasionally, but is not applicable to populations in the United States.

98

least the first factor is at work here. Both show sex ratios over 110 for 1970–1980 immigrants, who form the bulk of each group's total population. Immigration and Naturalization Service data (not shown) on immigration since 1970 indicate that immigration from India and Vietnam has been consistently male-dominant.

Koreans, on the other hand, with by far the lowest sex ratio among Asian American groups in 1980, have extremely low sex ratios among immigrants, no matter what their year of arrival. So do Japanese and Filipinos (except early immigrant Filipinos), and all are at least partly the result of marriages to American servicemen stationed abroad.[20] INS data show that since 1970 immigration from the Philippines, Korea, and Japan has consistently had very low sex ratios, and that from China, Taiwan, and Hong Kong as well has had more females than males.

The effects of immigration on the sex ratio of a population can be dramatic. For example, at the turn of the century the sex ratio for Chinese was 1,385 males per 100 females, the result of heavily male Chinese immigration in the preceding 50 years. Even by 1970, we find a sex ratio of 123 for Filipinos, another group that consisted initially mostly of male immigrants. By 1980, however, many of the older single male Filipino immigrants had died, and although the remaining elderly early Filipino immigrants still had a high sex ratio, the overall sex ratio for Filipinos was below 100.

Sex ratios for a total population can conceal important differences at various ages. In 1980, for example, the sex ratio of Asian Indians was very high at ages 35–49, the result of much migration of unaccompanied male Indians. The sex ratio for Koreans aged 25–39, on the other hand, was very low, as was the case for Japanese aged 40–54. Filipinos showed the effects of early male-dominant migration with high sex ratios for those over age 65 and the effects of recent female dominance with low sex ratios at ages 25–39.

Extreme imbalances in a population's sex ratio can have important effects on that population's functioning. For example, a preponderance of males in the marrying ages may mean a shortage of potential marriage partners, especially if marriage to other groups is not possible for various reasons. On the other hand, the current low sex ratios for some groups of Asian Americans does not necessarily mean a shortage of marriage partners. In fact, the more numerous females are mostly not looking for partners, having already married outside their ethnic group (generally to white servicemen).

While the overall sex ratios of Asian American populations in 1980

---

[20]Higher male mortality plays a part too, of course, especially for the older immigrants who arrived before 1960.

are close to normal, this was not always the case, and it is to a brief examination of age and sex composition in the past that we now turn.

Age and Sex Structures in the Past

The age and sex structures of Asian American populations have changed dramatically since Asians first arrived in the United States. For the country as a whole, immigration has not dramatically affected the age and sex composition because the numbers of immigrants have been small in relation to the total population of the country. For Asian American populations, on the other hand, immigration has often been of a magnitude large enough to affect strongly the age and sex structure.

The various histories of immigration have resulted in quite different patterns of median ages for the groups for which we have data. The Chinese provide a good example. Chinese median ages were very high during the early years of the twentieth century, the result of two factors: first, the remaining early immigrants were aging and almost no new immigrants were arriving, and second, there were few children being born because there were so few Chinese females in the country. There *were* some children being born, however, and as the original immigrants died out, gradually the median age of the Chinese population fell, only to rise again recently with the influx of a new wave of adult immigrants.

The median ages of the Asian American populations have differed quite a bit by sex because of the different immigration histories of the sexes. Until recently, without exception the male median ages were higher than those of the females. Immigrants were predominantly males in most cases, and the few females that came as adults were not enough to balance the males, so the female age structures were dominated by the children of these women. The Chinese of the early twentieth century are a prime example of this, with high and rising male median ages and low and falling female medians.

Immigration today is not the severely unbalanced process (in terms of males and females) that it was in the past, so that even high levels of immigration in the future will not distort the relationship of the median ages of the two sexes. In any case, large and growing native-born Asian American populations will balance any effects of sex-selective immigration.

The dependency ratios for Asian American populations have fluctuated substantially over the years of this century. The course of the total dependency ratio has reflected changes in both the old-age and the youth dependency ratio. Old-age dependency ratios have never risen above 12 (for Japanese in 1970), and were essentially zero early in the experience of a number of groups (for example, Japanese 1900–1920, Filipinos 1920–1940).

As they are today, in the past youth dependency ratios were substantially higher than old-age ratios. The highest value was 77 for Japanese in 1930, after the Japanese value was only 8 in 1900. Other groups show substantial variations as well.

Immigration has affected the sex structure of Asian American populations just as strongly as it has affected the age structure. In great contrast to the normal total population stand the Asian Americans, especially as we go far back in time (Table 3.11). The early immigration of Chinese, Japanese, and Filipinos was heavily male dominated, with resulting sex ratios that are unmatched for any groups at other times. The situation for Chinese in this respect was most extreme, with a recorded sex ratio for 1890 of almost 2,700 males per 100 females. The highest recorded Japanese sex ratio was a relatively low 957 in 1880. [21]

With increasing length of residence in this country, Asian American sex ratios became more normal. This happened because of the immigration of women, because of the aging and deaths of the unbalanced cohorts of immigrants, and because of the birth of children. Regardless of the sex ratio of the parental generation, a generation of children will have a normal sex ratio (except, of course, if there is outmarriage and resulting problems of definition). During periods when immigration for a group was low, as it was for all Asian groups after the restrictive legislation of the 1920s and the earlier restrictions on Chinese and Japanese, the sex ratio was bound to fall because of the rising proportions of native-born within the populations.

Recent heavy levels of immigration from Asia have not resulted in the unbalanced sex ratios of the past because recent immigration has been much more balanced in terms of the sexes. The main exceptions to this have been in a direction opposite to that observed historically: Japanese and Korean sex ratios dropped well below 100 after 1960, an effect of the immigration of young women of these groups who had married American servicemen abroad.

[21] Sex ratios at specific ages have been much more extreme than those for the total population. For example, in 1900 there were almost 7000 male Chinese ages 60–64 per 100 female Chinese in the same age group. The significance of the sex ratio is most important at the ages where marriages occur. These have been much more moderate but still extreme by current standards. In 1900, there were 500 Japanese males ages 20–24 for each 100 Japanese females. The Chinese ratio at the same ages was over 650.

TABLE 3.11

Sex Ratios, by Race, United States: 1860–1980

Year	All Races	White	Black	American Indians	His-panic[a]	Chi-nese	Japa-nese	Fili-pino[b]	Korean	Asian Indian	Viet-namese
1860	104.7	105.3	99.6	119.0	—	1,858.1	—	—	—	—	—
1870	102.2[c]	102.8[c]	96.2[c]	95.0	—	1,284.1	587.5	—	—	—	—
1880	103.6	104.0	97.8	104.8	—	2,106.8	957.1	—	—	—	—
1890	105.0	105.4	99.5	102.6	—	2,678.9	687.3	—	—	—	—
1900	104.6	105.0	98.6	101.5	—	1,385.1	487.1	—	—	—	—
1910	106.2	106.7	98.9	103.5	—	925.8	349.2	944.2	674.4[d]	—	—
1920	104.1	104.4	99.2	104.8	—	465.7	159.6	485.2	267.9	—	—
1930	102.6	102.9	97.0	105.1	—	296.4	128.9	706.1	168.5	—	—
1940	100.8	101.2	95.0	105.5	—	224.5	119.1	456.7	—	—	—
1950	98.7	99.1	94.3	108.5	—	168.1	108.6	271.3	—	—	—
1960	97.1	97.4	93.4	101.2	—	133.2	93.9	175.4	—	—	—
1970	94.8	95.3	90.8	96.2	98.0	110.7	84.8	123.4	67.7	107.2	—
1980	94.5	94.8	89.6	97.5	99.3	102.3	84.5	93.4	71.5	—	107.6

SOURCES: 1860–1890: United States Bureau of the Census, 1975, Series A91-104. Others, except as noted: PC80-1-B1, Tables 38–40. 1970 data for Koreans from 1970 Census of Population, PC(1)-D1, Table 190. Other data for Koreans: see sources in Table 2.4. 1970 data for Hispanics: 1970 Census of Population PC(1)-D1, Table 191.

NOTES: Data prior to 1900 do not include Hawaii or Alaska.

[a] Hispanics may be of any race.

[b] Data for Filipinos included with other races for Alaska in 1920 and 1950.

[c] Does not include adjustment for undercount in southern states.

[d] Excludes 13 Koreans in Alaska.

Implications of the Age and Sex Structure of Asian American Populations

We have examined the factors affecting the age and sex composition of a population, but what of the consequences of that composition? One important effect is that on fertility. A population that has a very high (or very low) sex ratio, as many of our immigrant-dominated populations have had, has two options. It must either adopt "celibacy" on the part of the relatively abundant sex, as happened to the early Chinese and Filipino males in the United States, or there must be outmarriage, as happened especially with the Chinese in Hawaii.[22]

It is extremely difficult for an ethnic group with an unbalanced sex ratio to function as a normal community. A large number of male Filipino plantation workers growing old together, with shared experiences and histories, does not constitute a complete enduring community. If outmarriage is not easy or is prohibited, the situation is even worse. On the other hand, if outmarriage can and does occur, then the sense of solidarity and togetherness that defined the group may erode.

This leads to the topic of persistence of ethnicity and ethnic identification. Do individuals and groups want to retain their ethnic identification? Do they care if there is outmarriage in large numbers or not, and does outmarriage lead inexorably to loss of community? This is not the place to explore these questions; we simply want to point out that the sex structure of a population can have important implications for its social functioning and even its continued existence.

The age structure of a population is also important. As with the current discussions of social security and the aging of the general population of the United States, the age structure can have effects throughout a society. The aging of the total U.S. population is due basically to declines in fertility, less so to rises in life expectancy, and very little to any effects of immigration, yet it is an important topic and likely to become more so in the coming years. How much more profound are the effects of an age structure determined by the vagaries of immigration flows, in turn determined in large part by immigration legislation and its changes!

Among Japanese Americans it seems likely that there will eventually be an older generation larger than the younger generation supposed to support it. What happens when the aged of a population group traditionally committed to caring for the old are dependent upon a relatively

---

[22]Theoretically, polygamy is another option, but not in the United States and not among the groups we are studying.

small number of working adults, all embedded in a larger society where the care of the aged, certainly the personal care, is not so firm? A similar question may be asked for Chinese and Filipinos, although the latter show a much livelier level of fertility than do the Japanese.

Another example of the importance of the age structure concerns the Vietnamese. The large proportions of Vietnamese in or soon to enter the childbearing ages probably means a large number of Vietnamese births in the near future and rapid increase in the number of Vietnamese in the country, especially since Vietnamese show relatively high fertility. In general, any population pyramid with a broad base has a potential for rapid growth. Looking at the different Asian American pyramids, we might conclude that the Vietnamese have the potential for the most age-structure-influenced growth in their future. Among non-Asian American groups, Hispanics, especially Mexican Americans and Puerto Ricans, have pyramids with broad bases and hence high potential growth (Davis et al. 1983). Future growth also depends, of course, on fertility and on future immigration patterns.

Asian American populations are not, of course, living alone. They are all part of the larger American society. Some second- and third-generation Japanese have married non-Japanese spouses, and together they may provide for the welfare of the aged Japanese (i.e., a high old-age dependency ratio for Japanese may conceal a larger number of children *plus* spouses willing to care for the elderly). The federal government may well provide much more of the support of aged Asian Americans than they would have dreamed of expecting from that source in the origin countries.

The strange shapes and patterns of the Asian American pyramids may mean difficulties in the years ahead, but they may also be relatively unimportant when we consider that Asian Americans are part of the overall American society, not isolated and alone. If there are problems of aging, they are national problems, not restricted to Asian Americans. If there are recognizably separate Asian American groups, they are still part of the larger society. And, of course, it is always a moot point whether there *are* functionally separate Asian American groups. It is doubtful that all Asian Americans see themselves as part of a particular ethnic community first and as Americans second. This may not be true, at least not yet, for recently arrived groups such as the Vietnamese, so their struggles and progress may be affected more by their age and sex structure than is true for other groups.

Summary

The above discussion makes clear that the Asian American population is a heterogeneous group. The differing histories of immigration, combined with different patterns of fertility and mortality, have resulted in populations that differ demographically in many ways. There is no typical Asian American fertility or mortality pattern, no age and sex structure common to all the groups, all of which factors have implications for the future growth rates of the different Asian American groups. And they also have important impacts on the socioeconomic characteristics of the populations. We examine the socioeconomic data on Asian Americans later in this volume.

4

THE GEOGRAPHY
OF ASIAN AMERICANS:
RESIDENCE AND MIGRATION

IN THIS chapter we shall examine facts about the geographic distribution of Asian Americans and how it has been changing.[1] A limited
number of demographic factors determine the geographic distribution of any population: where people are born and die, and where they
move.[2] Beyond the demographic factors are deeper causes: why people
locate and move as they do. Here we invoke history, the need for reliance on ethnic resources, "assimilation," and socioeconomic characteristics and trends as important factors.

In the case of Asian Americans, both historically and currently, the
most important demographic factor has been immigration: where have
newly arrived immigrants settled? The current concentration of Asian

[1]The discussion will be based primarily on 1980 census data, but 1990 data will be
incorporated where available.
[2]It is possible for the distribution of a population to change purely through differential natural increase: a region with high natural increase will come to have more and more
of the total population than a region with lower natural increase, all other factors being
equal. We make no attempt to assess the importance of this factor, implicitly assuming
that for our purposes the natural increase of Asian Americans is the same in all parts of
the country.
    One other group of factors in the apparent changes in a group's distribution, espe-
cially when contrasted to the distribution of whites, is "improvement in the ability of the
Census to locate and enumerate minority group members, changes in the definition of
different minority groups, and changes in self-identification" (Sandefur and Jeon 1988, p.
14).

106

Americans in certain states and regions, such as Hawaii and the West Coast, is due primarily to the fact that these were the places of residence after arrival from abroad of the earliest immigrants (discussed in Chapter 2; for other discussions, see Lyman 1977 and Allen and Turner 1988). The unusually scattered initial distribution of Vietnamese and other Indochinese across the country is the result of the efforts of the U.S. government to spread the impact of the refugees.

Americans are a notoriously mobile people, however, and Asian Americans are no exception. Immigrants do not always stay where they arrive, nor do their descendants, and the resulting internal migrations have had a substantial effect on the geographic distribution of the Asian American population.[3]

Data Sources

The Immigration and Naturalization Service publishes data on port of entry and on state of intended residence for newly arrived immigrants, but these are clearly not "hard" data: immigrants are under no obligation even to visit the intended state, much less settle there. Nevertheless, we will look briefly at some recent data on this topic. The INS once also collected data every January on the residences of all "aliens," but that practice has been discontinued; in any case it would not provide information on foreign-born Asian Americans who are naturalized citizens, nor of course on native-born Asian Americans.

For basic information on the geographic distribution and movement of Asian Americans, then, we depend mostly on the decennial census, which fortunately provides us with good information on the 1980 distribution of Asian Americans at state and regional levels, at a finer, metropolitan level, and on recent and lifetime migration patterns.

Geographic Distribution in 1980 and 1990

The 1980 and 1990 geographic distributions by region of Asian Americans and of the total Asian and total United States population are

---

[3]Emigration may also play a part in the changing distribution of a population. Unfortunately, there is almost no current data on emigration, certainly not on the areas of origin within the United States of Asian American emigrants. It is almost certainly true, however, that emigration is not a major factor affecting the distribution of Asian Americans today, whatever its effect on numbers.

shown in Table 4.1.[4] Compared to the distribution of the total U.S. population, the Asian American population was heavily concentrated in the West, slightly less so in 1990 than in 1980. The three other regions showed relatively few Asian Americans compared to the distribution of the total population (proportions were almost equal in the Northeast in 1990).

Among Asian Americans, the regional distribution varied considerably. For example, Chinese (in 1980 but not in 1990), Koreans (in 1990 but not in 1980), Asian Indians, Pakistanis, Sri Lankans, and especially Bangladeshis were more concentrated in the Northeast than was true for the total population or for Asian Americans as a whole. Filipinos, Japanese, and Okinawans in 1980 and 1990 and, additionally to a lesser extent, Cambodians, Hmong, and Indonesians in 1990, on the other hand, were somewhat more concentrated in the West than all Asian Americans and showed relatively low percentages in the other three regions. No Asian American groups were found in unexpectedly large proportions in the South, and only Malayans and Hmong (both years) and Laotians (1980) were at all concentrated in the Midwest.

Over the 1970–1980 decade, the distribution of Asian Americans became more like that of the total population (as shown by delta, the Index of Dissimilarity).[5] Values of delta fell for the four groups for which we have data for both 1970 and 1980 (Chinese, Japanese, Filipinos, and Koreans), as did the value for all Asian Americans. With both total U.S. and Asian American population distributions again changing between 1980 and 1990, values of delta fell for Asian Americans as a group and for Chinese, Japanese, and some of the less numerous groups as well; delta rose for Asian Indians, Koreans, and Vietnamese and some smaller groups. According to the assimilation model, decreasing distributional dissimilarity would indicate that Asian Americans were becoming more assimilated (cf. Sandefur and Jeon 1988). In both 1980 and 1990, among the major groups, Asian Indians showed the distribution most like that of the total U.S. population, while Japanese were the most dissimilar.

Regional distribution data concealed uneven concentrations of Asian Americans at the state level in 1980 and 1990 (Table 4.2 and Figure 4.1). California, which had more than 10 percent of the total national population and ranked Number 1 in this respect, contained a much higher

[4]Allen and Turner (1988) have fine maps showing in great detail the 1980 distribution of each Asian American group. They also have maps of lifetime migration patterns of U.S.-born Asian Americans, something with which we do not deal.

[5]The Index of Dissimilarity measures the percentage of one group that would have to move to other regions in order for its regional distribution to match that of the criterion group, in this case the total U.S. population. The index is affected by the number and, hence, size of geographical units used: The more and smaller the units, the higher the index. Thus, values in Table 4.8, which uses states as the geographical unit, are greater than corresponding values in Table 4.1, which uses regions.

proportion of Asian Americans: 36 percent in 1980 and close to 40 percent in 1990, placing it as Number 1. The state with the second largest number of Asian Americans in 1980, however, was Hawaii (13 percent), although Hawaii ranked only 38th in terms of national population, with less than one-half of 1 percent of the total. By 1990, New York had passed Hawaii and ranked second in the number of Asian Americans.

California was home to the most members of all the six most numerous Asian American groups except Asian Indians, who were found in greatest numbers in New York in 1980. The distribution among states after California of the six groups was varied, with Hawaii (Filipinos and Japanese), New York (Chinese and Koreans), and Texas (Vietnamese) all having the second largest accumulation of at least one group.

In 1980, 74 percent of the total U.S. population lived in urban areas (Table 4.3). Asian Americans were the most urban of any group, with almost 94 percent living in urban areas. Chinese were the most urban, with virtually all (97 percent) living in urban areas.

The concept "urban" often includes some areas that are not really urban in character, so the Census Bureau also employs the concept of "urbanized area."[6] In 1980, 61 percent of the U.S. population lived in urbanized areas, with 76 percent of the black, 79 percent of the Hispanic, and over 87 percent of the Asian American population living in such urban places. Differences among the separate Asian American groups paralleled the differences in percentages living in urban areas.

Urbanized areas can be divided into central city portions and urban fringe areas. The data on the percentage of each group's urbanized area population living in the central city reveal certain patterns. Only 42 percent of the white populations of urbanized areas lived in the central cities, in contrast to 62 percent of Hispanic and 75 percent of black urbanized area populations. Asian Americans fell between whites and Hispanics, with almost 54 percent in the central city portions of urbanized areas. Chinese showed the highest proportions in the central cities, while Asian Indians showed the lowest.

Asian Americans also differed from the total population in their being more concentrated in the nation's metropolitan areas Standard Metropolitan Statistical Areas, or SMSAs[7] (Table 4.3). Native-born Asian

---

[6]An urbanized area is "an incorporated place [or "census designated place" in Hawaii] and adjacent densely settled surrounding area that together have a minimum population of 50,000" (1980 Census of Population PC80-S1-14, p. 5). There are additional details, making the concept more exact in practice.

[7]An SMSA is "a large population nucleus, together with adjacent communities which have a high degree of economic and social integration with that nucleus . . . Each SMSA has one or more central counties containing the area's main population concentration: a UA [Urbanized Area: see note 6] with at least 50,000 inhabitants. . . . There are 318 SMSAs designated in the United States for the 1980 census" (1980 Census of Population, PC80-S1-14, pp. 5–6).

TABLE 4.1

Distribution of United States and Asian American Population, by Region: 1980 and 1990

1980

	Total United States		Percentage by Region				Delta[a]
	Number	Percent	Northeast	Midwest	South	West	
TOTAL UNITED STATES	226,545,805	100.0	21.7	26.0	33.3	19.1	0.0
Total Asians	3,466,421	100.0	17.1	12.3	14.2	56.4	37.3
Chinese	812,178	100.0	26.8	9.2	11.3	52.7	38.7
Filipino	781,894	100.0	9.9	10.4	11.0	68.8	49.7
Japanese	716,331	100.0	6.5	6.5	6.6	80.3	61.2
Asian Indian	387,223	100.0	34.2	23.1	23.4	19.2	12.6
Korean	357,393	100.0	19.1	18.1	19.9	42.9	23.8
Vietnamese	245,025	100.0	9.0	13.4	31.4	46.2	27.1
Laotian	47,683	100.0	9.8	28.0	16.5	45.7	28.7
Thai	45,279	100.0	15.9	18.6	22.5	43.0	24.0
Cambodian	16,044	100.0	14.3	14.1	16.0	55.6	36.6
Pakistani	15,792	100.0	32.7	21.2	22.6	23.5	15.5
Indonesian	9,618	100.0	19.6	11.3	12.8	56.2	37.2
Hmong[b]	5,204	100.0	6.8	53.4	2.4	37.4	45.8
Malayan	4,075	100.0	14.5	48.7	13.1	23.7	27.4
Sri Lankan	2,923	100.0	28.8	15.1	14.5	41.6	29.7
Burmese	2,756	100.0	15.3	17.3	26.6	40.8	21.8
Okinawan	1,415	100.0	3.0	2.3	8.1	86.6	67.6
Bangladeshi	1,314	100.0	52.7	10.5	22.2	14.6	31.1
Asian not specified[c]	12,897	100.0	22.4	16.9	20.4	40.3	22.0
All other Asian	1,377	100.0	19.8	22.4	21.8	36.0	17.0

TABLE 4.1 (*continued*)

	Total United States		Percentage by Region				
	Number	Percent	Northeast	Midwest	South	West	Delta[a]
			1990				
TOTAL UNITED STATES	248,709,873	100.0	20.4	24.0	34.4	21.2	0.0
Total Asians	6,908,638	100.0	19.2	10.9	15.8	54.1	32.9
Chinese	1,645,472	100.0	19.2	10.9	15.8	54.1	32.9
Filipino	1,406,770	100.0	10.2	8.1	11.3	70.5	49.3
Japanese	847,562	100.0	8.8	7.5	7.9	75.9	54.7
Asian Indian	815,447	100.0	35.0	17.9	24.0	23.1	16.5
Korean	798,849	100.0	22.8	13.7	19.2	44.4	25.6
Vietnamese	614,547	100.0	9.8	8.5	27.4	54.3	33.1
Laotian	149,014	100.0	10.7	18.6	19.6	51.0	29.8
Thai	91,275	100.0	12.9	14.2	26.0	46.8	25.6
Cambodian	147,411	100.0	20.5	8.8	13.1	57.7	36.6
Pakistani	81,371	100.0	34.3	18.9	26.5	20.4	13.9
Indonesian	29,252	100.0	12.7	10.5	16.1	60.7	39.5
Hmong	90,082	100.0	1.9	41.3	1.8	55.0	51.1
Malayan	12,243	100.0	18.9	24.6	29.5	27.0	6.4
Sri Lankan	10,970	100.0	25.2	14.9	21.6	38.3	21.9
Burmese	6,177	100.0	17.8	10.1	18.8	53.3	32.1
Okinawan	2,247	100.0	3.5	6.7	11.9	78.0	56.8
Bangladeshi	11,838	100.0	57.9	9.6	20.3	12.1	37.5
All other Asian	148,111	100.0	20.7	15.2	24.3	39.9	19.0

SOURCES: 1980: 1980 Census of Population, PC80-S1-12, Tables 1, 4. 1990: United States Department of Commerce News, release of June 12, 1991 (CB91-215).

NOTE: Regions are shown in Figure 4.1.

[a] Delta is the Index of Dissimilarity, compared with total U.S. See text for explanation.

[b] Evidence indicates this is a severe underestimate of Hmongs.

[c] Includes write-in entries such as Asian American, Asian, and Asiatic.

TABLE 4.2

States with the Most Asian Americans, by Race: 1980 and 1990

	Year	Total U.S. Population	Asian Americans	Chinese	Filipino	Japanese	Korean	Asian Indian	Vietnamese
POPULATION 1980	1980	226,545,805	3,446,421	812,178	781,894	716,331	357,393	387,223	245,025
POPULATION 1990	1990	248,709,873	6,908,638	1,645,472	1,406,770	847,562	798,849	815,447	614,547
Rank	Year	State (%)	State (%)	State (%)	State (%)	State (%)	State (%)	State (%)	State (%)
1	1980	CA(10.4)	CA(36.0)	CA(40.1)	CA(45.8)	CA(37.5)	CA(28.7)	NY(17.5)	CA(34.8)
1	1990	CA(12.0)	CA(39.6)	CA(42.8)	CA(52.0)	CA(36.9)	CA(32.5)	CA(19.6)	CA(45.6)
2	1980	NY(8.7)	HI(13.1)	NY(18.1)	HI(16.9)	HI(33.5)	NY(9.3)	CA(15.4)	TX(11.3)
2	1990	NY(7.2)	NY(10.0)	NY(17.3)	HI(12.0)	HI(29.2)	NY(12.0)	NY(17.3)	TX(11.3)
3	1980	TX(6.3)	NY(9.4)	HI(6.9)	IL(5.7)	WA(3.8)	IL(6.8)	IL(9.7)	LA(4.4)
3	1990	TX(6.8)	HI(7.6)	HI(4.2)	IL(4.6)	NY(4.2)	IL(5.2)	NJ(9.7)	VA(3.4)
4	1980	PA(5.2)	IL(4.9)	IL(3.6)	NY(4.6)	NY(3.5)	HI(4.9)	NJ(7.9)	VA(3.9)
4	1990	FL(5.2)	TX(4.5)	TX(3.8)	NY(4.4)	WA(4.1)	NJ(4.8)	IL(7.9)	WA(3.0)
5	1980	IL(5.0)	TX(3.7)	TX(3.3)	WA(3.3)	IL(2.6)	MD(4.1)	TX(6.0)	WA(3.6)
5	1990	PA(4.8)	IL(4.1)	NJ(3.6)	NJ(3.8)	IL(2.6)	TX(4.0)	TX(6.8)	LA(2.9)
6	1980	OH(4.8)	NJ(3.1)	MA(3.1)	NJ(3.1)	TX(1.7)	TX(3.9)	PA(4.4)	PA(3.3)
6	1990	IL(4.6)	NJ(3.9)	MA(3.3)	WA(3.1)	NJ(2.0)	MD(3.8)	FL(3.9)	FL(2.7)
7	1980	FL(4.3)	WA(3.0)	NJ(2.9)	VA(3.0)	CO(1.5)	WA(3.8)	MI(4.0)	FL(2.9)
7	1990	OH(4.4)	WA(2.8)	IL(3.0)	VA(2.5)	TX(1.7)	VA(3.8)	PA(3.5)	PA(2.6)
8	1980	MI(4.1)	PA(2.0)	WA(2.2)	TX(2.0)	NJ(1.4)	NJ(3.7)	MD(3.6)	IL(2.6)
8	1990	MI(3.7)	VA(2.3)	WA(2.1)	TX(2.4)	OR(1.4)	WA(3.7)	MD(3.5)	NY(2.5)
9	1980	NJ(3.3)	VA(2.0)	MD(1.9)	FL(1.9)	OR(1.2)	VA(3.6)	OH(3.5)	NY(2.4)
9	1990	NY(3.1)	FL(2.2)	MD(1.9)	FL(2.3)	CO(1.3)	PA(3.4)	MI(2.9)	MA(2.5)
10	1980	NC(2.6)	MD(1.9)	PA(1.7)	MI(1.8)	MI(0.9)	PA(3.0)	FL(2.9)	OR(2.3)
10	1990	NC(2.7)	MA(2.1)	FL(1.9)	MD(1.4)	MI(1.3)	HI(3.1)	OH(2.6)	IL(1.7)

SOURCES: 1980: 1980 Census of Population PC80-S1-12, Table 4. Data based on a sample. 1990: United States Department of Commerce News, release of June 12, 1991 (CB91-215); STF1a (Computer Summary Tape File 1A).

NOTE: CA = California; CO = Colorado; FL = Florida; HI = Hawaii; IL = Illinois; LA = Louisiana; MA = Massachusetts; MD = Maryland; MI = Michigan; NC = North Carolina; NJ = New Jersey; NY = New York; OH = Ohio; OR = Oregon; PA = Pennsylvania; TX = Texas; VA = Virginia; WA = Washington.

FIGURE 4.1

Number of Asian Americans, by State, 1980

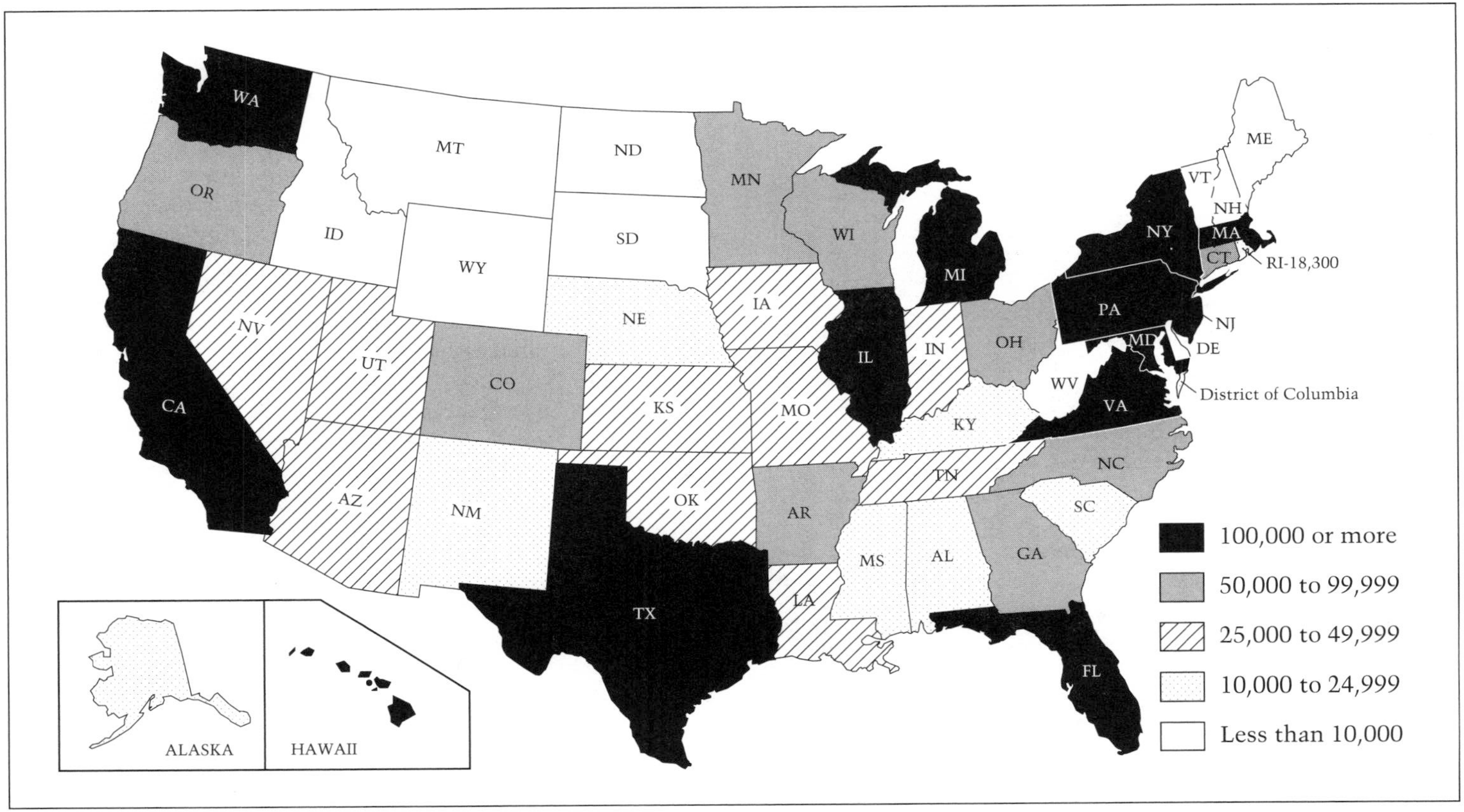

SOURCE: 1980 Census of Population, PC80-S1-12, p. iv.

NOTE: Includes Pacific Islanders (7.0 percent of total).

TABLE 4.3

Residential Distribution of United States and Asian American Population: 1980

	United States	White	Black	His-panic	Asian Amer-ican[a]	Chi-nese	Fili-pino	Japa-nese	Asian Indian	Korean	Viet-namese
TOTAL	100.0	100.0	100.0	100.0	100.0	100.0	100.0	100.0	100.0	100.0	100.0
Percent urban	73.7	71.3	85.3	89.9	93.7	97.0	92.4	91.7	92.6	93.0	95.4
Urbanized areas	61.4	58.5	75.9	79.1	87.2	93.1	84.6	83.2	86.3	86.9	88.6
Central city	29.6	24.6	57.2	48.8	46.7	58.1	43.4	44.2	37.9	40.5	48.9
Urban fringe	31.8	33.8	18.7	30.2	40.4	35.0	41.2	39.0	48.4	46.4	39.7
Percent of u.a. in central city	48.2	42.1	75.3	61.8	53.6	62.4	51.3	53.1	43.9	46.6	55.2
Percent rural	26.3	28.7	14.7	10.1	6.3	3.0	7.6	8.3	7.4	7.0	4.6
Percent in SMSAs[b]	74.8	73.3	81.1	87.6	92.1	96.1	90.9	88.7	92.1	92.5	92.4

SOURCE: 1980 Census of Population, PC80-1-B1, Tables 38, 39.

NOTE: This table uses complete count data; totals differ slightly from sample data.

[a] Sum of six groups listed only.

[b] Standard Metropolitan Statistical Area (see Note 4 for definition).

Americans, in turn, showed a greater degree of concentration than did recent immigrants, indicating that in spite of the lure of places where earlier immigrants and their descendants resided, recent immigrants were settling in a less-concentrated fashion (Bartel 1989).[8]

Changes in Geographic Distribution and Historical Trends

As already discussed with regard to Table 4.1, the geographic distribution of Asian Americans changed between 1980 and 1990; Table 4.4 shows similar data for 1970 and figures on growth rates for the intercensal periods 1970–1980 and 1980–1990.

The total U.S. population grew at an annual rate of 1.1 percent during the 1970–1980 decade and 0.9 percent the following decade, showing almost no growth in the Northeast and Midwest regions and growth rates of about 1–2 percent for the South and West. In contrast, the Asian American population as a whole grew annually from over 6 percent to almost 9 percent, depending on whether we limited our consideration to the four groups counted in both censuses or included in the 1980 figures all people counted as Asian Americans.[9] The fastest growth for Asian Americans was in the South (1970–1980) and the South and Northeast (both periods), whereas the slowest growth was in the West, home of most Asian Americans.

The recent changes were not unique. The West was the original home of 100 percent of Asian Americans (1860 census), and its share did not drop below 90 percent until after 1940. Since then, the West's share has fallen rapidly. No other region had even 10 percent of the total Asian American population until after 1960, and even by 1980 no other region had more than 20 percent. All this was quite different from what was going on for the total U.S. population.

Although the Chinese originally went to rural places in the United States (where railroads were being built and gold mined), they subsequently urbanized and, since at least 1910, have been more urban than the total U.S. population. Later-arriving groups similarly started out as less urban than the total population but eventually became more urban. Japanese passed the national urban average between 1940 and 1950, while Filipinos did this between 1950 and 1960. Spotty data on Koreans and Asian Indians indicated relatively low levels of urbanization in the early

[8]Bartel also found that "[t]he more educated Asians . . . were more geographically dispersed and less likely to choose cities based on the location of fellow ethnics" (p. 384).

[9]That is, we can calculate growth by comparing the number of Asian Americans in 1970 (four groups only) with the members of the same four groups in 1980, or we can compare Asian Americans in 1970 (four groups only but undoubtedly accounting for the vast majority of Asian Americans in that year) with *all* Asian Americans in 1980.

TABLE 4.4

Total and Asian American Population: 1970, and Intercensal Growth Rates, by Region and Ethnicity: 1970, 1980, and 1990

Region	United States	All Asian Americans	Chinese, Japanese, Filipinos, and Koreans	Chinese	Japanese	Filipino	Korean	Asian Indian	Vietnamese
1970									
UNITED STATES	203,211,926	c	1,426,148	431,583	588,324	336,731	69,510	—	—
Percent	100.0	c	100.0	100.0	100.0	100.0	100.0	—	—
Northeast	24.1	c	13.9	26.7	6.7	9.0	19.8	—	—
Midwest	27.8	c	8.5	8.8	7.3	8.1	19.0	—	—
South	30.9	c	7.2	7.5	4.8	8.7	17.0	—	—
West	17.1	c	70.5	57.1	81.3	74.2	44.2	—	—
1970–1980 Annual Growth Rate[a] (percent)									
UNITED STATES	1.1	8.9[b]	6.3	6.3	2.0	8.4	16.2	—	—
Northeast	*	10.8[b]	7.2	6.2	1.8	9.3	15.9	—	—
Midwest	0.4	12.6[b]	7.9	6.8	0.8	10.9	15.7	—	—
South	1.8	15.8[b]	10.6	10.3	5.2	10.9	17.8	—	—
West	2.2	6.7[b]	5.2	5.5	1.9	7.7	15.9	—	—
1980–1990 Annual Growth Rate[a] (percent)									
UNITED STATES	0.9	6.9	—	7.1	1.7	5.9	8.0	7.4	9.2
Northeast	0.3	8.1	—	7.2	4.7	6.1	9.8	7.7	10.1
Midwest	0.1	5.8	—	5.8	3.1	3.3	5.2	4.9	4.6
South	1.2	8.0	—	8.0	3.5	6.2	7.7	7.7	7.8
West	2.0	6.5	—	7.0	1.1	6.1	8.4	9.3	10.8

SOURCES: U.S., 1970: 1970 Census of Population, PC(1)-B1, Table 61; Chinese, Japanese, and Filipinos, 1970: 1970 Census of Population, PC(2)-1G, Tables 1, 16, 31; Koreans, 1970: 1970 Census of Population, PC(2)-1G, Table 48; PC(1)-D1, Table 270.

[a] Calculated according to the formula: P[1980 or 1990]/P[1970 or 1980]=e^{rt}, where t=10 years.

[b] Treats sum of four groups in 1970 as total for Asian Americans in 1970.

c Data for Asian Americans as a group are not available for 1970.

— means unavailable.

* Indicates less than 0.05 percent.

NOTES: Data are from samples except U.S. total. Totals for Chinese, Japanese, and Filipinos in 1970 do not agree with those in Table 2.4 because of differences in sample.

Percentages may not total exactly 100.0 percent because of rounding.

TABLE 4.5

Percent of the Asian American Population That Was Foreign-Born, by Region: 1980

	United States	Northeast	Midwest	South	West
ɹinese	63.3	71.4	69.0	69.7	56.9
lipino	64.7	73.0	73.6	67.8	61.6
panese	28.4	69.0	46.7	60.3	21.0
ɔrean	81.9	83.8	82.3	84.0	79.8
sian Indian	70.4	74.1	69.2	65.6	71.2
ietnamese	90.5	89.9	89.9	89.4	91.4
sian American[a]	60.9	74.3	71.3	73.1	51.8

ƆURCE: 1980 Census of Population, PC80-1-C, State volumes, Table 94.

ɔix groups listed only.

years of this century, but they, along with Vietnamese, were much more urban by 1980.

Place of Birth

Answers to the census question on place of birth provide information on what proportions of Asian Americans are native- and foreign-born, for the country as a whole and for each of the four geographic regions. We are also able to examine lifetime migration flows to the separate regions from the other regions and from abroad. Such data give us much information on the impact of immigration and on long-term flows of Asian Americans, but it is not possible to make any estimates of just when the migration occurred. Data in the next section are more useful for that.

Almost 61 percent of the population of the six largest Asian American groups in the United States in 1980 was foreign-born (Table 4.5). The percentage of foreign-born was highest, of course, for those groups who began arriving in the United States in large numbers most recently, as we saw in Chapter 2.

Patterns differed for the regions. Japanese, for example, showed only 21 percent foreign-born in the West, but 69 percent foreign-born in the Northeast. This might lead one to conclude that the recent Japanese immigrants mostly gravitated to the Northeast. This is not true, however; there are still almost four times as many foreign-born Japanese in the West as in the Northeast; the percentages show a different picture because of the small numbers of native-born Japanese in the Northeast.

Chinese and Filipinos showed patterns somewhat similar to those of Japanese, in that the largest numbers, yet the lowest percentages, of foreign-born are found in the West. Korean, Asian Indian, and Vietnamese foreign-born, on the other hand, showed patterns of even percentages of foreign-born in the four regions: Vietnamese around 90 percent, Koreans around 80 percent, and Indians around 70 percent.

Further insight on the impact of the foreign-born on the geographic distribution of Asian Americans is afforded by the information contained in Table 4.6. Here, we see where the lifetime immigrants (foreign-born Asian Americans) were living in 1970 and 1980. In 1970, almost 60 percent of foreign-born Chinese, Filipino, and Japanese as a group were living in the West region, with almost 22 percent in the Northeast and small percentages in the Midwest and South. The concentration of Chinese in the Northeast was the source of the overall high percentage there, for Filipinos and Japanese did not show much affinity for the Northeast. In contrast, the latter two groups had much higher percentages in the West than did Chinese, who had less than 50 percent of their foreign-born in that region.

By 1980 the situation had changed somewhat. The regional distributions of the "older" groups had not changed much, since they had a large number of foreign-born already here in 1970. Even so, the proportion of foreign-born living in the West fell for Filipinos and Japanese, and the South showed gains for all three groups of established Asian Americans. The foreign-born of the three newest groups, however—Koreans, Asian Indians, and Vietnamese—did not show as much tendency to concentrate in the West. Asian Indians, in fact, showed a strong liking for the Northeast and a disaffinity for the West, where less than 20 percent of them were found. Compared to other Asian groups, Vietnamese were concentrated in the South, the result of refugee location policies. Koreans were well represented in all regions.

These patterns and changes in the distribution of the foreign-born are, of course, the direct results of patterns of settlement among the recent immigrants (as well as the migration and dying-off of the older foreign-born); we shall turn to the patterns of recent immigration in a moment.

Foreign-born Asian Americans are becoming a large percentage of all foreign-born people in the United States, again a direct consequence of recent immigration patterns. In 1970, close to 9 percent of the total U.S. foreign-born population was Asian-born. In the West the figure was almost 17 percent. By 1980, some 18 percent of all the foreign-born in the United States had been born in Asia; again, the West led with over one-quarter of its foreign-born population being of Asian birth.

TABLE 4.6

Regional Distribution of Foreign-Born Population: 1970 and 1980

Region	United States	Asian American[a]	Chinese	Filipino	Japanese	Korean	Asian Indian	Viet-namese
UNITED STATES				1980				
Foreign-born population	14,079,906	2,010,070	514,389	505,504	203,338	292,573	272,617	221,649
Percent	100.0	100.0	100.0	100.0	100.0	100.0	100.0	100.0
Northeast	32.0	20.9	30.2	11.1	15.9	19.6	36.0	8.9
Midwest	15.0	13.8	10.0	11.8	10.6	18.2	22.7	13.4
South	20.6	16.8	12.4	11.5	14.1	20.4	21.8	31.0
West	32.4	48.5	47.4	65.6	59.3	41.9	19.4	46.7
				1970				
UNITED STATES								
Foreign-born population	9,619,302	505,702	204,232	178,970	122,500	—	—	—
Percent	100.0	100.0	100.0	100.0	100.0	—	—	—
Northeast	42.8	21.8	34.6	11.3	15.6	—	—	—
Midwest	19.5	10.6	10.7	10.3	11.0	—	—	—
South	13.7	9.5	8.5	10.0	10.4	—	—	—
West	24.0	58.1	46.2	68.4	63.0	—	—	—

SOURCES: 1980: 1980 Census of Population, PC80-1-C, State volumes, Table 94 and PC80-1-C1, Table 77. 1970: 1970 Census of Population, PC(2)-1G, Tables 3, 18, and 33 and PC(1)-C1, Table 136.

[a]Sum of the groups listed only.

— Not available.

TABLE 4.7

Percent of 1980 Population Aged Five and Over Who Were Abroad in 1975, by Ethnicity and Region

	United States	Northeast	Midwest	South	West
Chinese	22.2	20.2	28.2	31.0	20.4
Filipino	22.5	22.8	26.2	25.9	21.3
Japanese	10.2	36.9	19.0	23.3	6.3
Korean	41.0	40.2	36.1	43.4	42.1
Asian Indian	30.9	31.9	30.3	29.8	31.2
Vietnamese	70.1	66.1	69.3	68.8	71.9
Asian American[a]	25.9	28.7	31.8	37.0	21.3

SOURCE: 1980 Census of Population, PC80-1-C, State volumes, Table 94.

[a] Six groups listed only.

Residence in 1975 and 1975–1980 Migration

Answers to the census question on residence exactly 5 years prior to the census enable us to look at migration patterns over a well-defined and recent period of time. We are still hampered, however, by the fact that such retrospective migration questions do not capture all the movement during the previous 5 years: only the residence in 1975 and the 1980 residence are known; any intermediate residences are ignored as if they never existed. We also miss any migration by those under 5 years of age at the census, migration by those who died in the interval, and emigration out of the country since 1975. Nevertheless, much can be learned about recent internal migration and immigration by examining these data.

Almost 26 percent of the total populations of the 6 largest Asian American groups in 1980 aged 5 and over had been abroad 5 years previously (Table 4.7).[10] The range for the different ethnic groups was from 10 percent, for Japanese, to 70 percent, for Vietnamese. Koreans and Asian Indians trailed Vietnamese, while Chinese and Filipinos stood at about 25 percent who had been abroad in 1975.

As with the foreign-born, patterns for recent immigrants varied for

[10]Since the question simply asks where the respondent was 5 years earlier, we cannot distinguish between people who immigrated in the 5 years before the 1980 census and those who were already U.S. residents but had been out of the country in 1975. We will assume that most of those abroad were immigrants in the subsequent 5 years, and we will speak of them collectively as "immigrants," keeping in mind that not all were actual immigrants.

TABLE 4.8

Regional Distribution of 1975–1980 Immigrants

	Total	Percent	Northeast	Midwest	South	West
UNITED STATES	3,931,836	100.0	22.0	13.7	28.5	35.8
Chinese	167,589	100.0	24.1	11.6	15.4	48.9
Japanese	68,962	100.0	23.3	11.8	14.9	49.9
Filipino	158,353	100.0	9.9	12.0	12.6	65.5
Korean	130,604	100.0	18.4	14.8	21.2	45.6
Asian Indian	105,816	100.0	35.7	21.6	23.0	19.7
Vietnamese	150,447	100.0	8.2	13.5	30.5	47.8
Asian American[a]	781,771	100.0	18.7	13.9	19.7	47.6

SOURCES: United States: 1980 Census of Population, PC80-S16, Table 1; Asian Americans: 1980 Census Population, PC80-1-C, State volumes, Table 94.

NOTE: Asian American is total of six groups listed only.

the different regions. In the Northeast, Japanese actually ranked third in terms of proportion of the 1980 population 5 years old and over who had been abroad in 1975, behind Vietnamese (66 percent) and Koreans (40 percent). Chinese, on the other hand, showed only 20 percent abroad in 1975. This ranking was due to the fact that Japanese had relatively small numbers in the Northeast in 1975, whereas the Chinese had large numbers. Between 1975 and 1980 the Japanese population in the Northeast grew by only 14,531, while the Chinese population grew by more than twice that, 32,019.

Vietnamese, not surprisingly, had the highest proportions abroad in 1975 for all four regions, always followed by Koreans in second. Japanese are always the lowest except for the Northeast.

Data on the Asian Americans abroad in 1975 are presented in another way in Table 4.8. Here we see where the 1975–1980 immigrants were living at the time of the 1980 census. With the exception of Asian Indians, the highest proportion of recent immigrants for each group was found in the West region. Though only 20 percent of recent Indian immigrants were found in the West, at least 46 percent of all other groups were there, and over 65 percent of recent Filipino immigrants were in the West in 1980. Asian Indian immigrants, instead of concentrating in the West, were found in greatest concentrations in the Northeast, and also had higher than the average Asian American proportions in the Midwest region. Vietnamese stood out by their high proportion residing in the South.

The pattern of Asian Americans being distributed differently from the total U.S. population will probably not change anytime soon (Table 4.9). The Index of Dissimilarity calculated at the *state* level for 1980

TABLE 4.9

Indexes of Dissimilarity for Distribution of Asian Americans, by State, 1980

Comparison Distributions	Own 1980 U.S. 1980 (1)	U.S. 1980 INS 1980 (2)	Own 1980 INS 1980 (3)
Chinese	47.5	48.0	8.4
Japanese	62.6	—	—
Filipino	54.4	51.3	11.2
Korean	32.9	33.0	7.1
Asian Indian	25.8	31.8	9.4
Vietnamese	38.8	41.3	16.7

SOURCES: 1980 Census of Population, PC80-S1-12, Table 1; INS 1988 Statistical Yearbook, Table 16.

NOTES: Calculated by taking sum of positive differences between percentage distributions *by state* of 1980 census total U.S. population, specific ethnic group 1980 population, and 1988 distribution of intended state of residence. See text.

Japanese not shown for columns 2 and 3 because too few immigrate to appear in INS table.

showed that Asian Americans were moderately concentrated, with Japanese being distributed least like the total U.S. population and Asian Indians most (column 1 of Table 4.9). INS data for state of intended residence in 1988 indicated a continued difference between Asian American places of settlement and the U.S. distribution (column 2). By comparison, Asian immigrants in 1988 were intending to distribute themselves in a pattern quite close to the distribution of the same Asian American groups in 1980 (column 3).

Data on residence in 1975 could also be used to look at recent *net* . migration flows among the various regions of the country. For example, for the six most numerous Asian American groups as a whole, we found that between 1975 and 1980, 11,783 more moved from the Midwest to the West than moved from the West to the Midwest (Figure 4.2). Net flows to the West from the South (6,644) and the Northeast (14,650) also contributed to an overall growth of the Asian American population in the West from internal migration.

The South gained 6,715 from the Midwest and 12,731 from the Northeast, and thus had a net growth from internal migration of 12,802. The Midwest, gaining only from the Northeast, lost 16,669 Asian Americans due to internal migration, and the Northeast lost 29,210, with net migration flows going from it to all other regions.

The direction of these recent flows was the same as for the lifetime flows; patterns of internal migration did not seem to have changed in

FIGURE 4.2

Net Migration of Asian Americans among U.S. Regions: 1975–1980

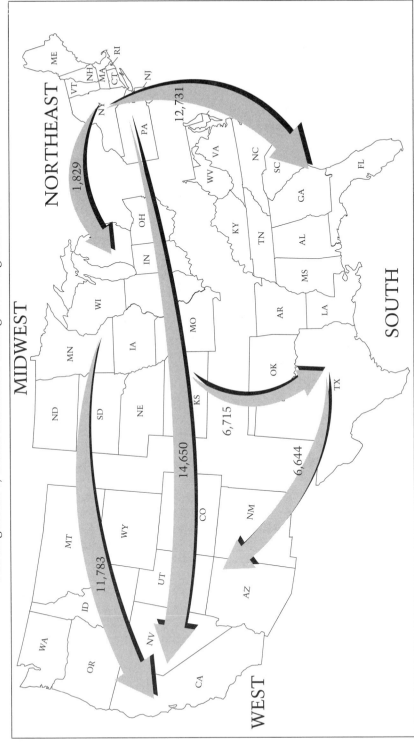

SOURCE: 1980 Census of Population, PC80-1-C, State volumes, Table 94. (Data on Asian and Pacific Islanders as a group can be found in PC80-S1-16.)

NOTE: Includes six largest Asian American groups only, and only those five and older in 1980. Also includes Hawaii and Alaska.

the 5 years preceding the 1980 census over what they were in earlier years.

All the six largest Asian American groups showed internal migration patterns for the 1975–1980 period that were the same as the total Asian American patterns: the Northeast losing population to all other regions, the Midwest losing to the South and the West, and the West gaining population through net migration from all the other three regions. The only exception: a small net flow of Koreans to the Northeast from the Midwest.

As their distribution patterns are becoming more similar to those of whites over time, so too are the migration patterns of (native-born) Asian Americans becoming similar to those of whites (Sandefur and Jeon 1988). "Minority groups . . . had regional net migration patterns similar to those of whites during the 1975–1980 period" (p. 16). This may be interpreted as evidence of the growing assimilation of Asian Americans, at least with regard to regional migration.

If we divide the amount of net in- or out-migration for the 1975–1980 period by the 1975 population of each region (i.e., that portion of the 1975 population still alive and in the United States in 1980), we get what might be called "net migration probabilities": the percentage of the 1975 population which would move out in the next 5 years.[11]

The data in Table 4.10 show the result of this procedure. Overall, the Northeast suffered a net loss of more than 7 percent of its 1975 Asian American population to internal migration during the following 5 years. The Midwest lost almost 7 percent, while the South gained more than 5 percent and the West, 2.5 percent. These figures are in the same direction (gain or loss) but slightly different in magnitude from the figures for the total U.S. population.

Patterns for the separate groups were varied: Vietnamese, who were relatively few in number in 1975, showed the largest net out-migration probabilities from the Northeast and the Midwest and the largest in-migration probability to the West. Asian Indians showed the highest in-migration probability for any group and region combination, 16.5 percent for the South.

An examination of migration between SMSAs revealed that Asians as a group were more mobile than either Hispanics or Europeans, that immigrant Asians were much more likely to change location than U.S.-born Asians, and that the more educated individuals within each ethnic

---

[11]Actually, the true "probability" would be the probability of gross out-migration: those who moved out divided by the original 1975 population. A similar "probability" of in-migration could be calculated, and the difference between these two is the net probability of internal migration.

TABLE 4.10

Net Internal Migration Probabilities: 1975–1980

	Northeast	Midwest	South	West
UNITED STATES	−3.8	−2.5	3.0	3.2
ASIAN AMERICAN	−7.4	−6.7	5.1	2.5
Chinese	−5.0	−8.6	4.2	3.5
Japanese	−5.4	−4.4	1.5	0.5
Filipino	−12.5	−7.4	4.2	2.5
Korean	−4.9	−6.7	−1.2	6.1
Asian Indian	−9.8	−2.8	16.5	5.0
Vietnamese	−15.2	−19.9	—	13.7

SOURCE: 1980 Census of Population, PC80-1-C, State volumes, Table 94.

NOTES: A "net internal migration probability" is the net internal migration divided by the 1975 population, expressed as a percent. See text.
— Less than 0.05.

group had the highest migration rates (Bartel 1989).[12] The movement of Asians, however, was not in general toward areas where there were *smaller* concentrations of Asians. Bartel assumed that "individuals who live in cities with small percentages of the ethnic population are, in effect, more assimilated into American society" (p. 388); she concluded that Asian migration patterns did not seem to be leading toward greater assimilation, in contrast to the impression based on regional data.

Finally, we examined the growth in the populations of the ethnic groups in the separate regions between 1975 and 1980 and divided that growth into the effects of internal migration and the effects of immigration (i.e., the effects of those abroad in 1975). This is shown in Table 4.11. Immigration dominated internal migration as the source of the growth of Asian American populations in all regions. Note that all the groups grew in all regions, in spite of the net out-migration from some of the regions, because of the overwhelming effect of immigration. For example, the Filipino population of the Northeast grew by 8,109 between 1975 and 1980. If only internal migration had been operating, the population would have fallen by almost 93 percent of that amount. Because of immigration, the Filipino population grew.

The opposite extreme is shown in the case of Asian Indians in the South. There, the population grew by 32,449; 25 percent of this growth was due to net internal migration, 75 percent to immigration. (We cannot distinguish here between immigrant Indians who moved, in the 5 years before the census, directly to the South and immigrant Indians

[12]Education is seen as providing an individual with more options and making him or her less dependent upon ethnic resources. See also Walker and Hannan (1989).

TABLE 4.11

Percentage of 1975–1980 Population Growth Due to Immigration and to Net Internal Migration, by Ethnicity and Region

	Chinese	Japanese	Filipino	Korean	Asian Indian	Vietnamese	Asian American
NORTHEAST							
Change	32,019	14,531	8,109	22,160	29,022	11,256	117,097
Percentage due to:							
Immigration	126.1	110.8	192.9	108.3	130.2	110.1	124.9
Internal migration	−26.1	−10.8	−92.9	−8.3	−30.2	−10.1	−24.9
MIDWEST							
Change	14,805	6,456	14,762	16,847	21,331	18,046	92,337
Percentage due to:							
Immigration	131.2	124.6	128.8	114.5	107.1	112.4	118.1
Internal migration	−31.2	−24.6	−28.8	−14.5	−7.1	−12.4	−18.1
SOUTH							
Change	24,048	10,771	22,338	27,268	32,449	45,892	166,766
Percentage due to:							
Immigration	91.8	95.3	89.6	101.6	75.0	100.0	92.3
Internal migration	8.2	4.7	10.4	−1.6	25.0	0.0	7.7
WEST							
Change	92,717	37,114	113,144	64,329	23,014	75,253	405,571
Percentage due to:							
Immigration	88.5	92.8	91.7	92.7	90.5	95.5	91.8
Internal migration	11.5	7.2	8.3	7.3	9.5	4.5	8.2
Total growth[a]	167,589	68,962	158,353	130,604	105,816	150,447	781,771

SOURCE: 1980 Census of Population PC80-1-C, State volumes, Table 94, and PC80-S1-16, Table 1.

NOTES: Immigration is defined as being abroad in 1975.

The population under consideration is all those five years old and over and in the United States in 1980, excluding those who emigrated and those under five in 1980.

[a]This is all due to immigration, since net internal migration must sum to zero.

who moved to other regions first and then moved internally to the South.)
This was by far the most important contribution of internal migration
to the growth of any group in any region. Overall, around 92 percent of
the growth of the Asian American populations of the South and the
West was due to immigration and only about 8 percent to internal migration. The situation was even more unbalanced in the Northeast and
Midwest regions, where net internal migration was out of these regions
yet Asian American growth was substantial because of the large influx
of immigrants.

Refugee Settlement and Resettlement

The situation of Asian Americans, primarily Vietnamese (and Sino-
Vietnamese), Laotians (including Hmongs), and Cambodians who came
to this country predominantly as refugees, deserves a short separate discussion because of the differences in distribution and migration between
this group and most other recent Asian arrivals.[13]

Initially, patterns of placement of Indochinese refugees were strongly
affected by U.S. government policies designed to disperse them across
the country, minimizing their impact on service providers and other aspects of community life and speeding their assimilation into the host
society. This policy resulted in an initial pattern of residence for the
first wave of refugees much less concentrated in certain areas than that
of other immigrants.[14]

The refugees were under no obligation to stay where they initially
settled, however, and redistribution began almost immediately. "Refu-
gees tended to prefer urban places with a warm climate and an existing
Asian population. . . . Movement tended to be toward the South and
West, particularly into California" (Gordon 1984, pp. 17–19; see also
Desbarats 1985). Desbarats and Holland noted that Orange County in
California had more refugees than any *state* except California itself (1983).

The initial placement of the second wave of refugees was somewhat
different from that of the first, in particular because attempts were made
to place new arrivals in areas where there were ties with first-wave individuals. Since the earlier arrivals had moved from their originally widely
dispersed locations, the second-wave arrivals were less dispersed to be-

---

[13]The following discussion is based almost entirely on Gordon 1984, and upon the
sources she cites in her work.

[14]Refugees were often sponsored by church groups and middle-class families. This
may have helped make their initial social adjustment less difficult and their later social
mobility easier.

gin with than had been the first wave. The same was not true, however, for the groups that had few members in the first wave, that is, Cambodians and Laotians. These were available for initial placement almost anywhere, and Cambodians were settled between 1981 and 1982 in twelve selected sites around the country. These nuclei may be successful in attracting other Cambodians. Meanwhile, California continues to be the major magnet for refugees of all backgrounds,[15] although, for Laotians and Cambodians, urban centers in the East and Midwest, such as Boston, Providence, and St. Paul, have attracted many newcomers.

Evidence indicates that after an initial period of redistribution and migration, the residence patterns of the first-wave refugees stabilized somewhat, and it is expected that the same will happen to the more recently arrived second-wave refugees.

Residential Segregation and Integration of Asian Americans

The distribution of Asian Americans by region or state is only one aspect of geographical distribution. Another aspect, and in some ways more important, is the distribution of Asian Americans within particular geographical areas, especially in the urban areas where they are mostly found. Residential segregation/integration is an important aspect of assimilation, and Langberg (1986) argues that it should be added to Gordon's classic (1964) list of the dimensions or phases of assimilation.[16]

Until the last decade or so, the focus of studies of spatial segregation in the United States was on blacks and whites. More recently a number of studies, first of Hispanic and then of Asian American residential patterns, have appeared, based on 1980 and 1970 census data. In this section we shall review the results of some of these studies, which typically look at distributions by census tract within a number of SMSAs; the figures we cite are averages for the SMSAs.

[15]A map of internal migration of refugees from 1981 to 1984 in Allen and Turner (1988, p. 194) shows this pattern vividly: *all* the arrows representing substantial flows of refugees migration go toward California.

[16]Gordon's seven phases were acculturation, structural assimilation, marriage, identification, attitude receptional, behavioral receptional, and civic assimilation (Langberg 1986, p. 7). Gordon argues that once there is acculturation and structural assimilation, other aspects of assimilation will follow automatically. Langberg argues that "[t]o achieve structural assimilation, there must be the opportunity for intergroup contact (p. 10)," i.e., residential assimilation. Massey and Mullan (1984), in discussing black and Hispanic spatial assimilation, also saw it as a necessary step between acculturation and other forms of assimilation.

Although there are at least five dimensions of residential segregation[17] (Massey and Denton 1988b), we shall focus here on the most widely used measure, the Index of Dissimilarity. As already discussed above, this index measures the percentage of one group that would have to change area of residence (for example, census tracts) in order for its distribution among those areas to be the same as that of a reference group.[18]

In our discussion we will first present information on the level of residential segregation for Asian Americans compared to whites, then examine whether these differences seem to be based on race or whether they can be explained on the basis of socioeconomic status.

Langberg (1986) and Langberg and Farley (1985) looked at indexes of dissimilarity between Asians and non-Hispanic whites in 38 Standard Metropolitan Statistical Areas (SMSAs) in 1980. They found the average level of the index to be 40, compared to 69 between blacks and non-Hispanic whites and 44 between Hispanics and non-Hispanic whites.[19] In every SMSA, Asians were less segregated from whites than were blacks; Asians were less segregated from whites than Hispanics, as well, in 23 of the 38 SMSAs. "The moderate segregation score for Asians—about 40—suggests that although they are a newly-arrived and easily identified

---

[17]These are evenness ("differential distribution of two social groups among areal units"), exposure ("degree of potential contact or . . . interaction between minority and majority groups members within geographic areas"), concentration ("the relative amount of physical space occupied by a minority group"), centralization ("the degree to which a group is spatially located near the center of an . . . area"), and clustering ("the extent to which areal units inhabited by minority members adjoin one another") (Massey and Denton 1988b, pp. 283, 287, 289, 291, and 293).

[18]For example, in the following table, the index between Asians and whites is 20; this means that 20 percent of the Asians would have to move to different census tracts (e.g., tract C to tract A) to achieve a distribution of Asians among the tracts the same as that of whites (or vice versa, with whites changing to match the Asian distribution).

Tract	Asians	Whites
A	20%	40%
B	40%	40%
C	40%	20%
Total	100%	100%

Note that no single measure can capture all aspects of distribution and segregation. For example, in the table above, we do not know whether Asians make up 5 percent or 95 percent (or some other percent) of the total population. In a situation where Asians make up only 5 percent, their "exposure" to other Asians would be much less than if they made up 95 percent, regardless of the fact that the index of dissimilarity is 20 in both cases.

[19]According to Kantrowitz (1973) (cited in Massey and Denton 1988a), a rough guide is that values between 0 and 30 represent low levels of residential segregation, those between 30 and 60 are moderate, and above 60 are high.

racial group, they do not cluster in predominantly Asian enclaves" (Langberg and Farley, p. 72).

The various Asian American groups had quite different levels of segregation. Japanese had the lowest index, 42, while Vietnamese had the highest, 69, indicating a high level of segregation from non-Hispanic whites. Filipinos, Koreans, Asian Indians, and Chinese all had moderate scores in the mid-50s. Langberg surmised that the Japanese level of segregation was low because the predominantly U.S.-born Japanese were not an immigrant group in the same sense that the other Asian groups were, whereas the Vietnamese had the highest proportion of foreign-born in 1980. For the Japanese, the forced relocation during World War II was undoubtedly a factor in their dispersed residence. "[T]he Vietnamese came to the U.S. mainly as war refugees with little time to prepare materially and emotionally for an orderly migration. Thus the need for institutional support derived from living in enclaves may be greater for the Vietnamese than for other Asians who have entered the U.S. for family reunification or occupational reasons" (Landberg, 1986, p. 174), and the Vietnamese may be "following the traditional ethnic pattern of settling in an ethnic enclave upon arrival in a new country" (p. 173).

Does socioeconomic status play any part in these patterns? If differences in income or education, for example, were at the root of residential segregation, then we would expect to find little or no segregation between Asians and whites of similar incomes or levels of education. This, however, does not turn out to be the case: by level of education, Asian-white indexes range between 53 (for those with less than a high school education) to 42 (for college graduates). There is thus a decline in segregation with level of education (income patterns are basically similar), but segregation by no means disappears.[20] In fact, the highest level of segregation between Asians of different levels of education or income is lower than the lowest level between Asians and whites of the same socioeconomic level.

These results from Langberg's study "indicate that the residential segregation of Asians is not entirely a social class phenomenon. After controlling for education or income, we find that Asians and whites are segregated from each other but the extent of the segregation is much less than that of blacks from whites" (Langberg and Farley, p. 73).

Factors that did seem to affect level of segregation in Langberg's study included nativity and English ability (which of course are highly related), which Langberg used as his indicators of acculturation. Denton and Massey (1988) also found nativity important, with Asian-"Anglo"

---

[20]Similar results are found by Denton and Massey 1988, in a study of 60 SMSAs.

dissimilarity falling from about 50 among immigrants to about 45 among the native-born.

The results of Langberg's study led him to suggest that different groups in the United States follow different models of assimilation.[21] Europeans, with low segregation indexes, generally follow the "Anglo-conformity" model, whereas Asians may adhere more to the "structural pluralism."

Other studies of residential segregation have come to similar conclusions. Massey and Denton (1987, 1988) looked at 60 SMSAs and found moderate levels of segregation between Asians and whites in 1970 (average of 44); the index declined to 34 by 1980.[22] Massey and Denton find that "[i]n spite of a decade of heavy Asian immigration, . . . densely settled and ethnically homogeneous Asian enclaves have not formed in U.S. metropolitan areas" (1988, p. 613). They expect, however, that "Asian enclaves [will] emerge and become poles of attraction for new immigrants" (1987, p. 817).

In attempting to explain their results, Massey and Denton invoke a perspective that finds spatial assimilation "driven by social mobility and, among immigrant groups, by acculturation" (1987, p. 817). That is, they assume that Asians (and other immigrant groups) will move out of enclaves as two processes occur: (1) a rise in the ability to live in better neighborhoods where the majority white population is found, and (2) acculturation, which means the group members identify less with the group and do not need to live so close to other members. "[T]hese variables affect spatial integration through the intervening step of suburbanization" (ibid.). "[T]he spatial assimilation of Hispanics and Asians occurs primarily through movement to the suburbs. Indicators of acculturation and assimilation are strongly related to suburbanization, but once suburbanization is controlled, they are weakly and inconsistently related to indicators of segregation" (1987, p. 823). Furthermore, "Asians appear . . . to deviate from the traditional American immigrant pattern by bypassing inner-city enclaves as a first step in the process of spatial assimilation" (1988, p. 601).

The studies by Langberg and by Massey and Denton do not answer all questions about Asian American residential patterns. For example, the use of census tracts is only a proxy for "true" suburbs which are more meaningful units of social organization (Gong 1989). Studies of particular areas can yield conflicting results or different insights. For example, White (1986) found a "surprising level of residential segregation *among* diverse Asian immigrant groups in Long Beach, California"

---

[21]These models are cited in Gordon (1964).
[22]Black levels fell from 79 to 69 and Hispanic levels fell only from 44 to 43 during the same period.

(p. 266; emphasis added), while Gong found the "level of segregation between Asian groups" to be quite low in Chicago suburbs (1989, p. 11). White found inter-Asian levels of segregation to be about as high as Asian-white levels, but Gong found higher levels of Asian-white segregation.

Discussion and Conclusion

In terms of geographic distribution and migration, Asian Americans generally seem to respond to the same forces as other individuals and groups. Economic opportunity and the location of friends and relatives are often cited as central to location decisions (DeJong and Fawcett 1981), and these are important to Asian Americans as well. There are, however, certain prominent features that are related to the unique history of Asian Americans, and these are responsible for the fact that Asian Americans are not distributed at all in the same way as are the white population or the total U.S. population. The historical fact of Asian immigration—most Asians arrived on the West Coast and in Hawaii and settled there first—is still the single most important factor affecting the distribution of Asian Americans. Migration out of the West and immigration to other regions have of course occurred, yet for the larger, older Asian American groups—Chinese, Japanese, and Filipinos—the majority still live in the areas where the first Asians arrived over a century ago. This is less true for the more recently arrived groups, Koreans and especially Asian Indians, whose indexes of dissimilarity are relatively low and who appear to be responding to the distribution of opportunities.

A second factor that has been cited as affecting the distribution of Asian Americans is "assimilation." Presumably, as a group becomes more assimilated into the majority society and as its education, occupations, and incomes become more like those of the total population, geographic assimilation will occur as well. Socioeconomic factors—the ability to live in better neighborhoods, for example—will come to outweigh the need to live in an ethnic enclave for support. Presumably, as well, middle-class Asians' identification with other Asian Americans may fall. Associated with all this are the factors of length of residence and generation. As noted above, the predominantly nonimmigrant Japanese had the lowest SMSA index of dissimilarity, while Vietnamese had the highest. Residential assimilation, as well as other aspects of adaptation, takes time to occur.

Thus, as time passes and as Asian Americans become more assimilated, it is possible and perhaps likely that their distribution patterns will become more similar to those of the majority population. This appears to have been happening at the regional level, but the evidence at the level of SMSA census tracts is not so clear.

The spatial assimilation of Asian Americans may well happen at a greater speed than for either Hispanics or blacks, who have other factors that might act to impede their geographic assimilation (the enclave nature of many Hispanic communities, which are bigger, stronger, and more linguistically homogeneous than Asian American enclaves, and the impacted socioeconomic situation of the blacks, who couldn't move to the suburbs whether they wanted to or not).

The recent history of refugees from Southeast Asia to some extent recapitulates the longer history of other Asian American groups. Certain factors (in this case, U.S. government policies) determined the original distribution of refugees, and some of these areas have remained focal points of subsequent settlement. However, the refugee situation is different in that the internal migration following initial settlement, the so-called secondary migration, has been much more important. Vietnamese and other refugee groups are concentrating in certain areas very quickly, and we may well see rises in their dissimilarity compared with whites and the total population.

FAMILY AND HOUSEHOLDS

DESPITE their many other dissimilarities, Asian Americans share strong traditions of extended kinship ties.[1] Historically, Chinese, Japanese, Koreans, and Vietnamese families differed somewhat from one another, but all derived their basic norms and values from Confucianism. These included obedience to and responsibility for parents, patrilinearity, patriarchy, a preference for sons, and considerable personal interdependence. Much the same is true of Asian Indian family norms. Filipinos differ most noticeably in a much more egalitarian role for women. With urbanization and industrialization, of course, Asian families have been undergoing changes that include nuclearization in their home societies. Nevertheless, all literature on contemporary Asian societies stresses the relative importance of the family when compared to the current American situation (Caces 1985; Kuo and Lin 1977; Hurh and Kim 1984; Caplan, Whitmore, and Bui 1985). Furthermore, the family is often cited as one of the chief determinants of the educational successes of Asian American children.[2] Added to this is the fact that the family is an essential adaptive mechanism for survival of Asian immi-

---

[1]Some materials in this chapter appeared in Gardner, Robey, and Smith (1985).

[2]For example, William Liu is quoted as saying, "In the Confucian ethic, there is a centripedal family orientation that makes people work for the honor of the family, not for themselves. In Confucianism, one can never repay one's mother and father, and there is a very strong sense of guilt. It is very compelling, like the Protestant ethic in the West, a great inducer of motivation." Quoted in Fox Butterfield (1986).

grants in the United States, so we wish to pay special attention to the condition of Asian American families and households, especially over periods of stay in the United States.

Asian immigrants entering the United States confront a situation where American households and families are displaying high rates of divorce and remarriage, increasing proportions of single-parent families, and household formations not based on the traditional family. Of course, the American family has been undergoing change for many years, but significant recent developments have led some social scientists to express uncertainty about its future (Epenshade 1985). Sociological literature since the 1950s has offered considerable debate about the possibly irreparable decline of the American family. Increases in divorce rates and other indicators have prompted some social scientists to voice pessimistic views about the future significance of the family (National Center for Health Statistics 1985; Glick 1984; Goode 1977; Westoff 1983). It is clear that the family has been "losing functions" in contemporary society, and that the American concentration upon the nuclear family has weakened the extended family system. However, not all scholars view these changes as destructive. William J. Goode insists, "Long after the last reader . . . has moldered into dust, the vast majority of human beings will continue to be born into a family unit with two spouses, male and female, with or without another child already there" (Goode 1977). Most scholars feel that, despite the loss of economic, educational, and religious functions, the family is still very active in the areas of reproduction, early socialization, and for the emotional support of individuals.

Census data cannot address many of these issues, but, fortunately, they can give us excellent information on family and household structures, and, possibly more important, they tell us a good deal about the economic well-being of Asian American households and families. These analyses are important, because very little demographic literature on the Asian American household exists (Staples and Mirande 1985; Huber and Spitze 1980). Some data can be found in Gardner, Robey, and Smith (1985); Xenos, Barringer, and Levin (1989); Barringer and Cho (1990); Yao (1985).

Before we proceed, it will be helpful to review some definitions. The *nuclear* family, of course, consists of a husband, wife, and children. The *extended* family refers to significant kinship ties beyond the nuclear family. The *primary* family refers to the principal family in a household, which may include other relatives and non-relatives. The *household* is a group of people who sleep and eat together. A *household unit* is a physical living area where a set of people share food and utilities. A *family household* is a household structured around kinship. A *non-family household* is composed of unrelated individuals, such as young workers sharing an apartment. A *householder* is usually the person who owns, rents, or leases and occupies a household.

The census term *family* refers to at least two related persons living together. This is a more restrictive definition than that used by most social scientists, because "living together" is not a common requirement for the existence of a "family" as understood by most sociologists or anthropologists. It does not include most nuclear family members living outside, such as college students in dormitories or husbands or wives working in and residing in other locations. This means that census information about family income and family size may be somewhat misleading. Furthermore, census data give us no information about extended family ties outside the household.

These matters are significant for our purposes, because Asian immigrant families often carry over some extended-family practices to the United States. For example, Korean, Chinese, and Vietnamese often enlist the services of grandparents in child rearing, and may share financial resources outside the immediate household (Hurh and Kim 1988). This suggests that income figures and family size estimates from the census are relatively conservative. Despite these problems, census data do allow us to compare Asian Americans with other American ethnic groups.

Marital Status of Asian Americans

As Goode's quote above suggests, the "ideal" American family is one with two married parents and their children living together. However, the trend in America since the 1950s, and accelerating into the 1970s, was for more single households, and for an increasing divorce rate, which began to taper off in the early 1980s (Glick 1984). Among American minorities, blacks experienced more marital disruption than whites (Epenshade 1983). Hispanic populations appear quite similar to whites, with some variations on particular measures (Bean and Tienda 1987). Bean and Tienda attribute this, in part, to the familism of Hispanic cultures. We might expect, then, that Asian Americans would display even more conservative characteristics.

Our data are less than ideal for some purposes, since our files did not permit examination of remarriages or total histories of remarriage and divorce.[3] However, Table 5.1 does show the present marital status of Asian Americans in 1980 by sex. Note that Koreans, Filipinos, and Asian Indians showed the highest percentages of married persons over

[3]This was a problem with our constructed files; such data can be gleaned from the census.

age 15, for both males and females. There was very little other variation, except for low marriage percentages for blacks and Vietnamese. Vietnamese males showed a low percentage married and separated, no doubt attributable to disruption and resettlement after the Vietnam war. As expected, Asian Americans showed lower percentages of divorced persons than did whites or Hispanics. Divorce percentages were higher for females than males, except for Filipinos, where gender differences were minimal. Among Asian Americans, male Japanese and Filipinos showed slightly higher divorces than other groups. Japanese and Korean females displayed the highest divorce percentages, but they were still far below percentages shown for whites, blacks, or Hispanics.

Table 5.2 shows the marital status of Japanese, Chinese, Filipinos, and whites over time, in 1960, 1970, and 1980. With the exception of Filipinos, the percentage of divorced and separated persons increased from 1960 to 1980, as we would expect. For all groups, the percentage of single females also increased over time. The percentage of married males dropped over time for Japanese and whites, but increased for Chinese and Filipinos, reflecting more favorable sex ratios in 1970 and 1980. There is some ambiguity in these figures, but in general, the trends indicate that although Asian American families showed fewer signs of family "instability" than whites, they also showed the same trends in general. However, whites showed consistently higher percentages of persons now married, probably because they included very few immigrants.

If assimilation theory has any credibility, we would expect that Asian Americans' marital status would become more like whites the longer the Asian Americans' residence in the United States. Table 5.3 shows present marital status of those Asian Americans immigrating between 1975 and 1980, compared to the total population of Asian Americans and to native Americans. Note that among recent immigrants, percentages of divorced persons were quite low, with only Japanese (11.5 percent) showing percentages approaching the total percentages for whites, blacks, and Hispanics. It is not known how many of those persons were divorced after immigrating to the United States, but it is likely that most were, since divorce rates are low in most Asian societies. For all groups, the divorce percentages are much higher for the general population than for immigrants. For example, about 1.6 percent of new Chinese immigrants are divorced, while the figure jumped to 3.9 percent for Chinese in the general population, and 6.9 percent for native Americans. When we compare divorces across the total population, note that all Asian Americans show lower percentages than whites, blacks, or Hispanics. When we compare native Americans, however, the percentage of divorced persons is higher for Asian Indians (15.6 percent), Koreans (13.1 percent), and Vietnamese (13.4 percent) than for whites (8.6 per-

TABLE 5.1

Marital Status, by Sex and Ethnicity in 1980, Standardized, by Age with 1980 White Distribution, by Sex as the Standard

(Percentage)

Ethnicity	Single	Now Married	Separated	Widowed	Divorced	Total
			Males			
Japanese	37.9	55.9	1.0	2.1	3.1	100.0
Chinese	35.5	59.1	1.0	2.3	2.1	100.0
Filipino	30.4	63.0	1.4	2.0	3.2	100.0
Korean	28.8	66.0	1.3	1.9	2.1	100.1
Asian Indian	30.5	62.4	1.0	3.44	2.6	99.9
Vietnamese	33.9	57.3	3.3	4.2	1.3	100.0
White	28.0	63.0	1.4	2.4	5.2	100.0
Black	34.1	48.0	6.3	4.7	7.0	100.1
Hispanic	27.7	61.6	2.7	2.9	5.1	100.0
			Females			
Japanese	26.7	54.9	1.1	12.7	4.6	100.0
Chinese	25.5	57.5	1.2	13.3	2.6	100.1
Filipino	23.6	58.5	2.0	12.7	3.2	100.0
Korean	17.1	57.2	1.9	19.7	4.1	100.0
Asian Indian	17.6	62.3	1.3	15.1	3.6	99.9
Vietnamese	22.0	53.6	3.1	19.1	2.3	100.1
White	21.2	57.8	1.7	12.5	6.8	100.0
Black	28.6	36.7	8.7	16.7	9.3	100.0
Hispanic	21.8	52.2	4.9	13.3	7.8	100.0

SOURCES: Housing Files, 5% PUMs "A" Tape and 0.17 "A" & "B" Tapes.

TABLE 5.2

Marital Status, by Sex for Japanese, Chinese, Filipinos, and Whites: Year 1960, 1970, and 1980 Standardized, by Age with 1980 White Distribution as the Standard

Ethnicity and Year	Single Male	Single Female	Now Married Male	Now Married Female	Separated Male	Separated Female	Widowed Male	Widowed Female	Divorced Male	Divorced Female	Total Male	Total Female
						Percentage						
JAPANESE												
1960	33.9	26.9	61.3	64.1	0.5	0.4	3.3	7.1	1.1	1.5	100.1	100.0
1970	33.6	26.7	60.9	59.2	0.7	0.9	2.8	10.3	2.0	2.8	100.0	99.9
1980	37.9	26.7	55.9	54.9	1.0	1.1	2.1	12.7	3.1	4.6	100.0	100.0
CHINESE												
1960	38.5	20.7	54.8	66.9	1.8	0.5	3.5	10.5	1.2	1.4	99.8	100.0
1970	34.7	23.9	59.0	59.4	1.0	1.0	3.7	13.8	1.5	1.8	99.9	99.9
1980	35.5	25.5	59.1	57.5	1.0	1.2	2.3	13.3	2.1	2.6	100.0	100.1
FILIPINOS												
1960	40.4	20.1	50.8	69.7	2.0	1.2	3.4	7.1	3.4	1.9	100.0	100.0
1970	34.0	25.3	57.9	59.8	1.7	1.6	2.9	10.6	3.5	2.7	100.0	100.0
1980	30.4	23.6	63.0	58.5	1.4	2.0	2.0	12.7	3.2	3.2	100.0	100.0
WHITES												
1960	24.3	18.6	69.3	65.4	1.0	1.3	3.3	11.9	2.1	2.8	100.0	100.0
1970	27.7	21.8	65.8	60.7	1.0	1.5	2.8	12.3	2.6	3.7	99.9	100.0
1980	28.0	21.2	63.0	57.8	1.4	1.7	2.4	12.5	5.2	6.8	100.0	100.0

SOURCES: PC80-1-2E, PC80-1-1C, PC(2)-4C.

TABLE 5.3

Marital Status of Household Heads, by Nativity/Year of Immigration for each Ethnicity in 1980 Standardized, by Age with 1980 White Distribution as the Standard

Ethnicity	Single	Now Married	Separated	Widowed	Divorced	Total
			Percentage			
ALL HOUSEHOLD HEADS						
Japanese	19.9	60.0	2.1	10.8	7.2	100.0
Chinese	17.1	68.3	1.6	9.1	3.9	100.0
Filipino	12.9	72.3	2.4	6.4	6.0	100.0
Korean	10.4	68.9	3.2	11.4	6.1	100.0
Asian Indian	14.0	59.0	1.6	19.5	6.0	100.1
Vietnamese	14.2	66.0	5.0	11.4	3.4	100.0
White	10.8	64.7	2.2	13.6	8.6	99.9
Black	16.6	41.7	10.2	18.2	13.4	100.1
Hispanic	10.9	61.3	5.5	12.0	10.3	100.0
IMMIGRATED 1975–1980						
Japanese	14.9	63.6	2.0	7.9	11.5	99.9
Chinese	15.0	74.8	1.8	6.7	1.6	99.9
Filipino	13.0	72.8	2.5	8.9	2.9	100.1
Korean	8.6	74.8	3.0	10.1	3.5	100.0
Asian Indian	13.0	71.8	2.2	10.6	2.4	100.0
Vietnamese	14.2	68.4	5.2	10.0	2.2	100.0
White	*	*	*	*	*	*
Black	*	*	*	*	*	*
Hispanic	*	*	*	*	*	*
NATIVE-BORN						
Japanese	21.6	62.3	1.8	7.8	6.5	100.0
Chinese	23.2	59.8	1.6	8.5	6.9	100.0
Filipino	15.2	58.7	4.1	11.1	10.9	100.0
Korean	17.0	57.1	3.4	9.4	13.1	100.0
Asian Indian	18.6	40.4	3.5	21.9	15.6	100.0
Vietnamese	20.8	32.3	14.5	19.0	13.4	100.0
White	*	*	*	*	*	*
Black	*	*	*	*	*	*
Hispanic	*	*	*	*	*	*

SOURCES: Housing Files, 5% PUMs "A" Tape and 0.1 "A" & "B" Tapes.

* Data not readily available.

cent). However, among native Americans, Chinese and Japanese still show lower percentages of divorced persons than is the case with whites. It would appear, therefore, that the longer Asian Americans remain in the United States, the more likely they are to be divorced, but of course part of that increase is simply due to age.

The percentage of now married persons is somewhat larger for new immigrants than for the total population. For example, of Koreans who immigrated between 1975 and 1980, 74.8 percent were married, as compared to 68.9 percent in the total population. Except for Japanese, the percentage of married Asian Americans was much higher than for blacks, whites, or Hispanics. The low percentage of married persons among Japanese was due to a very high percentage of divorced persons (around 14 percent) among those who immigrated before 1975. Figures for Vietnamese throughout were somewhat variable, again most probably because of their refugee status in 1980.

Figure 5.1 shows the percentage of persons now married among Asian Americans by age and sex. The percentage of early marriages was highest for Filipino males and for Asian Indian females. Koreans also showed relatively early ages for marriage. Note that the percentage of early marriages for both Japanese and Chinese females was much lower than for other groups. Koreans and Asian Indians showed the highest overall percentages of marriage, while Japanese displayed the lowest overall percentages. Japanese had the highest proportion of native Americans of all Asian American groups, and therefore appeared much more similar to whites in this regard. Early marriages among females were quite variable among Asian Americans. For example, only about 20 percent of Chinese and Japanese women were married at ages 20–24, compared to about 50 percent for Korean and 60 percent for Asian Indian women. A similar pattern existed for ages 25–29. White American women exhibited a pattern that appeared to lie about midway between the various Asian Americans. The same was true for males, with only Koreans and Asian Indians showing higher percentages of men married at most ages. All Asian American men marry later than white men, especially for Chinese and Japanese. These data reinforce the contentions of many family specialists that Americans like to be married, including whites.

By themselves, the foregoing data are somewhat misleading, because most divorced white Americans remarry, and we already suspect that divorces are more common among white Americans than among Asian Americans, especially new immigrants. Figure 5.2 certainly shows divorce incidences to be much higher for both white males and females, except for Asian Indians, who for some reason show high percentages of divorce in the 45-to-55 age range. Vietnamese data, again, may be distorted by their family disruptions caused by the Vietnam War. Apart

FIGURE 5.1

*Percentage of Asian Americans Married
Except Separated, by Age: 1980*

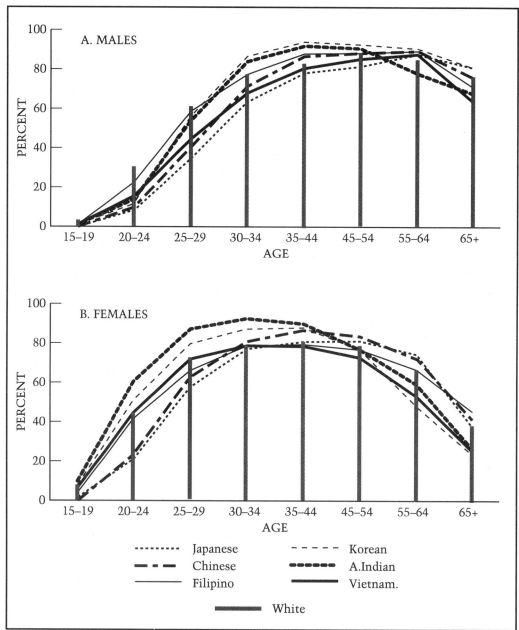

SOURCE: Special Census Tabulations.

FIGURE 5.2

*Percent Divorce Among Asian
Americans, by Age: 1980*

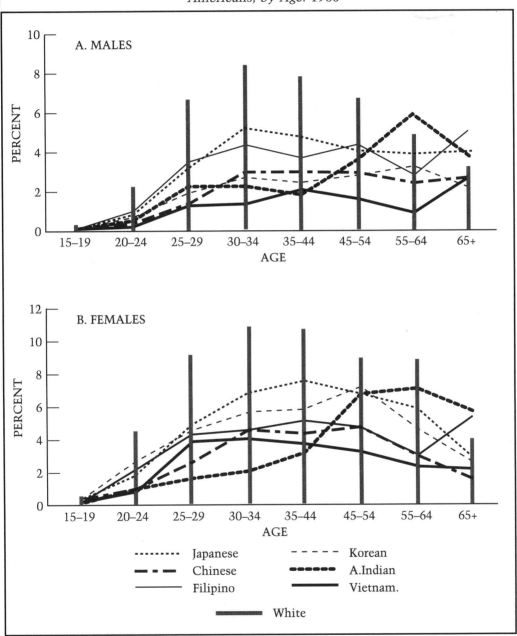

A. MALES

B. FEMALES

.... Japanese   – – – – Korean

— ·· — Chinese   •••••• A.Indian

——— Filipino   ━━━ Vietnam.

▨▨▨▨ White

SOURCE: Special Census Tabulations.

from those aberrations, Japanese and Korean females, in that order, show the next highest number of divorces, though both are well below the levels of whites. The same is true of Japanese males, but Korean men show low percentages of divorced persons. In all cases, female divorce percentages are higher than those of males. This is undoubtedly due to the fact that men find it easier to remarry, especially among Asian immigrants.

Figures 5.1 and 5.2, taken together, reinforce the notion that Asian American marriages may be more stable than those of whites. It is important to note that although Vietnamese immigrants share some other social characteristics with blacks and Hispanics, the incidence of divorce appears to be quite low among the Vietnamese.

Figure 5.3 shows outmarriages of male and female Asian Americans to other ethnic groups. In all cases, except Vietnamese, male outmarriage is twice or more that of females. Filipinos show the most outmarriage, Koreans, the least. The determinants of amalgamation are very complicated, and are beyond the scope of this study. But the subject is very important, and deserves careful study. In Hawaii, in 1985, 56.5 percent Filipino and 51.5 percent Japanese outmarried. For whites, the figure was only 13.3 percent (Hawaii State Department of Health 1988). Kitano and Daniels (1988) reported that 43.4 percent of Japanese males and 56.6 percent of Japanese females outmarried in 1984. They found that intermarriage rates had dropped somewhat from a high of 63 percent in 1977 to about 51 percent in 1984. Lee and Yamasake (n.d.) reported that intermarriage for Asian Americans is most likely with other Asian American groups, or with non-Hispanic whites or Hawaiians. Widespread intermarriage will produce some obvious problems for the classification of Asian Americans in the analysis of 1990 census data.

Family Composition

Part of the success enjoyed by Asian Americans has been attributed to strong family support. David Bell suggests, "All the various explanations of the Asian Americans' success tend to fall into one category: self-sufficiency. The first element of this self-sufficiency is family. The stability of the family contributes to success in three ways. First, it provides a secure environment for children. Second, it pushes those children to do better than their parents . . . and finally, it is a significant financial advantage" (Bell 1985). The composition of families in 1980 gives us further evidence of family stability and structure. Table 5.4 shows a number of statistics comparing Asian American families to whites and

FIGURE 5.3

Outmarriage of Asian Americans—Marriage to Members of Another Race: 1980

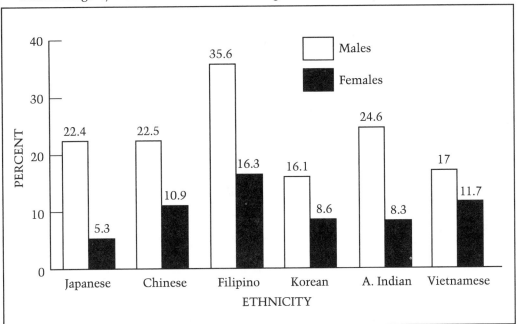

SOURCE: PC80-2-1E.

blacks. First, the percentage of families living with their own children under 18 was highest for Koreans (75.3 percent) and lowest for Japanese (47.1 percent). Whites were also low, at 49.5 percent. These figures related partly to the proportion of immigrants in each of the Asian American populations: Koreans, Filipinos, Vietnamese, and Asian Indian populations consist mostly of immigrants from countries with high fertility rates. The percentages of children residing with their own parents among Asian Americans were also very high (close to 90 percent), all exceeding whites except for Vietnamese, again because of disruption from the Vietnam War. Note that families with children residing with both parents were about twice as common among Asian Americans as among blacks. The percentages were also higher than for whites, again excepting Vietnamese.

The percentages of married-couple families were about the same for Asian Americans and whites, and were much higher than for blacks. Those married-couple families with their own children varied much more, again showing higher fertility for those Asian Americans with large proportions of recent migrants.

TABLE 5.4
Family Composition, by Ethnicity

Family Composition	Ethnicity							
	Japanese	Chinese	Filipino	Korean	Asian Indian (Percentage)	Vietnamese	White	Black
TOTAL NUMBER	167,795	191,640	167,513	67,596	97,596	42,261	59,190,133	6,105,698
Family with own children under 18	47.1	56.1	67.9	75.3	69.2	72.8	49.5	61.4
Children residing with two parents	87.3	88.2	84.5	89.4	92.7	74.1	82.9	45.4
Married couple	84.1	86.8	83.6	86.0	91.0	72.8	86.1	57.1
With own children under 18	48.4	59.3	71.5	77.7	72.5	81.4	49.2	58.4
Female householder, w/o husband present	11.9	8.5	11.8	10.8	5.7	14.8	10.8	37.2
With own children under 18	47.4	43.0	57.3	68.1	44.6	67.6	55.6	69.0
Employed	70.1	67.1	75.8	68.6	52.5	51.8	*	*
Persons/household	2.7	3.1	3.6	3.4	2.9	4.4	2.7	3.1
Persons/family	3.6	3.7	4.2	4.9	3.5	5.2	3.2	3.7

SOURCE: PC80-2-1E.

* Data not readily available.

One of the indicators of family instability having some objective consequences is the percentage of female householders with no husband present. Other measures of instability, even divorce, are controversial, but female householders, as we shall see, suffered dramatic income losses. In this respect, Asian Americans appeared similar to whites, with percentages hovering around 11 percent. Asian Indians appeared lower, at about 5.7 percent. Blacks had the highest percentage of single female householders, at 37.2 percent. Of households, Koreans, Vietnamese, and Filipinos had the highest percentage of children under 18, again a factor associated with fertility. Note that single female householders' employment varied from 75.8 percent for Filipinos to a low of 51.8 percent for Vietnamese and 52.5 percent for Asian Indians. With the exception of Vietnamese, again, Asian Americans had about the same percentage of single female householders as did whites. Both Asian Americans and whites were far better off in this respect than blacks. We will return to this subject when we examine household incomes.

Table 5.4 also shows mean family and household size. These figures were computed by the Census Bureau by dividing the total number of persons in families and households by number of families and households. The household figures were probably reasonable, but the family figures were misleading in that they took into account only family members residing in a particular household. Household size varied considerably among Asian Americans, with a low of 2.7 persons for Japanese (which, incidentally, was the same for whites), to 2.9 for Asian Indians, 3.1 for Chinese, 3.4 for Koreans, 3.6 for Filipinos, and 4.4 for Vietnamese. As we shall show subsequently, household size is also an important contributor to income.

Household Composition

Table 5.5 shows household composition for each Asian American ethnicity, compared to whites, blacks, and Hispanics. The most prevalent type, of course, was a family household with male householder. Asian Americans varied in percentages of male family household heads, with a low of 60.7 percent for Japanese, 66.7 percent for Asian Indians, 68.0 percent for Chinese, 69.5 percent for Vietnamese, 70.9 percent for Filipinos and 72.0 percent for Koreans. With the exception of Japanese, these percentages were much higher than for whites and Hispanics (63.4 percent) or blacks (42.7 percent).

The percentage of family households with female householders was about the same for most Asian Americans as for whites, around 10 per-

TABLE 5.5

Household Composition of Asian Americans, White, Black, and Hispanic Population: 1980

	Ethnicity								
Household Composition	Japanese	Chinese	Filipino	Korean	Asian Indian	Vietnamese	White	Black	Hispanic
					(Percentage)				
HOUSEHOLDERS BY TYPE									
Family household, male	60.7	68.0	70.9	72.0	66.7	69.5	63.4	42.7	63.4
Family household, female	10.1	11.1	12.3	11.2	6.4	14.2	10.1	29.8	18.1
Non-family household	29.2	20.9	16.8	16.8	26.9	16.3	26.5	27.5	18.5
Total	100.0	100.0	100.0	100.0	100.0	100.0	100.0	100.0	100.0
HOUSEHOLD MEMBERS RELATIONSHIP TO HOUSEHOLDER									
Householder	34.0	31.8	26.4	23.2	35.0	21.0	37.4	32.8	28.0
Spouse	27.6	21.9	21.1	26.4	23.8	16.5	23.6	12.2	17.5
Child	30.0	34.7	37.3	42.0	32.5	42.2	33.1	41.1	43.9
Other relative	4.8	7.9	11.6	6.2	6.5	14.3	3.3	9.5	7.2
Not related	3.6	3.7	3.6	2.2	2.3	6.0	2.6	3.4	3.4
Total	100.0	100.0	100.0	100.0	100.0	100.0	100.0	100.0	100.0
Total Number	11,937	12,423	10,164	4,021	6,690	2,534	2,680	2,127	2,189

SOURCE: PC80-C1, Tables 121, 131, 160, and special tabulations.

cent. Asian Indians appeared to have fewer female-headed family households (6.4 percent), and Vietnamese, more (14.2 percent). Blacks had the highest percentage of such households, at 29.8 percent, followed by Hispanics at 18.1 percent. Figure 5.4 shows the effect of length of stay in the United States on the percentage of female household heads. In general, the percentage increased with length of stay in the United States, and was highest for most groups among native Americans. Notable exceptions were among Japanese who immigrated before 1975. These groups were also marked by a very high percentage of divorced women. Filipinos immigrating from 1975 to 1980 contained a large proportion of young single women, and Filipino households of persons immigrating before 1965 contained large numbers of unmarried males. Koreans and Hispanics showed the most consistent patterns. Black and white immigrants were not shown because numbers were very small.

Non-family households were least common among Vietnamese (16.3 percent), Filipinos (16.8 Percent), and Koreans (16.8 percent) and most frequent among Japanese (29.2 percent) and Asian Indians (26.9 percent). The reasons for these disparities were not entirely clear, but Vietnamese, Koreans, and Filipinos had the largest numbers of recent immigrants. Most Japanese were native Americans, so it was no surprise that they resembled whites and blacks in this respect. Xenos, Barringer, and Levin (1989) attribute the high percentage of non-family households among Asian Indians to very high proportions of aged and young in their American population.

Relationship of Household Members

Children constitute a high proportion of household membership among Vietnamese (42.2 percent), Koreans (42.0 percent), and Filipinos (37.3 percent). These figures are similar to those for blacks (41.1 percent) and Hispanics (43.9 percent). Japanese, with 30.0 percent children, Chinese (34.7 percent), and Asian Indians (32.5 percent) more resemble white households (33.1 percent). These figures correspond to fertility rates reported in Chapter 2.

Relatives other than children were reported by the Census Bureau and gave us some notion of the extended family, at least within the household. Vietnamese reported the largest percentage of other relatives in the household (14.3 percent) followed by Filipinos (11.6 percent), Chinese (7.9 percent), Asian Indians (6.5 percent), Koreans (6.2 percent), and Japanese (4.8 percent). All these figures were appreciably higher than for whites (3.3 percent). Blacks (9.5 percent) and Hispanics (7.2 percent) fell somewhere between. These data suggest that although most family

FIGURE 5.4

Percentage of Female Household Heads, by Period of Immigration/Nativity: 1980

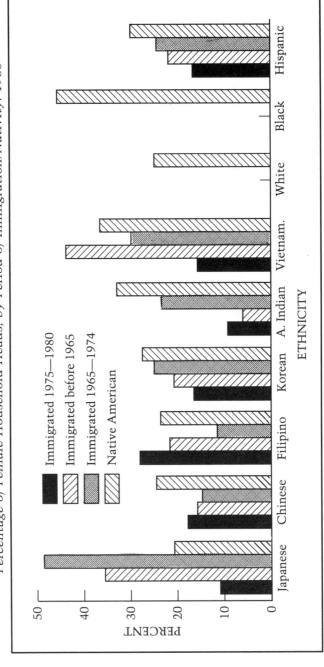

SOURCE: 5% PUMS "A" Tape.

households consisted only of a nuclear family, many Asian American households were extended. However, given the fact that very few Japanese households were made up of extended families, it is likely that this phenomenon was related to Asian ethnic groups with large numbers of recent immigrants (Gardner, Robey, and Smith 1985). Percentages of non-relatives in households were not much different from whites, blacks, and Hispanics, except for Vietnamese, who had a much higher percentage of households with non-relatives (6 percent), and Koreans, with a very low percentage (2.2 percent).

All the preceding figures support the widespread belief that Asian American families appear very stable, certainly when compared to black and Hispanic families. The exception is among Vietnamese, who, again, are unusual in that those in the United States in 1980 were mostly refugees from the Vietnam War, and could be expected to show signs of disruption.

Family and Household Incomes

Although much analysis of income is confined to personal income (which we pursue in Chapter 8), family and household incomes may be more significant for Asian Americans, and especially those who are immigrants. As we pointed out earlier, Asian immigrants appear to use family and household combined incomes as coping strategies. Table 5.6 shows data on incomes. First, both median household and family incomes were considerably higher for all Asian Americans than for whites (except Vietnamese, who had the *lowest* incomes of all, even lower than blacks and Hispanics). The highest incomes were for Asian Indians, followed by Filipinos, Chinese, Japanese, Koreans, and whites, in that order. These figures have not been adjusted for educational levels of household heads, number of household workers or household type, but they do suggest that the household strategy for income pays off. For married-couple families, the same situation holds.

Households with female householders with no husband present had much lower incomes; the Koreans and Vietnamese had slightly more than one-third of the incomes of married-couple families. Filipinos and Chinese single female householders had the highest household incomes, but even they were about half of the incomes of married-couple households.

Per capita family income is also instructive. Japanese, with small family sizes, had the highest per capita family incomes, at $9,068. Japanese were followed by Asian Indians ($8,667), whites ($7,635), Chinese

TABLE 5.6

Family and Household Income: 1979

Type of Income	Ethnicity								
	Japanese	Chinese	Filipino	Korean	Asian Indian	Vietnamese	White	Black	Hispanic
					(Dollars)				
MEDIAN HOUSEHOLD INCOME									
Median	21,368	22,559	23,687	20,180	24,993	12,840	17,680	11,020	13,495
Mean	25,225	26,600	27,194	24,367	29,591	15,271	21,173	14,206	16,044
MARRIED COUPLE FAMILY									
Median	23,820	23,908	25,228	21,450	25,924	15,263	21,005	12,598	14,510
Mean	27,876	27,668	28,873	26,119	30,854	16,718	23,702	15,684	16,947
FEMALE HOUSEHOLD, NO HUSBAND PRESENT									
Median	11,740	13,433	14,401	8,533	11,599	6,940	8,947	*	*
Mean	14,639	17,149	17,317	11,601	14,901	10,358	*	*	*
Per capita									
Family income	9,068	7,476	6,915	5,554	8,667	3,382	7,635	4,674	4,920
Total number	167,795	191,640	167,513	67,457	97,596	42,261	59,190,133	6,105,698	2,168,649

SOURCE: PC80-1-2E and PC80-1-1C.

* Data not readily available.

TABLE 5.7

Median and Mean Family Income, by Selected States and for the Total U.S. Population: 1979

State	\multicolumn{6}{c}{Ethnicity}
	Japanese	Chinese	Filipino	Korean	Asian Indian	Vietnamese
	\multicolumn{6}{c}{(Dollars)}
TOTAL U.S.						
Median	27,354	22,559	23,687	20,459	24,993	12,840
Mean	30,527	26,600	27,194	24,670	29,591	15,271
CALIFORNIA						
Median	27,388	24,409	23,586	20,713	23,772	11,852
Mean	30,716	28,008	25,727	24,052	27,342	15,144
HAWAII						
Median	29,215	28,433	20,519	19,463	*	*
Mean	31,994	32,388	22,921	22,754	*	*
ILLINOIS						
Median	28,109	23,785	32,255	22,981	25,998	*
Mean	31,009	28,634	36,260	26,865	31,112	*
NEW YORK						
Median	30,038	16,100	27,904	19,930	22,709	*
Mean	36,442	20,844	32,227	24,837	27,697	*

SOURCE: PC 80-2-1E.

* Numbers too few for accurate data.

($7,476), Filipinos ($6,915), and Koreans ($5,554). Hispanics ($4,920) and blacks ($4,674) trailed, with Vietnamese showing by far the lowest per capita family income (only $3,382). One can quibble about the meaning of these figures, but in general, those groups with the highest family incomes also had the highest per capita incomes; variations undoubtedly were related to the numbers of children in families.

Incomes were known to vary in various regions of the United States, so we constructed Table 5.7, which shows median and mean family incomes for various States with large proportions of Asian Americans. Variations were minimal for Japanese, but Chinese showed considerable variation, with the highest incomes in Hawaii, but very low median incomes in New York (28.6 percent less than the total U.S. median income for Chinese).[4] Filipinos fared better in Illinois and New York, less well in California, and least well in Hawaii, where nearly all were relatives or descendants of plantation workers from the poor region of Ilocos

[4] We have been told by Chinese informants that New York City's Chinatown contains many recent poor immigrants from Hong Kong and Taiwan. It certainly resembles a ghetto in many respects.

Norte. Koreans and Asian Indians showed little variation, and there were too few Vietnamese outside California to give good data.

Average-income figures tend to obscure what may be going on with very low and high incomes. Unfortunately, the Census Bureau published income data with a cutoff point of only $75,000, so we cannot look at the really well-to-do. However, we picked an arbitrary upper-household income figure of $40,000, which was a comfortable income in 1980, and compared it with the poverty level. Table 5.8 makes this comparison, and also shows figures by recency of arrival in the United States and for native-born Americans. Looking first at those who immigrated to the United States between 1975 and 1980, all groups except Filipinos displayed about twice as many households below the poverty level as white natives. However, 34.3 percent of Vietnamese and 30.9 percent of Chinese households were below the poverty level. This is about the same proportion as black and Hispanic natives. Koreans and Asian Indians had about twice as many households below the poverty level as did white natives. However, these figures dropped dramatically for immigrants who entered from 1965 to 1974, suggesting relatively successful adaptation, again excepting Vietnamese. Native Americans, Japanese, Chinese, and Koreans showed lower percentages than did whites. However, Filipinos showed somewhat higher percentages than whites, and Asian Indians the highest percentage of all (33.3 percent). Native American Asian Indians consisted of large numbers of very old and very young, as we pointed out earlier.

At the other end of the spectrum, recent Japanese immigrants showed a high percentage (15.8) of households with over $40,000 in income. Percentages were relatively low for other groups except Filipinos (8.5 percent) and Asian Indians (7.4 percent). But all were higher than Hispanics (only 1.2 percent). Excepting Japanese, all groups showed a substantial increase in higher incomes for those who immigrated from 1965 to 1974, most much higher than for native whites (9.7 percent). Again, except for Japanese, Asian Americans who immigrated before 1965 showed very high percentages of higher incomes. Koreans and Asian Indians in those brackets had three times as many households with incomes above $40,000 as did whites. These percentages dropped for most natives, except Japanese, who seemed to have about twice as many households with higher incomes than was the case with whites. All native Asian Americans except Vietnamese fared much better than blacks and Hispanics. On all measures, Vietnamese fared worst of all. In general, this table indicates that household incomes increased the longer Asian immigrants have been in the United States, and that immigrants who have been here for over 5 years or so have done better than natives. Poverty levels, on the other hand, decrease, the longer immigrants remain in the United States.

TABLE 5.8

Percentage of Households Below the Poverty Level and Percentage of Households with $40,000 or More Income, by Period of Immigration: 1979

Immigrated	Japanese	Chinese	Filipino	Korean	Asian Indian (Percentage)	Vietnamese	White	Black	Hispanic
Total number	11,937	12,423	10,164	4,021	6,690	2,534	2,680	2,127	2,189
1975–1980									
Below poverty	21.6	30.9	11.5	22.7	17.0	34.3	*	*	35.9
Above $40,000	15.8	4.1	8.5	4.2	7.4	3.9	*	*	1.2
1965–1974									
Below poverty	13.8	10.9	4.3	10.6	4.7	16.8	*	*	20.8
Above $40,000	10.7	13.5	21.3	18.0	21.6	10.0	*	*	4.0
BEFORE 1965									
Below poverty	12.8	9.0	7.7	8.8	8.1	11.1	*	*	18.0
Above $40,000	10.2	20.8	14.4	28.0	27.8	*	*	*	4.7
NATIVE AMERICANS									
Below poverty	5.3	7.7	11.6	8.9	20.6	33.3	10.1	29.7	31.8
Above $40,000	0.1	17.9	10.2	14.9	3.7	*	9.7	4.2	4.5

Ethnicity

SOURCE: PUMs "A" 5% Tape.

*Numbers less than 100.

Determinants of Household Income

We now show three variables that have strong effects upon household income: household type, number of household workers, and period of immigration/nativity.[5] Rather than treat them all separately, we shall show their simultaneous, or adjusted, effects as determined by multiple classification analysis. Table 5.9 shows household income gains and losses from the grand mean income for each category of the three predicting variables, along with the strength of prediction for each variable (Beta), and the total strength of the model (R^2) for each ethnicity.

First, observe the variable, household type. Note that for all ethnicities, married-couple families were well above the grand mean income. Japanese, especially, benefited by being married couples, with an average household income of $31,150 ($27,366 + $3,784). Vietnamese benefited the least, by far (+$965). Households with single male householders generally suffered losses, the highest loss for Asian Indians (−$4,618). In general, the greatest losses were for households with single female householders, followed closely by non-family households. The losses here were all severe, but especially for Koreans (−$8,268) and Asian Indians (−$8,268). Non-family households of Koreans, Asian Indians also suffered strong losses. Overall, this variable had the strongest effects for Japanese and Koreans, and the least for Vietnamese.

Overall, however, the number of household workers had even stronger effects, with significant losses for one worker, and enormous gains for 4 or more workers. For example, Filipinos with only one household worker averaged only $18,350, but households with 4 or more workers averaged $41,990, an increase of 229 percent. This effect varied from ethnicity to ethnicity, but all showed strong effects, from Vietnamese (B = .57) to blacks (.49) and Filipinos(.42). For some reason, Koreans and Asian Indians received less benefit from additional household workers (B = .23).

Period of immigration/nativity also showed strong effects, except for Japanese, whites, and blacks (who were almost all natives). Koreans and Asian Indians benefited most for longer periods of stay in the United States, followed by Chinese, Filipinos, and Hispanics. Vietnamese figures may be distorted because almost all Vietnamese entered the United States between 1975 and 1980. In general, natives did slightly less well than longtime resident immigrants. Native Filipinos and Asian Indians did very poorly, probably because they were either very young, or very old agricultural workers. The one exception was Chinese, where natives seemed to be better off than immigrants.

[5]This variable was constructed by adding immigrant/native as the last category of period of immigration.

156

TABLE 5.9

Determinants of Household Income, Adjusted Gains and Losses in Dollars, Aged 25–64: 1979

Type	Ethnicity								
	Japanese	Chinese	Filipino	Korean	Asian Indian	Vietnamese	White	Black	Hispanic
EFFECTS HOUSEHOLD TYPE									
Married couple family	3,784	2,195	1,706	2,628	1,932	965	2,432	2,122	1,418
Family householder male, no wife	381	-2,499	-2,316	181	-4,618	-890	-1,914	615	611
Family householder female, no husband	-6,010	-6,450	-5,371	-8,476	-8,268	-8,243	-6,589	-3,321	-4,915
Non-family householder	-7,475	-5,741	-4,238	-9,372	-5,889	-1,115	-5,192	-785	-1,958
Beta coefficient	0.31	0.21	0.17	0.29	0.20	0.11	0.24	0.19	0.19
NUMBER OF HOUSEHOLD WORKERS									
1	-4,656	-4,915	-7,869	-3,377	-3,698	-6,698	-3,400	-5,328	-4,816
2	-522	1,090	539	616	2,071	733	122	3,127	1,920
3	7,779	5,945	6,272	6,881	6,926	7,095	9,700	9,385	7,318
4 or more	16,339	11,520	15,771	10,345	11,422	17,878	14,991	15,837	12,087
Beta coefficient	0.34	0.30	0.42	0.23	0.23	0.57	0.32	0.49	0.41
PERIOD OF IMMIGRATION/ NATIVITY									
1975–1980	489	-8,166	-5,382	-6,587	-6,522	-510	-3,982	-6,384	-5,941
1965–1974	-1,308	-499	3,308	3,302	2,480	4,357	-4,799	258	-1,539
Before 1964	-1,843	2,312	268	9,766	9,927	4,667	-929	3,612	1,545
Native	289	3,890	-2,651	4,017	-4,550	4,164	106	-9	670
Beta coefficient	0.04	0.25	0.19	0.34	0.31	0.12	0.04 *	0.04 *	0.15
GRAND MEAN	$27,366	$24,777	$26,219	$22,980	$26,703	$18,043	$23,486	$16,933	$17,945
R2	0.291	0.230	0.301	0.290	0.237	0.348	0.195	0.328	0.243
Total number	10,284	10,667	8,226	3,572	5,462	2,390	2,680	2,127	2,184

SOURCE: 5% PUMs "A" Tape.

* Insignificant at 0.05 level.

This model is incomplete at this point, because we have not been able to discuss the effects of other variables, such as education or occupational prestige of the household head. We shall return to it in Chapter 8.

Housing

Kwitko (1986) analyzed a number of aspects of Asian American housing. Table 5.10 shows tenure of Asian Americans, compared with blacks, whites, and Hispanics. Whites had the highest rates of owner-occupancy (69.6 percent), followed by Japanese (58.7 percent), Filipinos (56.6 percent), Asian Indians (51.9 percent), Koreans and blacks (45.9 percent), Hispanics (43.1 percent), and finally, Vietnamese (27.2 percent). The very low figures for Vietnamese no doubt reflected the fact that almost all were recent arrivals. These figures showed Asian Americans lagging far behind whites for reasons not altogether clear. However, groups with large numbers of recent immigrants such as Koreans have difficulty establishing down payments and credit ratings for home mortgages during their first 5 years or so of residency in the United States. It is rather difficult to explain why Japanese should lag behind whites on this measure, since they are nearly all natives and have higher household incomes than whites. This may be due to the fact that Japanese reside in areas of high living costs, such as Hawaii, California, and New York.

Table 5.11 shows mortgage payment as a ratio of the 1979 annual household income for each ethnicity.[6] In general, the ratios were highest for Vietnamese (.28), Koreans (.27), Asian Indians (.24), and Chinese (.23). The ratio was lowest for Japanese (.16). This is no doubt due to the fact that Japanese were mostly natives, and probably purchased their homes with lower mortgage payments much before the new immigrants.

Table 5.12 shows the number of persons per room in Asian American households, compared to whites, blacks, and Hispanics. The least dense households were among whites and Japanese. Overcrowding did not appear to be a problem except with Vietnamese. Filipinos and Koreans had fairly dense housing, probably because of larger numbers of children. Still, Asian Americans lived in more crowded conditions than blacks, but this appears not to have been a serious problem except for the Vietnamese. Figure 5.5 shows the median value of homes for Asian Americans in 1980, compared to the total United States average. The

---

[6]These ratios were computed for each household and not as aggregates for each ethnicity.

158

TABLE 5.10
Tenure of Asian American Households

Tenure	Ethnicity							
	Japanese	Chinese	Filipino	Korean	Asian Indian (Percentage)	Vietnamese	White	Black	Hispanic
Number	11,937	12,423	10,164	4,021	6,690	2,534	2,680	2,127	2,189
Owner-occupier	58.7	54.9	56.6	45.9	51.9	27.2	69.6	45.9	43.1
Renter: cash	39.1	43.6	41.5	53.1	46.8	71.5	69.6	45.9	43.1
Renter: no cash	2.1	1.5	1.9	1.1	1.3	1.3	2.2	1.9	2.0

SOURCE: PUMs "A" 5% Tape; Table 7.

TABLE 5.11
Mortgage Payments as a Ratio of 1979 Annual Household Income for Asian Americans

Household Income $	Ethnicity (Monthly Mortgages $)					
	Japanese	Chinese	Filipino	Korean	Asian Indian	Vietnamese
$1–$4,999	301.50	387.03	353.70	384.75	318.72	218.00
	1.45 *	1.86	1.70	1.85	1.53	1.05
$5,000–$9,999	254.65	321.36	270.51	360.14	269.49	279.20
	0.41	0.51	0.43	0.48	0.43	0.45
$10,000–$19,999	283.18	370.63	355.42	428.90	367.15	344.27
	0.23	0.30	0.28	0.34	0.29	0.28
$20,000–$29,999	329.46	411.11	407.55	478.18	443.04	398.79
	0.16	0.20	0.20	0.23	0.21	0.15
$30,000–$39,999	362.15	470.55	485.81	556.68	510.03	442.01
	0.12	0.16	0.17	0.19	0.17	0.15
$60,000+	472.38	594.44	591.93	727.81	665.43	514.31
	0.09	0.11	0.11	0.13	0.12	0.09
Mean income $	25,718	23,315	24,960	22,313	24,122	16,225
Mean mortgage $	351.53	446.64	440.38	510.75	482.33	383.89
Ratio	0.16	0.23	0.21	0.27	0.24	0.28
Total number	11,937	12,423	10,164	4,021	6,690	2,534

SOURCE: 5% PUMs "A" Tape.

* Midpoints of income categories were used to calculate ratios of annual household income to mortgage.

TABLE 5.12
Density* in Asian American Households

Household	Ethnicity								
	Japanese	Chinese	Filipino	Korean	Asian Indian (Percentage)	Vietnamese	White	Black	Hispanic
Number of persons	2.67	3.14	3.74	3.47	2.97	4.43	2.7	3.1	3.5
Number of rooms	4.89	4.71	4.25	4.20	4.75	3.86	5.4	4.9	4.5
Persons/room	0.55	0.67	0.88	0.83	0.63	1.15	0.54	0.63	0.78
Total number	11,937	12,423	10,164	4,021	6,690	2,534	2,680	2,127	2,189

SOURCE: Kwitko, Table 12 (PUMs 5% Tape).

* Crowding is defined as more than one person per room (Department of Health, Education, and Welfare, 1974).

FIGURE 5.5

Median Value of Homes for Asian Americans: 1980

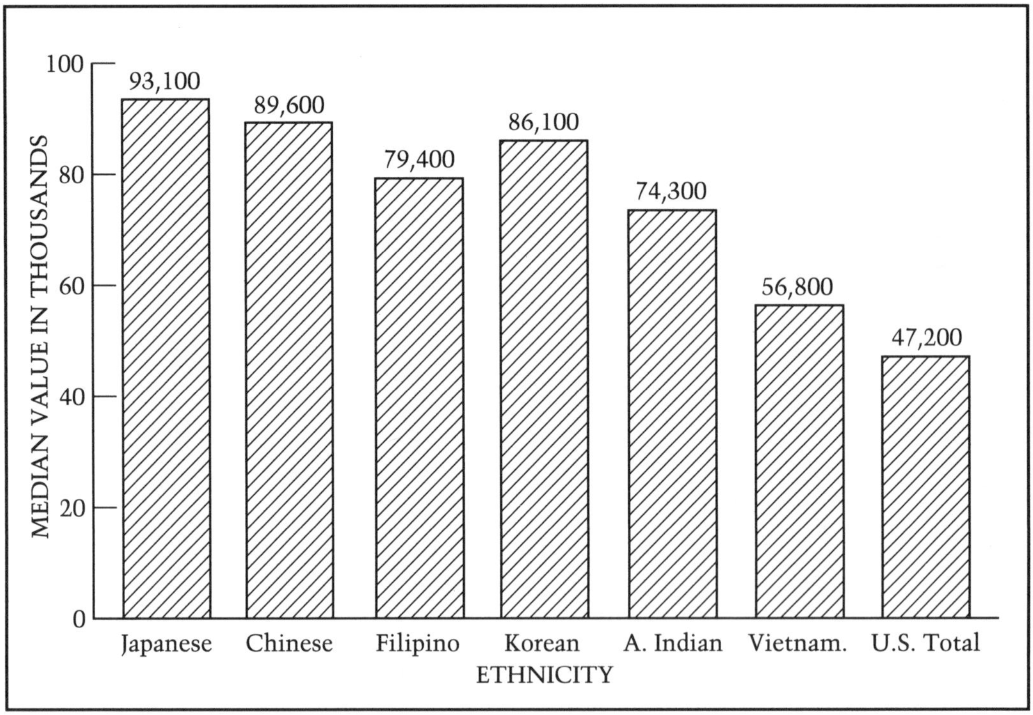

SOURCE: Johnson, Levin, and Paisano (1988).

figures showed Asian Americans to own homes valued high above the U.S. average of $47,200, but this must be qualified by the fact that many Asian Americans were immigrants and had purchased homes quite recently. Also, nearly all Asian Americans lived in cities with high housing costs. The most expensive homes were owned by Japanese; the least expensive, by Vietnamese.

Conclusions

In this chapter we have examined several U.S. Census statistics relating to the family and household. Given the importance of the family to Asian Americans, and its function in helping new immigrants to adapt to American society, we were especially concerned about these investigations. It is satisfying, therefore, to report that our data indicate a high degree of stability in most Asian American families and households.

On almost all measures concerning marriage and divorce, Asian Americans showed more signs of stability than whites, and certainly more than blacks. There is some variation, which deserves comment. First, Japanese seemed most like whites: we attribute this to the fact that nearly all Japanese are native-born Americans. Second, as migrants stay in the United States, they appeared to become more like whites in terms of these characteristics. Third, Vietnamese showed some signs of instability, but this may be the result of their refugee status stemming from the Vietnam War.

The same is true of family and household composition measures. Asian Americans had very high percentages of married-family households. Large percentages of their children under 18 lived at home with two parents. Perhaps more important, Asian Americans generally had fewer households led by female householders with no husband present. Data on household incomes suggest that Asian Americans had put the household to work, literally, to their advantage. Generally, their household incomes were higher than those of whites, and were much higher than those of blacks and Hispanics. Much of this is due to larger numbers of household workers, but is also in part due to the prevalence of married-family households. There seemed to be little regional variation in incomes, excepting the case of Chinese in New York and Filipinos in the West, where both experienced significant losses. Regional variations will again be examined in Chapter 8.

A brief examination of housing also indicates that Asian Americans appeared to have decent housing facilities, although there are significantly fewer owner-occupiers among Asian Americans than among whites. The cost of Asian American housing was higher than the nationwide average, probably because most Asian Americans live in cities, and most of them are recent immigrants, and so have purchased housing at higher prices.

Before we depart with a rosy picture, however, there are serious problems that need to be addressed. First, Vietnamese were an exception to almost everything we have indicated above (except for family stability). Their incomes were lower than those of blacks and Hispanics, and they ranked high on poverty indicators. No doubt much of this is the result of the Vietnam War, but they deserve special examination in the 1990 Census. Second, new immigrants to the United States (at least for the first 5 years) showed many signs of adjustment problems. These problems appear to be overcome after some time in America, but it should be understood that many Asian Americans have reached comfortable family and household status only after some very trying adjustment periods.

EDUCATIONAL ATTAINMENT

T HIS CHAPTER begins an examination of the achievements of Asian Americans in the areas of education, occupation and employ-ment, and earnings, and continues in Chapters 7 and 8. Each chapter can stand alone, but for full impact, they probably should be read together. The phenomenon we shall be exploring begins with edu-cation, which, for most Asian Americans, is quite extraordinary.

As we pointed out in Chapter 5, the Confucian ethic is often cited as an important determinant of the desire for education among Asian Americans. This may be seen as a result of history, because East-Asian societies made education a prerequisite, at least ideally, for high-status positions. It also works through the family, with obedience to elders and respect for status. However that may be, neither Filipinos nor Asian Indians can be said to be influenced by Confucianism, and they equal or surpass East Asians in educational attainment.

The achievements of Asian Americans in education have been well documented in both scholarly articles (Hirschman and Wong 1981, 1986; Mare and Winship 1988; Barringer, Takeuchi, and Xenos 1990) and in the popular press (Bell 1985; Lindsey 1982; McBee 1984; Doerner 1985; Time 1987). The widespread public interest in Asian American educa-tional levels stems mostly from comparisons with other minorities, par-ticularly blacks and Hispanics. This comparison is not necessarily wel-comed by Asian Americans themselves (Kim and Hurh 1983; Hsia 1987–

1988), partly because it obscures differences among Asian Americans, and also because it tends to pit the "model minority" stereotype against other disadvantaged minority groups.

Sociologists have long been interested in the effects of minority and immigrant status upon educational achievements. Several historical strands emerge: assimilation, human capital, status attainment, structural critiques, and a more recent return to cultural explanations.

Assimilation

The general role of education in the achievements of immigrant minorities was important for assimilation theorists (Gordon 1964, 1978; Park 1950). Assimilation theory generally assumed that education would help immigrants to become acculturated and subsequently attain other forms of assimilation, culminating in biological amalgamation. Examples of research dominated by this viewpoint are common (Hurh and Kim 1984; Kitano 1976; Kuo 1977; Montero 1981; Montero and Tsukashima 1977; Peterson 1971; Wang 1981; Yu 1977). Although each of these studies concentrated upon some variant of assimilation theory, most of them questioned some or all of the outcomes one would expect from assimilation theory. Hurh and Kim, for example, found Koreans to be relatively unassimilated and were led to the concept of "adhesive adaptation," which in many respects is similar to the concept "ethnic enclave." On the other hand, most of these studies showed strong relationships between education and socioeconomic status, especially in the case of Japanese Americans. Kitano and Daniels have retained an assimilation model in their recent work on Asian Americans (1988).

Human Capital

Human capital theory asserts a direct and unequivocal role of education in the advancement of minorities. It asserts that success in school and high levels of formal education increase the prospects for better paying, higher status, and more satisfying employment (Berg 1969; Parsons 1968). This approach appears to have dominated American educational policy toward minorities. Its advocates cite the high levels of both educational achievement and economic success among Jews and Asian Americans in support of the theory (Peterson 1971; Sklare 1971; Sung 1967; Nelson 1988). Portes and Stepick (1985) pointed out that many of the positive aspects of human capital are supported in ethnic enclaves, a position disputed by Nee and Sanders (1987), especially in the case of Chinese.

Status Attainment

The relationships between status origins (family backgrounds) and educational achievement are well known in the work of Blau and Duncan (1967), Featherstone and Hauser (1978), Sewell, Hauser, and Wolfe (1976), and others. Jenks (1972) minimized the importance of status origins, but Bowles and Gintes (1976) argued their importance. Hauser and Mossel (1985) attributed most of the effects of status origins upon common family factors such as parents' education, occupations, and the like. Miller, Kohn, and Schooler (1986) argued that the common factor is the learning of self-direction, which leads to better school performance and subsequent occupational choice. As we argued in Chapter 5, it is widely believed that Asian family stability has had a major influence on educational success. The precise effects of some of these factors on Asian Americans are shown by Mare and Winship (1988). They found that although Asian families show some (minor) disadvantageous characteristics compared to whites, Asian American children still excel in school, a finding for which they had no ready explanation.

Census data do not allow examination of parents' socioeconomic status, but status attainment is important for our purposes because of the attention paid to the interrelationships of education and occupation.

Structural Critiques

In part because of neo-Marxist influence in American sociology, and in part because of the failure of most existing theories to explain the continued poor performance of blacks, Native Americans, and Hispanics in education, many scholars began to question the role of education in the successful adaptation of immigrants. Lieberson (1980) and Steinberg (1981) supported structural arguments by showing that the social and economic entry of a generation into American society *preceded* the higher levels of formal education of their children. Bonacich and Cheng (1984) made a very similar argument for Asian minorities, demonstrating that their immigration to the United States was tied to exploitation in the economic periphery. The high levels of education of the children of early immigrants came after their parents' initial adjustments. Hirschman and Wong (1986) pointed to some structural factors which may have helped the early Asian immigrants. Among these were a favorable pre-selection of well-educated persons (certainly among Japanese and Koreans), residence in areas of easy access to education (California), changes in social-class composition of Asian Americans, and real payoffs on educations and occupations. This last point was important for Ogbu (1978), who pointed to the "castelike" situations of blacks and Hispanics, as opposed to the more upwardly mobile conditions of immigrants. Others who have questioned the positive effects of education on occupation and income include Bowles and Gintis (1976), Collins (1971), Mayes (1977), and Scimecca (1980).

The relatively low educational advancements of some American minorities contrast with the high levels of education and high visibility of Asian Americans as petite bourgeoisie and professionals. This has led to explanations popularized by the terms "model minorities" (Kitano 1976) and "middlemen" (Bonacich 1973), explanations roundly attacked by Suzuki (1977) and E. Wong (1985). In general, these theories assert that Asian Americans have benefited from selective immigration, relatively favorable entry conditions, and favorable niches in the host economy. There is no question that most Asian Americans are well-educated (Hirschman and Wong 1984, among others) and that they tend not to experience severe extreme residential segregation (Langberg and Farley 1985; Massey and Denton 1987). Some enclaves do exist, however. We pointed to New York in Chapter 5, and Nee and Sanders (1987) demonstrate negative aspects of San Francisco's Chinatown. Whatever one makes of "model minorities," there is abundant evidence that the high levels of education of Asian Americans are not always translated into other measures of success, as we shall see in Chapters 7 and 8.

Cultural Explanations

Recently, the academic pendulum is swinging away from structural theories, and scholars once again are looking for explanations of differential education in cultural or social-psychological factors. Trueba (1988) attacked Ogbu's structural position, maintaining that language, culture, and cognition must be taken into account at the level of the ethnic groups as a whole, and also at the individual level. Trueba appeared especially concerned about English-language abilities of immigrant minorities. However, a recent study of Southeast Asian immigrants in San Diego found no significant effects of language or adjustment problems upon school performance (Rumbaut and Ima 1987). We noted earlier that Miller, Kohn, and Schooler (1986) attributed family effects upon education to the learning of self-direction. Finally, Bidwell and Friedkin (1988) proposed a theory that opts for cultural explanations of decisions students make during their whole academic careers which affect outcomes: "students' criteria for decisions and willingness to follow through." Some of these ideas may help to explain the apparent ability of Asian Americans to overcome structural blockages that have been so detrimental to other minorities. Unfortunately, the census data offer precious little in support of cultural theories, although we shall examine some aspects of language.

Some Institutional Blockages

Hsia (1988), Wilson and Justiz (1988), Tsuang (1989), and Divoky (1988) have all described some negative aspects of the Asian American educational experience. *Time* (1987) quoted a Cambodian student who earlier had attempted suicide: "I go to bed at 1 or 2 and get up early to study. You study so hard and still you don't have time to complete all the work. For me, whatever I do, I want to be perfect." Such devotion appears to pay off.

A report from the California Post Secondary Education Commission (1988) found that Asian high school students are twice as likely as white students and six times as likely as blacks and Hispanics to meet the entrance requirements for the state's public universities. The study also found that 33 percent of Asian high-school graduates, 16 percent of whites, 5 percent of Hispanics, and about 5 percent of blacks qualified for the freshman classes in 1986 at the state's eight major university campuses.

These and other similar statistics may have prompted some universities to establish limits on Asian (including Asian American) enrollments. Bunzel and Au (1987) investigated a sudden decrease in Asian American admission rates at some major universities and found that although Asian Americans are overrepresented at the most prestigious schools (8 percent of the freshman classes as compared to 2.1 percent in the total population), their admission rates were lower than for white applicants. Apparently no overt biases have been uncovered in investigations of universities, but some observers believe that Asian American applicants must show higher credentials for admissions than are required of whites. It is also widely believed that Asian Americans are discriminated against because they do not qualify for affirmative action.

Most universities have attributed these discrepancies to simple institutional racism,[1] but it is quite clear that many Asian Americans do not believe that, or find it irrelevant. Furthermore, Asian Americans are wary of policies such as that in the State of California which changed educational emphasis away from sciences to the English language. Whatever the effects of such discrimination, Asian Americans made up almost 14 percent of Harvard's freshman class, 20 percent at the Massachusetts Institute of Technology, and 25 percent at the University of California at Berkeley in 1987 (Bunzel and Au 1987).

A recent report from the University of California at Berkeley (Almaguer et al. 1990) showed that the percentage of white undergraduate registrants dropped from 66.1 percent in 1980 to 44.9 percent in 1989. During that same period, the percentage of Asians increased from 20.7 percent to 27.3 percent. These figures were compared with the projected population for California in 1990: whites, 58.1 percent; Asians, 9.7 percent. Whatever charges were brought against Berkeley for discriminating against Asians, the report pointed out that in the fall of 1989, only 3,500 slots were open to the freshman class. There were 21,300 applicants, 5,800 of whom had straight "A" averages in high school. The *median* high-school grade point average for Asian applicants from 1985 to 1988 was 4.0., as compared to a range of 3.85 to 4.0 during the same years for whites. Other minorities ranged from 3.4 to 3.5. Given the need for minority representation, these data obviously posed a dilemma for the administration at Berkeley.

There appears to be no direct evidence for blatant discrimination against Asian students at most of the large universities,[2] but it is clear that Asians are at some disadvantage because of institutional racism: that is, many Asian Americans feel that they should gain admission solely on the basis of their higher credentials, but university admissions are geared to ethnic and minority representation. Obviously, given their startling academic credentials, Asian Americans will be discriminated against if some sort of ethnic and/or racial equity is the goal of a university.

---

[1]"Institutional racism" refers to institutional practices—for example, giving preference to children of alumni in admission procedures—which militate against minorities, with or without intent.

[2]Some of the public statements of college administrators do indicate some hostility and/or prejudice, without question. However, these statements have not been shown necessarily to reflect school admission policies. The real problem lies with informal procedures of departments or colleges, which we know very well can depart from administration policies.

Educational Achievements

Census data from 1980 show educational levels of Asian Americans which generally fit the popular image. Figure 6.1 shows high-school and college completion rates by ethnicity.[3] High-school completions varied much less than college completions. Asian Americans, except Vietnamese, exceeded or equaled whites, and all exceeded blacks and Hispanics in terms of high-school completion. For college completion the Asian American groups all exceeded whites, blacks, and Hispanics, excepting, again, Vietnamese.

Table 6.1 shows school completion rates in more detail, comparing educational levels of Asian Americans with those of whites, blacks, and Hispanics. Vietnamese educational levels throughout this study were quite low, but it is noteworthy that a recent study of Southeast Asians in San Diego found that Vietnamese high-school juniors and seniors earned higher grades than whites. Vietnamese also made up 23 percent of the valedictorians and salutatorians in the class of 1986. Given language and cultural handicaps, it is surprising that Hmongs ranked third in grades, better than whites, Hispanics, Filipinos, and blacks (Rumbaut and Ima 1987). It is ironic that these authors attributed the relatively low showing of some other Asian American groups to assimilation.

Asian Indians in the United States are particularly well educated, with 58 percent of those over 25 having graduated from college. A surprising 20 percent completed 20 or more years of education. The high figures for groups with large percentages of immigrants (Chinese, Koreans, Filipinos, and Asian Indians) are in part due to selective immigration (Barringer and Cho 1990, Fig. 6.1). Chinese, Koreans, and Filipinos also show large percentages of persons with little or no education, reflecting lower educational requirements in their home countries.

Table 6.2 shows differences in educational levels by gender. Males received better educations than females in most Asian American groups. However, the reverse was true of Filipinos, reflecting the relative power of females in Philippine society.[4] The gender differences appeared greatest among Koreans, with 54 percent of males and only 22.7 percent of females completing 4 years or more of college. Differences were also

---

[3]Strictly speaking, the census data give us years completed, not actual completion of degrees. We assume here that nearly all persons with four years completed will have graduated.

[4]Filipino figures here may be somewhat misleading, because high school requires only three years to complete in the Philippines, compared to four years in most societies. Therefore, some Filipinos in the 1–3 year college category may actually have completed college.

FIGURE 6.1

Percentage High-School and College Completion, Aged 25–64: 1980

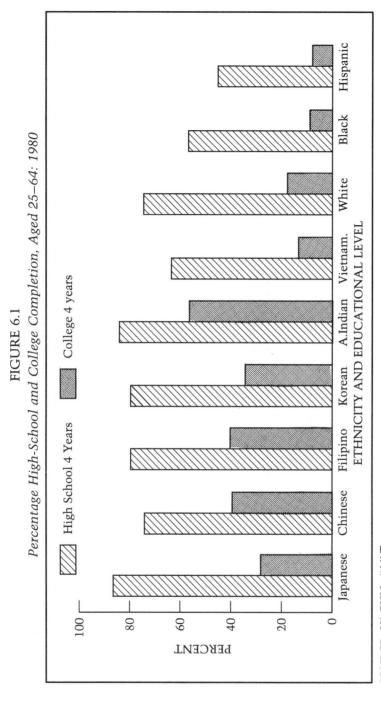

SOURCE: 5% PUMs "A" Tape.

TABLE 6.1
Years of Education, by Ethnicity, Aged 25–64: 1980

Years of Education	Ethnicity								
	Japanese	Chinese	Filipino	Korean	Asian Indian (Percentage)	Vietnamese	White	Black	Hispanic
NUMBER	21,129	21,725	19,689	8,833	10,477	4,916	4,887	4,151	4,186
Total	99.9	99.9	100.0	100.0	100.1	100.0	99.9	100.0	101.0
None (no formal education)	0.5	4.7	0.8	2.2	1.4	4.7	0.5	0.9	3.7
1–6 (primary school)	1.2	8.4	6.9	5.4	3.1	11.6	3.5	8.9	21.9
7–11 (some middle school and some high school)	10.8	11.4	11.7	12.0	10.5	19.5	20.7	32.7	28.2
12 (high-school degree)	37.0	19.6	19.1	29.1	13.4	29.7	39.9	33.2	25.1
13–15 (some college)	21.7	15.7	20.6	16.3	14.0	21.5	17.3	15.5	13.2
16 (college degree)	15.6	15.8	21.7	21.2	14.1	6.1	9.4	4.9	3.5
17–19 (some graduate school or more)	10.5	17.2	14.1	9.4	23.1	4.9	6.5	3.4	3.2
20 or more (doctorate or equivalent)	2.6	7.1	5.1	4.4	20.5	2.0	2.1	0.5	1.2

SOURCE: PUMs "A" 5% Tape.

NOTE: Since the numbers come from a 5 percent sample, the actual figures will be about 20 times larger.

great for Asian Indians, but still 41.7 percent of Asian Indian women completed 4 years of college or more. White women had a much higher percentage of high-school graduates than any of the Asian Americans, but many fewer college graduates than any group except Vietnamese. These gender differences, however, were much less than for incomes, as we shall see in Chapter 8. Figures 6.2 and 6.3 show high-school and college completion for both sexes in 1960, 1970, and 1980. Note the difference in college completion as compared to high-school completion. As Table 6.3 indicates, since 1960, Japanese, Chinese, and Filipinos have all improved their levels of education considerably. So have whites, blacks, and Hispanics. Asian Americans maintained a substantial lead over other groups in both decades.[5] Asian Americans were much better represented among the college-educated than other groups in 1960 and 1970, and were gaining as of 1980. The ratios of male and female levels of education appeared about the same in 1960, 1970, and 1980, which is to say, extremely unfavorable for both Japanese and white women. However, the relative educational levels of Filipino females to males showed some tendency to equalize in 1980. The better educations for Filipino females take on a special significance in Chapter 8, where it will be seen that even with much better educations, Filipino women earn much less than Filipino men.

Table 6.4 shows educational levels of Asian Americans, blacks, and whites in 1989, based upon the Current Population Survey. Unfortunately, the Asian American sample was too small to break down into individual ethnicities, so Asian Americans and Pacific Islanders were lumped together. Nevertheless, the data showed the significant differences between Asian American educational levels and those of whites and blacks. It is difficult to tell from the figures whether Asian Americans have gained or lost since 1980, but with a college completion rate of 44.1 percent for men and 33.3 percent for women, it seems unlikely that there has been much overall change. This alleviates some concerns that the overall levels of education were decreasing for recent cohorts of immigrants (Barringer, Takeuchi, and Xenos 1990). There has been some reason to believe that educational levels of newer immigrants, especially those who had migrated between 1975 and 1980, were lower than those of their predecessors, because a higher percentage of the later migrants were entering the United States for family completion (See Chapter 2).

[5]In comparisons over time, we are limited to an examination of Japanese, Chinese, and Filipinos. Other Asian American groups were too small for detailed analysis prior to 1980.

TABLE 6.2

Gender and Education, Asian Americans, Blacks, Whites, and Hispanics: 1980,
Aged 25–64

Level of Education	Ethnicity (Percentage)							
	Japanese		Chinese		Filipino		Korean	
	M	F	M	F	M	F	M	F
NUMBER	9,104	12,025	10,796	10,929	8,534	11,115	3,484	5,347
Total	100.1	100.2	99.9	100.1	99.9	100.0	100.0	100.0
Less than high school	4.2	6.4	13.9	20.3	8.6	13.2	3.8	16.7
High school 1–3 years	6.0	8.1	7.1	7.7	8.5	7.9	4.6	10.1
High school 4 years	30.6	41.8	16.8	22.4	20.9	17.6	20.4	34.7
College 1–3 years	21.0	22.3	14.7	16.7	24.5	17.6	17.2	15.8
College 4 years or more	38.3	21.6	47.4	33.0	37.4	43.7	54.0	22.7

SOURCE: PUMs "A" 5% Tape.

Figure 6.4 shows the expected curvilinear relationship of education
with age. Some truncation appeared at the lower age ranges, because we
had limited samples to ages 25–64.[6] Except for Chinese, the modal age
category for 16 or more years of education was 35–39. However, Japanese and Chinese both showed large percentages across the 25-to-39 age
range. In all ethnic groups, a noticeable decline in percentage of college
graduates began at age 55, and earlier for Japanese and Chinese. The
high percentage of college graduates in the 25–29 year age group among
Japanese, Chinese, and Asian Indians is remarkable. Filipinos and Koreans have significantly fewer college graduates in that age bracket, which
may have something to do with the characteristics of incoming cohorts
of immigrants.

---

[6]We have used this age limitation because we will be analyzing the effects of education on occupations and incomes, best done if our samples can be presumed to have completed their educations. See Blau and Duncan for precedent.

	Ethnicity (Percentage)								
₁sian Indian		Vietnamese		White		Black		Hispanic	
M	F	M	F	M	F	M	F	M	F
₅41	4,836	2,375	2,541	2,384	2,503	1,840	2,311	2,007	1,099
₁0.0	100.0	100.0	100.0	100.0	100.0	100.1	99.9	100.0	100.0
4.5	11.5	15.2	30.3	11.2	10.0	22.5	17.9	36.2	37.0
4.4	10.6	10.9	14.5	13.6	14.6	20.2	24.5	16.7	17.8
8.5	19.1	28.6	30.7	35.0	44.5	31.1	34.8	22.7	27.3
1.3	17.1	27.7	15.7	17.9	16.8	17.4	14.0	13.9	12.5
1.3	41.7	17.6	8.8	22.3	14.1	8.9	8.7	10.5	5.4

Educational Levels by Period of Immigration/Nativity

Table 6.5 shows college completion rates for various ethnic groups by period of immigration and nativity.[7] The overall pattern for Chinese, Filipinos, Koreans, and Asian Indians did show some decline in the percentage of college graduates in the 1975–1980 cohort. For example, in 1980, 54.8 percent of Filipino immigrants in the 1970–1974 group had completed college, as compared to only 45.4 percent in the 1975–1980 group. Japanese, on the other hand, showed a large increase (22.5 percent) for the same period. As we have pointed out elsewhere, many of the Japanese entering the United States from 1975 to 1980 are managers and other employees of Japanese firms, and are not, strictly speaking, immigrants. There is no way we can distinguish them from true immigrants from Japan. Otherwise, the highest percentages of college graduates appear among older immigrants, especially those who entered between 1960 and 1970. This reflects the larger percentages of persons

[7]Percentages of Japanese, blacks, and whites in the immigrant categories are based upon very small numbers, so should be interpreted with some caution.

FIGURE 6.2

Percentage High-School Graduates: 1960, 1970, and 1980, Aged 25 +

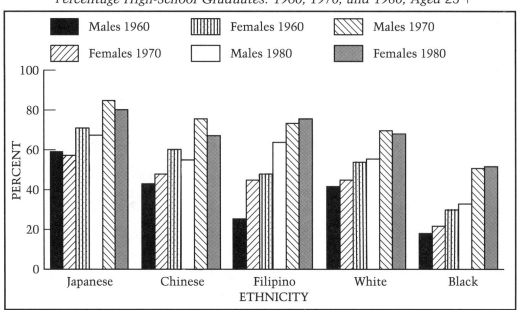

SOURCES: PC80-1-D1-A; PC80-2-1E.

entering for employment, rather than for family completion, immediately after the immigration reforms of 1965.

Both Japanese and Chinese native Americans showed college completion percentages about equal to the total percentages. But among Filipinos, Koreans, and Asian Indians, native-born Americans were not nearly so well-educated as immigrants. This reflected both the fairly recent agrarian backgrounds and the age structures of those groups. The overall pattern for Asian groups with large proportions of immigrants showed a much higher percentage of college graduates among immigrants than for natives. However, in the aggregate, the Asian American natives were still better educated than whites, blacks, and Hispanics.

High-school completions (not shown) demonstrated about the same patterns as college completions. Among Chinese, Filipinos, Koreans, and Asian Indians, there was a significant decrease in the percentage of high-school graduates in the 1975–1980 cohort of immigrants compared to the 1970–1974 and 1965–1969 cohorts. Chinese had fewer high-school graduates than other Asian American groups (again, excepting Vietnamese), and were about equal to whites in this respect, but remember that their college completion percentages are much higher than those of whites. Without knowing something about the origins of Chinese immigrants,

FIGURE 6.3

Percentage College Completion or More: 1960, 1970, and 1980, Aged 25 +

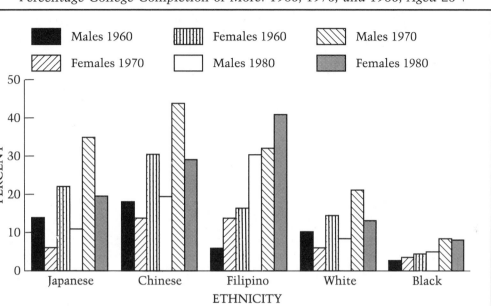

SOURCES: PC80-1-D1-A; PC80-1-2E.

it is impossible to speculate about the reasons for the relatively poor showing on high-school completion. The percentage of high-school graduates is dramatically high for all Asian American groups compared to blacks or Hispanics. Japanese, Filipinos, Koreans, and Asian Indians all make a better showing than whites with respect to high-school completion.

School Enrollment

The above figures for immigrants are for persons aged 25–64, and tell us nothing about the school performance of young people. Figure 6.5 shows school enrollment of a restricted age range (16–24) in graphic form. Note that a high percentage of Japanese, Chinese, Koreans, and Asian Indians were in pre-school (aged 3–4). Fewer Filipinos and Vietnamese of that age appeared to be in school, with approximately the same percentage as whites (32.0 percent). By age 7, nearly all children in each of the ethnic groups were in school. However, for whites and blacks, the percentage in school began to decline markedly at ages 16–17, pre-

TABLE 6.3

Educational Levels of Selected Ethnic Groups: 1960, 1970, and 1980, Aged 25 Years and Over

Years of Education Completed	Ethnicity					
	Japanese	Chinese	Filipino	White	Black	Hispanic
1960						
			Males			
Total	100.1	100.0	100.0	100.0	100.0	*
0–8	26.9	46.6	62.3	39.5	64.5	*
9–11	14.3	10.9	12.7	18.9	17.3	*
12	34.6	15.5	12.7	22.2	11.3	*
13–15	10.4	8.8	6.3	9.1	4.1	*
16+	13.9	18.2	6.0	10.3	2.8	*
			Females			
Total	100.0	100.1	100.0	100.0	99.9	*
0–8	29.6	42.4	39.0	35.7	57.7	*
9–11	13.6	10.1	16.9	19.6	20.5	*
12	41.4	24.3	20.0	29.2	14.3	*
13–15	9.1	9.4	10.4	9.5	4.1	*
16+	6.3	13.9	13.7	6.0	3.3	*
1970						
			Males			
Total	100.1	99.9	100.0	100.0	100.1	100.0
0–8	17.9	29.0	38.0	27.8	47.0	44.6
9–11	11.2	10.7	13.9	18.2	22.9	17.5
12	34.8	18.8	19.5	28.5	20.0	20.9
13–15	13.9	10.6	12.0	11.1	6.0	9.2
16+	22.3	30.8	16.6	14.4	4.2	7.8
			Females			
Total	99.9	100.0	100.0	100.0	100.1	100.0
0–8	19.8	36.5	23.6	25.6	41.1	47.9
9–11	13.0	8.7	12.7	19.4	26.4	18.0
12	42.7	23.8	20.4	35.5	22.2	23.1
13–15	13.3	11.4	12.8	11.1	5.8	6.7
16+	11.1	19.6	30.5	8.4	4.6	4.3
1980						
			Males			
Total	100.1	100.0	100.0	100.0	100.0	100.0
0–8	8.6	17.4	18.0	16.9	28.8	39.1
9–11	7.2	7.4	8.9	13.6	20.5	15.5
12	30.0	17.2	19.4	31.8	28.3	22.6
13–15	19.1	14.2	21.5	16.4	14.0	13.4
16+	35.2	43.8	32.2	21.3	8.4	9.4
			Females			
Total	100.1	99.9	99.9	99.9	100.0	100.0
0–8	11.7	35.2	16.9	16.4	25.6	41.3
9–11	8.8	7.4	8.0	15.5	22.9	16.1
12	40.1	22.0	17.0	39.1	30.0	26.0
13–15	19.8	15.8	16.8	15.6	13.2	10.6
16+	19.7	19.5	41.2	13.3	8.3	6.0

SOURCES: PC(1)-1C, Table 76; PC(2)-1C Table 19, 21, 22, 23, PC(2)-5C, PC80-1-2E.

* Data not readily available.

TABLE 6.4

Education Update: Current Population Survey: March 1989
Educational Level, by Sex and Ethnicity, Aged 25 or More

| | Ethnicity and Sex (Percentage) | | | | | |
| | Asian and Pacific Islanders | | Whites | | Blacks | |
Level of Education	Male	Female	Male	Female	Male	Female
Total	100.0	100.0	100.1	100.1	100.1	100.0
None	3.3	5.2	0.6	0.6	1.4	0.9
1–4 years	1.5	2.3	1.6	1.4	4.4	3.2
5–7 years	3.7	4.9	4.1	3.8	8.2	7.1
8 years	2.5	4.0	5.1	5.4	4.6	5.9
1–3 years	4.8	5.0	10.9	11.2	17.7	19.5
High school, 1–3 years	21.8	28.9	35.9	42.8	37.2	37.5
High school, 4 years	18.3	16.4	16.9	17.6	15.5	14.5
College, 4 years or more	44.1	33.3	25.0	17.3	11.1	11.4

SOURCE: Special Tabulations from the March 1989 CPS.

sumably before high-school graduation. By ages 18–19, only 52.8 percent of whites and 51.7 percent of blacks were enrolled, probably reflecting high-school graduation. For the same age periods, Asian Americans varied from Chinese, with 82.1 percent enrolled, to 67 percent of Vietnamese. By ages 22 to 24, a high percentage of Chinese (53.0), Japanese (38.9), Koreans (30.5), Asian Indians (39.2), and Vietnamese (38.1) were still enrolled in school as compared to 17.4 percent whites and 15.9 percent blacks. Among Asian Americans, only Filipinos showed a diminishing percentage of enrollments after age 22. The decline in enrollments for Filipinos actually began at ages 18–19, suggesting that fewer young Filipinos would be finishing college. Note the relatively high percentage of Vietnamese (13.1 percent) enrolled in school at ages 35 and above.

The comparatively high enrollments for Asian Americans in school in 1980 help to account for the high educational levels of Asian Americans in 1989 (Table 6.3). Many of the younger persons shown in Figure 6.3 will appear in the 25–64 age group in the 1990 Census, where we will again be able to break down educational levels by Asian ethnicity. Certainly, compared to whites and blacks, Asian Americans have maintained very high levels of school enrollments.[8] It is striking that al-

[8]Hispanics show a pattern very similar to whites and blacks, but with even lower enrollment rates (Bean and Tienda 1987, 248–256).

FIGURE 6.4

Percentage Completing 16 or More Years of Education, by Age: 1980

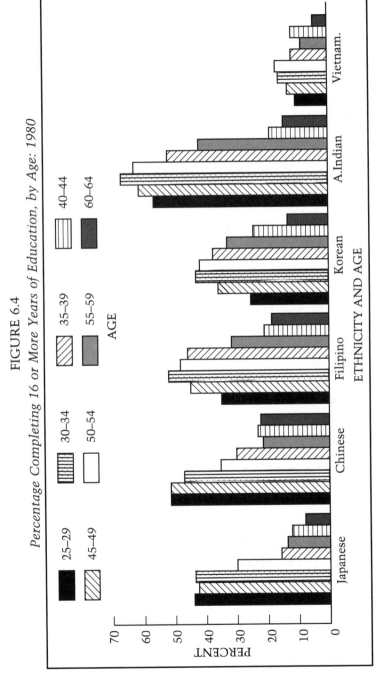

SOURCE: 5% PUMs "A" Tape.

TABLE 6.5

College* Completion, by Period of Immigration/Nativity, Aged 25–64: 1980

Period of Immigration	Ethnicity and School Completed									
	Japanese	Chinese	Filipino	Korean	Asian Indian	Vietnamese	Whites	Blacks	Hispanics
1975–1980	49.1	33.9	45.5	29.5	52.4	11.4	17.2	3.6	5.9
1970–1974	26.6	41.2	54.8	34.7	64.5	16.2	7.7	15.8	7.5
1965–1969	23.1	45.1	51.9	50.6	73.7	44.1	19.4	7.9	8.4
1960–1964	14.5	43.6	35.6	44.5	77.0	44.8	11.4	16.7	18.0
1950–1959	14.0	41.9	27.1	56.8	72.5	66.7	12.2	15.4	9.8
Before 1950	18.7	26.7	10.0	45.2	36.8	40.0	8.2	—	5.2
Natives	29.3	44.5	24.3	27.9	19.0	20.7	18.4	8.8	7.1
Total	28.8	40.2	41.0	35.0	57.6	13.0	18.1	8.8	7.9

SOURCE: PUMs "A" 5% Tape.

* 4 or more years.

— Too few cases for tabulation.

FIGURE 6.5

Percentage of Persons Enrolled in School, by Age and Ethnicity: 1980

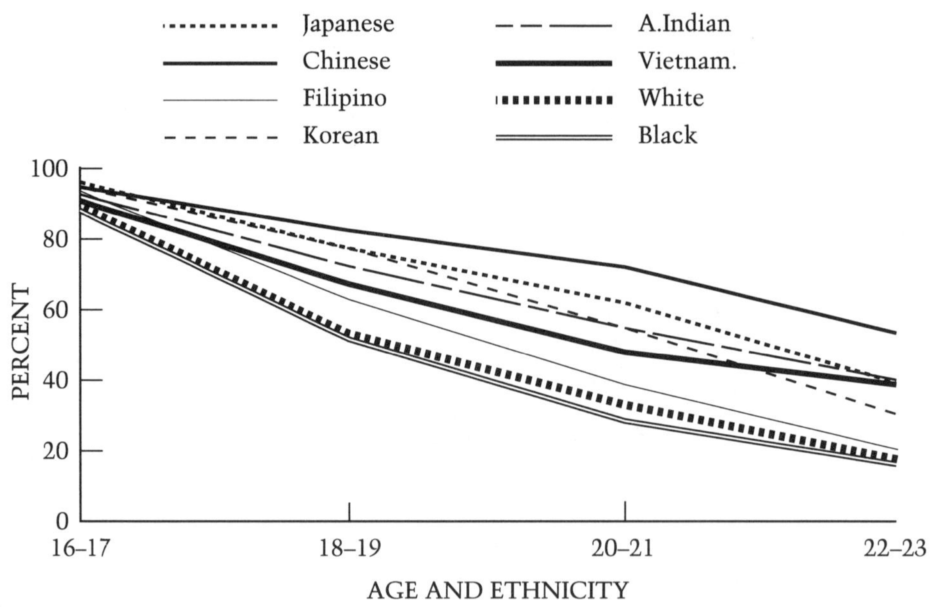

SOURCES: PC80-1-2E and PUMs "A" 5% Tape.

though Chinese have the highest percentages of poorly educated adults over 25, their school enrollment percentages in the critical ages of 16 to 24 are the highest of all groups. This suggests that at least some immigrants and their children are obtaining good educations, placing them in the "immigrant" rather than "castelike" category of John Ogbu's model.

English Ability and Language Spoken at Home

Most of the literature on immigrant adjustment points to language difficulties as one of the most important problems facing newcomers to the United States. We would expect language ability to be tied closely to education for two reasons: one, English is normally learned in Asian schools, especially in high school and college; second, inability to command English may affect one's ability to study in the United States.[9] So,

[9]However, Rumbaut and Ima, in their study of Southeast Asians in San Diego, found

TABLE 6.6
School Enrollment for Asian Americans, Whites, Blacks, and Hispanics, by Age: 1980

				Ethnicity				
Age	Japanese	Chinese	Filipino	Korean	Asian Indian	Vietnamese	White	Black
				(Percentage Enrolled in School)				
3–4	58.0	41.2	27.6	42.1	51.4	29.1	32.0	38.8
5–6	94.6	85.6	89.1	88.4	92.3	83.4	86.1	87.3
7–13	99.2	97.5	98.8	98.3	98.3	96.7	99.0	97.9
14–15	98.7	97.4	98.6	98.6	97.6	96.4	98.1	96.9
16–17	96.2	95.2	92.8	94.9	92.2	90.4	89.0	87.9
18–19	77.0	82.1	62.7	77.7	72.0	76.0	52.8	51.7
20–21	61.6	71.7	38.3	54.8	54.3	47.6	33.3	28.4
22–24	38.9	53.0	20.2	30.5	39.2	38.1	17.4	15.9
25–34	14.6	23.1	9.6	13.2	14.8	22.5	8.5	9.6
35 or older	2.8	3.9	5.2	5.3	5.2	13.1	2.0	2.6

SOURCES: PC80-1-2E and PUMs "A" 5% Tape.

TABLE 6.7

Years of Education Completed, by Ethnicity and Ability to Speak English, Aged 25–64: 1980

Education Completed	Japanese		Chinese		Filipino	
	Not well or not at all	Well or only English	Not well or not at all	Well or only English	Not well or not at all	Well or only English
NUMBER	1,712	19,417	5,344	16,381	886	18,803
Total	99.9	100.1	99.9	100.0	100.0	100.0
Less than high school	9.5	5.7	53.6	5.8	68.2	8.1
High school 1–3 years	11.9	6.8	9.4	4.8	6.8	8.8
High school 4 years	36.9	38.4	22.8	19.5	10.2	19.1
College 1–3 years	19.0	21.0	6.1	19.4	9.1	21.4
College 4 or more	22.6	28.2	8.0	50.5	5.7	42.6

SOURCE: 5% PUMs "A" Tape.

English ability can be seen both as a determinant of educational level, and as a result of education, particularly in the home country. Table 6.6 shows the relationship for most ethnicities quite clearly. For example, among Chinese who speak English not well or not at all, 53.6 percent completed less than high school, as compared to 5.8 percent who speak English well or who speak only English. On the other hand, only 8.0 percent of those who speak English poorly completed college, as compared with 50.5 percent who speak it well or exclusively. This relationship is especially strong for Chinese, Filipinos, Asian Indians, and Vietnamese, but not so clear for Koreans. Why this should be so for Koreans is a mystery. There seems to be almost no relationship between these two variables among Japanese, probably because most Japanese were born in the United States.[10]

that, among school children, ability to speak English was not an important factor in educational success. Young immigrants learn English faster than adults, so the negative effects of poor English would be felt more strongly with age. Certainly, in our experience, Asian undergraduate and graduate students from abroad are hampered by poor English during their first year or so in school, but most overcome language problems sufficiently to do excellent research work after one year.

[10]We would like to caution the reader at this point that these data may not be terri-

Korean		Asian Indian		Vietnamese		Hispanic	
Not well or not at all	Well or only English	Not well or not at all	Well or only English	Not well or not at all	Well or only English	Not well or not at all	Well or only English
2,606	6,229	650	9,827	1,996	2,820	1,105	3,001
100.0	100.0	100.0	100.0	101.1	100.0	100.1	100.1
17.5	8.3	43.2	5.4	40.6	10.7	71.2	24.2
12.3	7.1	23.5	6.7	18.4	8.7	11.8	18.3
38.7	24.5	10.6	12.6	25.7	33.3	12.0	29.9
11.9	18.4	10.6	15.8	11.0	28.9	2.7	17.0
19.6	41.7	12.1	59.5	4.4	18.4	2.4	10.7

We should also expect ability to speak English to improve the longer immigrants stay in the United States. Table 6.7 shows English ability by period of immigration and nativity. The data show that for all groups, the percentage of those persons who speak English poorly or not at all decreased with time spent in the United States. For example, 49.5 percent of Koreans who entered the United States between 1975 and 1980 spoke English poorly or not at all, compared with 2.5 percent who immigrated between 1950 and 1959. Conversely, 47.5 percent of the 1975–1980 cohort reported speaking English well, as compared with 65.8 percent of those entering between 1950 and 1959. Of course, the ability to speak English well varies from group to group, with Asian Indians and Filipinos reporting the greatest ability to speak well and Chinese, Kore-

bly reliable. The Census Bureau asks whoever fills out the census form (or who is interviewed) to estimate this information for every member of the household. It is a rather subjective matter at best. But it is not clear to us how an objective assessment of, say, Korean and Asian Indian English ability can be made from these data. Many Asian Indians speak English as a second language, as do Filipinos and Chinese from Hong Kong. Koreans and Chinese from the PRC or Taiwan learn English in school, but it is seldom spoken except in cases of necessity. So what does it mean when a Korean says he or she speaks English "very well?" Does that have the same meaning as for a Filipino?

TABLE 6.8

English Ability, by Period of Immigration/Nativity, Aged 25–64: 1980

Ethnicity and Ability to Speak English	Period of Immigration/Nativity							
	1975–1980	1970–1974	1965–1969	1960–1964	1950–1959	Before 1950	Native	Number
JAPANESE Total	100.0	99.9	100.0	100.0	100.0	99.9	100.0	21,129
Not well or not at all	34.7	17.6	13.8	16.6	9.3	12.8	2.7	1,770
Well or very well	61.4	72.3	70.5	67.0	61.6	52.9	28.2	8,566
Speaks only English	3.9	10.0	15.7	19.4	29.1	34.2	69.1	10,793
CHINESE Total	100.0	100.0	100.0	100.0	100.1	99.9	100.0	21,725
Not well or not at all	45.8	28.7	25.2	26.5	25.3	24.5	3.0	5,598
Well or very well	51.1	67.8	70.7	68.9	66.7	66.7	43.2	12,692
Speaks only English	3.1	3.5	4.1	4.6	8.1	8.7	53.8	3,435
FILIPINO Total	100.0	100.0	100.1	100.0	100.0	100.0	100.0	19,689
Not well or not at all	10.5	3.6	3.1	2.3	2.2	7.9	1.6	967
Well or very well	85.9	91.4	91.1	87.9	76.7	67.5	25.1	15,119
Speaks only English	3.6	5.0	5.9	9.8	21.1	24.6	73.3	3,603
KOREAN Total	100.0	100.1	100.1	100.0	100.0	100.0	100.0	8,833
Not well or not at all	49.5	23.7	7.0	5.4	2.5	19.4	3.6	2,683
Well or very well	47.5	71.6	83.2	75.9	65.8	67.7	12.6	5,235
Speaks only English	3.0	4.8	9.9	18.7	31.7	12.9	83.8	915
ASIAN INDIAN Total	100.0	100.0	100.0	100.0	100.0	100.0	99.9	10,477
Not well or not at all	11.6	4.5	1.7	3.0	3.4	7.0	1.7	656
Well or very well	76.4	83.2	79.6	74.7	66.1	47.4	19.3	7,645
Speaks only English	12.0	12.3	18.7	22.3	30.5	45.6	78.9	2,176
VIETNAMESE Total	100.0	100.1	100.0	99.9	100.0	100.0	100.0	4,916
Not well or not at all	45.5	8.0	4.5	3.4	*	*	12.6	1,975
Well or very well	52.7	79.9	80.2	93.1	77.8	60.0	36.8	2,743
Speaks only English	1.8	12.2	15.3	3.4	22.2	40.0	50.6	198
HISPANIC Total	100.0	100.1	99.9	99.9	100.1	100.1	100.0	*
Not well or not at all	74.2	56.4	46.5	36.3	28.8	29.2	10.8	*
Well or very well	24.8	39.7	51.4	57.1	62.9	59.4	64.7	*
Speaks only English	1.0	4.0	2.0	6.5	8.3	11.5	24.5	*

SOURCE: 5% PUMs "A" Tape.   * Data not readily available.

TABLE 6.9

Language Spoken at Home, and Nativity, 5 years and Older: 1980

Language Spoken at Home and Nativity	Japanese	Chinese	Filipino	Korean	Asian Indian	Vietnamese
Only English	55.9	19.4	32.6	20.5	31.3	5.0
Other language	44.1	80.6	67.4	79.5	68.9	95.0
Native language *	42.9	79.5	63.8	76.8	60.1	83.4 **
Percent born in U.S.	71.1	32.7	29.9	12.7	23.1	3.7

SOURCE: PC80-1-2E.

* Includes all dialects recorded by the census.

** 8.1% speak some Chinese dialect.

ans, and Vietnamese the least well. This, again, reflects the fact that most educated Asian Indians and Filipinos use English as a second language in their home countries, while Koreans and Vietnamese do not. Chinese show a confusing pattern which we cannot interpret without knowing their countries of origin. The data for native Americans are interesting: for most Asian Americans, natives report few persons with poor English. But for Vietnamese and Hispanics, over 10 percent of natives report difficulties with language. Of those who speak only English, Asian Indian, Korean, and Filipino natives show the greatest percentages, Vietnamese and Chinese, the least.

This leads us to another question: Which languages do Asian Americans use at home? The data here are instructive, and give some support to the notion of a multicultural, rather than an assimilated, adaptation to American society. Table 6.8 shows language spoken at home by ethnicity, and also the percentage of persons over 5 years of age who were native Americans. Note that although 71.1 percent of Japanese were born in the United States, 44.1 percent reported speaking a language other than English at home.[11] A large 80.6 percent of Chinese and 79.5 percent of Koreans reported speaking a language other than English at home. It is especially significant that, although many were adept with English, about two-thirds of Filipinos and Asian Indians also spoke languages other than English at home.

[11]How well they speak it is another matter. Many young Korean and Chinese immigrants speak their own languages only to parents or to other relatives who are not comfortable with English. Immigrant parents often find themselves in conflict with their children over the question of retaining their native languages. This is a question which deserves some careful research, with far richer data than that offered by the census.

Education of Household Heads

In a survey of families in Texas, Yao (1985) found that Asian American families had more structure and were more likely to push their children to study than did white ("Anglo") families. Her sample was of stable middle-class families, so we do not know what effects family or household structure might have on education. Census data cannot answer that question, but we can examine the educational levels of different kinds of householders, with the implied suggestion that parents with higher levels of education might be better able to support education for their children. We are also interested in how householders' educations might affect their occupations and incomes (Chapters 7 and 8). Table 6.9 breaks down the educational levels of householders of different kinds of families for the various ethnic groups. First of all, the overall level of education of Asian American householders (except Vietnamese) was much higher than that of whites, blacks, and Hispanics. Even for single female householders, Asian Americans had at least double the number of college-degree holders than did whites, blacks, and Hispanics. It is also true, however, that married-couple households exhibited the highest overall educational levels for all ethnicities. Note that 70 percent of Asian Indian and 55.6 percent of Korean married-family householders completed college, as compared with 18.8 percent for whites, 8.8 percent for blacks, and 9.3 percent for Hispanics. One interesting phenomenon was the very high percentage of college graduates in Asian American non-family households. For example, 46.5 percent of Chinese non-family householders have completed 4 years of college. Since this sample was limited to ages 25–64, most of the single householders must have been young professionals or students. If we examine those householders with fewer than 4 years of college, it is apparent that the lowest percentages were among married-couple householders. In general, single female householders had the highest percentage of those with fewer than 4 years of education, though for some ethnicities, single male householders or non-family householders also showed high percentages with low educational levels.

Conclusions

Whatever may be true of other aspects of the Asian American "success" story, there is no question about their standing with respect to education. Except for Vietnamese, Asian Americans are much better educated than whites, blacks, or Hispanics. Even in the case of Vietnamese, the recent San Diego study by Rumbaut and Ima indicates that Vietnamese children are doing extremely well in high school, overcoming the handicaps of their parents. This bodes well for their future.

There have been some concerns that the 1975–1980 cohort of immigrants from Asia were not as well-educated as their predecessors. Our data show this to be true, but the census data from 1989 indicate that Asian Americans still have much higher levels of education than do whites. Since these data are not disaggregated for each Asian ethnicity, we must wait for the 1990 data to determine trends for each of the ethnic groups. If the Vietnamese experience is true of other groups, it would appear that the children of less well-educated Asian Americans obtain high levels of education, indicating that Asian Americans fit Ogbu's "immigrant" classification, rather than the "castelike" status of blacks and Hispanics.

The superior educations of Asian Americans hold up when we control for gender. Here, Filipinos become unusual in that females are better educated than males. Although male-female discrepancies in education are great for Chinese, Koreans, and Asian Indians, still women of those groups are much better educated than white women.

School enrollment figures for Asian Americans are higher than for whites at all ages past 17, and are much higher than for blacks. It is significant that although Filipino and Asian Indian immigrants are better educated than Chinese, school enrollment data show that Chinese have the largest percentage of children enrolled in school in critical age categories. In general, it appears that children of Asian immigrants are receiving high levels of education. Asian American householders, too, are better educated than whites, blacks, and Hispanics, even for single female families. Married-couple family householders have the highest levels of education, and since they are more prevalent among Asian Americans than for whites, blacks, and Hispanics, there is even more reason to suspect that children of Asian American households are receiving superior educations. From what we know about the effects of family on status attainment, we would certainly expect children from educated families to become educated themselves.

The ability to speak English is highly correlated with years of formal education, both because Asian immigrants learn English in school, and also because inability to speak English may hinder the ability to study in the United States. However, ability to speak English improves greatly the longer immigrants remain in the United States, giving some obvious support to assimilation theory. On the other hand, most Asian Americans (Japanese excepted) speak a language other than English at

TABLE 6.10

Level of Education of Household Heads, by Household Type and Ethnicity, Aged 25–64:1980

Ethnicity and Household Type	Ethnicity and Education Completed (Percentage)						
	Less than High School	High School 1–3 years	High School 4 years	College 1–3 years	College 4 years	Total	Number
JAPANESE							
Married couple family	8.1	7.3	32.3	18.1	34.2	100.0	7,128
Family hh head male, no wife present	10.5	10.8	35.6	19.5	23.6	100.0	343
Family hh head female, no husband present	13.1	9.4	45.0	19.9	12.7	100.0	971
Non-family household	9.8	6.3	25.2	24.3	34.3	99.9	3,495
CHINESE							
Married couple family	17.5	8.1	17.2	12.9	44.3	100.0	8,271
Family hh head male, no wife present	16.1	8.2	20.0	21.6	34.1	100.0	440
Family hh head female, no husband present	26.9	8.7	26.3	17.4	20.7	100.0	783
Non-family household	16.2	3.7	13.6	20.0	46.5	99.9	2,929
FILIPINO							
Married couple family	13.3	8.8	20.3	22.1	35.5	100.0	7,036
Family hh head male, no wife present	20.3	10.8	16.5	21.0	31.4	100.0	424
Family hh head female, no husband present	14.5	9.1	20.9	18.4	37.1	100.0	986
Non-family household	17.5	7.2	16.4	19.4	39.6	100.0	1,718
KOREAN							
Married couple family	4.4	4.8	19.1	16.0	55.6	99.9	2,894
Family hh head male, no wife present	5.1	9.4	30.8	20.5	34.2	100.0	117
Family hh head female, no husband present	22.2	13.2	36.6	14.8	13.2	100.0	325
Non-family household	12.0	8.3	26.9	23.8	29.1	100.1	1,892

TABLE 6.10 (continued)

Ethnicity and Ability to Speak English	Period of Immigration/Nativity							
	1975–1980	1970–1974	1965–1969	1960–1964	1950–1959	Before 1959	Native	Number
ASIAN INDIAN								
Married couple family		5.8	5.1	8.9	10.3	70.0	100.1	4,491
Family hh head male, no wife present		11.5	8.1	16.2	18.2	45.9	99.9	148
Family hh head female, no husband present		25.4	18.0	22.1	12.1	22.4	100.0	272
Non-family household		18.0	11.7	16.2	15.6	38.4	99.9	1,779
VIETNAMESE								
Married couple family		17.6	10.7	26.5	27.0	18.2	100.0	1,532
Family hh head male, no wife present		12.5	14.8	32.0	29.3	11.3	99.9	256
Family hh head female, no husband present		28.7	19.8	29.0	14.5	8.0	100.0	647
Non-family household		14.7	12.8	13.0	26.3	15.2	82.0	398
WHITE								
Married couple family		15.6	14.6	34.8	16.3	18.8	100.1	2,221
Family hh head male, no wife present		28.0	9.3	45.3	12.0	5.3	99.9	75
Family hh head female, no husband present		16.9	18.5	39.6	18.5	6.4	99.9	313
Non-family household		21.3	14.1	30.4	17.0	17.2	100.0	882
BLACK								
Married couple family		26.5	20.3	29.9	14.5	8.8	100.0	1,258
Family hh head male, no wife present		31.9	21.6	31.0	11.2	4.3	100.0	116
Family hh head female, no husband present		21.2	29.3	31.8	31.2	4.6	118.1	844
Non-family household		30.8	19.6	23.4	16.4	9.8	100.0	858
HISPANIC								
Married couple family		37.3	18.5	22.4	12.5	9.3	100.0	1,701
Family hh head male, no wife present		44.0	15.6	23.3	12.2	4.4	99.5	90
Family hh head female, no husband present		43.1	23.4	21.7	8.8	3.0	100.0	466
Non-family household		35.0	12.3	23.8	15.6	13.3	100.0	512

SOURCE: 5% PUMs "A" Tape.

home, giving support to multicultural arguments that seem to be at odds with the assimilation theory.

All the evidence we have examined sustains the image of Asian Americans as having very high levels of education. There is variance, of course, both among individuals and among different ethnicities, but overall, Asian Americans are much better educated than whites, blacks, or Hispanics. There is reason to believe that this will continue to be the case, but we should point out that Japanese Americans, who include the highest percentage of native Americans, exhibit educational levels most like whites. If this is an assimilation effect, perhaps succeeding generations of Asian Americans will display somewhat less spectacular educational achievement.

7

EMPLOYMENT AND OCCUPATIONS

W E HAVE seen that Asian Americans are generally well educated, and that their families tend to be stable. Still, those strengths must be converted to desirable jobs. This is problematic enough for white Americans, but may be especially difficult for immigrants, who must overcome problems of language, culture, information, and possible discrimination to obtain employment commensurate with their backgrounds and skills. Most American employers are ignorant of the status of various Asian universities or other symbols of prestige accrued from occupations in Asian countries. Information networks available to native-born Americans may be closed to immigrants, so newcomers must rely on family or friends for information concerning employment. This can be very restrictive, as Caces (1985) has shown for Filipinos. These and other factors can put new immigrants in an unfavorable position in the job market, but, as we shall demonstrate, Asian Americans appear to reach near parity in occupations with white Americans after 5 or 10 years' stay in the United States.

The importance of occupational choice or opportunity cannot be overemphasized. Occupations convert education to income, but they also carry with them prestige, which extends far beyond the occupational sphere itself. Occupations largely determine life-styles and are a major contributor to personal identity. They also help to define networks of acquaintances, and, therefore, further opportunities for success.

Literature on occupational opportunities for immigrants and minorities is closely tied to education and income, so much of the relevant literature is discussed in Chapters 6 and 8. Obviously, these subjects cannot be disentangled easily, so it is no surprise that frameworks for the discussion of occupations appear similar to and overlap with the theories discussed in Chapter 6 for education. Scholars seem to agree that three or four major orientations subsume most of the studies of immigrants and jobs (Model 1988; Treiman, Lew, Lee, and Brown 1986; Nelson 1988). These are: *cultural* explanations, which purport to show how cultural orientations such as devotion to hard work have benefited certain groups over others; *resources and demographic differentials*, which concentrate on skills, niches in the host economy, age, and gender, and the like; and *discrimination* explanations, which argue that barriers to access to desirable occupations discriminate against some minorities and immigrants. Any particular study may share one or more of these orientations, but one can usually be found to dominate. For example, Light, Kwuon, and Zhong (1988) examine the role of rotating credit associations *(kye)* in Korean enterprises in Los Angeles. They clearly emphasize rotating credit associations as resources, though they also share some cultural attributes that cannot be ignored.

Cultural Explanations of Occupational Differences

The classic statement of cultural factors in occupational success is to be found in Weber (1958), who found much of the essence of capitalism in the norms and values of Calvinism. Bellah (1957) found similar traits in the culture of Tokugawa Japan. Woodrum (1985) attempted to tie religion to income and self-employment of Japanese immigrants. A number of cultural factors are cited by Light and Bonacich (1973, 1988) which are said to help Korean enterprises in competition and labor exploitation. The "middleman" hypothesis has been widely criticized as a cultural explanation (E. Wong 1985), although that was not the main thrust of Bonacich's work. The clearest examples of cultural explanations relating to Asian Americans can be found in Peterson (1971), Kitano (1976), and Kitano and Sue (1973). The "model minority" hypothesis, as we reported in Chapter 6, has been roundly criticized, and, except in the popular press, is in bad repute. In general, current literature has been critical of cultural orientations, looking instead for explanations in structural or socioeconomic characteristics of immigrants and of the host society. Since the census is largely mute on culture, we shall discuss only English ability, and even that as a resource.

Resource Differentials among Minorities and Immigrants

First and foremost among resources thought to influence success is, of course, education. We have reviewed this literature in Chapter 6. One point needs to be made in the context of occupations, however: With the exception of the status attainment studies of Blau and Duncan and their colleagues, very little of this literature makes occupations the central focus.[1] Rather, more attention is paid to the relationship of education and income. The work of Hirschman and Wong (1986) and that of Chiswick (reviewed in Chapter 8), the U.S. Commission on Civil Rights (1988), and Barringer, Takeuchi, and Xenos (1990) examine occupations as intervening variables between education and income in various groups of Asian Americans. It is clear that the role of occupation in converting education to income is central.

Related to this is the question of selectivity of immigrants to the United States. Literature suggests that Asian immigrants are highly selective with respect to education and occupation (Gardner, Robey, and Smith 1985; Xenos, Gardner, Barringer, and Levin 1987; Barringer and Cho 1990; Koo and Yu 1981). With respect to occupations, evidence suggests that immigrants may experience some downward mobility upon arrival in the United States, but recover after a period of residence (Hurh and Kim 1984; Chiswick 1983; Gordon 1987; Barringer, Takeuchi, and Xenos 1990).

Occupations can be seen as a resource of immigrants in assuring the educational attainment of their children (Lieberson 1980; Steinberg 1981; Cheng and Bonacich 1984). It also can be pointed out that Asian immigrants to the United States since 1965 are mostly from highly modernized urban societies. They have already been socialized into the core occupational sector before immigrating, and therefore are not required to face some of the handicaps of earlier generations, who immigrated from pre-modernized, peripheral economies (Barringer, Takeuchi, and Xenos 1990).

Ethnic enclaves may provide resources for immigrants that parallel human capital (Portes and Bach 1985; Hurh and Kim 1984), but they can also have negative effects (Nee and Sanders 1987). In general, immigrants can be helped by favorable niches in the host society (Lieberson 1980). Niches make possible middlemen minorities (Bonacich 1973; Bonacich and Modell 1980; Bonacich and Light 1988). Middlemen oc-

---

[1]One notable exception is the work of Nelson (1988), which we will discuss subsequently.

cupy entrepreneurial niches between the lower and upper classes, primarily in small businesses or in self-employed professions. They are characterized by hard work, frugality, and a strong sense of ethnic solidarity, coupled with hostility to the host society. Much research in this area has concentrated on small Korean enterprises in Los Angeles, Chicago, and New York (Bonacich and Light 1988; Hurh and Kim 1988; Il-Soo Kim 1981). Both lack of resources (poor educational backgrounds and English ability) and positive factors (openings in the American economic structure) are said to influence entry into middlemen positions. Choi (1988), however, disputes many of the contentions of Bonacich et al., citing Hurh and Kim, among others, that Korean entrepreneurs often have very high levels of education and have no special problems with English.

Whatever the case, it apparently is true that Koreans are overrepresented in the small business arena. As we shall see, Koreans have the highest percentage of self-employed workers of major Asian ethnic groups. There are nearly 90 Korean-owned businesses for every 1,000 Koreans in the United States, as compared with 64 per 1,000 for all Americans. Asian Indians follow (70 businesses per 1,000), Japanese (68.5 businesses per 1,000) and Chinese with 65.1 businesses per 1,000 (Manning and O'Hare 1988). The largest numbers of Asian-owned businesses are in Los Angeles–Long Beach (33,180), Honolulu (21,583), and San Francisco–Oakland (18,312). Manning and O'Hare found that the rate of Asian American businesses in various locales was not related to the proportion of Asian Americans in those areas, but rather to the average sales of the enterprises. Sales appear highest on the West Coast and in Hawaii, and lowest in the Northeast. This gives very strong support to the resources arguments. Reports of ethnic violence related to Asian American small businessmen abound (*U.S. News & World Report*, Nov. 24, 1986; U.S. Commission on Civil Rights 1986, Chapter 5).

Asian Americans are not as prevalent in the corporate board rooms of America as they are in big-city ghettos. Kitano and Daniels (1988, p. 171) point out that of 29,000 directors of the 1,000 largest U.S. firms in 1985, only 159 (0.5 percent) were Asian Americans.

The literature on Asian American entrepreneurship is voluminous, so we shall not pursue it in our own analysis. However, we would like to point out that the high visibility of some Asian Americans as petite bourgeoisie should not obscure the simple fact that the vast majority are engaged in other occupations.

Demographic Factors

Early Asian immigrants to the United States suffered from extremely unbalanced sex ratios. Recent immigrants show a preponderance of females among Koreans and Filipinos, and a preponderance of males among Vietnamese and Asian Indians (Xenos et al. 1989; Barringer and Cho 1990). Nee and Wong (1985) argue that the delayed family life of early Chinese immigrants delayed their progress economically. This may prove a handicap to Vietnamese, also. Fertility rates vary among Asian Americans (Chapter 2), but are still much lower than for Hispanics. Research indicates that restriction of family size aids in economic progress (Chiswick 1983, 1986). However, as we shall indicate in Chapter 8, some groups, especially Filipinos, appear to capitalize on family workers. Clearly, the number of family workers is closely related to income but, conversely, large families are characteristic of groups with low incomes.

Discrimination and Exploitation

Discrimination against Asian Americans in the marketplace is difficult to establish empirically. In one survey of Asian American immigrant businessmen in Honolulu, investigators were repeatedly told that respondents did not wish to reply to questions about discrimination because they did not wish to appear "ungrateful to Americans." It is widely believed to be a factor in hiring practices, however (*Newsweek*, May 11, 1987). Academics are more likely to invoke exploitation (Bonacich 1987; Barringer, Takeuchi, and Xenos 1990) from unexplained differences between ethnic groups. The census gives no direct evidence of either exploitation or discrimination against Asian Americans, of course, but it would be naive to assume it is not an important factor in the adaptation of Asian Americans to the United States.[2]

Occupational Distribution of Asian Americans

Previous reports based on the 1980 Census have suggested that Asian Americans compared favorably with white Americans in terms of oc-

---

[2]For example, several Asian American engineers from Silicon Valley firms have told us that companies recruit young engineers from Asia at lower wages than Americans are paid. As they move up to higher wages, they are replaced with new immigrants. The networks that lead to this process should be studied.

TABLE 7.1

Occupational Distribution, by Ethnicity and Sex, Aged 25–64: 1980

Occupation of Worker	Ethnicity and Sex (Percentage)							
	Japanese		Chinese		Filipino		Korean	
	M	F	M	F	M	F	M	F
NUMBER	8,734	9,016	10,254	8,642	7,257	9,389	3,284	3,923
Total	99.9	99.9	100.1	99.9	100.0	99.9	100.0	100.1
Executive, administrative, and managerial	18.1	8.6	15.7	10.3	10.4	6.7	15.3	5.6
Professional specialty	18.7	15.7	25.6	16.3	15.7	22.6	20.1	11.3
Technical and related support	5.7	2.8	6.9	5.8	6.1	5.8	5.0	2.3
Sales	8.6	9.5	7.4	8.5	4.3	5.6	14.7	11.6
Administrative support	8.2	29.3	6.7	22.3	14.2	25.8	4.7	13.1
Service, household	*	1.2	0.3	0.9	0.1	1.0	*	0.5
Service, other	6.8	16.9	21.2	12.5	13.6	15.6	7.4	23.2
Farm, forest, fishery	7.0	1.7	0.8	0.4	3.9	1.6	1.4	0.7
Precision production, craft and repair	16.9	4.0	8.1	3.0	14.7	3.6	14.6	5.9
Operators, assemblers, inspectors	3.9	8.1	4.4	18.7	8.2	9.5	11.8	22.4
Transportation, equipment, material movers	3.0	0.2	1.4	0.1	4.2	0.2	1.8	0.2
Handlers, helpers, cleaners	3.0	1.9	1.6	1.1	4.6	1.9	3.2	3.3

SOURCE: 5% PUMs "A" Tape.

* N/A.

cupational distribution (Gardner, Robey, and Smith 1985; Barringer, Takeuchi, and Xenos 1990; Barringer and Cho 1990). Table 7.1 shows the occupational distribution of Asian Americans by sex, compared to whites, blacks, and Hispanics. All Asian American males except Filipinos and Vietnamese fared about as well in managerial positions as did whites, and all did much better in this regard than blacks or Hispanics. Asian women fared less well, although Chinese women were better represented than white women in management positions.[3] In professions, however, Asian American men far outnumbered whites proportionately. Asian Indian men, especially, with 43.0 percent occupied as profession-

[3]This may be misleading in one respect, because the census classification of executive, management, and administrative position does not distinguish management of large firms or organizations from that of small firms or offices.

sian Indian		Vietnamese		White		Black		Hispanic	
M	F	M	F	M	F	M	F	M	F
458	3,387	3,097	1,737	2,252	1,838	1,600	1,738	1,879	3,295
0.0	100.2	100.0	100.1	100.0	99.9	100.0	100.1	100.0	99.8
5.8	6.0	6.2	4.8	15.5	8.1	5.8	6.0	7.4	4.5
3.0	28.0	11.3	7.5	11.3	15.1	5.0	11.9	6.8	7.5
7.5	6.8	9.7	3.7	2.8	2.7	1.3	3.3	1.4	1.6
5.9	7.7	3.4	6.8	10.3	12.7	3.4	5.1	4.9	8.1
6.9	24.1	7.8	17.5	5.9	31.8	8.7	21.5	6.9	22.6
0.1	0.8	*	0.1	*	0.9	0.2	5.4	0.1	2.3
4.4	11.1	10.0	18.8	6.8	13.0	14.9	25.8	12.1	19.4
1.4	0.8	2.3	0.7	4.4	0.9	4.2	0.7	6.9	2.6
6.8	2.2	20.6	9.7	22.4	2.5	16.8	2.1	21.7	4.4
5.9	10.0	20.9	26.1	9.8	9.0	15.9	13.8	14.5	22.1
1.0	0.3	1.6	1.3	7.2	1.0	12.3	1.0	7.8	0.9
1.3	2.4	6.2	3.1	3.6	2.2	11.5	3.5	9.5	3.8

als, showed a concentration far above that of other groups. Here, even Vietnamese men appeared equal to whites. In general, men outnumbered women in professions, with the notable exception of Filipinos, where females (22.6 percent) exceeded males (15.7 percent).

Generally, fewer Asian Americans were engaged in sales than were whites (Koreans being the notable exception).[4] In administrative support positions, females far outnumbered males, but Filipinos showed a relatively high percentage of males (14.2 percent) as compared to white males (5.9 percent). Very few persons of any ethnicity, except for black women (5.4 percent), appeared as household servants. In other service occupations, however, Asian Americans appeared to be overrepresented, except by comparison with blacks. There was a high percentage (21.2 percent)

[4]As we shall see subsequently, much of the Korean concentration in sales is in small businesses.

of Chinese males in service positions.[5] Non-white women were also much more likely to be employed in service occupations, giving support to split labor market theory (Bonacich 1972). It is interesting that only Japanese men were more heavily represented than whites, blacks, or Hispanics in farming, fishing, and forestry occupations, though Filipinos came close. Note the extreme sex disparity in these occupations: men far outnumbered women for all ethnicities.

Japanese, Filipino, Korean, and Vietnamese men were fairly well represented in precision production occupations, but none as heavily concentrated as whites (22.4 percent). Women were uniformly underrepresented in precision production. In the category of operators, assemblers, and inspectors, Asian Americans showed great variation, from 3.9 percent Japanese men to 11.8 percent Koreans (as compared to 9.8 percent white). In this category, Asian women outnumbered men, sometimes by a large percentage (18.7 percent of Chinese women as compared to 4.4 percent men). Asian Americans were underrepresented across all ethnicities in transportation. Note, however, that there was some overrepresentation among Filipinos in the unskilled occupations of handlers, helpers, and cleaners. Otherwise, however, Asian Americans showed about the same percentages as whites in unskilled occupations, and much less representation than blacks or Hispanics.

To summarize, Asian Americans were best represented in the professions and white-collar occupations. They seemed to come close to whites in management positions. Whites were more heavily concentrated than Asian Americans in labor, especially in the upper echelons of precision production. Asian Americans, especially women, were overrepresented in service occupations. There was much variation among ethnicities in each category, however. As we expected, women were less well represented than men in professions and management, with the notable exception of Filipinos.

Figures 7.1 and 7.2 show the above in a simplified graph form. The bar charts reinforced the general observations that Asian American men (except Vietnamese) generally did about as well in management and professions as did whites. Chinese, Filipino, and Vietnamese men were overrepresented in services compared to whites. In fact, Chinese men showed higher percentages in services than did blacks or Hispanics. Asian American women (again excepting Vietnamese) did about as well in professional and management positions as did white women, but Japanese, Filipino, Koreans, and Vietnamese women were all overrepresented in services compared to whites.

[5]We checked this by individual occupations, and yes, many of these men are cooks. Chung (1987) also reports this to be true of a survey in the Boston area.

FIGURE 7.1

Percentage of Males in Selected Occupations, Aged 26–64: 1980

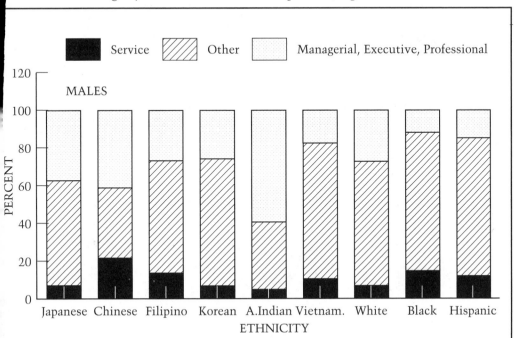

OURCE: Table 7.6.

In all these measures, Vietnamese made the poorest showings among Asian Americans, followed by Koreans. Asian Indians, by far, had the most impressive occupational distributions. Chinese appeared to be bimodal, with large percentages in both management and professions on one hand, and in services on the other.

Occupational data in broad categories usually obscure important internal differences. Table 7.2 breaks down professional and sales occupations in greater detail. Note that the highest percentage of Japanese professionals were in education, Chinese were more represented among scientists, and Filipinos were very heavily concentrated in health fields. Koreans were evenly distributed among various specialties, and Asian Indians were concentrated in science and health specialties. Vietnamese were underrepresented in health specialties. White and black professionals seemed to be concentrated in education.

In sales, note the high percentage of Koreans (34.9 percent) among supervisors and proprietors, reflecting their propensity for petite entre-

FIGURE 7.2

Percentage of Females in Selected Occupations, Aged 26–64: 1980

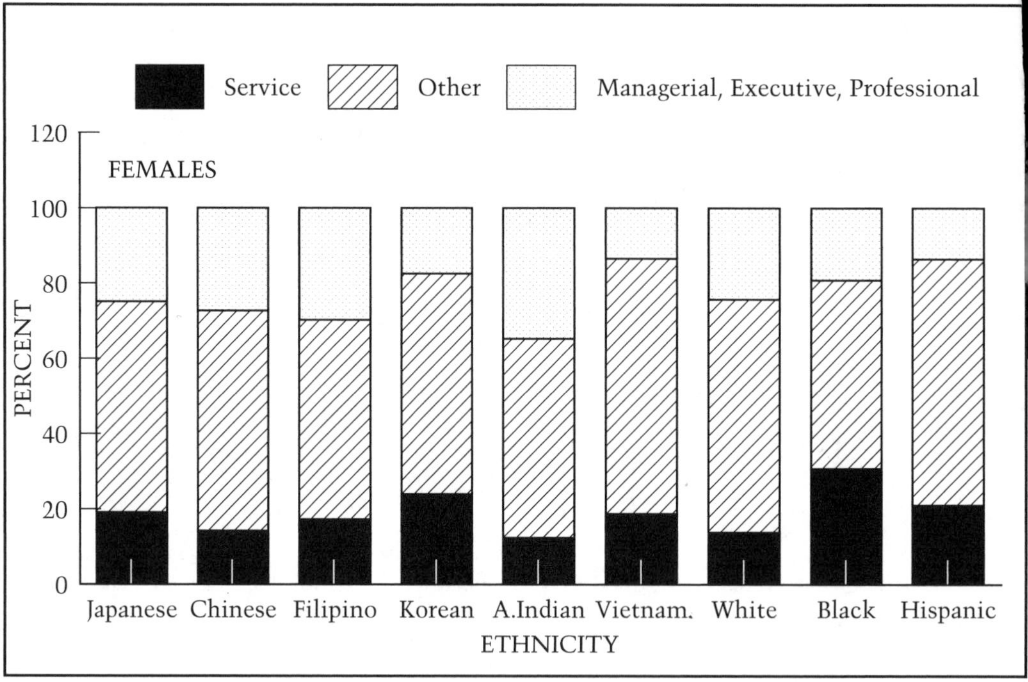

SOURCE: Table 7.6.

preneurship. Filipinos (9.3 percent) made the poorest showing in this category, lower than blacks and Hispanics. Other ethnicities were more evenly divided between sales supervisors and sales representatives. Except for Filipinos, Asian Americans equaled or surpassed whites in sales supervision and proprietorship. It appeared that the "middleman" hypothesis might apply best to Koreans, Asian Indians, Chinese, and Vietnamese, in that order.

Occupations are unequally distributed geographically in the United States (Nelson 1988). We have not attempted an exhaustive study of this phenomenon, but Table 7.3 shows occupational differences among Asian Americans in California and New York. Note that Japanese were more heavily represented in management in New York (29.5 percent) than in California (12.6 percent). Chinese were more heavily concentrated in service in New York (21.0 percent) than in California (15.7 percent). Note also that Chinese were more likely to be found in white-collar occupations in California, and as laborers in New York. Filipinos were much

TABLE 7.2
Breakdown of Professional Specialty and Sales Occupation, by Ethnicity, Aged 16+: 1980

Occupations	Ethnicity (Percentage)							
	Japanese	Chinese	Filipino	Korean	Asian Indian	Vietnamese	White	Black
PROFESSIONAL SPECIALTY	59,886	78,496	62,644	21,055	62,500	7,112	10,731,198	829,648
Total	100.1	100.0	100.0	100.0	99.9	99.9	100.0	100.0
Engineers and scientists	26.0	41.1	16.7	18.1	39.8	34.2	18.4	8.1
Health diagnosis	6.6	11.2	17.9	22.1	27.4	9.1	13.3	2.2
Health assessment and treating	11.4	10.7	45.0	24.5	10.8	6.1	13.9	15.9
Teachers, librarians and counselors	34.9	23.0	11.8	18.9	15.6	24.4	38.4	51.2
Other	21.2	14.0	8.6	16.4	6.3	26.1	16.0	22.6
SALES OCCUPATIONS	39,416	34,345	20,876	18,851	10,055	4,481	9,998,463	468,564
Total	100.0	100.0	100.0	100.0	100.0	100.0	100.0	100.0
Supervisors and proprietors	16.7	21.1	9.3	34.9	22.0	17.4	16.0	11.2
Sales representative, commodities and finance	26.0	25.3	25.3	13.3	28.3	11.0	32.5	19.2
Other	57.3	53.6	65.4	51.8	49.7	71.6	51.5	69.6

SOURCES: PC 80-1-2E and PC 80-1-C1.

TABLE 7.3

Differential Distributions of Occupations in California and New York, Aged 16+: 1980*

Occupations	Japanese		Chinese		Filipino		Korean		Asian Indian	
	CA	NY	CA	NY	CA	NY	CA	NY	CA	NY
TOTAL NUMBER	15,807	11,176	161,981	73,343	171,185	18,550	44,678	12,949	26,443	30,488
Total	100.1	100.0	100.2	100.1	100.0	100.0	100.0	99.9	100.0	100.1
Managerial	12.6	29.5	13.3	10.7	8.1	12.7	12.4	13.1	13.6	12.7
Professional specialty	16.7	21.3	17.6	13.5	12.0	34.9	11.1	22.3	25.9	33.4
Technical, sales, and administrative support	34.6	27.4	34.6	24.1	38.4	35.2	30.8	36.1	30.2	32.2
Service	10.8	11.1	15.7	21.0	15.0	8.5	11.8	9.9	8.5	7.8
Farm, forest, fishery	7.1	0.2	0.7	0.1	2.7	0.1	1.4	0.1	4.5	0.1
Precision production, craft and repair	8.5	3.7	6.9	4.7	9.3	3.9	12.6	5.3	7.2	4.4
Other labor	9.8	6.8	11.4	26.0	14.5	4.7	19.9	13.1	10.1	9.5

SOURCE: PC 80-1-2E.

*Vietnamese have been omitted from this analysis because no data were available for New York.

more concentrated as professionals in New York (34.9 percent) than in California (12.0 percent). Koreans and Asian Indians showed no major differences in these two states. Vietnamese were not shown because of low representation for New York. In general, Japanese and Filipinos fared better in New York; Chinese did better in California. Other such differences occurred, and they seemed to vary greatly by ethnicity, and in some cases, by sex. Since the variation seemed greater state by state than by broad regions (such as Northeast or West), a detailed study of geographic variations in occupation would seem in order.

Table 7.4 shows changes in occupational distributions over time for Japanese, Chinese, and Filipinos.[6] In general, several patterns emerged from this comparison. First, between 1960 and 1990, there was a decided shift away from agriculture, particularly for Filipino males. Second, the percentage of all three groups in management and professions increased over this period. The percentage of persons in service occupations has decreased somewhat, but all three groups still had substantial percentages in service occupations in 1980. Figures for 1989 suggest little change overall, but of course we do not know about distributions by ethnicity.

Percentages of persons in white-collar occupations (clerical and sales) increased among Japanese and Filipinos, particularly for males, but changed very little for Chinese. Percentages in labor categories decreased slightly over time.

Females showed the greatest changes in professions from 1960 to 1970, and in management from 1970 to 1980. Notice that the percentage of employed women increased for each group between 1960 and 1970. The percentage of women in labor has remained quite constant. Women outnumber men in white-collar occupations, mainly because so many are employed as administrative assistants.

In general, Table 7.4 shows a gradual, if not spectacular, improvement in the occupational distributions of Asian Americans between 1960 and 1980. The data for 1989 are ambiguous, but they do suggest that no catastrophic changes will be seen in the 1990 Census. Data for 1960, 1970, and 1980 are shown in Figures 7.3 and 7.4. Note the gains in management for both men and women from 1970 to 1980.

---

[6]Other groups were not classified or were too small to count in 1960 and 1970. We employed the occupational classifications of 1960 and 1970 for this table for purposes of comparison. Occupational classifications changed in 1980. To compensate, we aggregated major classifications and reclassified some of the 1980 groups. There still may be some problems of comparison, but we believe that this grouping minimizes them. Note that 1989 scores are for all Asian Americans and Pacific Islanders combined. This may or may not be useful, because Pacific Islanders probably depress the Asian American rankings. On the other hand, Asian Americans make up most of the group.

TABLE 7.4

Occupations of Japanese, Chinese, and Filipino Americans by Gender, Employed Persons Aged 16+: 1960, 1970, 1980

	Year					
	1960		1970		1980	
Occupations	Male	Female	Male	Female (Percentage)	Male	Female
Japanese						
Total number	113,472	71,271	147,054	116,918	199,016	183,518
Total	100.0	100.1	99.9	100.0	100.0	100.0
Manager, official	10.2	3.8	11.7	3.8	17.0	8.3
Professional technical	15.4	12.3	21.4	19.4	22.0	17.8
Clerical and sales	13.8	37.2	15.1	36.9	17.9	42.9
Labor (all)	37.6	19.0	39.9	24.6	27.1	12.5
Farm, fishery, forestry	17.2	6.7	5.2	0.5	7.2	1.3
Service	5.8	21.1	6.6	14.8	8.8	17.2
Chinese						
Total number	66,704	25,630	114,433	69,129	225,100	174,864
Total	100.1	99.9	100.2	100.0	99.9	100.1
Manager, official	16.6	5.8	11.4	3.8	15.0	10.4
Professional technical	19.7	17.9	28.9	19.4	30.3	20.4
Clerical and sales	14.7	40.6	13.8	36.9	15.5	34.4
Labor (all)	22.6	24.0	21.4	24.6	16.3	20.8
Farm, fishery, forestry	1.3	0.7	0.7	0.5	0.6	0.3
Service	25.2	10.9	24.0	14.8	22.2	13.8
Filipino						
Total number	53,937	11,572	64,936	48,286	170,417	191,052
Total	100.1	100.1	100.2	100.0	99.9	100.0
Manager, official	1.9	1.7	3.4	1.7	9.3	6.4
Professional technical	6.6	26.4	20.7	33.5	19.1	27.1
Clerical and sales	6.2	30.0	12.9	33.8	18.9	34.7
Labor (all)	38.9	17.4	35.4	12.3	31.9	13.8
Farm, fishery, forestry	24.4	4.3	5.1	0.7	4.3	1.4
Service	22.1	20.3	22.7	18.0	16.4	16.6

SOURCES: PC80-1-2E; PC(1)-1C; PC(2)-1C.

206

FIGURE 7.3

Occupations of Japanese, Chinese, and Filipino Males: 1960, 1970, 1980

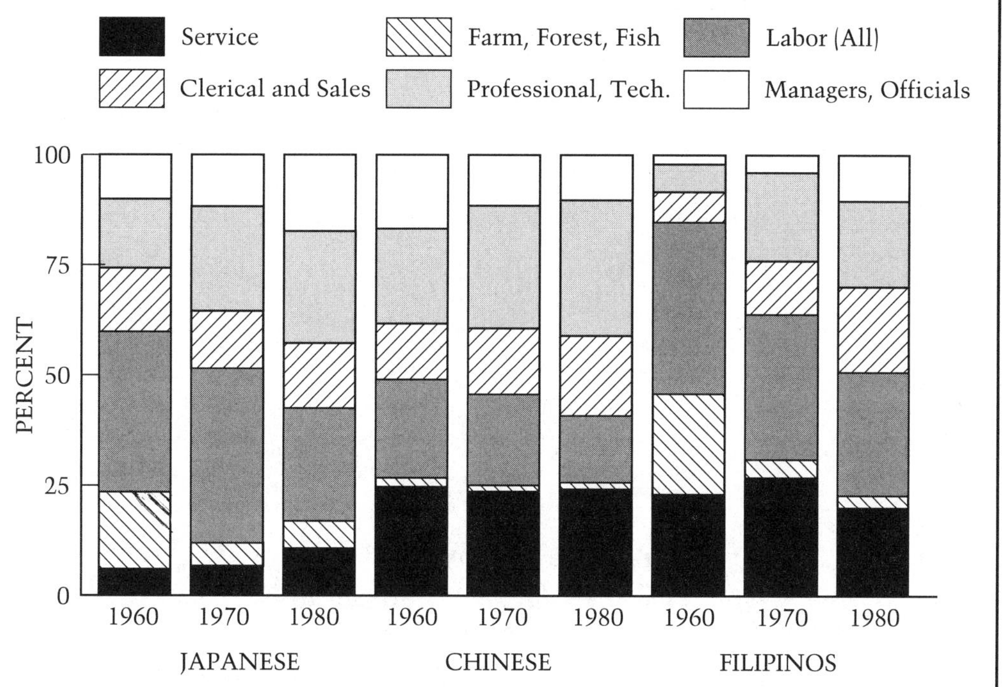

OURCES: PC80-1-2E; PC(1)-1C; PC(2)-1C.

Industry of Workers

Table 7.5 shows distributions of workers by industry. Overall, industry showed less variation than among occupations, except in areas such as professional services and in retail trades, which we have already discussed. One notable exception was the very heavy concentration (42.7 percent) of Vietnamese in manufacturing. Koreans and Chinese were overrepresented in retail trades. Otherwise, Asian Americans were less heavily concentrated in insurance, real estate, and finance than were whites, by about half. This is an important category, because high incomes are generated there. Banking and credit industries were not shown for whites and blacks in census tables, so we have not made that comparison.

FIGURE 7.4

Occupations of Japanese, Chinese, and Filipino Females: 1960, 1970, 1980

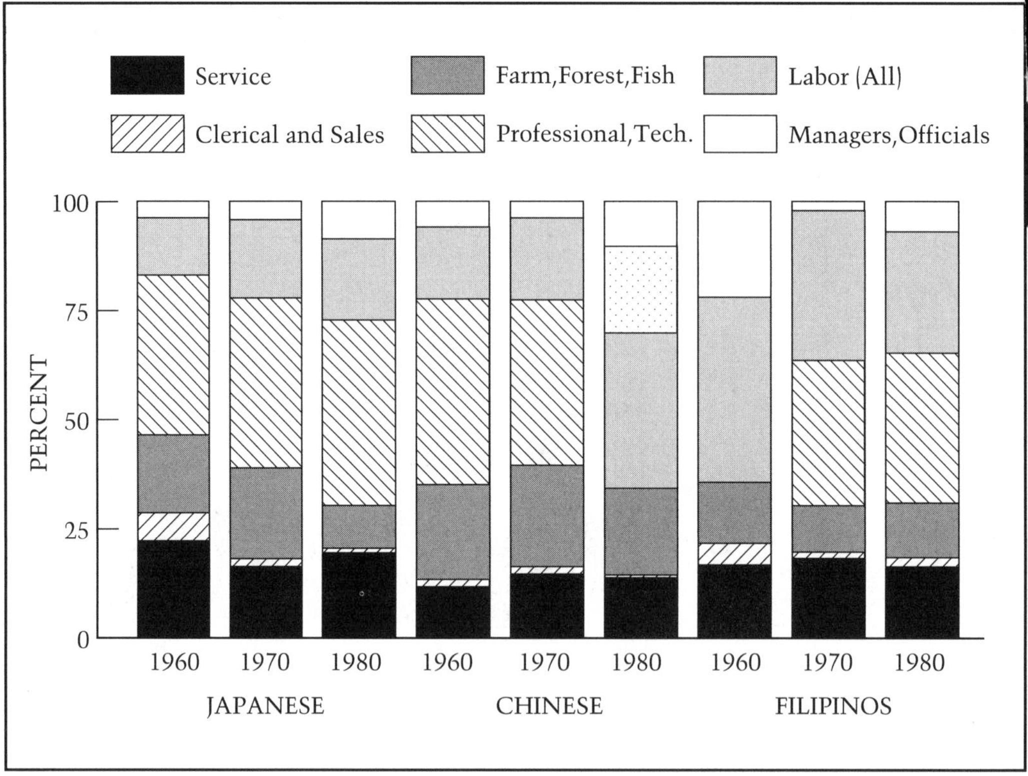

SOURCES: PC80-1-2E; PC(1)-1C; PC(2)-1C.

Class of Worker

Table 7.6 shows class of workers broken down by sex. Korean, Japanese, and Chinese males appeared underrepresented as private wage workers, largely because many were self-employed, showing their involvement in entrepreneurial activities. Vietnamese and Hispanics had the highest percentages of private wage workers. Filipinos and blacks had the highest numbers of federal workers, and Japanese and black women were visible in state government employment. Women, especially white, black, and Hispanic women, were more commonly engaged in local government employment than were men. A fair percentage of Korean and Chinese women were unpaid family workers, which is probably related to small businesses. Generally speaking, Asian Americans appeared to be equitably distributed across the class patterns, except for

TABLE 7.5
Industry of Workers, Employed Persons Aged 16+

Industry	Japanese	Chinese	Filipino	Korean	Asian Indian	Vietnamese	White	Black
				(Percentage)				
Total	100.1	99.9	100.0	100.0	100.0	100.0	100.0	99.9
Agriculture	4.8	0.5	2.8	1.0	1.1	0.7	3.0	1.7
Mining	0.2	0.3	0.2	0.2	0.4	0.6	1.1	0.5
Construction	3.8	1.9	2.9	2.1	2.8	2.3	6.1	4.3
Manufacturing (all)	14.3	20.3	19.2	26.3	23.0	42.7	22.3	23.2
Transportation with communication	6.8	5.3	6.3	3.3	3.8	2.9	7.2	8.9
Wholesale trade	5.7	3.4	2.8	3.6	3.4	3.3	4.5	2.8
Retail trade	9.8	26.7	11.9	25.9	11.1	16.8	16.6	11.1
Banking and credit	3.1	3.4	4.3	2.1	3.2	2.2	*	*
Insurance, real estate, and other finance	3.2	3.8	4.3	2.4	3.5	2.0	6.2	4.8
Business and repair services	4.1	3.8	3.7	4.4	4.3	3.8	4.2	3.6
Private households	0.8	0.6	0.7	0.3	0.5	0.4	*	*
Other personal services	4.0	3.1	4.8	5.3	2.8	3.2	2.8	6.1
Entertainment and recreation	1.2	0.7	1.0	1.2	0.5	0.8	1.1	0.8
Professional service	0.7	21.3	29.2	19.4	36.4	15.4	19.9	24.6
Public administration	7.6	4.8	5.9	2.5	3.2	2.9	5.0	7.5

SOURCE: PC80-1-C1.

* Data not readily available.

TABLE 7.6

Class of Worker, by Sex and Ethnicity, Aged 16+: 1980

	Ethnicity (Percentage)							
	Japanese		Chinese		Filipino		Korean	
Class of Worker	M	F	M	F	M	F	M	F
EMPLOYED PERSONS aged 16+	199,016	183,518	225,100	174,864	170,417	191,052	67,185	73,563
Total	100.1	99.9	100.0	100.1	99.9	100.0	100.1	100.0
Private wage and salary worker	70.7	70.8	75.1	76.9	78.1	79.9	72.7	79.4
Federal gov't worker	6.3	4.3	5.1	3.5	8.8	5.4	3.1	3.2
State gov't worker	6.6	11.6	6.2	6.6	3.6	5.2	4.2	3.6
Local gov't worker	5.0	7.8	4.0	6.6	5.7	7.3	2.8	3.7
Self-employed worker	11.2	4.5	9.0	5.0	3.6	1.9	16.5	7.8
Unpaid family worker	0.3	0.9	0.6	1.5	0.1	0.3	0.8	2.3

SOURCES: PC80-1-C; PC80-1-2E.

the preponderance of Korean, Japanese, and Chinese self-employed workers. Underrepresentation appeared mostly in Asian American women as local government workers.

Education and Occupation

Educational requirements exist for many occupations and are most noticeable in the professions. Given an abundance of workers, educational requirements may be established for no justifiable reasons; often minority workers complain of being locked out of occupations because of poorer educations. This is not likely to be the case for Asian Americans, however, since they appear to be better educated than whites, blacks, or Hispanics in most occupational categories. Table 7.7 shows average years of education for various occupational categories.[7] Note that for

[7]Mean or median years of education are not the happiest choices for this purpose.

| Asian Indian | | Vietnamese | | White | | Black | | Hispanic | |
M	F	M	F	M	F	M	F	M	F
17,172	59,683	47,174	33,541	48,843,987	35,183,388	4,674,871	4,659,177	3,287,208	2,168,649
100.0	100.0	100.1	99.9	100.0	100.1	99.9	99.9	100.1	99.9
77.6	77.5	87.4	83.8	76.1	76.0	73.4	67.2	82.2	78.9
3.0	2.5	1.6	2.6	3.7	3.0	7.2	7.6	3.8	3.6
8.4	7.0	4.1	4.3	3.7	5.3	4.8	8.5	2.6	4.5
4.2	8.0	4.6	6.0	6.3	10.9	10.9	15.3	6.4	10.4
6.6	4.0	2.1	2.6	9.9	4.0	3.5	1.2	4.9	2.1
0.2	1.0	0.3	0.6	0.3	0.9	0.1	0.1	0.2	0.4

executive and administrative positions, all Asian American groups except Vietnamese were better educated than whites, blacks, or Hispanics. The same was true for professions, though Japanese were very close to whites in this regard. As we move through white-collar, service, and labor, note that educational discrepancies appeared greater. Asian Americans seemed to be overeducated for many occupational categories when compared to whites, blacks, and Hispanics, but of course their overall educational levels were higher to begin with. Looked at in another way, whites, blacks, and Hispanics could be said to have some advantages over Asian Americans in that they apparently needed less education for most occupational categories. It is difficult to know what this means, however, until we look at incomes in the next chapter.

Educational requirements usually are stated in terms of high-school, college, or post-graduate degrees, which are not shown with central tendencies of years of schooling completed, rectified in the 1990 Census. Also, mean differences of a year or two do not appear very large, but may mask enormous differences in degree completions (see Chapter 5). However, for purposes of clarity in such a complex table, we chose the mean.

TABLE 7.7

Mean Years of Education, by Occupation, Aged 25–64: 1980

Ethnicity and Mean Years of Education

Occupations	Japanese	Chinese	Filipino	Korean	Asian Indian	Vietnamese	White	Black	Hispanic
NUMBER	17,750	18,896	16,646	7,207	8,845	3,834	4,090	3,338	3,295
Total	13.6	13.3	13.9	13.5	15.7	11.8	12.6	11.4	10.1
Executive, administrative, managerial	14.7	14.8	15.4	15.2	16.3	13.9	14.1	13.2	13.3
Professional specialty	16.5	17.5	17.0	16.9	18.2	15.6	16.1	15.2	15.0
Technical and related support	15.0	16.4	15.6	16.0	16.8	14.3	13.6	12.9	13.4
Sales	13.3	13.2	13.8	13.8	14.3	11.2	12.8	12.1	11.5
Administrative support	13.4	14.0	14.5	13.9	14.5	12.9	12.6	12.5	12.1
Service, household	11.0	8.4	9.5	7.4	9.5	6.7	10.4	9.5	7.3
Service, other	12.9	11.5	12.5	11.3	13.7	10.7	11.2	10.5	10.1
Farm, forest, fishery	12.0	10.3	8.8	11.4	12.1	9.2	10.7	8.1	6.0
Precision production, craft and repair	12.2	11.5	12.5	12.6	8.7	11.0	11.4	10.9	9.5
Operators, assemblers, inspectors	11.6	7.9	11.7	11.5	13.5	10.6	10.7	10.6	8.3
Transportation, equipment, material movers	11.9	11.9	11.2	13.0	11.9	10.5	10.9	10.6	9.3
Handlers, helpers, cleaners	11.7	10.7	10.4	11.7	12.9	9.8	10.3	9.9	8.4

SOURCE: 5% PUMs "A" Tape.

Occupational Prestige

The subject of occupational prestige has long occupied the attention of sociologists, and for good reason. Occupational prestige has replaced family lineage as the primary indicator of social status in industrial societies. Unfortunately, it is difficult to measure objectively, although many attempts are made (see Blau and Duncan 1967 for the most complete discussion). Basically, prestige scores are a composite of a national prestige study with education and income. We have used a measure designed by Lloyd Temme (1975) for the report of the U.S. Commission on Civil Rights (1978).[8] In Temme's measure, physicians have a high score of 88; farm workers a low of 10. The possible scores range from 100 to 0. Scores of 52 and above generally are for professionals, managers, and executives. Scores from 33 to 51 are found among white-collar workers and precision labor. Scores below 33 are generally ascribed to labor, farm, and service workers. There is some overlap in this, but we find it convenient to label those ranges "high," "medium," and "low," respectively.

Table 7.8 shows average prestige scores for each of the major occupational categories. This is useful information, because it allows us to observe how occupations are distributed *within* each of the occupational groupings. Note, for example, that the prestige scores of Asian Indians in the professions (70.3) were much higher than for Japanese (63.5) or whites (63.3). This is because many Asian Indians were scientists, engineers, and physicians, while more Japanese and whites were teachers. Likewise, many Filipinos were nurses or nurses' aides.

In general, prestige scores were evenly distributed among managers and executives, with Asian Americans equaling or surpassing whites, blacks, and Hispanics. Although professional prestige scores were more variable, Asian Americans surpassed whites, blacks, and Hispanics. Among sales occupations, Koreans showed the highest scores, presumably because so many of them were managers and proprietors. In the farm, forest, and fishing category, whites excelled, probably because nearly all large farm owners were whites. Note that whites appeared to have a slight edge in most of the labor categories. There seemed to be no consistent differences in the service categories. To summarize, Asian Americans appeared to occupy higher prestige occupations than whites in the professions and about the same in management, supervision, service,

[8]Because the Census Bureau changed occupational codes in 1980, we adapted the Temme scores to the 1980 codes. Since that time, Stevens and Cho (1985) published a new prestige score based on Featherman's work. We found that the Temme scores provided better correlations with income, so we retained that measure.

TABLE 7.8

Occupational Prestige Score,* by Occupation, Aged 25–64: 1980

Occupations	Ethnicity and Mean Prestige Score								
	Japanese	Chinese	Filipino	Korean	Asian Indian	Vietnamese	White	Black	Hispanic
NUMBER	17,750	18,896	16,646	7,207	8,845	3,834	4,090	3,338	3,295
Total	43.5	45.1	42.4	41.1	52.1	37.6	42.3	35.1	35.1
Executive, administrative, managerial	57.7	57.9	58.6	57.5	58.0	58.1	57.5	57.3	57.7
Professional specialty	63.5	66.4	63.6	66.0	70.3	65.5	63.3	62.0	63.7
Technical and related support	50.1	51.6	49.0	49.7	49.1	50.5	48.4	46.5	48.8
Sales	40.6	41.4	37.8	43.1	40.4	37.9	40.6	37.1	37.2
Administrative support	42.7	42.6	42.0	41.8	42.1	40.6	43.1	40.6	41.0
Service, household	13.4	15.6	17.0	19.3	14.6	16.9	15.9	12.7	14.0
Service, other	28.6	27.9	26.8	25.9	28.9	24.7	27.4	27.3	26.0
Farm, forest, fishery	21.9	21.6	15.0	17.3	18.2	16.4	25.4	16.2	15.6
Precision production, craft and repair	38.5	38.0	38.2	36.3	39.4	37.0	39.3	38.3	37.8
Operators, assemblers, inspectors	29.8	28.6	29.6	29.6	29.7	29.8	30.1	19.0	29.3
Transportation, equipment material movers	29.2	28.6	28.0	26.7	26.5	27.2	30.8	28.9	27.9
Handlers, helpers, cleaners	19.3	19.7	20.3	19.9	20.9	19.8	20.2	20.2	20.1

SOURCE: 5% PUMs "A" Tape.

* Temme Prestige Score (see text).

214

and in white-collar occupations. Whites did somewhat better than Asian Americans in labor.

Because so many Asian Americans are recent immigrants, we examined the effect of period of immigration and nativity on prestige scores (Table 7.9). The effect was fairly dramatic. The general trend for Chinese, Filipinos, Koreans, and Asian Indians was a dramatic change of 5 points or more for those who had been in the United States for 5 or more years, over those who had immigrated between 1975 and 1980. Japanese showed just the reverse, again because most of the Japanese who entered between 1975 and 1980 were managers of Japanese firms. Even so, most recent Asian American immigrants had prestige scores higher than had blacks or Hispanics, and some were higher than those of whites. It is important to observe that Hispanics showed much fewer dramatic increases over the same time periods. Chinese, Japanese, and Korean native Americans had higher prestige scores than whites, blacks, or Hispanics. Native Filipinos had lower scores than whites, because many of them were still engaged in agriculture. The figures for natives were interesting, because native Asian Americans tended to be either very young or very old.

It is possible that the lower prestige scores of recent immigrants could be the result of a new trend, with persons entering with lower occupational qualifications, but that seems unlikely, given the fact that there appears to have been a gradual improvement in the occupational distribution of Asian Americans between 1960 and 1980 (Figure 7.4). More likely, new immigrants need a period in which to locate satisfactory jobs. That, plus promotions, is a much more likely explanation of increases over time in residence.

Sectoral Differences

Dual-market labor theory (Bonacich 1972; Bonacich and Cheng 1984) suggests that immigration to the United States is due in part to a shortage of labor in the peripheral economy.[9] This suggests that Asian Americans might be concentrated in periphery occupations. Dual-market labor theory also predicts that immigrant women should appear most commonly in the periphery.

[9]The "periphery" refers to labor-intensive, generally small-scale enterprises using simple technology. Service and farming occupations are examples. The "core," on the other hand, refers to large-scale, capital-intensive, and technologically sophisticated firms, such as electronics and car manufacturing. We have used the Tolbert, Horan, and Beck (1972) classification of industry for this analysis.

TABLE 7.9

Occupational Prestige, by Period of Immigration/Nativity, Aged 25–64: 1980

	Ethnicity							
	Japanese		Chinese		Filipino		Korean	
Period of Immigration/Nativity	Prestige Score	N	Prestige Score	N	Prestige Score	N	Prestige Score	N
Total	43.5	17,750	45.1	18,896	42.4	16,646	41.1	7,207
NATIVE	44.5	12,686	48.7	4,539	39.4	2,913	45.0	402
FOREIGN-BORN	241.7	5,064	267.9	14,357	255.0	13,728	268.0	6,805
Immigrated:								
1975–1980	48.4	1,473	40.7	4,181	39.0	4,087	37.2	2,991
1970–1974	40.1	825	44.2	3,439	44.7	4,357	41.4	2,405
1965–1969	39.4	612	46.1	2,906	46.4	2,938	47.9	765
1960–1964	37.3	651	46.4	1,414	46.5	849	46.5	386
1950–1959	36.9	1,360	46.7	1,326	43.4	1,007	50.7	240
Before 1950	39.6	143	43.8	1,091	35.0	490	44.3	18

SOURCE: 5% PUMs "A" Tape.

* N/A.

Table 7.10 shows the distribution of males and females of various ethnicities occupied in the core and periphery. Data appeared to support the theory, but there was considerable variability by ethnicity. The differences by sex were often striking, with Japanese, Filipino, Korean, Vietnamese, and white women overrepresented in the periphery. For combined sexes (not shown), Japanese, Chinese, Filipinos, and Koreans were overrepresented in the periphery, as were blacks and Hispanics. Whites (sexes combined) appeared to be equally distributed in the periphery and core.

Other Determinants of Occupational Prestige

Table 7.11 shows prestige scores by class of worker, industrial sector, schooling, and gender. First, examining class of worker, recall that most workers were private wage workers. In this category, Korean and Vietnamese prestige scores fell below those of whites, but other Asian Americans did better. Black and Hispanic prestige scores were lowest by far. In various government occupations, Asian Americans generally

		Ethnicity							
Asian Indian		Vietnamese		White		Black		Hispanic	
Prestige Score	N	Prestige Score	N	Prestige Score	N	Prestige Score	N	Prestige Score	N
52.1	8,845	37.6	3,834	42.3	4,090	35.1	3,338	35.1	3,295
41.9	737	42.7	69	42.4	3,895	35.1	3,216	36.0	1,993
304.0	8,108	249.8	3,765	*	*	*	*	203.7	1,302
38.9	3,019	37.1	3,270	*	*	*	*	31.5	240
54.0	3,017	37.9	368	*	*	*	*	32.8	332
57.6	1,381	48.4	90	*	*	*	*	32.9	282
58.9	433	45.2	26	*	*	*	*	37.7	210
55.9	216	49.4	7	*	*	*	*	34.6	166
48.7	42	31.8	4	*	*	*	*	34.2	72

showed the highest prestige scores, probably because education pays off in the hierarchy of bureaucracies. Where most Asian Americans really excelled, however, was as self-employed workers or as employees of their own corporations. Note the extreme difference between Filipinos (71.6) and whites (52.2) in the latter category.

With respect to the industrial sector, it is interesting that prestige scores in the periphery and core were about the same for whites and blacks, but for Asian Americans, scores were higher in the core than in the periphery. For Chinese, particularly, core prestige scores averaged about 10 points higher than in the periphery.

As we would expect (because education associated with occupations entered into the makeup of prestige scores), education was related to prestige. However, most of the advantage in prestige gained by education came from college completion. Whites gained more prestige from education than did Asian Americans, except for Asian Indians and Chinese, both with very high educational levels beyond college. This is significant, given the fact that whites showed lower educational levels than most Asian Americans past college. It is one area where whites appeared to have some advantage. One interesting phenomenon among many Asian American groups was that persons in the lowest educa-

TABLE 7.10

Percent Employment in Periphery and Core, by Sex, Aged 25–64: 1980

Occupational Sector and Gender	Ethnicity (Percentage Employed)								
	Japanese	Chinese	Filipino	Korean	Asian Indian	Vietnamese	White	Black	Hispanic
PERIPHERY									
Number	10,065	11,951	9,012	4,763	4,761	1,966	2,071	1,865	1,818
Total	100.0	100.0	100.0	100.0	100.0	100.0	100.0	100.0	100.0
Male	41.3	50.7	34.1	40.5	52.3	46.9	42.9	37.4	48.0
Female	58.7	49.3	65.9	59.5	47.7	53.1	57.1	62.6	52.0
CORE									
Number	7,685	6,945	7,634	2,444	4,084	1,868	2,019	1,473	1,477
Total	100.0	100.0	100.0	100.0	100.0	100.0	100.0	100.0	100.0
Male	59.6	60.4	54.8	55.5	72.6	62.8	67.5	61.2	68.2
Female	40.4	39.6	45.2	44.5	27.4	37.2	32.5	38.8	31.8

SOURCE: 5% PUMs "A" Tape.

TABLE 7.11

Occupational Prestige Scores, by Class of Worker, Sector of Employment, Years of Education, and Sex, Aged 25–64: 1980

	Ethnicity (Occupational Prestige Scores)								
	Japanese	Chinese	Filipino	Korean	Asian Indian	Vietnamese	White	Black	Hispanic
NUMBER	21,129	21,725	19,689	8,833	10,477	4,916	4,887	4,151	4,091
Class of worker									
Private wage worker	41.7	42.5	40.5	37.7	49.7	36.2	40.5	32.6	33.3
Federal gov't worker	50.9	52.7	66.8	53.1	60.1	45.4	54.1	50.5	53.0
State gov't worker	51.8	55.8	49.5	57.4	60.0	49.8	49.6	41.7	42.3
Local gov't worker	49.5	53.0	47.6	49.6	55.7	44.6	47.2	41.9	39.8
Self-employed unincorporated	40.6	48.7	52.8	48.5	58.8	40.6	44.0	38.4	43.0
Employee own corporation	51.2	53.7	71.6	55.0	66.1	52.1	52.2	49.8	47.8
Unpaid family worker	32.7	38.7	44.0	36.8	40.3	36.4	36.5	40.7	30.5
Sector									
Periphery	41.1	41.5	40.8	40.5	50.7	36.1	41.7	34.5	33.5
Core	46.7	51.3	44.3	42.4	53.7	39.2	42.9	35.9	37.1
Years of education									
Less than high school	51.5	43.8	47.8	52.3	57.6	59.4	49.9	50.9	46.5
High school, 1–3 years	48.3	44.7	45.5	45.9	50.7	48.3	50.2	47.2	46.4
High school, 4 years	48.8	48.1	48.6	46.1	52.3	46.3	48.4	42.5	46.2
College, 1–3 years	51.4	49.9	49.3	49.9	53.7	46.0	51.7	47.5	47.9
College, 4 years or more	58.7	59.8	54.7	58.1	63.5	56.4	59.9	56.3	58.3
Sex									
Male	45.9	47.2	43.7	47.4	55.7	39.3	42.5	34.1	35.5
Female	41.1	42.5	42.3	37.1	46.1	35.7	41.0	36.4	34.4

SOURCE: 5% PUMs "A" Tape.

219

tional category (less than high school) showed higher prestige scores than high-school graduates. This was probably due to petite entrepreneurial activities. In fact, in perusing data, a handful of Chinese and Korean women with *no* formal educations showed up in the 55–58 prestige score bracket.[10]

Last, in the case of most Asian Americans, women had lower prestige scores than men. Filipinos, whites, and Hispanics showed little gender difference. Only black women had higher prestige scores than black men, but both were very low. Recall that Asian American women were generally less well educated than men, were overrepresented in the periphery, and that the periphery generally had lower prestige occupations than the core. Asian American women, therefore, have had many handicaps in occupations.

Employment, Unemployment, and Underemployment

Table 7.12 shows the labor force status of males and females aged 25 to 64 in 1979. Generally speaking, the percentage of employed Asian American women was higher than for whites, with 52.7 percent of women employed. Filipinos, with 69.7 percent of women employed, far outnumbered other groups. Except for Japanese (1.7 percent), however, Asian American women had higher unemployment rates than whites (2.4 percent), but generally were lower than for blacks (5.4 percent) and Hispanics (4.1 percent). Unemployment rates were generally lower for women than for men.

Among males, only Filipinos (76.8 percent) and Vietnamese (71.5 percent) showed fewer employed than white males (82.1 percent). All had higher employment rates than blacks. Except for Vietnamese (5.5 percent), all Asian American men had lower unemployment rates than whites (3.8 percent), blacks (7.0 percent), or Hispanics (5.6 percent).

Figure 7.5 shows the percentage of persons with some unemployment, and the average number of weeks unemployed for males, aged 25 to 64, in 1979. Chinese, Filipinos, Koreans, and Vietnamese all showed higher percentages of persons with some unemployment than did whites, though all but Vietnamese had less unemployment than blacks and Hispanics. Vietnamese, particularly, with about 32 percent with some unemployment, stood out from the Japanese, with around 12 percent. However, when we look at the average number of weeks unemployed, Asian Americans all looked better than whites (at about 14 weeks). Ko-

---

[10]They also had very high incomes.

TABLE 7.12
Labor Force Status, by Sex, Aged 25–64: 1979

Labor Force Status	Japanese	Chinese	Filipino	Korean	Asian Indian	Vietnamese	White	Black	Hispanic
					Ethnicity (Percentage)				
MALE									
Number	9,104	10,796	8,534	3,484	5,641	2,375	2,384	1,840	2,007
Total	100.0	100.0	100.0	100.0	100.0	100.1	99.9	100.0	100.0
Employed, at work	87.0	83.9	76.8	83.7	87.9	71.5	82.1	67.7	79.5
Employed, not at work	1.7	1.6	1.6	1.5	1.5	1.3	2.0	2.6	3.1
Unemployed	1.9	2.1	3.2	3.0	3.7	5.5	3.8	7.0	5.6
Armed forces, total	1.1	0.4	11.4	1.3	0.3	0.2	1.3	2.6	1.1
Not in labor force	8.3	12.0	7.0	10.5	6.6	21.6	10.7	20.1	10.7
FEMALE									
Number	12,025	10,929	11,155	5,349	4,836	2,541	2,503	2,311	2,099
Total	100.0	100.0	100.0	100.0	100.0	100.0	100.0	99.9	99.8
Employed, at work	60.1	61.2	69.7	54.4	49.9	48.9	52.7	56.0	45.5
Employed, not at work	1.8	2.1	2.5	1.3	2.0	2.0	1.9	3.1	2.6
Unemployed	1.7	2.7	3.0	3.7	4.8	4.6	2.4	5.4	4.1
Armed forces, total	0.1	0.1	0.2	0.2	0.1	*	0.1	0.2	0.1
Not in labor force	36.3	33.9	24.6	40.4	43.2	44.5	42.9	35.2	47.5

SOURCE: 5% PUMs "A" Tape.

* N/A.

221

FIGURE 7.5

Measures of Unemployment for Males, Aged 64 + : 1979

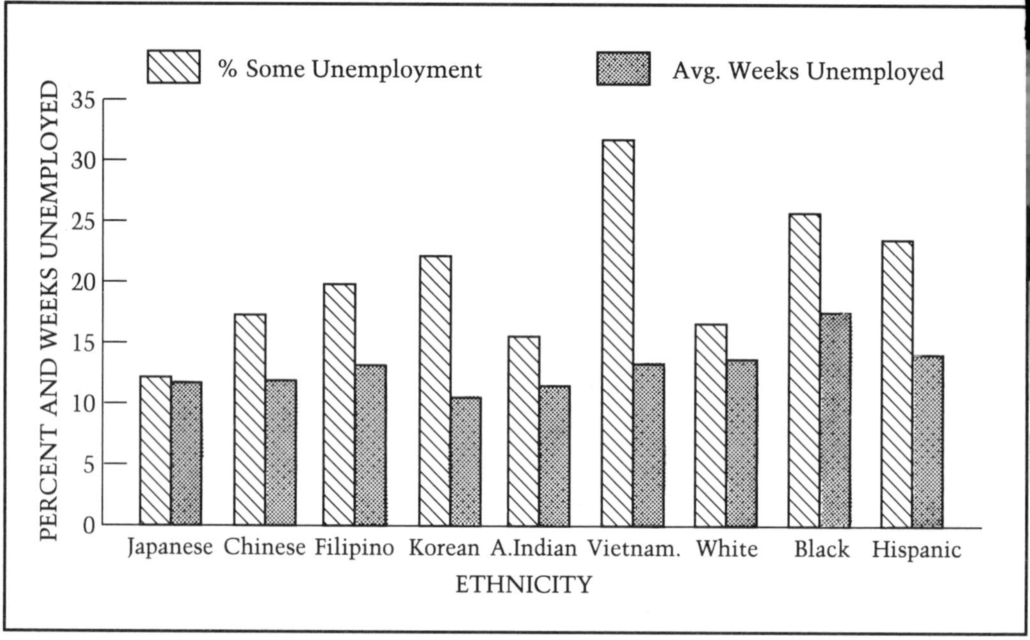

SOURCES: PC80-1-2E and PC-80-1C.

reans showed the fewest weeks unemployed (around 11 weeks), but if we consider 50 weeks complete employment, Koreans were still out of work 22 percent of 1979. As we might expect, blacks (14.5 weeks) and Hispanics (18 weeks) had the longest periods of unemployment. To summarize, Asian Americans were more likely than whites to experience some unemployment in 1979, but for shorter periods of time.

Unemployment figures often mask the problem of underemployment, which the census measured as number of weeks worked in 1979, and average hours per week worked during that same year. Table 7.13 shows weeks worked and hours worked in 1979 by sex.

Except for Koreans, Asian American men all worked slightly fewer hours per week than did whites, and except for Japanese, all Asian Americans worked fewer weeks than did whites. However, all Asian American men experienced fewer weeks unemployed than whites.[11]

Asian women, on the other hand, worked longer hours than white women. Japanese, Chinese, and Filipino women also worked more weeks

[11]The figures shown here are somewhat different from those in Figure 6.2 because of different age specifications.

TABLE 7.13

Measures of Underemployment: Average Hours Worked per Week, Weeks Worked, and Number of Weeks Unemployed, by Sex, in the Labor Force, Aged 25–64: 1979

Measures of Underemployment	Ethnicity (Hours and Weeks)								
	Japanese	Chinese	Filipino	Korean	Asian Indian	Vietnamese	White	Black	Hispanic
MALE									
Average hours worked per week	42.5	42.6	41.3	43.7	43.0	40.9	43.7	39.7	40.8
Weeks worked	48.6	46.6	47.0	45.2	47.0	43.0	48.2	45.4	45.8
Weeks unemployed *	12.9	12.7	12.8	12.4	12.9	13.5	15.2	17.5	13.8
Number	8,492	9,667	7,896	3,144	5,265	1,791	2,173	1,487	1.782
FEMALE									
Average hours worked per week	36.4	37.5	38.4	38.6	37.4	37.9	35.0	36.1	36.3
Weeks worked	44.9	42.4	43.7	40.5	40.3	40.0	41.0	42.7	40.3
Weeks unemployed *	12.4	13.8	12.4	14.0	15.0	14.5	16.0	17.2	**
Number	8,088	7,581	8,592	3,319	2,812	1,405	1,572	1,516	1,186

SOURCE: 5% PUMs "A" Tape.

* Based upon the numbers who experienced some unemployment.

** Not computed for Hispanic females.

than white women; Koreans, Asian Indians, and Vietnamese, slightly less. All had fewer weeks of unemployment than did white women.

We suspected that part of the underemployment of Asian Americans might be due to large numbers of recent immigrants among Chinese, Filipinos, Koreans, Asian Indians, and Vietnamese. Table 7.14 shows the numbers of weeks worked in 1979, by period of immigration and nativity. It is clear that among Asian Americans, recency of immigration was extremely important. Except for Japanese, who had few recent immigrants, Asian Americans who immigrated between 1975 and 1980 worked about 5 weeks less than those who immigrated before 1975. Vietnamese, again, were an exception, but since they were refugees, their situation was somewhat different. Asian Indian and Vietnamese natives did not fare so well, but other native Asian Americans worked more weeks than whites, blacks, or Hispanics.[12] It is clear that once Asian Americans were in the United States for some time, their time at work was longer than was the case for whites, blacks, or Hispanics. Unemployment showed the same pattern (Barringer and Cho 1990).

The industrial sector of employment also affected the number of weeks worked. Jobs in the core offered more work time than in the periphery for all ethnicities. But since new immigrants were more likely to work in the periphery, this also had a negative effect upon the employment of immigrant groups of Asian Americans.

Prediction of Occupational Prestige[13]

Nelson (1988) regressed occupational status on work experience (age), education, nativity, length of residence, and industrial sector. She found that when all adjustments had been made, education played the largest part in determining status, followed by industrial sector. Whites and Japanese received the greatest benefit from education. Length of residence, after adjustment, remained significant for Chinese, Filipinos, and Koreans, but not for Asian Indians and Vietnamese. She concluded that only Japanese had reached parity with whites with respect to returns on human capital investment.

---

[12]We do not show figures for black or white immigrants here, because the numbers are small.

[13]Readers with some statistical background may raise eyebrows at this procedure, because education is used as an independent variable. As we pointed out earlier, education goes into the production of prestige scores, so the procedure may appear partially tautological. It is; however, the purpose of this prediction is not only to show the strength of education in determining occupational prestige, but also to show how education affects other variables, such as gender or the industrial sector. We beg indulgence in this matter.

TABLE 7.14

Number of Weeks Worked in 1979, by Period of Immigration/Nativity, and Industrial Sector, in the Labor Force, Aged 25–64

	Ethnicity (Weeks Worked in 1979)								
Determinants	Japanese	Chinese	Filipino	Korean	Asian Indian	Vietnamese	White	Black	Hispanic
PERIOD OF IMMIGRATION/ NATIVITY									
1975–1980	43.6	39.1	41.5	40.0	41.4	41.6	*	*	41.0
1965–1974	44.0	45.3	46.8	44.2	46.5	41.1	*	*	43.7
Before 1965	45.3	46.9	46.3	45.9	47.9	44.9	*	*	43.9
Native	47.7	46.8	45.7	45.6	44.4	44.6	45.2	*	43.8
INDUSTRIAL SECTOR									
Periphery	45.6	43.7	44.1	42.2	43.3	40.2	43.2	42.7	41.8
Core	48.3	46.4	46.2	43.7	46.3	43.0	47.0	45.7	45.6
Number	16,467	17,201	16,646	6,405	8,077	3,196	3,711	2,949	2,968

SOURCE: 5% PUMs "A" Tape.

* Data not readily available.

Our own model adds class of occupation, and combines period of immigration and nativity into a single variable. The model regresses occupational prestige on sex, industrial sector, period of immigration/nativity, years of education, and class of work. Results are shown in Table 7.15. The mean prestige score for each group is shown at the top of the table. Beta, the regression coefficient, is shown for each independent variable. Beta values that were not significant at the .01 level appear with an asterisk. Betas are followed by departures in prestige scores from the mean prestige score, again for each category of the independent variables. For example, sex, when adjusted for all the other variables, had only a slight effect (or in the cases of Filipinos, whites, and Hispanics, no effect) on occupational prestige. Even in the case of Koreans, with Beta equaling .12, females lost only about 2.3 points on a prestige scale. The meaning of that 2.3 points was extremely ambiguous, so for practical purposes we can say that sex lost nearly all its effects upon prestige when adjusted for other variables. This is significant, because, as we shall see, adjusted income effects by sex are great.

Industrial sector remained significant for all groups except Asian Indians. The effects were generally small, and most noticeable for Japanese and Chinese.

Period of immigration/nativity was significant for all Asian American groups, but not for whites, blacks, or Hispanics. The effects were not strong, but they did show the pattern discussed earlier: except for Japanese, new immigrants received lower-prestige occupations. The longer they remained in the United States, the greater their prestige scores. These effects were strongest for Koreans. The effects of age (a proxy for work experience) were either not significant, or were very minor.

Two variables, however, do have significant and strong effects upon occupational prestige when adjusted: education and class of work. The Beta scores for education ranged from a high of .55 for whites to a low of .42 for Koreans. One possible explanation for that magnitude of difference was that many Koreans were self-employed, whereas whites were more likely to be found in firms or bureaucracies, where education had a greater payoff. Vietnamese, also, received low returns on education. The differences between, say, Japanese and whites with fewer than 4 years of high school, and those with a college degree or better, were striking—differences of around 20 prestige points. It does seem to be the case that whites had some advantage over other groups with respect to returns on education.

Class of work also had some interesting effects, independent of education. The effects seemed strongest for Filipinos and Koreans, with those employees of their own corporations receiving the greatest benefit. In fact, all Asian Americans received the highest status from self-employment. Note that private wage workers, by far the largest category, had the greatest loss in status.

In summary, education remains the best predictor of occupational prestige, when adjusted for other variables. Class of employment is also important, with self-employment giving Asian Americans the highest status. Other socioeconomic variables such as sex, industrial sector, age, and period of immigration retain some predictive power when adjusted, but their effects are much diminished when adjusted for education and class of employment.

Conclusion

Asian Americans are well represented among the professions, and appear to be making gains as executives and managers, though apparently not on the boards of the nation's largest corporations. Some, especially Koreans and Chinese, are active as petite bourgeoisie, with relatively high prestige. It appears that Asian Americans, except for Vietnamese, are reasonably distributed across occupational categories, with some overrepresentation in service occupations, and underrepresentation only in labor, as compared to whites. It is difficult to make very much out of the 1989 Current Population Survey data, because all Asian Americans and Pacific Islander Americans are lumped together. However, the data suggest that Asian Americans should continue to maintain a reasonable distribution in the occupational sphere.

However, Asian Americans, especially women, tend to be employed in the periphery, and many are new immigrants, with lower-prestige occupations. Regression analysis shows that much of the magnitude of those differences is accounted for by levels of education and class of employment. Whites appear to receive higher status from education, especially compared to Koreans and Vietnamese.

Asian Americans may be disadvantaged compared to whites in unemployment, and in several measures of underemployment. But these disadvantages also appear to be tied closely to recent immigration and concentration in the periphery. Also, Asian Americans tend to be unemployed for shorter periods of time than do whites, blacks, and Hispanics.

All these generalizations vary from group to group. Koreans and Vietnamese appear at a disadvantage compared to whites on some measures, and Vietnamese are often in the same company as blacks and Hispanics—on the bottom of the ladder. Japanese are most like whites,

TABLE 7.15
Prediction of Occupational Prestige Scores: 1980

		Ethnicity							
	Japanese	Chinese	Filipino	Korean	Asian Indian	Vietnamese	White	Black	Hispanic
MEAN (PRESTIGE SCORE)	43.5	45.1	42.4	41.1	52.1	44.4	42.3	35.1	35.1
SEX									
Male	0.6	1.0	**	2.3	1.1	0.5	-0.1	-1.3	-0.3
Female	-0.5	-1.1	**	-1.9	-1.7	-0.6	0.1	1.2	0.4
Beta	0.04	0.06	0.00*	0.12	0.07	0.04	0.01*	0.09	0.02*
SECTOR									
Periphery	-1.9	-1.9	-1.4	-0.5	-0.1	-1.4	-1.0	-1.0	-1.2
Core	2.5	3.3	1.6	1.0	0.1	1.4	1.1	1.3	1.5
Beta	0.14	0.15	0.09	0.04	0.01*	0.09	0.08	0.08	0.09
PERIOD OF IMMIGRATION									
1975–1980	0.97	-2.1	-3.5	-2.5	-0.7	-0.4	0.4	0.3	-0.5
1965–1974	-2.3	-0.1	0.6	1.1	1.1	1.9	-1.5	1.5	-0.9
Before 1965	-2.8	1.5	2.4	4.1	-0.6	0.6	-0.8	1.5	0.3
Native	0.6	0.8	1.5	3.7	-0.2	3.7	**	**	0.3
Beta	0.08	0.07	0.09	0.14	0.06	0.06	0.02*	0.02*	0.03*
AGE									
25–34	-1.0	-0.1	0.2	**	-0.7	-0.4	-1.5	**	**
35–44	1.3	1.0	0.8	0.2	1.1	0.9	1.0	0.7	0.7
45–54	0.8	-0.5	-0.9	-0.1	-0.6	**	1.0	**	-0.3
55+	-0.9	-0.9	-2.1	-1.6	-0.2	-0.2	0.1	-1.4	-1.1
Beta	0.06	0.04	0.5	0.02*	0.05	0.06*	0.08	0.04*	0.04*

TABLE 7.15 (continued)

					Ethnicity				
	Japanese	Chinese	Filipino	Korean	Asian Indian	Vietnamese	White	Black	Hispanic
YEARS OF EDUCATION									
Less than high school	-10.6	-11.4	-13.1	-8.6	-16.9	-6.3	-9.0	-5.8	-5.6
High school	-6.0	-6.9	-8.1	-6.0	-11.8	-2.9	-3.0	-1.2	0.3
College, 1–3 years	-0.3	-1.7	-2.4	0.2	-7.6	2.5	2.3	4.6	6.5
College, 4 years	10.6	9.8	9.0	8.4	7.3	13.7	13.9	17.7	19.2
Beta	0.50	0.53	0.53	0.42	0.51	0.45	0.55	0.50	0.52
CLASS OF WORKER									
Private wage worker	-1.1	-1.6	-1.3	-2.0	-1.7	-1.1	-0.9	-1.6	-0.9
Federal gov't worker	0.5	**	-0.2	1.5	3.5	2.8	0.7	2.5	1.7
State gov't worker	4.3	4.6	4.1	9.3	3.4	7.6	2.5	3.9	2.3
Local gov't worker	2.7	3.4	2.9	5.3	3.4	4.9	1.9	3.7	1.4
Self-employed, unincorporated	-0.4	5.4	9.3	4.7	6.5	4.7	1.6	6.6	7.0
Employee of own corporation	7.5	7.9	21.9	8.3	10.3	11.7	8.5	15.1	9.0
Unpaid family worker	-6.4	-0.3	-2.5	-3.0	-2.2	1.7	-5.1	8.2	-1.6
Beta	0.14	0.17	0.22	0.22	0.17	0.18	0.12	0.19	0.14
R	0.597	0.659	0.623	0.611	0.602	0.539	0.575	0.576	0.582
R^2	0.357	0.435	0.388	0.373	0.363	0.291	0.330	0.332	0.339

SOURCE: 5% PUMs "A" Tape.

* Not Significant at the 0.01 level.

** Data not readily available.

229

TABLE 7.16

Occupations of Asian Americans and Pacific Islanders, by Gender, Aged 16+

Occupations*	Year (Percentage)	
	Male	Female
Total	100.0	100.0
Executive, administrative, managerial	11.9	11.4
Professional specialty	22.7	15.8
Technical	5.5	4.8
Sales	11.0	10.9
Administrative assistance	9.0	20.4
Service (all)	13.1	15.2
Farming	1.7	0.3
Precision production	10.8	3.9
Machine operator	6.8	8.8
Transportation	2.5	**
Handler, helper	2.2	2.5
Armed forces	**	**
Never worked	2.8	6.0

SOURCE: Current Population Survey, 1989.

*Data were not disaggregated by ethnicity.

**Data not readily available.

probably because most of them are native-born Americans. Still, occupational data indicate that Asian Americans are holding their own compared to whites, and have escaped the "castelike" status of blacks and Hispanics. This is not necessarily the case with income, however, as we shall see.

INCOMES: THE QUESTION OF PARITY

OUR EXAMINATION of Asian Americans to this point shows that most groups have more stable households and families, compared to other Americans. Asian Americans far excel other Americans in terms of education. Finally, with a few exceptions, they appear to hold their own in terms of occupational status. These points are not ordinarily disputed, but there is great debate about how well those strengths are converted into earnings.

Income is the ultimate criterion in the literature for the success of immigrants or minorities in American society. There are several reasons why this is so: first, income is undeniably the first indicator of success in a capitalist society; and second, income is seen as an "objective" indicator, less subject to interpretation than, say, occupational prestige. There are a number of reasons why income is not quite as objective as some may believe, however, and one must maintain a proper dose of skepticism about the data.[1]

There are several other potential problems with income data. Most

[1]Informants may not have an accurate estimate of their various incomes. After all, the person responding to the census questionnaire or interview is being asked about the personal, investment, and welfare incomes of every member of the household. Even if a respondent knows the answer to all those questions, he or she may underreport certain types of income, not believing that the response is confidential. Acknowledging these problems, we will beg off with the assumption that misinformation is distributed equally among respondents. This would allow comparability, if not absolute accuracy.

studies of income have used wages and salaries, or personal income, as the basis for analysis. However, others have used total income. Occasionally, household or family incomes are cited. It makes a difference if studies cite hourly, or annual incomes, and so on. Small but sometimes significant shifts due to sampling error occur when one uses the 5 percent public use tapes, as compared to the ⅙ sample reported by the Census Bureau.[2] Most studies of personal income restrict the age of samples from 25 to 64, so that the assumption of completed educations can be made. However, census tables and most household data restrict ages from 15 or 16 and above. Also, it makes a great deal of difference if samples are limited to all persons, to the work force, or to only those persons in the work force with incomes. Finally, the dispersion of incomes is so great that one must be cautious about making assertions about minor differences in mean or median incomes, even with the large sample sizes involved.

Literature on the incomes of immigrants and minorities in the United States is extensive. The particular line of investigations relevant to Asian Americans began with an examination of the costs of being "black" (nonwhite) from 1950 and 1960 Census data (Siegel 1965). Siegel found that although occupational differentiation between whites and non-whites decreased between 1950 and 1960, the rate of income return on education was less for non-whites. About 40 percent of income differentials were attributed to the "cost of being black."

The U.S. Commission on Civil Rights (1978) conducted similar investigations with the 1960 and 1970 Census data, plus data from the 1976 Social Indicators Survey (Survey Marketing Services, 1978). They concluded that adjusted incomes for minorities and women had actually declined relative to whites from 1959 to 1969. The commission found some improvement in 1975, but pointed out that regional differences caused Japanese and Chinese male incomes to decline. Their general conclusions were that, although Asian American incomes were quite high, when adjusted for education, whites had a decided advantage. Similar findings were reported for Hispanics (Poston, Alvirez, and Tienda 1976).

Suzuki (1977) raised objections to reports of equity in Japanese American and white incomes, pointing out that Japanese were far better educated than whites, and lived in urban areas with higher living costs. Subsequently, Morrison Wong (1980) compared Chinese males from samples in the 1960 and 1970 Census data. He found also that although Chinese men were much better educated than whites, their earnings

---

[2]For example, in this study, we used the ⅙ sample to report household incomes in Chapter 4, and the Public Use Sample in Chapter 7. Differences are slight, but they create somewhat different pictures.

were relatively uncompensated. Hirschman and Wong (1981) compared Japanese, Chinese, Filipino, and white males' incomes, using 1960, 1970, and 1975 Census data. They reported that older generations of Asians were less well-educated than were whites, but that younger generations were far better educated than whites. Asian Americans were overrepresented in the professions. Japanese most closely resembled whites; Chinese, the least, largely because about twice as many Chinese were professionals. Filipinos were the most disadvantaged, but had made considerable progress from 1960 to 1975. Controlling for education, Asian Americans earned far less than whites.

Wong (1982), using the same data base, reported that, as of 1969, only Japanese had reached income equity with whites, but that by 1975, both Filipinos and Japanese had reached parity. Chinese were far behind. Wong and Hirschman (1983) examined women's incomes and found that Asian American women had modest income advantages over whites because they were younger, had better educations, and were more likely to live in SMSAs than their white counterparts. But although white women tended to be professionals, Asian women were more likely to be found in service and blue-collar occupations. Some of their interpretations were questioned by Woo (1985).

Once more, Hirschman and Wong (1984) examined the 1960, 1970, and 1980 Census data to compare Japanese, Chinese, and Filipino workers with whites and blacks. Except for Chinese, they found a decline in direct negative effects on earnings during the 1970s, attributing this phenomenon to less overt discrimination. However, when adjusted, all the minorities' incomes except Japanese suffered by comparison with whites.

Chiswick (1983), using the 1970 Census data, found that overall, Asian American employment, education, and earnings equaled those of whites. However, Filipinos were found to suffer some disadvantages. Fujii and Mak studied Asian American men in Hawaii, using data from a 1976 Office of Economic Opportunity Census Update Survey (Survey Marketing Services, 1978). They found that Chinese and Korean men had higher incomes than whites, but that all Asian Americans enjoyed fewer returns on education than did whites. They also found that all immigrants except whites suffered relative disadvantages to natives. They concluded that "It pays to be white in Hawaii."

Cabezas, Shinagawa, and Kawaguchi (1986) made one of the most comprehensive surveys of literature on this subject, accompanied by a study of personal earnings, which finds evidence of economic disadvantages of Asian Americans in California.

Studies of the 1980 Census data show the same conclusions and contradictions found in earlier data. The U.S. Commission on Civil Rights

(1988), however, reversed its 1978 conclusions and argued that Asian Americans had reached essential parity with whites. They pointed out that family incomes of most Asian American groups were higher than those of whites. Many of their conclusions were based upon controlled comparisons of *native men* only. The commission tended to ascribe other differences to disadvantages of recent immigrants, whom they acknowledged but dismissed in favor of natives for analysis. Their actual findings were very similar to what we report here, but we are somewhat puzzled by their conclusions, especially with regard to Koreans and Vietnamese. In any case, the report was not well received by Asian Americans, as its published review indicates (U.S. Commission on Civil Rights 1988, 119–131).

Poston and Zhongke (1989) agreed with the commission in general, noting that Asian American immigrant men often showed higher human capital returns than did native whites. They pointed out, however, that some Asian Americans, notably Koreans, Vietnamese, and other smaller groups, were very disadvantaged compared to whites. Trieman and Lee (1988), in a study of Los Angeles, showed findings that contradicted the commission. They concluded that Asian Americans do less well than average if their higher skills and educations are taken into account. Tienda and Lii (1987) also show findings that tend to disagree with the commission, but we would discount the Asian American data because all groups were lumped together. The problem of aggregating Asian Americans is also true of a study by Sandefur and Pahari (1989), which tends to agree with the commission.

Finally, Barringer, Takeuchi, and Xenos (1990), using some of the material reported here, concluded that only Japanese Americans had reached parity with whites as of 1979, and, in some respects, even that was open to challenge. They also concluded that Asian Americans were too heterogeneous to be studied as a single entity.

In summary, although Asian American incomes appear higher than those of whites, Asian Americans are also much better educated. When a number of factors are controlled, whites still appear to have some advantages, except possibly in the case of Japanese Americans. Data on Japanese, Chinese, and Filipinos (the only groups large enough for such comparisons) indicate relative improvement since 1960. In any case, there is a wide disparity among Asian Americans, so generalizations must be made cautiously.

Most of the literature on this subject has been for males only, or has treated males and females separately. In the following analyses, we shall include both males and females, with gender breakdowns where relevant.

FIGURE 8.1

Personal Income, by Sex, Wage, and Salary, Aged 25–64: 1979

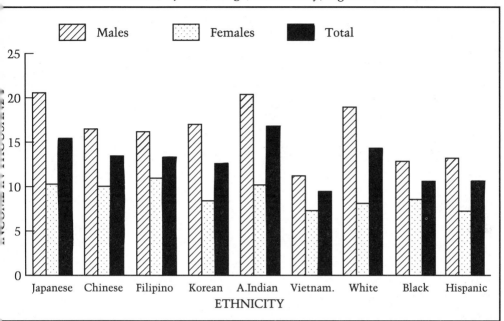

SOURCE: PUMS "A" 5% Tape.

Personal Incomes

Although some literature gives the impression that Asian Americans' unadjusted personal incomes are higher than those of whites, this depends in part on data used. Figure 8.1 shows that the personal incomes of only Japanese ($15,256) and Asian Indians ($16,757) exceeded those of whites ($14,233). These figures were for employed persons aged 25 to 64. Incomes of Chinese ($13,326), Filipinos ($13,194), Koreans ($12,347), and Vietnamese ($9,429) were all at least $1,000 less than whites'. Vietnamese personal income, in fact, was less than for blacks and Hispanics. Both Japanese and Asian Indian males showed slightly higher incomes than did white males. However, Japanese, Chinese, Filipino, and Asian Indian females all had much higher personal incomes than those of white females. Vietnamese men and women had the lowest incomes of all.

More conventional data, for employed persons aged 16 and over, are shown in Table 8.1. These data were directly from census tables (PC80-

TABLE 8.1

Personal Income Distribution of Employed Asian Americans, Aged 16+: 1980

Income Category	Ethnicity					
	Japanese	Chinese	Filipino	Korean (Percentage)	Asian Indian	Vietnamese
TOTAL PERSONS WITH INCOME	495,711	517,301	471,472	172,471	222,629	112,805
MEDIAN	$10,287	$8,133	$9,406	$7,977	$10,319	$5,886
MEAN	$13,104	$11,738	$11,468	$11,489	$15,074	$7,347
TOTAL	100.0	100.0	99.9	99.9	100.1	99.9
Less than $5,000	28.0	34.8	27.2	34.0	28.0	45.5
$5,000–$9,999	20.8	22.4	26.0	25.2	20.9	25.8
$10,000–$11,999	7.9	6.8	9.7	7.7	6.6	8.1
$12,000–$14,999	9.9	8.0	11.0	8.5	7.9	8.7
$15,000–$19,999	12.3	10.1	12.9	9.3	11.2	7.2
$20,000–$24,999	9.1	7.1	6.7	6.2	8.2	2.8
$25,000–$34,999	7.3	6.6	3.8	4.4	9.2	1.3
$35,000–$49,999	2.8	2.5	1.2	2.2	4.3	0.3
$50,000 or more	1.9	1.7	1.4	2.4	3.8	0.2

SOURCES: PC 80-1-2E and PC 80-1-1C, Table 95.

1-2E) and were probably better figures for citation. Here, figures *did* in-. dicate that Asian Americans, except Vietnamese, had higher mean incomes than did whites. However, only Japanese and Asian Indian mean incomes were sufficiently higher to draw notice. For all practical purposes, Chinese, Filipino, and Korean mean incomes were the same as those of whites. Distributions of incomes were shown for Asian Americans. Note the high percentage of Asian Indians (3.8 percent) with incomes over $50,000, and the high percentage of Vietnamese (45.5 percent) with incomes less than $5,000.

The U.S. Commission on Civil Rights (1988) showed the depressing effects of recent immigration upon income, and the rising incomes of immigrants with longer periods of stay.[3] Table 8.2 shows personal incomes by period of immigration and nativity. With the exception of Japanese, who enjoyed a very high increase in income for the period, Asian Americans all showed a similar pattern: incomes were much lower for

[3]The commission also analyzed the effects of immigration upon whites, which we have not done, because of small numbers. The effects of immigration upon whites are in fact insignificant (see our regressions).

TABLE 8.2

Personal Income, by Period of Immigration/Nativity, Persons in the Work Force, Wage and Salary Only: 1979

Period of Immigration/Nativity	Ethnicity								
	Japanese	Chinese	Filipino	Korean	Asian Indian (Dollars)	Vietnamese	White	Black	Hispanic
NUMBER	21,129	21,725	19,689	8,833	10,477	4,916	4,106	4,151	4,887
Total	15,215	13,309	12,315	13,013	16,667	9,391	14,186	10,542	10,638
Immigrants									
1975–1980	19,236	7,946	9,074	9,027	11,414	9,298	*	*	6,811
1970–1974	13,330	11,797	13,588	12,609	17,522	8,406	*	*	8,352
1965–1969	12,593	14,333	15,643	16,975	23,753	12,132	*	*	10,510
1960–1964	11,370	15,837	15,846	16,822	26,791	11,100	*	*	11,182
1950–1959	10,897	16,663	15,494	20,128	25,101	18,338	*	*	13,662
Before 1950	13,602	16,205	13,363	17,425	18,739	13,435	*	*	11,723
Natives	15,656	15,971	12,756	15,909	11,396	13,618	*	*	11,144

SOURCE: 5% PUMs "A" Tape.

* N/A.

those who immigrated between 1975 and 1980, and then increased to a high for those who immigrated somewhere between 1950 and 1960. Again excepting Japanese, natives earned less than immigrants in 1979. Hispanics showed a similar pattern. Among natives, Japanese, Chinese, Koreans, and Asian Indians all earned considerably more than whites. These data suggest that Asian immigrants suffered earnings losses during their first 5 to 10 years in the United States, but made up those losses after a stay of 10 years or more. Japanese were an exception because, as we noted earlier, their recent "immigrants" were apparently highly paid employees of Japanese firms.

It is possible, although unlikely, that the phenomenon observed in Table 8.2 is an artifact of cross-sectional analysis, and that, in fact, succeeding cohorts of immigrants are earning less. Table 8.3 shows the median personal incomes of Japanese, Chinese, and Filipino males and females in 1959, 1969, and 1979. The longitudinal data showed that, although Chinese and Filipino males still lagged behind white males in 1979, their incomes relative to whites showed a steady increase since 1969. In all cases, Asian American females earned more than white females in 1979. Furthermore, unagreggated data from the 1989 Current Population Survey, shown in Table 8.4, suggested that the incomes of Asian American men as a whole equaled white men's incomes. Asian women, as in 1979, earned more than did white women. These data did include Asian and Pacific Islanders, which probably depressed the Asian figures somewhat.

The figures shown above were unadjusted for other factors that affect earnings. But Table 8.5, taken from the U.S. Commission on Civil Rights (1988) report, shows an increase in both hourly and annual earnings of Japanese, Chinese, and Filipino native-born men, relative to whites, from 1960 to 1980. These data all suggested that earnings of Asian Americans were improving over time, despite the temporary income losses of new immigrants. Of course, disaggregated data from the 1990 Census will give more definitive data on this subject.[4]

Education and Income

The very high levels of education of Asian Americans have led to much speculation about the contribution of education to earnings. Ta-

[4]The Public Use Samples are promised for 1993. Some Asian Americans have complained about the lack of detail about Asian Americans in the yearly population surveys. Census Bureau spokespeople are perfectly correct in replying that the samples are too small for further breakdown, but it does seem odd that Pacific Islanders are still included with Asian Americans.

TABLE 8.3

Personal Incomes for Japanese, Chinese, and Filipino: 1959, 1969, 1979, Aged 15+, Adjusted to 1980 Dollars

	1959		1969		1979	
Ethnicity	Median	Ratio to White	Median	Ratio to White	Median	Ratio to White
JAPANESE						
Male	10,035	1.00	14,998	1.19	15,026	1.17
Female	4,893	1.40	6,408	1.39	7,410	1.38
CHINESE						
Male	8,634	0.86	10,343	0.82	10,749	0.83
Female	5,142	1.46	5,319	1.15	8,253	1.54
FILIPINO						
Male	7,595	0.76	9,939	0.79	10,797	0.84
Female	3,776	1.07	6,956	1.51	6,064	1.13
WHITE						
Male	10,000	1.00	12,579	1.00	12,881	1.00
Female	3,524	1.00	4,609	1.00	5,356	1.00

SOURCES: PC80-1-2E and PC80-1-1C; Tables 96, 97, 98, PC(2)-5A, PC(2)-1C.

TABLE 8.4

Income Update: Total Personal Income: March 1989

	Ethnicity (Percentage)					
	Asian and Pacific Islanders		Black		White	
Income in Dollars	Male	Female	Male	Female	Male	Female
TOTAL NUMBER	2,122	2,093	8,610	10,380	75,246	77,494
MEAN	$22,090	$13,550	$14,410	$9,930	$22,500	$11,518
Total	100.0	100.1	99.8	100.1	100.2	100.0
1–10,000	37.7	61.2	51.5	68.1	32.4	61.9
12,500–20,000	20.2	19.2	23.9	20.2	23.7	21.8
22,500–30,000	16.9	9.6	13.8	8.2	18.2	10.0
32,500–40,000	9.3	5.4	6.3	2.5	11.3	3.8
42,500–50,000	5.3	2.4	2.3	0.6	6.3	1.3
52,500–60,000	4.6	1.1	0.7	0.3	2.8	0.5
62,500–70,000	1.7	0.6	0.5	0.1	1.8	0.2
72,500–80,000	1.6	0.1	0.1	*	1.1	0.2
82,500–97,500	1.4	0.4	0.2	*	0.9	0.1
100,000+	1.3	0.1	0.5	0.1	1.7	0.2

SOURCE: Current Population Survey, March 1989.

* Values missing, or too few cases.

ble 8.6 shows the marginal increase in earnings for various progressive levels of education in 1979. Note that at the lowest levels of education shown (fewer than 12 years), Japanese and whites had a noticeable advantage over other groups, averaging $3,000 or more over others. Marginal increases for a high-school education were greatest for Chinese ($2,985) and Hispanics ($2,502). Increases for some with college completion were low except for Koreans ($2,520). In general, increases were greater for college completion, and here, Japanese ($5,824), Hispanics ($3,913), and whites ($4,031) showed the greatest advantage. The greatest income increases came with the equivalent of a doctorate, with income jumps of from $11,634 for Filipinos, $10,845 for Hispanics, and $8,819 for Asian Indians, to a low of around $3,500 for Vietnamese and blacks. Census data cannot tell us how much of these differences are due to discrimination, but it seems unlikely that there would be greater discrimination against Japanese than against Filipinos. More likely, occupation and choice determine income differences at this educational level. These data suggest that Asian Americans in general gain the greatest in income with higher levels of education, especially with postgraduate educations.

Turning again to analysis from the U.S. Commission on Civil Rights (1988), Table 8.7 shows earnings of Japanese, Chinese, and Filipino native men relative to whites, for various levels of education for 1960 and again in 1980. For 8 years of education, all groups increased from 1960 to 1980, relative to whites. The same was true of a high-school education. Japanese, Chinese, and Filipino men with a college education showed increases from 1960 to 1980, with only Filipinos lagging behind whites. Given the fact that Filipino immigrants were much better educated than natives, these figures would be different if immigrants had been included. Still, an improvement in returns on education for Asian Americans appeared to be taking place over time.

TABLE 8.5

Ratio of Japanese, Chinese, and Filipino Yearly and Hourly Earnings to Whites, Native–Born Men, Aged 25–64: 1960 and 1980

	1960		1980	
Ethnicity	Yearly	Hourly	Yearly	Hourly
Japanese	0.99	0.92	1.07	1.09
Chinese	1.14	1.06	1.08	1.17
Filipino	0.65	0.70	0.85	0.91

SOURCE: U.S. Commission on Civil Rights, 1988, p. 102.

TABLE 8.6
Marginal Increase in Income for Additional Education Completed, by Race: 1979*

Years of Education	Ethnicity								
	Japanese	Chinese	Filipino	Korean	Asian Indian (Dollars)	Vietnamese	White	Black	Hispanic
Fewer than 12									
Total income	11,187	7,587	9,124	7,603	8,430	7,309	11,346	8,827	8,550
12 (high school)									
Total income	12,921	10,573	10,731	8,881	10,255	8,730	12,604	10,136	11,052
(marginal increase)	(1,734)	(2,985)	(1,607)	(1,278)	(1,824)	(1,421)	(1,258)	(1,309)	(2,502)
13–15									
Total income	14,036	12,408	11,865	11,401	11,046	9,454	14,095	11,690	12,346
(marginal increase)	(1,115)	(1,835)	(1,134)	(2,520)	(791)	(724)	(1,491)	(1,554)	(1,294)
16 (college)									
Total income	19,860	14,612	13,024	13,670	13,614	12,274	18,126	14,796	16,259
(marginal income)	(5,824)	(2,204)	(1,159)	(2,269)	(2,568)	(2,820)	(4,031)	(3,106)	(3,913)
17–19									
Total income	18,144	16,841	16,179	20,005	17,951	14,203	20,183	15,919	15,387
(marginal income)	(−1,716)	(2,229)	(3,155)	(6,335)	(4,338)	(1,929)	(2,057)	(1,123)	(−872)
20 or more (doctorate or equivalent)									
Total income	24,706	25,056	27,813	26,918	26,771	17,939	29,560	19,485	26,232
(marginal increase)	(6,562)	(8,215)	(11,634)	(6,913)	(8,819)	(3,736)	(9,377)	(3,566)	(10,845)
N	15,215	13,309	13,013	12,315	16,677	9,391	14,186	10,542	10,638

SOURCE: 5% PUMs "A" Tape.

* Mean personal income (wages and salaries only).

TABLE 8.7

Hourly Earnings of Japanese, Chinese, and Filipino Men by Years of Education Relative to Whites, Aged 25–64: 1960 and 1980

Ethnicity	8 Years of Education		12 Years of Education		16 Years of Education	
	1960	1980	1960	1980	1960	1980
Japanese	0.75	1.05	0.77	1.04	0.78	1.04
Chinese	0.80	0.90	0.85	0.94	0.91	0.99
Filipino	0.83	1.07	0.79	0.96	0.75	0.86

SOURCE: U.S. Commission on Civil Rights, 1988, p. 107.

Occupations and Income

Table 8.8 shows mean personal incomes for each major occupational category, broken down by sex. First of all, the uniform discrepancies between men's and women's pay were striking. Even among Filipinos, where sex differences were minimal on other measures, the income differentials were enormous. Recall in Chapters 6 and 7 that educational and occupational differences between men and women occurred, especially in some groups like Koreans, but those disparities paled compared to the income gap. Although there was some fluctuation from category to category, white women did not fare much better than Asian American women. As we shall see, the sex gap in income does not disappear when we control for other factors, such as time worked.[5]

Japanese men earned more in managerial positions than white men, but other Asian American men earned much less as executives and managers. In the professions, where Asian Americans often made the strongest showing, only Filipino, Korean, and Asian Indian men earned more than whites. Asian women earned far more than white women in the professions, however. As we moved into white-collar occupations, white men began to show advantages over all Asian Americans, except for Japanese. This discrepancy was particularly noticeable in service occupations, where Asian American men took a real income loss compared to whites. In service occupations, Chinese, Korean, and Vietnamese men earned the same as or less than blacks and Hispanics. Asian

[5]It is striking how much more men earn in occupations once dominated by women. Even in administrative support, for example, men earn roughly 50 percent more than women.

women did somewhat better in service, but their wages were nevertheless low. Throughout labor categories, only Japanese men and women did as well as whites. Recall that large numbers of Koreans and Filipinos were employed as laborers, and in those jobs, they took a large income loss.

These data are important, especially when taken together with educational data from Chapters 6 and 7, where we saw that Asian Americans were much better educated than whites across the board. In these terms, Asian American men, excepting Japanese, appeared very disadvantaged relative to whites. The only occupational category where Asian American men showed near parity with whites is in the professions. By comparison, Asian women were better off than white women, but their wages were still very low. Still, excepting Vietnamese, Asian Americans earned more in almost all occupational categories than did Blacks or Hispanics. The exception is in service occupations, where the low wages of Asian Americans gave some support to the dual labor market theory of Bonacich and Cheng (1984).

Table 8.9 shows personal incomes by class of worker. There are several significant points to be made about these data. First, note that private wage workers were generally paid less than workers in any other category, except unpaid family workers.[6] Whites and Japanese earned more as private wage workers than any other group. But as federal government workers, Japanese, Chinese, and Asian Indians earned more than whites. Except for Vietnamese, Asian Americans did as well as or better than whites as state and local government workers. Except for Koreans and Vietnamese, Asian Americans' wages equaled white wages in the self-employed categories. The relatively poor showing of Chinese and Koreans as employees of their own corporations reflected the small scale and marginality of the petite bourgeoisie. The high incomes of Filipinos and Asian Indians resulted from a large proportion of self-employed professionals.

Examining data from the 1980 Census, Kan and Liu (1986) noted an increase in the educational levels of Asian Americans that was partially attributable to the high educational levels of recent migrants. They concluded that the relatively high proportions of Asian Americans in professional and managerial positions were mismatched (overeducated), a finding noted in the 1978 report of the U.S. Commission on Civil Rights. We were curious to know if this was accompanied by lower incomes. Table 8.10 breaks down managerial and professional occupational cate-

---

[6]This really has become a contradiction in terms. What should the income of an "unpaid" family worker be called?

TABLE 8.8

Personal Income, by Occupational Category and Sex, Aged 25–64, Wages and Salaries

Occupational Category	Japanese		Chinese		Filipino		Korean	
	Male	Female	Male	Female	Male	Female	Male	Female
					(Dollars)			
NUMBER	7,563	7,662	8,856	7,149	6,726	8,387	2,624	2,992
Total	20,341	10,184	16,348	9,540	16,080	10,855	16,952	8,287
Executive, administrative, managerial	26,854	14,821	19,666	13,462	18,314	13,161	20,504	12,810
Professional specialty	22,864	13,540	23,227	14,149	27,403	16,513	25,423	15,269
Technical and related support	19,694	13,078	16,388	12,436	16,130	13,510	16,390	10,415
Sales	20,723	8,236	15,371	8,883	14,267	7,871	15,644	7,569
Administrative support	18,179	10,501	14,527	9,697	13,019	9,778	12,523	8,481
Services (all)	11,526	6,493	8,215	6,203	10,370	6,907	8,286	5,762
Farm, forest, fishery	15,298	7,164	13,392	5,345	9,965	5,884	9,809	5,115
Precision production, craft and repair	18,689	9,541	16,175	7,462	16,426	8,791	15,578	7,570
Operators, assemblers, inspectors	16,438	7,782	9,968	5,433	13,242	7,245	12,310	7,012
Transportation, equipment material movers	16,079	8,811	13,289	5,781	13,711	7,984	11,682	6,588
Handlers, helpers, cleaners	14,337	7,347	10,988	8,373	12,604	6,623	8,770	7,399

SOURCE: 5% PUMs "A" Tape.

gories by class of worker, and gives mean educational levels and mean personal incomes for each of the resulting subcategories. The results generally confirmed the arguments of Kan and Liu, but they also reinforced what other tables have shown, namely, that Japanese were better compensated for their educations than whites, but other Asian Americans were not. Vietnamese, as might be expected, were the least compensated. Except for Japanese, whites were better paid for managerial positions, and were less well-educated than Asian Americans. However, in the professions, Asian Americans were better educated *and* better compensated than whites. It was very clear from this table that Asian Americans found themselves best off as self-employed professionals.[7]

[7]In most Asian countries, there is a semi-humorous stereotype of mothers urging

Ethnicity									
Asian Indian		Vietnamese		White		Black		Hispanic	
Male	Female	Male	Female	Male	Female	Male	Female	Male	Female
4,956	2,598	1,736	1,365	1,929	1,508	1,400	1,492	1,665	1,144
20,264	10,122	11,125	7,242	18,915	8,090	12,727	8,564	13,061	7,148
21,676	10,529	14,581	8,426	25,584	11,446	17,547	12,558	18,778	12,084
25,916	16,603	15,844	10,894	24,408	9,890	16,623	12,319	18,166	9,775
16,178	10,346	11,741	8,578	20,780	7,796	13,856	10,112	18,181	10,542
14,837	5,837	8,666	6,105	18,641	6,532	13,110	7,442	15,054	5,706
12,623	7,471	9,119	7,584	16,818	8,651	14,233	9,984	12,223	8,397
9,316	6,804	6,500	5,456	11,646	4,583	8,794	5,878	9,088	4,846
7,728	4,134	6,389	3,717	13,688	2,948	6,818	10,071	7,662	3,427
16,299	7,566	11,867	7,421	17,517	9,596	13,702	9,393	14,246	9,137
11,806	5,856	10,745	6,562	15,079	7,570	13,908	7,963	12,056	6,071
11,759	3,921	9,513	4,002	16,980	7,589	12,895	7,474	12,591	5,767
9,103	4,768	9,204	5,760	13,005	6,432	10,282	7,143	10,493	8,418

Recall that dual labor market theory (Bonacich 1972) makes much of the double disadvantage of women employed in the periphery. Table 8.11 gives some support to these theories, for in addition to the overall wage gap between men and women, women also earned less in the periphery than in the core. However, the differences were not as great as those between males and females, and were virtually nonexistent for Filipino and Asian Indian women. But men also earned less in the periphery. Note especially the income losses of Chinese and Filipino men in the periphery. This probably reflected the high percentage of employment of Chinese men in service occupations, and Filipino men in service and agriculture.

their children to enter professional schools such as law or medicine rather than liberal arts colleges. Table 8.10 suggests that they may have been wiser than some of their children believed.

TABLE 8.9

Personal Incomes, by Class of Worker and Ethnicity, Aged 16+: 1979

Class of Worker	Ethnicity								
	Japanese	Chinese	Filipino	Korean	Asian Indian (Dollars)	Vietnamese	White	Black	Hispanic
NUMBER	5,354	16,070	16,098	5,681	7,687	3,114	3,474	2,953	2,837
TOTAL	15,215	13,309	13,013	12,315	16,667	9,391	14,186	10,452	10,639
Private wage and salary worker	14,675	12,453	12,283	11,219	15,916	9,336	13,971	10,073	10,259
Federal gov't worker	18,347	18,846	13,246	14,301	20,337	9,653	17,005	13,624	13,192
State gov't worker	14,401	13,559	14,133	16,117	16,137	9,711	13,965	10,223	9,869
Local gov't worker	14,414	14,054	13,195	13,434	14,742	8,752	12,066	11,039	11,164
Self-employed worker, unincorporated	15,816	15,591	17,323	13,187	16,984	10,284	15,486	5,203	16,278
Employee of own corporation	25,637	20,778	40,866	23,311	34,529	18,080	22,605	18,856	17,391
Unpaid family worker	9,584	5,859	5,046	6,127	4,346	4,048	5,627	2,365	6,391

SOURCE: 5% PUMs "A" Tape.

TABLE 8.10

Mean Years of Education and Personal Income, by Class of Worker (Executives and Professionals), by Race: 1979*

Class of Worker	Japanese	Chinese	Filipino	Korean	Asian Indian	Vietnamese	White	Black	Hispanic
TOTAL SAMPLE (NUMBER)	21,129	21,725	19,689	8,833	10,477	4,916	4,887	4,151	4,106
Executives, administrators, and managers (number)	2,352	2,492	1,385	720	1,064	213	497	197	203
Private wage worker									
Mean years of education	14.9	15.3	15.5	15.4	16.7	14.1	14.1	13.2	13.3
Mean income	$23,918	$17,371	$15,767	$18,375	$20,489	$13,648	$21,826	$15,226	$16,239
Government workers (all)									
Mean years of education	15.1	16.2	15.5	16.2	16.5	14.0	14.7	13.7	14.2
Mean income	$19,698	$18,492	$16,059	$15,530	$16,728	$14,407	$18,801	$14,855	$17,789
Self-employed (all)									
Mean years of education	13.4	13.0	14.6	14.8	15.0	13.2	13.5	10.9	11.6
Mean income	$25,163	$16,635	$21,241	$20,112	$19,191	$14,104**	$22,533	$8,498**	$19,078**
Professional specialty (number)	3,055	4,034	3,259	1,102	3,295	368	529	286	234
Private wage workers									
Mean years of education	16.0	17.4	16.7	16.6	18.0	15.6	15.4	14.7	14.0
Mean income	$18,195	$20,741	$18,371	$19,120	$22,698	$14,687	$17,378	$13,163	$14,659
Government workers (all)									
Mean years of education	16.7	17.5	17.0	17.2	18.3	15.6	16.4	15.6	15.7
Mean income	$17,384	$17,147	$18,181	$21,002	$20,268	$13,091	$15,051	$13,767	$12,519
Self-employed (all)									
Mean years of education	17.3	17.9	18.8	17.5	19.0	15.7	17.4	13.7	16.7
Mean income	$35,483	$36,438	$46,314	$37,978	$45,781	$22,635**	$30,018	**	$26,754

SOURCE: 5% PUMs "A" Tape.

* Mean personal income (wages and salaries only).

** N<20.

247

TABLE 8.11

Personal Income, by Sex and Industrial Sector, Wage and Salary

Sex and Industrial Sector	Ethnicity								
	Japanese	Chinese	Filipino	Korean	Asian Indian (Dollars)	Vietnamese	White	Black	Hispanic
MALE									
Total	20,341	16,348	16,080	16,952	20,264	11,125	18,915	12,727	13,061
Periphery	17,780	12,969	13,825	15,467	17,644	9,369	16,760	10,636	10,377
Core	22,288	20,772	17,688	18,709	22,323	12,341	20,148	14,268	15,283
Number	7,563	8,856	6,726	2,624	4,956	1,736	1,929	1,400	1,665
FEMALE									
Total	10,184	9,540	10,855	8,287	10,122	7,242	8,091	8,564	7,148
Periphery	9,337	8,425	10,756	7,920	10,068	6,565	7,130	7,462	6,133
Core	11,650	11,718	11,021	9,133	10,025	8,110	9,712	10,666	9,013
Number	7,662	7,149	8,387	2,992	2,698	1,365	1,508	1,492	1,111

SOURCE: 5% PUMs "A" Tape.

Age and Geographical Variation

As with most other dependent variables, income has a curvilinear relationship with age. Figure 8.2 confirms this for all ethnic groups.

The differences showed up in modal age categories. For most Asian Americans, incomes were highest in the 35-to-44 age brackets. However, for Koreans, whites, and Hispanics, the modal category was age 45 to 54. Note also that Koreans and Vietnamese in the 25-to-34 age bracket had lower incomes than blacks or Hispanics in the same age range.

Figure 8.3 shows broad geographical variations in incomes. The patterns generally corresponded to what we found about occupational prestige: incomes were generally higher for Asian Americans in the East (and also in the northern Midwest) than in the West. The most notable exception were the Chinese, who were very poorly paid in the East. These data were very broadly categorized, and no doubt lost interesting information.[8] A careful study of Asian American occupations and incomes in the largest SMSAs is badly needed.

The Prediction of Personal Income

As we noted in the beginning of this chapter, there have been a number of multivariate studies of Asian American incomes. Ours departs from other such studies primarily because female data are included in the model. We have also employed occupation[9] as a predicting variable rather than occupational prestige, because a previous study found occupational prestige to mask the effects of education (Barringer, Takeuchi, and Xenos 1990).

Table 8.12 shows the results of regressing personal income on sex, industrial sector, period of immigration/nativity, age (as a proxy for job experience), occupation, and education. Because the effects of weeks worked in 1979 and average hours worked in 1979 were quite straightforward, we entered those variables as covariates. Their effects could be

---

[8]These differences fade into insignificance in a multivariate model, so we have not pursued the matter of geographical variation further.

[9]For this purpose, we combined managerial and professional occupations in one category; technical, sales, and administrative support in "white collar"; precision manufacturing and operatives in "precision labor"; operators, transportation workers, and handlers in "labor"; and, finally, combined service and farm into a single category, largely because there were so few farm employees among Asian Americans. We tried other combinations, but the above seemed most sensible. The overall effect of substituting occupation for occupational prestige is negligible, except for removing the masking effects on education as noted in the text.

FIGURE 8.2

Effects of Age upon Personal Income, Age 25–64: 1979

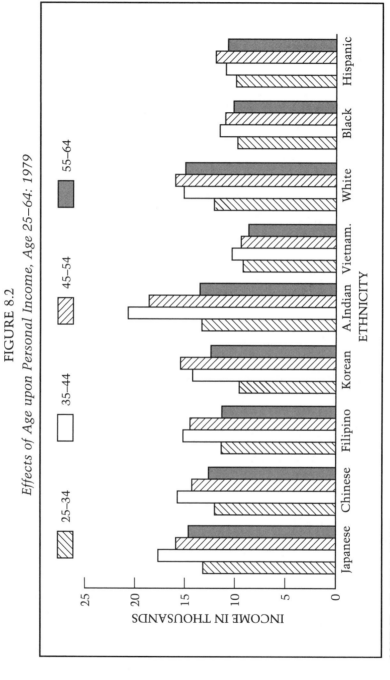

SOURCE: 5% PUMs "A" Tape.

FIGURE 8.3

Effects of Geographical Region upon Personal Income, Aged 25–64: 1979

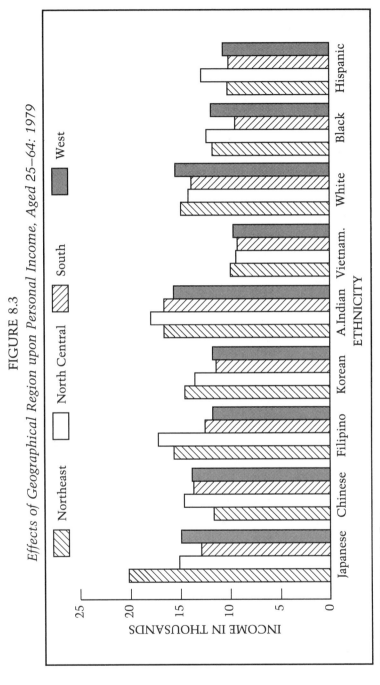

SOURCE: 5% PUMs "A" Tape.

TABLE 8.12

Determinants of Personal Income, Wage and Salary only, Aged 25–64: 1979

					Ethnicity				
Variable/Statistic	Japanese	Chinese	Filipino	Korean	Asian Indian	Viet-namese	White	Black	Hispanic
Grand mean income ($)	15,215	13,309	13,013	12,315	16,667	9,391	14,186	10,452	10,639
Number	15,225	16,005	15,113	5,616	7,654	3,101	3,426	2,976	2,806
Weeks worked in 1979 (covariate)									
F ratio	1,731	4,034	2,108	1,128	1,492	1,098	658	418	608
Average hours worked in 1979 (covariate)									
F ratio	2,154	730	1,545	486	978	299	429	172	238
Sex									
F ratio	1,792	712	798	218	124	112	395	140	197
Eta (unadjusted)	0.45	0.31	0.26	0.37	0.35	0.28	0.47	0.27	0.35
Beta (adjusted)	0.30	0.17	0.19	0.17	0.11	0.16	0.31	0.20	0.22
Deviation in dollars									
Male	3,411	1,700	2,161	2,180	1,100	961	3,052	1,629	1,567
Female	−3,366	−2,105	−1,733	−1,913	−2,023	−1,225	−3,905	−1,521	−2,285
Industrial sector									
F ratio	304	439	116	65	86	50	93	87	98
Eta	0.23	0.29	0.14	0.15	0.18	0.21	0.25	0.27	0.30
Beta	0.11	0.14	0.08	0.09	0.08	0.11	0.13	0.16	0.16
Deviation in dollars									
Periphery	−1,205	−1,197	−712	−812	−1,125	−763	−1,575	−1,144	−1,251
Core	1,406	1,865	809	1,348	1,204	693	1,453	1,361	1,423
Period of immigration									
F ratio	23	149	156	44	106	13	0.25**	0.60**	12
Eta	0.17	0.28	0.24	0.26	0.34	0.10	0.05	0.03	0.16
Beta	0.05	0.13	0.15	0.13	0.17	0.09	0.01	0.02	0.09

252

TABLE 8.12 (continued)

					Ethnicity				
Variable/Statistic	Japanese	Chinese	Filipino	Korean	Asian Indian	Viet-namese	White	Black	Hispanic
Deviation in dollars									
1975–1980	1,879	-2,519	-2,487	-1,701	-2,782	-162	1,346	-1,275	-2,280
1965–1974	539	-225	530	842	1,161	368	-527	-670	-565
Before 1965	-768	1,572	1,919	2,363	4,873	2,291	-168	661	1,022
Native	-137	1,180	499	1,960	-588	3,799	5	17	223
Age (experience)									
F ratio	335	137	60	20	61	5**	47	23	16
Eta	0.15	0.14	0.19	0.21	0.25	0.07	0.15	0.10	0.09
Beta	0.21	0.13	0.09	0.08	0.12	0.05	0.16	0.13	0.10
Deviation in dollars									
25–34	-3,269	-1,563	-993	-1,107	-1,794	16	-2,309	-1,270	-924
35–44	1,600	1,425	765	726	1,797	321	625	793	337
45–54	2,147	1,413	1,072	1,291	1,187	-284	2,063	1,055	1,238
55–64	1,253	634	-145	-491	688	-1,524	1,201	542	946
Occupation*									
F ratio	135	162	259	70	105	28	18	22	13
Eta	0.35	0.42	0.38	0.43	0.45	0.34	0.30	0.31	0.29
Beta	0.17	0.19	0.24	0.20	0.21	0.16	0.13	0.17	0.12
Deviation in dollars									
Service and farm	-2,501	-2,831	-2,450	-1,947	-2,931	-1,295	-1,084	-1,728	-1,208
Labor	-2,338	-1,419	-1,519	-3,071	-3,339	-233	-1,387	-845	-582
Precision labor and operators	-1,212	-785	-855	-1,041	-2,934	2	-914	340	389
White collar	-605	-843	-1,262	-1,069	-2,925	-634	-579	467	-345
Professional and management	2,740	2,609	3,743	4,067	2,818	2,384	2,454	2,329	1,972

TABLE 8.12 (continued)

Variable/Statistic	Ethnicity								
	Japanese	Chinese	Filipino	Korean	Asian Indian	Viet-namese	White	Black	Hispanic
Education									
F ratio	111	204	187	53	65	25	48	26	40
Eta	0.28	0.40	0.34	0.42	0.42	0.33	0.30	0.26	0.32
Beta	0.17	0.23	0.21	0.18	0.17	0.16	0.22	0.19	0.23
Deviation in dollars									
Less than high school	-2,297	-3,115	-1,933	-1,448	-3,362	-712	-2,593	-1,345	-1,618
High school	-1,520	-1,655	-1,579	-1,107	-2,604	-460	-902	-77	470
College 1–3 years	-483	-445	-849	-437	-2,148	-140	30	520	1,603
College 4 years	2,601	408	-310	-648	-1,513	1,207	3,162	3,279	3,497
College postgraduate	2,628	3,597	3,783	4,659	2,300	3,133	5,601	4,177	5,143
R	0.654	0.667	0.630	0.651	0.669	0.661	0.673	0.579	0.643
R²	0.427	0.445	0.397	0.424	0.448	0.437	0.453	0.335	0.414

SOURCE: 5% PUMs "A" Tape.

* See Text.

** Not Significant at 0.01 level.

seen in the F ratios for each ethnicity.[10] The table showed unadjusted effects for each of the predicting variables through the statistic *Eta*, which is comparable to the correlation coefficient. Adjusted effects were shown both through *Beta*, the standardized regression coefficient, and more directly by gains and losses in income for each category of the predicting variables. For example, for Japanese, the importance of gender could be seen in the relatively large *Beta* (.30) and the very large difference in adjusted male and female incomes ($18,635 for males, as compared to $11,859 for females).

Generally, gender retained its predictive power for income, even after other variables were accounted for. Adjusted gender effects were strongest for whites (B = .31) and for Japanese, as noted above. Gender effects were weakest for Asian Indians (B = .11). Industrial sector had a weaker, but significant, effect, ranging from relatively weak effects for Filipinos and Asian Indians (B = .08) to quite strong effects for Chinese (B = .14) and for blacks and Hispanics (B = .16). In general, whites (B = .13) were more affected by industrial sector than were Asian Americans.

Period of immigration/nativity had the greatest adjusted effects for those Asian American groups with large numbers of recent immigrants—Chinese and Koreans (B = .13), Filipinos (B = 15), and Asian Indians (B = .17). The adjusted effects of immigration/ nativity for those groups showed the same pattern as noted previously, that is, new immigrants earned the least, and older immigrants earned more than natives.

Age showed variable effects and was more important for Japanese (B = .21) and whites (B = .16); less important for Koreans and Filipinos, and least for Vietnamese (B = .05).

Occupation and education both made large contributions to income, comparable to gender in magnitude. Occupation had the greatest effect for Filipinos (B = .24), Asian Indians (B = .21), and for Koreans (B = .20). The effects were least for whites (B = .13) and Hispanics (B = .12). Note, however, that education was correspondingly important for whites (B = .22) and for Hispanics (B = .23). Education also had strong effects for Chinese (B = .23) and Filipinos (B = .21). Taken together, these data suggested that education *and* occupation were both important for Asian Americans in the determination of personal incomes. Practically, persons of Asian ancestry must have good educations, plus the proper occupational opportunities or choices, in order to obtain high incomes. To illustrate, a Korean could gain around $4,600 with 20 years of education,

---

[10]F ratios vary by sample size, so they should not be compared across ethnicities. They can be compared within each ethnicity, however. In doing so, note the strong contributions of weeks worked in 1979. This was expected, of course, because of the direct consequences in wages for lost time at work.

but lose around $3,000 if engaged in labor. On top of that, a Korean woman could lose another $2,000. These are not trivial gains and losses where the mean Korean income is just above $12,000.

Note that whites gained more income with college educations and above than did any of the Asian American groups. This seems ironic, given the superiority of Asian Americans' educations. However, Asian Americans gained more earnings in the occupations of professions and management[11] than did whites. The upshot seemed to be that whites gained more from education directly than Asian Americans, and that Asian Americans must translate their superior educations to appropriate occupations to gain commensurate incomes.

All in all, these models appear satisfactory, but still account for somewhat less than 50 percent of the variance in personal income. The census cannot give us direct data on such important matters as job discrimination, parents' backgrounds, work performance, conscientiousness, and so on. A well-designed study of such factors would give us invaluable insights.

Household Income

As we noted in Chapter 5, households are important for Asian Americans. The U.S. Commission on Civil Rights (1988) noted that Asian American family incomes generally were greater than those of whites. This appears to be corroborated by Figure 8.4. First, note that average household incomes *were* higher for Asian Americans (again excepting Vietnamese) than for whites, blacks, or Hispanics. Japanese showed the highest household incomes ($25,719), closely followed by Filipinos ($24,960) and Asian Indians ($24,122). Koreans fared less well ($22,312), but still earned more than whites ($20,572). This figure also showed per capita household incomes. Because Asian American households usually contained more children, their per capita incomes dropped relative to those of whites.[12] However, Japanese and Asian Indians still showed higher per capita incomes than whites, probably because of lower fertility.

The income gains from additional workers (Table 8.13) were remarkable for all groups, but the real advantage for Asian Americans was that their households contained more workers than did those of whites. Japanese, Chinese, Filipinos, and Koreans, especially, had higher percentages of 2, 3, 4, and 5 or more workers than did whites. Since the

[11]Likely only in professions, except for Japanese. See Table 8.10.
[12]Per capita household income seems particularly difficult to interpret, and in any case would always be affected by fertility.

FIGURE 8.4

Household Income and Per Capita Household Income, Householders, Aged 16 + : 1980

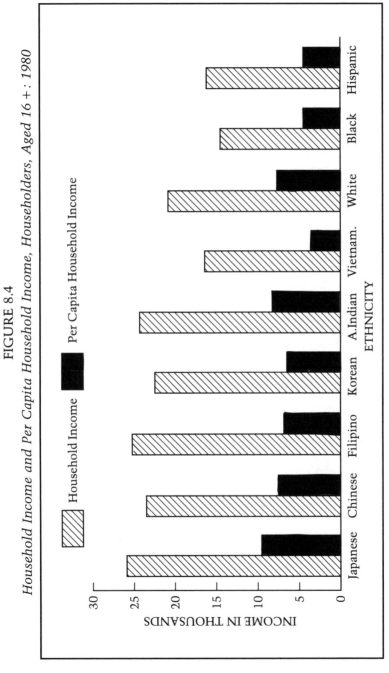

SOURCE: 5% PUMS "A" Tape.

increase for each additional worker averaged around $4,000 (in some cases, much more), the advantage of large households was obvious.

Furthermore, Asian Americans, except Japanese, had the largest percentages of married-family households, and these households had much higher incomes than other types. Married-family households, on the average, earned $10,000 or more over households headed by single females, and even more over non-family households. Part of the reason for the advantage of married-family households was a larger potential for workers, as we shall see.

Whatever advantages Asian American households might have in incomes, a large percentage of Asian American families were below the poverty level in 1979. Table 8.13 shows that Japanese (4.2 percent) had the fewest families in poverty, but Chinese (10.5 percent), Koreans (13.1 percent), and Vietnamese (35.1 Percent) all had larger percentages of families in poverty than did whites (7.0 percent). Except for Vietnamese, however, Asian Americans were far better off in this regard than blacks and Hispanics. Table 8.14 also shows us that the high poverty rates for Asian Americans were all accounted for by recency of immigration. Those Asian Americans who entered the United States before 1970 all showed poverty rates lower than the total rate for whites. But *all* the Asian American groups who immigrated between 1975 and 1980 had higher poverty rates than whites.

During the 1970s, there was some public concern expressed about the high numbers of non-whites on public assistance. Table 8.14 shows data reported in the 1980 Census. Japanese showed the lowest percentage of families with some public assistance income (4.2 percent). Among Asian Americans, Vietnamese (28.1 percent), Filipinos (10.2 percent), Chinese (6.6 percent), and Koreans (6.2 percent) showed somewhat higher rates than whites (5.9 percent), but all Asian Americans (except Vietnamese) showed lower percentages than blacks and Hispanics. We have not shown the data here, but public assistance income showed the same pattern as poverty: most of the Asian Americans receiving public assistance income were new immigrants, and, in some groups, natives. The table also showed social security income, which varied primarily with the age structures of the various ethnicities.

Prediction of Household Income

In Chapter 5, we introduced a truncated model of household determinants of household income. We will now introduce a more complete model, with most of the variables used to predict personal income, plus household variables. The predicting data are for household heads only.

TABLE 8.13

Percentage of Families below the Poverty Level, by Period of Immigration: 1979

	Japanese	Chinese	Filipino	Korean	Asian Indian	Vietnamese	White	Black	Hispanic
					Ethnicity				
TOTAL	4.2	10.5	6.2	13.1	7.4	35.1	7.0	26.5	21.3
FOREIGN BORN	5.6	11.8	5.3	7.9	5.0	30.3	*	*	*
Period of immigration									
1975–1980	10.1	22.8	8.8	11.1	10.7	35.7			
1970–1974	6.2	6.1	3.8	6.6	3.2	8.7			
Before 1970	4.3	2.8	4.6	4.0	2.2	6.8			

SOURCE: Xenos, Gardner, Barringer, and Levin (1987), pp. 276–277.

* Data not readily available.

TABLE 8.14

Reliance of Households on Public Assistance and Social Security for Income, by Ethnicity: 1979

Percent of Households	Japanese	Chinese	Filipino	Korean	Asian Indian	Vietnamese	White	Black	Hispanic
With no income	9.5	10.2	7.0	8.1	16.3	20.1	18.4	23.4	15.7
With income from									
public assistance	4.2	6.6	10.0	6.2	4.5	28.1	5.9	22.3	15.9
Social security	18.5	13.9	16.1	5.7	16.9	5.2	26.8	23.1	14.6

SOURCE: PC 80-1-1C, Tables 128, 138, 164.

Sex has been omitted, because it is highly correlated with household type. We lose some information by omitting sex, because although only a very few married-couple households are headed by females, many non-family household heads are females.

Table 8.15 displays the regression of household income on indus-trial sector, number of household workers, household type, period of immigration/nativity, occupation, and education of household heads. Age, weeks worked in 1979, and average hours worked in 1979 were entered as covariates. Their relative effects can be seen in the F ratios.[13]

A comparison with Table 8.12 demonstrates that the attributes of household heads (sector of employment, age, weeks worked, education, and employment) showed almost identical patterns as for personal in-come, but with slightly reduced effects upon household income, as com-pared to personal income.

The major contributor to household income, however, as shown on Table 8.15, was the number of household workers, with *Betas* from .41 for Filipinos to .21 for Koreans. There was relatively little difference between *Eta* and *Beta* coefficients for number of household workers, indicating that the variable was not much affected by other predictors, such as education of the household head. It is important to point out, however, that despite the contributions of extra household incomes for Asian Americans, whites still showed an impressive income gain for 4 or more workers ($13,842), more than Asian Indians ($12,848) or Kore-ans ($11,096). Among Asian Americans, Vietnamese showed impressive gains ($17,024) for 4 or more workers, suggesting an obvious coping strategy.[14]

Household type loses some of its predictive power when adjusted, probably because married-couple households have more workers than other types. Still, married-family incomes, even adjusted, are much higher than for any other type of household. This effect varies by ethnicity. For example, Japanese (B = .25) gained the greatest advantage; Vietnamese (B = .06) the least. As with the number of household workers, blacks and whites gained more advantage in married-family households than did Asian Americans, except for Japanese. It appeared then that Asian American advantages in household income came from larger numbers of household workers and a higher percentage of married-family house-holds, rather than in any inherent advantages over whites.

[13]We actually entered these variables in some MCA runs, but their patterns were the same as for personal income, and are not particularly revealing beyond what we already know. And, Table 8.15 is complex enough as it stands.

[14]One of our earlier readers expressed surprise that we stress the number of house-hold workers as a variable, apparently attributing this as naïveté on our part. As obvious as it may seem, however, the contributions of household members to household income have important social and policy implications.

TABLE 8.15

Determinants of Household Income, Household Heads, Aged 16+: 1979

Variable/Statistic	Ethnicity								
	Japanese	Chinese	Filipino	Korean	Asian Indian	Vietnamese	White	Black	Hispanic
Grand mean income ($)	27,476	24,916	27,169	23,337	27,049	18,313	23,320	17,525	17,995
Number	10,284	10,667	8,226	3,572	5,462	2,390	2,680	2,127	2,189
Weeks worked in 1979 (covariate)									
F ratio	497	1,022	406	397	436	387	134	210	179
Average hours worked in 1979 (covariate)									
F ratio	131	45	148	62	290	5**	18	9	22
Age (experience)									
F ratio	140	62	24	4	10	5	52	31	27
Industrial sector									
F ratio	212	192	92	42	52	28	50	22	65
Eta (unadjusted)	0.18	0.22	0.18	0.12	0.15	0.15	0.14	0.20	0.23
Beta (adjusted)	0.12	0.11	0.08	0.09	0.08	0.09	0.12	0.09	0.15
Deviation in dollars (adjusted)									
Periphery	−1,898	−1,569	−1,469	−1,252	−1,503	−1,338	−1,937	−1,022	−1,842
Core	2,016	2,265	1,336	1,933	1,321	1,051	1,568	1,115	1,774
Number of household workers									
F ratio	491	505	702	69	142	287	100	175	128
Eta	0.46	0.36	0.48	0.27	0.27	0.57	0.37	0.53	0.41
Beta	0.34	0.32	0.41	0.21	0.24	0.52	0.28	0.42	0.35

TABLE 8.15 (continued)

Variable/Statistic	Ethnicity								
	Japanese	Chinese	Filipino	Korean	Asian Indian	Viet-namese	White	Black	Hispanic
Deviation in dollars									
One worker	−4,759	−5,108	−7,350	−3,241	−3,855	−5,880	−3,400	−4,676	−4,045
Two workers	995	620	−456	732	1,807	−25	754	2,113	1,387
Three workers	7,534	6,286	6,159	5,726	7,947	6,135	6,779	7,948	6,223
Four or more workers	15,677	14,014	15,562	11,096	12,848	17,024	13,842	15,614	11,351
Household type									
F ratio	261	138	111	47	40	4	43	31	22
Eta	0.46	0.31	0.35	0.33	0.30	0.22	0.32	0.40	0.27
Beta	0.25	0.18	0.17	0.19	0.13	0.06	0.20	0.18	0.15
Deviation in dollars									
Married family household	3,115	1,828	1,822	1,773	1,234	496	1,850	2,223	1,022
Household head male, no wife present	491	825	−158	−783	−1,244	535	130	532	2,704
Household head female, no husband present	−5,314	−3,393	−4,535	−4,878	−2,215	−1,157	−4,560	−2,849	−3,316
Non-family household	−5,797	−5,250	−4,834	−6,369	−4,818	−1,407	−4,785	−1,861	−2,581
Period of immigration									
F ratio	4.2	210	102	70	98	3**	0.3**	2**	7
Eta	0.15	0.28	0.23	0.30	0.35	0.05	0.03	0.08	0.13
Beta	0.03	0.20	0.15	0.21	0.20	0.05	0.01	0.04	0.08
Deviation in dollars									
1975–1980	−312	−5,672	−4,918	−4,162	−4,630	−215	919	−1,393	−3,352
1965–1974	−142	−1,416	752	1,852	1,478	1,373	−1,838	−2,560	−733
Before 1965	−1,305	3,027	2,748	5,473	6,201	962	104	2,749	561
Native	216	2,877	−227	4,245	−94	3,462	16	31	396

TABLE 8.15 (continued)

Variable/Statistic	Ethnicity								
	Japanese	Chinese	Filipino	Korean	Asian Indian	Vietnamese	White	Black	Hispanic
Occupation*									
F ratio	62	88	84	23	45	15	14	8	11
Eta	0.21	0.31	0.29	0.34	0.34	0.26	0.30	0.25	0.25
Beta	0.14	0.17	0.18	0.15	0.17	0.14	0.14	0.10	0.13
Deviation in dollars									
Service and farm	-3,590	-4,380	-3,209	-2,910	-3,366	-1,716	-1,636	-1,878	-1,413
Labor	-2,066	-2,974	-2,037	-4,816	-3,828	-64	-1,344	-529	-1,361
Precision labor and operators	-1,493	-1,050	-846	-910	-3,943	-269	-1,344	835	-93
White collar	-302	-861	-1,338	-1,302	-3,333	-1,299	-683	466	-78
Professional and management	2,916	3,116	4,578	3,390	2,538	3,551	3,489	1,856	3,602
Education									
F ratio	46	117	135	37	43	10	40	25	29
Eta	0.14	0.28	0.32	0.36	0.34	0.26	0.30	0.22	0.29
Beta	0.13	0.21	0.23	0.19	0.17	0.12	0.24	0.20	0.22
Deviation in dollars									
Less than high school	-2,916	-5,028	-3,752	-2,678	-5,392	-1,262	-3,618	-2,240	-2,321
High school	-1,530	-2,267	-2,763	-2,113	-3,198	-409	-1,331	2	1,042
College 1–3 years	-783	-535	-1,683	-1,799	-2,728	-343	1,105	1,730	2,403
College 4 years	2,438	447	76	-1,125	-2,666	1,065	3,763	4,966	3,696
College postgraduate	3,249	4,651	6,803	6,055	2,509	4,129	8,312	6,839	7,051
R	0.649	0.653	0.687	0.623	0.616	0.701	0.616	0.675	0.635
R²	0.421	0.427	0.471	0.388	0.379	0.492	0.379	0.456	0.404

SOURCE: 5% PUMs "A" Tape.

* See Text.

** Not Significant at 0.01 level.

In this model, period of immigration, education, and occupation of household heads still retained salience when adjusted, and as we pointed out, the patterns were almost identical to those discussed for personal income.

In summary, the number of household workers and household type are the most important predictors of household income, though attributes of the household head also have great predictive power. As is the case for personal incomes, whites show a general pattern of advantage over Asian Americans, except Japanese. The fact that Asian Americans have higher household incomes than whites stems not from any inherent advantages Asian Americans have over whites, but because of a larger number of household workers, a greater proportion of married-family households, and a better educated population.

Conclusions

Our analyses have produced results similar in some respects to the studies conducted by the U.S. Commission on Civil Rights (1988), but our conclusions are quite different. The commission concluded:

> Taken together, the annual and hourly earnings (of Asian American males) suggest that almost all of the negative effect of Asian descent upon earnings was a result of Asians being disproportionately employed in lower paying occupations and industries (given their skills and characteristics). There is little evidence that Asians earned less than whites within the same occupation and industry.

Our results indicate that when other factors were controlled, whites earned more than Asian Americans in almost all occupational categories except in the professions, where Asian Americans had much higher incomes, but even there they bested whites only among the self-employed. In almost every category we have explored, whites showed advantages over most Asian Americans. There was of course some variation, group by group and among categories, and Japanese Americans did seem to have reached essential parity with whites .

Much of the income disadvantage experienced by Asian Americans can be explained away by recent immigration, but not all: even when immigration/nativity was accounted for, whites showed income advantages over most Asian Americans. Even Asian Indians, with a very large proportion of very well-educated professionals, showed income losses compared to whites (see also Barringer and Kassebaum 1989).

We must also point out that Koreans, and especially Vietnamese, showed lower incomes than whites in almost all categories of employment. Vietnamese consistently displayed incomes as low as, or lower than, blacks and Hispanics. A perusal of census data (PC80-1-2E) will show that Laotians, Hmongs, and other Southeast Asian groups had incomes similar to those of Vietnamese.

These disadvantages occur despite the fact that Asian women seem to enjoy some advantages over white women (though that is hardly consolation, given the generally low incomes of women of any ethnicity). Despite Woo's (1985) objections, we must conclude that Asian American women more than hold their own with white women, even when hours and weeks worked are controlled.

Household income data show some advantage of most Asian Americans over whites, but when we control for other variables, it becomes clear that this is due to the fact that Asian Americans employ more household workers, and have larger proportions of married-family households than do whites.

Studies of income over time suggest that Asian Americans have made improvements relative to whites since 1960. What we can see from the 1989 data suggest that no dramatic changes have taken place since 1980, but the 1989 data are aggregated for Asian Americans and Pacific Islander Americans, so we can say nothing about individual Asian American ethnic groups.

One of the most interesting findings here is that many Asian Americans (here we except both Japanese and Vietnamese) are far better educated than whites; they seem to convert their educations into high-status occupations; but they are nevertheless paid less than whites for the same or comparable occupations. This of course suggests that the problem is similar to the exploitation of women. This may or may not involve ethnic discrimination: certainly the census data are silent on that point. To put forward the most favorable interpretation: most Asian Americans are overeducated compared to whites for the incomes they earn.

In the long run, what one makes of all this depends upon the comparisons one wishes to emphasize. It is very clear that the Asian Americans we have studied, except Vietnamese, have certainly done much better with incomes than have blacks and Hispanics, for the most part even when their superior educations are accounted for (although well-educated Hispanics appear to do quite well). There is no question that blacks and Hispanics continue to fare poorly in the American economy. Vietnamese made even a poorer showing, probably because of their refugee status, as of 1980. They may show decided improvements in the 1990 Census.

Given that comparison, most Asian Americans can be seen to be closer to whites in income attainment, especially when we account for recent immigrants. However, except for Japanese, there seems to be no compelling reason to argue for parity. Perhaps even more to the point, the term "Asian Americans" confounds the issue: there is a very great difference between Japanese Americans on one hand, and Vietnamese or Koreans on the other.

PACIFIC ISLANDERS
IN THE UNITED STATES

When Micronesians of today leave their islands for higher education abroad they also leave behind this sense of place and belonging and enter a social context that not only fails to give definition, but also encourages the expression of one's own needs and desires, one's individuality. . . . In the social context of the islands control is clear, enforced, and external; in the new context control is unclear, sporadic, and expected to be much more internal than external. The result, not infrequently, is a sense of lost security and realization that a strange, if not confusing world must be confronted (Workman et al 1981:5).

I N 1990, the 365,024 Pacific Islanders recorded in the United States Census were 5 percent of the total Asian and Pacific Islander population. In 1980 the census counted 259,566 Pacific Islanders, constituting 7 percent of the Asian and Pacific Islander population. Although the absolute number of Pacific Islanders in the United States increased by 46 percent during the decade, their part of the total Asian and Pacific Islander population decreased because of the very large number of Asian immigrants, as seen in the earlier chapters.

Census publications before 1980 did not show any Pacific Islander group separately except Hawaiians. Therefore, data for specific Pacific Islander immigrants were available for the first time after the 1980 Census. After all 1990 results are available, we will be able to see trends for the first time. Unfortunately, as of this writing, only limited Pacific Islander counts are available for various geographic levels.

Three large geographical areas identify Pacific Islanders. Polynesia, the largest in area, covers a large triangle with Hawaii, New Zealand, and Pitcairn Islands forming the three points. The United States territory of American Samoa is in Polynesia.

Micronesia is a large oval at the equator, consisting of the U.S. territory of Guam, the Commonwealth of the Northern Mariana Islands

(CNMI), the freely associated states of the Federated States of Micronesia (FSM) and the Republic of the Marshall Islands, and the Republic of Palau (held as a strategic trust territory by the United States for the United Nations), and Kiribati, a former British colony.

Melanesia, the largest in population, is south of Micronesia and to the west of Polynesia.

No 1990 counts are yet available for these three areas. In 1980, the Pacific Islander population in the United States was about 85 percent Polynesian, 14 percent Micronesian, and 1 percent Melanesian. Of the 270,278 Polynesians in 1980, Hawaiians (172,346), Samoans (39,520), and Tongans (6,226) were the largest groups. Among the 35,508 persons of Micronesian background, more than 8 of every 10 were Guamanian. The Fijian population was the largest Melanesian group, with a total of 2,834.

The largest groups in 1990 were the same—Hawaiians (211,014), Samoans (62,964), Guamanians (49,345), Tongans (17,606), and Fijians (7,036). Of these groups, Tongans increased the most (183 percent during the decade), and Fijians, second (146 percent). These groups experienced immigration at rates similar to those seen among the Asians. The other large groups—Hawaiians (22 percent increase in the decade), Samoans (59 percent), and Guamanians (61 percent)—increased less, but the percentage increases were still considerable compared to the total U.S. population. The Samoan and Guamanian increases were less than Tongans and Fijians because larger numbers were present at the beginning of the decade. They were also less than the Asian increases partly because the populations of the sending populations were relatively small. The Hawaiian increase, although smaller than the others, was also probably larger than could be expected by natural increase alone, so it must indicate some reidentification to Hawaiian from other groups.

This chapter will focus on characteristics of Samoans, Tongans, Guamanians, and other Micronesians. The "Micronesian" category as defined for this paper includes all non-Guamanian Micronesians. Data on Hawaiians, the native American Polynesian group, show comparisons.

Estimates of all Pacific Islander groups except Hawaiians in the United States have been little more than approximations based on a limited supply of poor-quality migration statistics, some community-level studies, and assessments of community leaders. The 1980 Census was the first actual count of Pacific Islander immigrants using specific categories. The census was also the first to describe the demographic and socioeconomic characteristics of these groups.

The largest recent migration stream has been from (and through) American Samoa (Ahlburg and Levin 1990). The United States and Germany divided Samoa into American Samoa and Western Samoa at the turn of the twentieth century. The United States controlled American Samoa continuously in the 1900s, and New Zealand controlled Western Samoa from World War I until independence in 1962. From 1900 to 1951 the U.S. Department of the Navy administered American Samoa. The American naval base at Pago Pago in American Samoa employed many Samoans. An economic boom in Samoa after World War II continued for several years after the war. The naval presence and good economic times ended, however, when the base moved to Hawaii in 1951. The navy allowed Samoans connected with the naval base to migrate. Many did leave rather than return to subsistence farming (and a reduced standard of living). In the 1950s, unbalanced trade, a drought, and increasingly unrealistic economic expectations increased Samoans' desire to migrate to Hawaii and to the United States mainland.

Since 1951, the U.S. Department of Interior has administered American Samoa as an unincorporated territory. Military service has continued to attract Samoans, providing prestige at home, adventure abroad, education, and an American salary scale. After the early 1960s, enhanced employment and educational opportunities have also been motivations for emigration.

Persons born in American Samoa are United States nationals. This status gives them right of free entry into the United States, but has fewer privileges than citizenship. American Samoans, for example, cannot vote in federal elections.

Western Samoans made up 30 percent of American Samoa's population in 1980. Many Western Samoans migrate to American Samoa and the United States because of the lower standard of living in Western Samoa. In the 1980 U.S. Census, in fact, almost 13,000 persons had been born in Western Samoa compared to about 9,000 American Samoan-born.

Tongans, like Western Samoans, do not have free access to the United States. Much of the Tongan immigration has been reaction to the general economic situation in Tonga. Mormon Church activities also bring students and other potential migrants to the United States for extended periods. Also, like Western Samoans, many Tongans migrate to American Samoa and then on to the United States. About 800 persons born in Tonga were living in American Samoa in 1980 (2.5 percent of the resident population).

Migration from Guam has been similar to that from American Samoa. Guam became a U.S. territory after the Spanish-American War in 1898. In 1950, the Organic Act of Guam gave United States citizenship to Guam's inhabitants. Guamanians then had unrestricted entry into the United States. Guam is now negotiating for commonwealth status similar to that of Puerto Rico and the Northern Mariana Islands. Economic motives for immigration have been most important. Guamanians travel to the United States for relatively high-paying jobs by enlisting in the armed forces.

Migration from the rest of Micronesia has been much more recent. The Spanish (from the 1500s until 1898), Germans (until 1914), and Japanese (until the end of World War II) successively governed Micronesia. In 1947, the United Nations created the United States–controlled, strategic Territory of the Pacific Islands (TTPI). The United States neglected Micronesia until the Kennedy administration, when it appropriated relatively large amounts of money for economic development. In the late 1960s the educational system expanded, partly because of importation of Peace Corps volunteers. Until the Federated States of Micronesia and Marshall Islands compacts took effect in late 1986, most Micronesians came to the United States for postsecondary education. We will see the extent and characteristics of the long-term migrants only after the 1990 census. Palauans remain aliens.

Western Samoans and Tongans use American Samoa as a stopover migration point. The new freely associated states of the Federated States of Micronesia, and the Marshall Islands are likely to serve as conduit for persons from Kiribati, the Philippines, and Korea. Migrants from these areas and Palau already come for jobs and later intermarry and have children. Migration from all other Pacific Islands has been minor.

Who Are the Pacific Islanders?

Except for the information of totals for the large groups from the 1990 Census, the data used in this chapter come from answers to item 4 (race of individuals) on the 1980 Census questionnaire. The sample data from the 1980 Census showed 172,346 Hawaiians, 31,393 Guamanians, and 39,520 Samoans. A special tabulation displayed information for race, ancestry, language, and birthplace. The tabulation helps assess how different methods of counting Pacific Islanders affect the estimated populations for the various groups. Table 9.1 shows some of these data.

On a sample basis, 172,346 persons were Hawaiian race. However, 202,556 persons were Hawaiian by ancestry, either alone (a single ancestry response), or in combination with other ancestry groups (a multiple response). This number was 118 percent of the race response (18 percent more).

We compare the two items to see consistency in reporting. The two items together showed 239,546 persons reported as Hawaiian in either the ancestry and race items (139 percent of the race only response). Another 135,356 persons reported in *either* the race *or* the ancestry item (78 percent). These data show that some persons reported a race other than Hawaiian in item 4, but selected Hawaiian, either by itself or in combination with other ancestries, in the ancestry item.

The data also show that most of the persons reporting ancestry only (58 percent) reported a multiple ancestry response (Hawaiian and other groups).

Data for Guamanians differ. Ancestry responses of Chamorro and Guamanian were only 86 percent as frequent as the Guamanian race response. Also, a larger proportion of Guamanians reported a single ancestry group ("Guamanian" or "Chamorro") than reported in combination with some other ancestry group. The data for Samoans more closely resembled that of the Hawaiians. Although 39,520 persons reported Samoan as the race response, 51,283 wrote in a Samoan ancestry response, with 44,190 reporting only Samoan ancestry (86 percent of the Samoan ancestry responses). That is, more persons reported a single Samoan ancestry response than reported Samoan race.

Only 13,405 persons in the United States reported speaking Hawaiian at home (8 percent of Hawaiians by race). Another 27,581 persons reported speaking Samoan (70 percent), and 11,909 persons reported speaking Chamorro (38 percent). Chamorros and Samoans are often first-generation migrants, so are more likely to speak the language at home.

Data for Hawaiian birthplace are not compatible with the other responses since we cannot disaggregate non-natives from natives. Similarly, although most of the persons born on Guam were Guamanian, the census includes babies born to military personnel. On the other hand, it is likely that most of the Samoa-born persons were Samoan.

Race and ancestry items produce comparable data, but language and birthplace produce much less comparable data. Neither the 1980 nor the 1990 Census collected parental birthplace, so that item does not classify these groups.

Table 9.1 also shows similar comparisons for all Pacific Islanders, the major geographical areas of the Pacific Islands, and Tongans and Fijians, as well as the groups discussed above. As with the selected racial groups already discussed, the geographical areas showed similar numbers for race and ancestry responses, but smaller numbers for language and birthplace. Since Hawaiians make up most of the Polynesians, the relationships for Polynesian are similar to those found for Hawaiians. Tongans' and Fijians' relationships are more like those found for Samoans.

TABLE 9.1

Pacific Islanders in the United States, by Race, Ancestry, Birthplace, and Language: 1980

Pacific Island Group	Race	Ancestry	Race or Ancestry	Race and Ancestry	Single Ancestry	Multiple Ancestry	Language	Birth-place
TOTAL	259,566	345,276	406,413	198,429	192,561	152,715	83,800	320,251
Polynesian	220,278	303,517	349,698	174,097	164,940	138,577	48,843	265,319
Hawaiian	172,346	202,556	239,546	135,356	84,186	118,370	13,405	236,192
Samoan	39,520	51,283	58,303	32,500	44,190	7,093	27,581	21,943
Tongan	6,226	8,548	9,698	5,076	6,782	1,766	4,646	5,619
Melanesian	3,311	6,046	7,709	1,648	3,349	2,697	2,309	8,241
Fijian	2,834	3,571	4,862	1,543	2,462	1,109	985	7,538
Micronesian	35,508	33,325	46,149	22,684	23,081	10,244	27,125	45,384
Chamorro	31,393	27,023	38,115	20,301	18,683	8,340	11,909	38,919

SOURCE: U.S. Bureau of the Census unpublished tabulations.

273

Geographic Distribution

Table 9.2 shows the geographic distribution of the largest Pacific Islander groups on the basis of racial response for the states with the largest numbers of Pacific Islanders in 1990. About 44 percent of the Pacific Islanders in the United States in 1990 were living in Hawaii. Another 30 percent lived in California, and 4 percent lived in Washington.

The largest proportion of any group living in Hawaii were the Hawaiians, of course. Almost 2 out of every 3 Hawaiians were living in Hawaii in 1990, down from slightly more than 2 out of every 3 in 1980 (Table 9.3). No other group had more than half its residents living in Hawaii.

On the other hand, about half of all Samoans and Guamanians lived in California in 1990, down 5 percentage points during the decade for Guamanians, but up 5 percentage points for Samoans as they became more heavily concentrated in California. More than 4 in every 5 Fijians lived in California, and about 1 in every 4 Tongans lived in Utah.

Table 9.3 also shows the same geographic distribution for 1980, but including groups not yet tabulated for 1990. The percentage of Pacific Islanders increased by 18 percent in Hawaii during the decade. Of the states shown, the number of Pacific Islanders in Washington more than doubled (an increase of 115 percent); the Pacific Islander populations in the other states all increased considerably as well (from 67 percent in California to 74 percent in Utah).

The characteristics of Samoan migrants to Hawaii differ considerably from those who have migrated to California (Hayes and Levin 1984). Part of the reasons for the differences are historic, part are cultural, part are undoubtedly climatic. Hawaiian Samoans keep traditions more intact. Those in California find "as economic pressures increase, and Samoans move into the larger society [traditional values], as well as the typical demographic patterns, will tend to disappear" (Harbison 1986, p. 91).

Pacific Islanders adapt more easily to suburban and rural communities than to large urban areas (Rolff 1978, Kotchek 1977, 1978). Kotchek, who studied Samoans in Seattle, attributes this adapting to less ethnic visibility and freedom of choice. Pacific Islands networks there are not as strong or as extensive. She does find that some Samoans have abandoned the *faaSamoa*, but others see it as a unifying force.

San Francisco and Los Angeles, on the other hand, already reached levels of cultural density in the late 1960s to permit forming descent groups. Samoans held their first large funerals in San Francisco after a

TABLE 9.2
Pacific Islanders in Selected States by Group: 1990

Group	Number	Percentage	Hawaii	California	Washington	Texas	Utah	All Other
TOTAL	365,024	100.0	44.5	30.3	4.1	2.1	2.1	17.0
Hawaiian	211,014	100.0	65.8	16.3	2.6	1.4	0.7	13.3
Samoan	62,964	100.0	23.9	50.7	6.6	1.5	2.5	14.9
Guamanian	49,345	100.0	4.3	50.8	7.7	4.5	0.3	32.5
Tongan	17,606	100.0	17.5	45.0	2.5	3.6	22.2	9.2
Fijian	7,036	100.0	3.7	81.6	4.2	0.8	0.7	9.0
Palauan	1,439	100.0	24.9	27.6	7.9	5.1	0.3	34.3
All other	15,620	100.0	17.1	32.8	5.5	4.3	3.8	36.5

SOURCE: CB91-215, U.S. Bureau of the Census, June 12, 1991.

TABLE 9.3

Pacific Islanders in Selected States by Type: 1980

Group	Number	Percentage	Hawaii	California	Washington	Texas	Utah	All Other
TOTAL	259,566	100.0	53.0	25.5	2.7	1.7	1.7	15.4
POLYNESIAN	220,278	100.0	61.1	20.6	2.2	1.3	1.9	12.9
Hawaiian	172,346	100.0	68.6	14.1	1.6	1.4	0.5	13.8
Samoan	39,520	100.0	36.3	45.8	4.6	1.0	3.0	9.3
Tahitian	791	100.0	34.0	32.9	0.9	0.0	6.1	26.2
Tongan	6,226	100.0	23.8	37.8	1.4	0.5	29.1	7.4
All other	1,395	100.0	24.1	30.0	4.8	3.2	19.0	19.0
MICRONESIAN	35,508	100.0	7.5	51.3	5.4	4.2	0.4	31.2
Guamanian	30,695	100.0	5.3	55.4	5.7	4.2	0.2	29.2
C.N.M.I.	698	100.0	8.0	46.1	4.9	13.6	2.4	24.9
Marshallese	474	100.0	16.5	18.1	1.1	14.3	0.0	50.0
Palauan	692	100.0	44.1	29.5	2.0	4.3	0.0	20.1
All other	2,949	100.0	19.6	20.0	4.7	0.5	2.0	53.1
MELANESIAN	3,311	100.0	10.7	67.0	4.7	2.2	0.0	15.5
Fijian	2,834	100.0	9.2	72.8	5.2	1.7	0.0	11.2
All other	477	100.0	19.9	32.5	1.7	4.8	0.0	41.1
P.I. Not Reported	469	100.0	1.3	80.4	0.0	2.1	1.1	15.1

SOURCE: U.S. Bureau of the Census, PC80-S1-12, 1983.

1965 fire in a Catholic parish hall (Ablon 1970). Formation of similar Samoan descent groups in San Diego and Oceanside occurred later.

Demography

Because no characteristics for Pacific Islanders are yet available from the 1990 Census, the rest of the chapter will present data from the 1980 Census. All these data are now more than a decade old. Because they are also the first data available on Pacific Islands from a decennial census, they serve as benchline.

Age and Sex: Pacific Islanders in the United States are a very youthful population, consistent with their high mobility. For example, the median age for each of the specified Pacific Islander groups was lower than the United States median age of 30.0 years in 1980. The median age for Hawaiians was 24.3 years. Among the immigrant Pacific Islander groups, the median age was highest for Guamanians (23.0 years), followed by Micronesians (22.8 years), Samoans (19.2 years), and Tongans (18.9 years).

Tongan males (20.9 years) were older than females (17.2 years), probably because of selective migration. The median for Samoan males and females (19.3 years) was about the same. However, females in the other groups were older than males, as in the total United States. In all cases, the medians by sex were lower than for the total U.S. population.

We also see Pacific Islander youthfulness in the large proportions under 15 years old, and the small proportions 65 years old and over. Although about 7 percent of the total U.S. population was under 5 years old, almost 11 percent of the Pacific Islander population fell in this group. These figures included 12 percent of the "other" Micronesians, 14 percent of the Samoans, and more than 16 percent of the Tongans (Table 9.4).

Although 11 percent of the total U.S. population was 65 years old and over, only 4 percent of the Pacific Islanders were in this age group. Even here, the 6 percent elderly of the Hawaiians skewed the total Pacific Islander distribution. Only 2 percent or less of the other selected groups were elderly. Since the elderly are less likely to migrate, and since migration of Pacific Islanders is relatively recent, these proportions are not surprising.

The distribution by age shows differences among the groups. Almost half of all "other" Micronesians were between 20 and 34 years old, primarily a student-aged population. Samoans and Tongans were younger, Hawaiians and Guamanians, in slightly older groups.

The 98 males per 100 females for Pacific Islanders in 1980 was more

TABLE 9.4

Age of Pacific Islander Persons: 1980

Age	United States (in 000's)	Total Pacific Islander	Hawaiian	Samoan	Tongan	Guamanian	Other Micronesian
TOTAL PERSONS	226,546	259,566	172,346	39,520	6,226	30,695	4,813
MALES/100 FEMALES	94.5	98.0	95.0	103.4	113.7	102.5	119.3
Percent	100.0	100.0	100.0	100.0	100.0	100.0	100.0
Under 5 years	7.2	10.8	10.0	14.1	16.3	9.1	11.8
5 to 9 years	7.4	9.9	9.2	12.4	13.0	9.7	7.4
10 to 14 years	8.1	10.5	10.0	13.3	13.0	10.2	7.4
15 to 19 years	9.3	11.7	11.6	12.0	9.0	12.7	13.1
20 to 24 years	9.4	11.4	10.8	10.5	8.3	13.9	23.9
25 to 34 years	16.4	17.4	16.4	16.9	17.1	21.7	24.7
35 to 44 years	11.3	11.3	11.7	10.4	12.8	10.5	6.7
45 to 54 years	10.0	7.5	8.5	5.3	6.2	6.2	3.3
55 to 64 years	9.6	5.1	6.1	3.1	2.3	3.5	1.1
65 years and over	11.3	4.4	5.6	2.1	2.2	2.4	0.5
Median age	30.0	23.1	24.3	19.2	18.9	23.0	22.2

SOURCES: U.S. Bureau of the Census, PC80-1-C1, Table 98, and PC80-2-1E.

balanced than the 94 males per 100 females in the United States. The ratio for Hawaiians was similar to that of the United States total, but all others had more males than females in 1980. The 103 Samoan males for every 100 Samoan females was more balanced than the 114 Tongan males and 119 "other" Micronesian males to 100 females of the respective groups.

The distributions by age for total Pacific Islanders and for Hawaiians were similar to those for the total United States population. The distributions for the other groups were more erratic. For example, although not shown here, almost 50 percent more Tongan males than females aged 25 to 44 years old were present, and almost twice as many "other" Micronesian males as females aged 15 to 19 years old.

Household and Family Size and Composition: Traditional social structure and the physical structure of the housing units influence Pacific Islander household and family size in the United States. Pacific Islander immigrant extended families remain strong and cohesive, with fluid household composition. Relatives come and go, the duration of their stays mainly dependent on their reasons for being in the household and the area (Ablon 1970, Lewthwaite et al. 1973).

The structure of houses in the United States limits the size, composition, and fluidity of the Pacific Islander households (particularly outside Hawaii). Builders construct American houses and apartments for nuclear families, with many walls and areas which can easily be "privatized," frequently a priority for Westerners. Pacific Islanders, on the other hand, often find others' desire for complete privacy verging on craziness. The Samoan *fale,* for example, "is more suited for extended family life, because it appears spacious, even when filled with people; it has no subdivisions and little or no furniture; and it is open to all sides, weather permitting" (Rolff 1978, p. 155). Daily life occurs outside the house, so as long as air can flow freely through the house, the structure is relatively unimportant. People go inside mainly to sleep.

In 1980, the composition of the Pacific Islander household and distribution of relatives within it was very different from the distribution in U.S. households in general. Although 22 percent of all U.S. household members were male family householders, only 16 percent of the persons in Pacific Islander households were in this category. This difference in these percentages is due to the larger Pacific Islander families and households. Although about 1 in every 3 persons in all U.S. households were children, more than 4 in every 10 Pacific Islanders in households were children. About half of Samoans and Tongans in households were children.

Pacific Islanders frequently stay in their parents' or a sibling's home after marriage. They may even have several children before setting up their own household. "This type of arrangement frequently occurs when the husband is a serviceman stationed out of the area, is in the merchant marine, or is employed by one of the shipping or passenger lines" (Ablon 1970, pp. 79–80). Also, the percentage of other relatives in Pacific Islander households (10 percent) was more than twice that for the total U.S. population (4 percent). More than 13 percent of Samoans and 12 percent of "other" Micronesians living in households were "other" relatives.

The average U.S. household in 1980 had 2.74 persons and the average family 3.27. However, as in other transitory transitional populations, all Pacific Islander groups (based on the race of the householder) had larger average households (3.69 persons) and families (4.25 persons). For Samoans, especially, the differences were very large (4.86 persons per household and 5.16 persons per family). However, even Samoan family sizes are decreasing rapidly (Albon 1970; Shu and Satele 1977).

About half of all U.S. families in 1980 had a child 18 years of age or younger compared to more than two-thirds of all Pacific Islander families. The 63 percent for Hawaiians was slightly lower, presumably as a result of reduced fertility. More than 8 in every 10 Tongan and Samoan families had children under 18 in the family, as well as more than 7 in 10 Guamanians. Similarly, more than one-third of the Pacific Islander families had children under 6, as was the case with more than half of all Samoan families and more than 60 percent of Tongan families.

Marital Status: No long history of intermarriage between groups and with non-Pacific Islanders exists because most Pacific Islander immigration is recent. Hawaiians are the major exception. Data from the vital statistics for Hawaii showed 58 percent of full- and part-Hawaiian males marrying non-Hawaiian females between 1980 and 1985. About 60 percent of full- and part-Hawaiian females married non-Hawaiian males during the same period. Since Hawaiians are indigenous, unlike the other groups, the marriage experience may not be transferrable.

The data from the Hawaii vital statistics also showed 44 percent of Samoan males marrying non-Samoan females in 1980 to 1985 and 40 percent of Samoan females marrying non-Samoan males. Comparable numbers from other states are not yet available. Intermarriage reduces fertility (as seen in the fertility section), but also has other effects on individuals and the community in general. For example, "Non-Samoan spouses almost invariably reduce Samoans' involvement in *aiga* and church and often discourage the formation of extended kin households" (Rolff 1978:85). Rolff also reports that when families want to reduce their involvement in Samoan group activities they will often actively promote marriages with non-Samoans.

Micronesians, particularly the males who predominate in the marriage ages, often marry non-Micronesians, and often have unexpected problems. Frequently, young Micronesian males away from home for the first time experience "suspended adolescence," a phenomenon derived from their traditional cultures. Pacific Islanders, in general, have respect for authority, and follow adolescent behavior patterns, even into their late 20s and 30s, until they marry. Once they marry, whether at age 20 or 40, they assume the role of "married," with the authority and respect that role demands.

Many of the non-Pacific Islander women, infatuated with these individuals because of their domesticity and compliance, create a kind of "teddy-bear complex." Husband and wife sometimes have rude awakenings when the newly married male expects his wife to stop acting with authority and start acting like a more passive Pacific Islander wife. Sometimes the resulting conflicts lead to separation and divorce.

Fertility: Although Hawaii and California collect some data on deaths, the United States has no reliable mortality data for all Pacific Islanders. Data on children ever born collected in the 1980 census, however, permit the estimation of fertility levels. The 1980 Pacific Islander immigrant population arrived in the United States very recently, so a high proportion of the children they report were born outside the United States. All the Pacific Islander groups except Micronesians (with 1.2 children per woman aged 15 to 44) had higher fertility rates than the 1.3 for the total United States. The rates ranged from a low of 1.6 (per woman) for Guamanian women of this age group to highs of 2.1 for Tongans and 1.9 for Samoans.

Since most women complete their childbearing by the time they reach the 35–44 age group, it is useful to compare data for women at these ages. The U.S. average was 2.6 children per woman 35 to 44 in 1980. All the Pacific Islander groups at 3.5 children per woman had higher fertility rates (including the Hawaiians at 3.3). Micronesians (3.5), Guamanians (3.7), Samoans (4.3), and Tongans (4.4) all had higher fertility levels than the Pacific average.

Pacific Islander fertility in the United States Pacific Islands territories declined at least since the mid-1960s (Levin and Retherford 1986). The own-children method of fertility estimation was used for that study and for the analysis of fertility of Asians in the United States (Retherford and Levin 1989). The latter paper also discusses fertility information for the three largest groups of Pacific Islanders in the United States— Hawaiians, Guamanians, and Samoans.

Immigrant Pacific Islander women living in the United States in 1980 had the same fertility decline seen among Pacific Islander women in their home areas. Fertility levels for Pacific Islanders were higher than those for Asians, and for the total United States population. For all Pacific Islanders, the Total Fertility Rate (TFR) declined from 3.7 children per woman in 1965–1969 to 2.5 children per woman in 1975–1979. The TFR of Guamanians dropped precipitously over the same period, from 4.0 to 2.1. Hawaiians showed a more modest decline, from 3.3 to 2.3. Samoans decreased from 6.1 to 3.8 children per woman.

The data by urban and rural residence showed the expected relationships between the two areas. That is, urban fertility was lower than rural fertility. Total Pacific Islander urban fertility decreased from 3.6 to 2.5 between the years 1965 to 1969 and 1975 to 1979. Comparable rural TFRs declined from 4.1 to 2.8. Within urban and rural categories, fertility fell over the three periods. For the own-children method, the characteristic is as of census day. That is, women may have moved from rural areas (where they had some of their children) to urban areas (where they may have had other children) during the 15-year periods. The own-children method, however, assumes that the women were in the residential area of enumeration during the whole period.

The fertility of both native-born and foreign-born women declined between 1966 and 1980. The fertility of native-born was lower than the fertility of foreign-born for all Pacific Islanders and for Samoans. For Guamanians, however, the fertility of native-born women was consistently higher than for the "foreign-born" women. These data are consistent for the fertility rates Levin and Retherford found for Guam (1986).

These data show that differential fertility conformed to usual patterns: urban fertility was lower than rural fertility. Fertility of native-born was less than fertility of foreign-born. Fertility tended to fall not only for each group, but also for each category of urban-rural residence and nativity.

Comparisons with the total U.S. population suggest that assimilation occurred between 1965 and 1980. Fertility of the various racial minorities converged toward the fertility of the majority. However, especially for some groups of Pacific Islanders, differences in fertility had not disappeared by 1980.

Reproductive attitudes and values formed in the islands have more effect on fertility than U.S. sociocultural conditions because large proportions of the Pacific Islander immigrant populations arrived recently. Fertility levels in American Samoa decreased steadily for two decades. Some parts of Micronesia (notably the Northern Mariana Islands and Palau) also experienced recent decreases in fertility rates. Other Micronesian areas maintained high fertility levels (Levin and Retherford 1986). We lack information on contraceptive use for any of the Pacific Islander immigrant groups except Samoans, and only for Samoans in Hawaii. However, survey data show that in the late 1970s two-thirds of Samoan women in Hawaii had used contraceptives at some stage of their reproductive lives (Harbison and Weishaar 1981, p. 270). The relationship between improved socioeconomic status and later fertility decline seen in other developing countries and ethnic groups in the United States applies to Pacific Islanders as well. As contraceptive use increases, Samoan (and other Pacific Islander) household and family sizes should decrease to approach total United States levels.

Migration

Mobility—the First Step: Pacific Islander immigration is partially an unintended manifestation of traditional movements, the wanderlust, part of the transition to adulthood. The "trip" has been important in most Pacific Islands societies for generations. Historically, young voyagers left in canoes or other boats to explore and settle distant islands. Historically, groups of people "moved readily between islands and valleys in search of new land, disease-free sites, wives, trading goods, etc." Connell (1984, p. 12).

Frequently in the past, young men (at least in Micronesia) would hail a passing fishing boat to request to sail and leave the island for several years. They got experience and maturity (and stories to last a lifetime, many of them true). They then returned to the island to marry, have children, and settle down (Leinwald 1981, p. 85, Levin 1976, p. 187). This pattern continues, but transformed by newer forms of travel. For example, "just as their great-grandfathers signed aboard trading and whaling vessels a century ago to 'see the world', so Namoluk young persons today, (especially young men) set off to 'see the world' on a Boeing 727" (Marshall 1979, p. 7; also, Hezel 1978, p. 26).

Levin and Naich (manuscript), in writing about civil redemption in the atoll areas of Micronesia, however, note that the "trip" has both positive and negative aspects. In the past, when young men went on canoe voyages or fishing boats, no one knew (including the young person), when or whether he would ever return. A different kind of challenge replaced the traditional danger. Many islander immigrants lack preparation for dealing with "other" world problems, both scholastic and financial.

Levin and Naich also note that the "trip" both traditionally and in the contemporary situation, can serve as a form of redemption. A young person in conflict can lessen stress in these still-communal societies by leaving the island until tempers and memories have cooled.

The stress can also come at the other end of the trip. Sometimes students drop out of school in the States, for either financial or scholastic reasons. The shame involved with not finishing a degree often makes return to the islands difficult. By waiting, the elders on the island might "forget" the transgression, with redemption occurring. In either case, expiation of real or imagined sins results.

The United States government has encouraged this kind of travel with universal education through high school in the United States Pacific. Now many Pacific Islander students leave their islands to come to the United States for schooling, using the Basic Education Opportunity (Pell) Grant as their ticket. The school year BEOG pays about $2,000 per school year based on parental income. Since many Pacific Island families have low-pay pursuits such as copra collecting, most Pacific Islander students receive the full grant. Although $2000 does not cover most expenses for a year at school, students can usually scrape together airfare to the United States to claim the grant. Costs of books, food, and housing cause financial problems later.

The United States As Safety Valve: Emigration, then, is a kind of safety valve for increased pressure on human and natural resources in the Pacific Islands. Many Pacific Islanders have left for education. The safety valve works both ways. Pacific Islanders can settle in the United States. Also, the sending islands can avoid the potential problems both of returning migrants and many new participants joining the local labor force. As Connell notes, "as long as the 'safety valve' of emigration remains open there will be reduced pressure on South Pacific states to provide employment opportunities and welfare services in a more self-reliant context" (1984, p. 32).

Several channels of Pacific Islander immigration seem to be developing: (1) service in the armed forces; (2) school attendance followed by employment; and (3) employment during periodic stays in the United States. All groups except the Hawaiians, who are not immigrants, use the military channel for migration. The second channel, education followed by employment, might be called the "Micronesian" model; the third channel, employment combined with circular mobility, is the "Samoan" model, a model likely to become more widespread throughout the United States' Pacific Islands. These second and third channels will be discussed later.

Migration for Military Service: We cannot measure immigration for Hawaiians since they are native. Hawaiians and Guamanians had proportions of veterans in 1980 that did not differ much from the proportion for the total United States. On the other hand, much of the early Samoan immigration was the result of military activity in American Samoa, attracting young males into the service. Others moved as part of the *fitafita* guards in the mid-1950s. Many of these Samoans later retired to the States. The military continued to be attractive to Samoans into the 1970s because of the opportunity to leave Samoa (often to escape the *faa'Samoa*), and as a source of adventure. In 1980, more than 18 percent of Samoan males (many of whom were U.S. nationals) had served in the military. However, fewer than 6 percent of Micronesian males and only about 3 percent of Tongan males—few of whom were citizens—were veterans.

One example illustrates use of military service for migration. Ala'ilima describes the case of a man who lived with different relatives in Hawaii, and delivered his entire paycheck to them. When he decided to keep a small part, this uncle accused him of cheating, so he moved in with his sister, who was to send some of his paycheck to his parents. She did not follow through, so he joined the armed forces. "This, he says, was the best decision he ever made" (1986, p. 125).

In recent years, however, the pull of the military for Samoans has diminished somewhat. Rolff notes, for example, "during the 1970s, most high school seniors in . . . American Samoa were insufficiently prepared to pass the military entrance examinations" (1978, p. 177). The school system in American Samoa seemed to be unable, for cultural or educational reasons, to prepare students for the exams. Rolff also found "many contemporary young Samoans do not like the regimented life of enlisted men. And . . . they want to avoid long periods of separation from their families" (1978, p. 177).

In many cases, young Micronesian males join the military for the same reasons as Samoans. Under the compacts of free association, Micronesians enlist because the military gives increased income, an escape from family or other problems, and the chance for adventure.

What starts as "military" migration can turn into a more general migration. Janes (1984), for example, finds three waves of Samoan migrants: those migrating under military auspices in the 1950s, family-oriented migration from the late 1950s to the late 1960s, and a more recent immigration of elderly.

Birthplace: A total of 83,037 Pacific Islander persons were born outside the United States, but had immigrated before 1980 (Table 9.5). Of these, 45,669 (55 percent) were born in Micronesia, 29,127 (35 percent) in Polynesia, and 8,241 (10 percent) in Melanesia.

Fiji made up the largest proportion of Melanesia-born (more than 90 percent). Since a much smaller proportion reported as Fijian, many of these immigrants were Fijian Indian, about half of Fiji's population. These persons presumably reported as Asian Indian on the race item. Very few persons were born in the other areas of Melanesia. The United States has never had the close, formal ties with Melanesia that it has had with American Samoa in Polynesia or Guam and the rest of Micronesia.

More than 4 out of every 5 persons born in Micronesia were born on Guam. Unfortunately, the census cannot distinguish between chil-

TABLE 9.5

U.S. Population with Pacific Islander Birthplace: 1980

Birthplace	Number	Percent	Percent Excluding Guam	Percent of Group
TOTAL (1)	83,037	. . .	46,255	. . .
Percent	. . .	100.0	100.0	. . .
POLYNESIA	29,127	35.1	63.0	100.0
American Samoa	9,361	11.3	20.2	32.1
Cook Islands	130	0.2	0.3	0.4
French Polynesia	1,014	1.2	2.2	3.5
Norfolk	188	0.2	0.4	0.6
Tonga	5,619	6.8	12.1	19.3
Western Samoa	12,582	15.2	27.2	43.2
Other Polynesia	233	0.3	0.5	0.8
MICRONESIA	45,669	55.0	98.7	100.0
Guam	36,782	44.3	79.5	80.5
Kiribati	106	0.1	0.2	0.2
Northern Marianas	2,137	2.6	4.6	4.7
Trust Terr. of P.I.	5,066	6.1	11.0	11.1
Fed. St. Micronesia	1,401	1.7	3.0	3.1
Chuuk	542	0.7	1.2	1.2
Kosrae	110	0.1	0.2	0.2
Pohnpei	378	0.5	0.8	0.8
Yap	371	0.4	0.8	0.8
Marshall Islands	1,197	1.4	2.6	2.6
Palau	1,003	1.2	2.2	2.2
Other T.T.P.I.	1,465	1.8	3.2	3.2
Other Micronesia	1,584	1.9	3.4	3.5
MELANESIA	8,241	9.9	17.8	100.0
Fiji	7,538	9.1	16.3	91.5
New Caledonia	144	0.2	0.3	1.7
Papua New Guinea	425	0.5	0.9	5.2
Other Melanesia	134	0.2	0.3	1.6

SOURCE: U.S. Bureau of the Census unpublished data.

(1) Excludes Hawaii, Australia, New Zealand, Oceania, not elsewhere classified, and the American territories of Canton and Enderbury Islands, Johnston Atoll, and Midway Islands.

dren of military and children of civilians. These statistics include some births to parents who were military (or on civilian contract) temporarily on Guam. Persons from the former Trust Territory of the Pacific Islands made up the largest proportion of the rest of the Micronesian immigrants. Interpretation of the numbers shown for the constituent areas of the Federated States of Micronesia, Marshalls, and Palau, however, requires some caution. The relatively large number of "other" Micronesians were persons who presumably wrote "Micronesia" for birthplace.

Western Samoa was the largest Polynesian sender of migrants, with 43 percent of the total (and 15 percent of all Pacific Islander immigrants). Western Samoa is not a U.S. territory, but migrants move from Western Samoa to American Samoa, and then on to Hawaii and the United States mainland. The second largest group of migrants was from American Samoa. The 9,361 persons were 32 percent of the Polynesians. Tongans, who use essentially the same route as the Western Samoans, were the third largest Polynesian immigrant group (19 percent).

Short-term Migration: Another measure of migration, this time measuring shorter-term migration, comes from the question on residence in 1975. Both the U.S. and Pacific Islands censuses included this question. We can look at migration between the areas, but here we will be looking at migration to the United States. Of the 180,765 Pacific Islander persons 5 years and over in 1980, 82,934 (46 percent) were living in the same house in 1980 as in 1975 (Table 9.6). More than half of all Hawaiians were living in the same house, but less than 30 percent of the Tongans and Guamanians, and only 1 in 10 of the other Micronesians.

Persons living abroad 5 years before the census presented the opposite case. While about 2 percent of all persons in the United States had lived abroad in 1975, almost 10 percent of the Pacific Islanders fell in this category. The percentage for Hawaiians abroad was even less than the U.S. average, but other Pacific Islanders had very high rates. More than 6 out of every 10 "other" Micronesians were abroad in 1975, as well as 3 out of every 10 Guamanians, 1 in 3 Tongans, and 1 in 6 Samoans. These data show that a large part of the migration for some groups occurred in the 5 years before the census.

Of those in a different house in 1975, more than half of each group continued to live in the same county. Of those who lived in a different county, however, more marked differences existed between the groups. About half of the persons in the United States who lived in a different county lived in the same state. However, only about 4 in every 10 Pacific Islanders (and about the same proportion of Hawaiians and Micronesians) lived in the same state if they lived in a different county in 1975. Only 3 in every 10 Samoans were in this category, and only 1 in 6 Tongans. If Samoans and Tongans moved out of the county between 1975 and 1980, they were also likely to move out of the state altogether.

Of those who did move out of the state, most had lived in the West in 1975. Only 20 percent of those in this category for the whole United States lived in the West in 1975 compared to 71 percent of the Pacific

TABLE 9.6

Residence in 1975 for Pacific Islanders: 1980

Residence in 1975	United States (in 000's)	Total Pacific Islander	Hawaiian	Samoan	Tongan	Guamanian	Other Micronesian
PERSONS 5 YEARS+	210,323	180,765	124,358	22,855	3,815	22,196	3,567
Same house	112,695	82,934	65,322	8,556	1,116	6,260	433
Percent	53.6	45.9	52.5	37.4	29.3	28.2	12.1
Diff. house in U.S.	93,696	80,452	57,349	10,214	1,424	9,433	953
Same county	52,750	51,027	37,590	6,033	843	5,438	495
Percent	56.3	63.4	65.5	59.1	59.2	57.6	51.9
Different county	40,946	29,425	19,759	4,181	581	3,995	458
Same state	20,588	11,608	8,177	1,221	97	1,670	170
Percent	50.3	39.4	41.4	29.2	16.7	41.8	37.1
Different state	20,358	17,817	11,582	2,960	484	2,325	288
Percent	100.0	100.0	100.0	100.0	100.0	100.0	100.0
Northeast	22.5	6.4	5.7	7.1	3.5	9.1	16.0
Midwest	25.5	6.4	6.2	5.8	0.0	7.1	13.5
South	31.4	16.1	13.2	15.4	5.0	32.6	27.4
West	20.5	71.1	74.9	71.6	91.5	51.2	43.1
Abroad	3,932	17,379	1,687	4,085	1,275	6,503	2,181
Percent	1.9	9.6	1.4	17.9	33.4	29.3	61.1

SOURCE: U.S. Bureau of the Census, PC80-1-C1, Table 101, PC80-2-1E.

Islanders, and 92 percent of the Tongans. Micronesians became more dispersed over time, perhaps partly because of the lessening of the family bonds with migration. Further, many of the Micronesians were students.

A detailed analysis of the Pacific Islanders by year of immigration does not yet exist. However, if the Samoa-born respondents in Shu and Satele's 1976 survey of Samoans in southern California were representative of Samoan migrants in the United States, two-thirds had immigrated during the previous 15 years, and 24 percent in the previous 5 years (1977, p. 74). Of the 50 householders interviewed in Hawaii by Franco in 1983, 40 percent had immigrated during the previous 9 years (1983, p. 9). No secondary sources of information were available on year of immigration for other Pacific Islander groups.

Also, surveys have been fairly unsuccessful at seeking information on the subjective motivations of Samoan migrants. In Franco's recent survey of Samoans living in the Kalihi area of Oahu, for example, 23 of the 50 respondents cited "kinship-related" reasons for migration, and 17 cited their children's or their own education (1983, p. 11). Education of children appears in several surveys as either the primary reason for immigrating or among the most important (Baker 1976; Ala'ilima 1966; Ablon 1971; Enesa 1977), but the relative weight given to this motivation depends on the way of getting the information. Some of the surveys emphasized "economic" motivations such as the desire for wage employment and the opportunity to increase prestige by the generosity that a money income permits (Ala'ilima 1966; Baker 1976; Forster 1956), whereas others found little evidence of such motivations (Franco 1983; Enesa 1977).

Also, much variation exists in the emphasis placed on Samoan social structure as a specific motivation for migration. Shu and Satele stress the desire of many young Samoans to escape "traditional constraints" (1977, p. 10), and Rolff mentions the wish to escape the "matai system" (1978, p. 58). Although these data refer only to Samoans (no data are yet available for other groups), Samoans continue to be a special case since they carry their social structure within them; most other Pacific Islander immigrants do not have the same set social structure.

Many Pacific Islanders have trouble abandoning their traditional societies as they move into American society. For example, at one Oregon college, faculty found that Micronesian students have difficulties budgeting their money, tend to be reluctant to try different foods, and some male students have drinking problems. "A Micronesian who gets drunk, exhibits disruptive behavior, and is taken down to the police station, stands out in a way that an American student would not simply because of his physical appearance. The professors felt that, as a result, the entire Micronesian student population suffers for the action of a handful" (Leinwand 1981, pp. 118–119).

Social Characteristics

Educational Attainment: Education, in fact, may be the cause of a brain drain for several of the Pacific Island nations. Ballendorf describes the Micronesian school system as essentially a type of education mill with export to the United States as its product. "The total school age population participating is one of the highest in the world for a developing area: well over 90 percent" (Ballendorf 1977, p. 5).

This democratization of the school system caused an education explosion; "the total population of Truk District may be doubling every 22 years, but its high-school graduate population has been doubling every four" (Hezel 1978, p. 26). In 1967 about 300 Micronesians studied outside Micronesia. About 900 Chuukese studied outside in 1973, 2200 in 1975, and 3000 by 1977. A brain drain develops because of "frustration at home, higher living standards in the United States and the ability of Micronesians to adjust to the American culture and society as a result of their exposure during stateside college attendance" (Hezel 1978, p. 7).

Similarly, a study of high-school students in American Samoa in 1974 found that 62 percent intended to go to the United States after graduation. "Only 37 of the almost 400 graduating students said they planned to attend the Community College of American Samoa" (*Pacific Islands Monthly* 1974 45 [August]:9).

Naich (personal communication), among other of the newer Micronesian-cum-analysts, disagrees with Hezel and Ballendorf's assessment of the cause of Micronesian migration. "The limited job opportunities back home and other factors are probably the most convincing explanations; education itself is not. . . . Those who drop out of college tend to remain in the U.S., and those who complete their college education generally return home." Little evidence exists yet to support these positions for Pacific Islanders who come first for education and then stay on. The 1990 census should give us longitudinal data to enlighten us somewhat further.

Although a larger proportion of Pacific Islanders were enrolled in high school (26 percent of all Pacific Islanders 3 years old and over and enrolled in school) than the total U.S. population (25 percent), a smaller proportion of Pacific Islanders were enrolled in college (17 percent compared to 20 percent for the total population). These figures show indirectly that a smaller proportion of Pacific Islanders continued to college.

Ample evidence shows Micronesians are coming to the United States to attend college. Almost 1 in 4 enrolled Guamanians and 6 in 10 enrolled "other" Micronesians were in college in 1980.

Pacific Islanders attended public colleges in the same proportions as the total U.S. population. More than 80 percent of the United States population enrolled in college in 1980 were in public colleges. Only 39 percent of Tongans, however, were enrolled in a public college, probably because such a large proportion were enrolled at Brigham Young University in either Utah or Hawaii.

Also, a smaller percentage of Pacific Islanders 3 and 4 years old were enrolled in school (30 percent) than the U.S. population (33 percent). For 5- and 6-year-olds, however, the percentages reversed (90 percent for Pacific Islanders compared to 86 percent for the total United States). The percentages for ages 7 through 17 were fairly similar for the two groups, but then a divergence occurred. Only 45 percent of the Pacific Islanders 18 and 19 were in school, compared to 52 percent for the total United States population. Many Pacific Islanders who finished high school did not go on to college. Although more than half of all Tongans and "other" Micronesians in this age group were attending school in 1980, less than half of the Hawaiians, Samoans, and Guamanians were in school.

Of the 20- and 21-year-olds, only "other" Micronesians were attending school in the same proportions as the total U.S. population. While 1 in every 3 persons in this group were enrolled in school, only 1 in 4 persons in the other groups were enrolled.

"Other" Micronesians stayed in school, or came to the United States at older ages for schooling. Only 9 percent of the United States population 25 to 34 were enrolled in schools (and 10 percent of the Pacific Islanders), but 20 percent of the other Micronesians were in school. Also, 7 percent of the other Micronesians 35 years and over were in school compared to 2 percent of the total United States population.

Part of the larger proportion of dropouts among Pacific Islanders comes from the cultural tendency to coddle young children. Pacific Islanders have high expectations for youths, often reinforced with physical violence, particularly among Samoans. Often inherent conflicts exist between this relationship and that found between the teachers and students in the schools.

Ala'ilima, for example, describes these difficulties of moving from the Samoan family structure into the classroom. She notes that the teacher wants the students to speak up. The teacher "is forbidden by her morality and by our law to give him a blow on the head when he has gone too far" (1972, p. 58). Rules become obscured.

Similarly, Rolff (1978, p. 211) notes that migrant families keep adolescents busy "to the point of exhaustion." Family concerns always precede individual ones. Education becomes difficult, "even though many parents verbally urge their children to do well in school" (Rolff 1978, p. 211).

Only a few studies look at employment expectations of Micronesians while in school. In one study, Larson found that 18 of his small sample of 26 students intended to stay in the United States after graduation. Of t'_se 18, 12 said they would take a job "for the money." In fact, "half of the students who would take a job 'for the money' gave some indication that they needed the money in order to buy their return trip back to Truk" (Larson 1979, p. 30).

Naich (personal communication), once again, is at the other end of the continuum. In tracing his redemption hypothesis, he finds that many Micronesian former students in North Carolina, Oklahoma, Oregon, and Arizona who have been in the United States for a long time do want to return home "some day." Many did not want to go home right away because they were ashamed to go. Rather, either they did not do well in school or they did something in the United States to damage their own or their family's reputation. They decide to wait it out a little longer in the (often vain) hope of getting back into school or repairing the damaged reputation. Especially for those students given a feast by their islands before leaving for the United States, the parental admonition—to study hard, remember why they are away from home, not to come back without a degree—can have long-term effects. Many feel guilty about returning home empty-handed.

In any case, many Pacific Islanders immigrated to the United States for education. The proportions of high-school graduates among Pacific Islander immigrants were similar to the proportion for the total United States population in 1980. Although 16 percent of the United States population 25 years and older had attended college for 4 or more years, the proportion was almost as high for Micronesians (15 percent). Percentages were somewhat lower for Tongans (13 percent) and much lower for Samoans, Guamanians, and Hawaiians.

Pacific Islander males were more likely to graduate from high school and college than Pacific Islander females (Table 9.7). About 67 percent of all United States males and 66 percent of the females 25 years and over were high-school graduates, compared to 69 percent for Pacific Islander males and 65 percent for the females. On the other hand, only 11 percent of the Pacific Islander males were college graduates (only slightly more than half the 20 percent for the total United States). About 8 percent of the Pacific Islander females were college graduates (compared to 13 percent for the United States).

The individual groups also showed differences. Although 11 percent of all Pacific Islander males were college graduates, more than 13 percent of the Tongans and 22 percent of the "other" Micronesians were in

TABLE 9.7

Cumulative Level of School Completed for Pacific Islanders: 1980

Years of School Completed	United States (in 000's)	Total Pacific Islander	Hawaiian	Samoan	Tongan	Guamanian	Other Micronesian
MALES 25+ YRS	62,416	56,712	38,917	7,514	1,427	6,704	899
Elementary							
0 to 8 yrs	100.0	100.0	100.0	100.0	100.0	100.0	100.0
High school							
1 to 3 yrs	81.5	85.1	85.8	85.0	82.4	83.8	84.8
4 yrs	67.3	69.4	70.0	65.7	67.7	71.2	78.1
College							
1 to 3 yrs	36.1	30.2	29.7	26.8	34.8	29.7	61.2
4 yrs	20.1	11.2	11.5	9.8	13.1	8.9	21.9
5+ yrs	10.3	5.4	5.4	4.6	7.8	3.7	9.3
FEMALES 25+ YRS	70,420	62,106	44,464	7,393	1,094	6,906	853
Elementary							
0 to 8 yrs	100.0	100.0	100.0	100.0	100.0	100.0	100.0
High school							
1 to 3 yrs	82.0	83.0	84.8	78.9	76.4	79.8	78.1
4 yrs	65.8	65.2	67.0	56.6	64.0	64.7	63.5
College							
1 to 3 yrs	28.1	23.5	23.7	19.0	28.2	24.6	34.8
4 yrs	12.8	7.6	7.9	4.8	12.6	7.5	10.0
5+ yrs	5.3	3.5	3.7	2.2	5.6	3.7	2.9

SOURCE: U.S. Bureau of the Census, PC80-1-C1, Table 102, PC80-2-1E.

this category. Similarly, 13 percent of Tongan females and 10 percent of "other" Micronesian females were college graduates. Since "other" Micronesians moved to the United States for schooling, the small number of college graduates showed that some continued to stay in the United States after graduation.

Education information in the form of school attendance and educational attainment showed the heterogeneity of the Pacific Islander groups. Hawaiians showed one pattern—lower participation rates for higher ages being consistent with long-term residence. Hawaiians showed the spectrum of training leading to a large variety of occupations (albeit a large number at the lower end of the continuum). Guamanians and other Micronesians immigrated largely for educational training, many expecting to return after schooling. Their distribution was heavier at the other end. Samoans and Tongans were intermediate, some migrating for schooling with the intention of returning to the sending islands. Others intended to remain, or already were second- and third-generation migrants, so looked statistically more like the Hawaiians. It was unclear whether the Samoans and Tongans would become even more like the Hawaiians over time. Also, the 1990 census will help show whether Micronesians have also become permanent residents in large numbers, and also move in that direction as well.

Of the Pacific Islander immigrant groups, Micronesians were the most prominent in the education statistics, since the largest proportion of their population came to attend college. Some Micronesians approached tertiary education rather haphazardly. In fact, a superficial reading might lead to the conclusion that many were enjoying the "trip" referred to earlier in the migration section. A study published in 1977 noted that a "review of the colleges attended by most Micronesian students reveals that acceptance is not a major obstacle since most of the institutions, with all due respect, are likely candidates for the 'Who's Who' of obscure American Colleges" (Harlan 1977, p. 3). In fact, Harlan further noted that many of these colleges were "low quality institutions that are dependent on federally aided students for a large part of their income" (1977, p. 17).

On the other hand, many of the Micronesian students had no specific educational goals or selected unrealistic paths of study. For example, Tun and Sigrah (1975, p. 21) noted for Hawaii "that 90 percent [of the Micronesian students] want to be teachers, even though there are too many teachers in Micronesia." (What was true in 1975 may no longer be true.)

A later study found that students in business accounted for 21 percent of college students, while others studied education (17 percent), political and social science (13 percent), health sciences (12 percent), agriculture and marine resources (4 percent), and engineering and law (4 percent) (TTPI Bulletin of Statistics 1977, p. 32). Part of the selection probably came from job expectations as perceived by the students or as dictated by their governments.

Why Some Can't Adapt: The Problem of Language Acquisition and Use: Although the 1980 census data showed that Pacific Islander immigrants were proficient in English (Table 9.8), each respondent assessed his or her own ability. That is, no objective measure of English language ability for non-English speakers existed.

Only about 7 out of every 10 Pacific Islanders in the United States in 1980 spoke English at home, compared to 89 percent of the general population. Hawaiians skewed the Pacific Islander data since more than 90 percent of that group spoke English at home. Some "noise" may be in the data, in fact, since only 81 percent of the Hawaiians who spoke a language other than English at home spoke an Asian or Pacific Islander language.

Only half of the Guamanians spoke English at home, less than one-fourth of the Samoans, one-fifth of the "other" Micronesians, and only 1 in 8 of the Tongans.

Most of those who did not speak English at home spoke an Asian or Pacific Islander language, ranging from 96 percent of the Samoans to 77 percent of the Guamanians. Almost 80 percent of the Hawaiians who spoke an Asian and Pacific Islander language spoke Hawaiian. About 98 percent of the Samoans in this category spoke Samoan, 96 percent of the Guamanians spoke Chamorro, and most Tongans spoke Tongan. About 11 percent of the "other" Micronesians spoke Chamorro at home (presumably persons from the Northern Mariana Islands), and most others spoke other Micronesian languages.

The 6 in 10 of the Pacific Islanders over 17 years old and speaking an Asian or Pacific Islander language in 1980 who also spoke English very well included more than 7 of every 10 Hawaiians and Guamanians. On the other hand, only slightly more than half of the adult Samoans spoke English very well. This lack of English-speaking ability was more prominent among "other" Micronesians (only 46 percent speaking English very well), and Tongans (36 percent) (Table 9.9).

The standard of English proficiency that many migrants achieve on their home islands is often inadequate for employment in the United States. Samoan immigrant parents often cite their children's improved English ability as a primary reason to immigrate to the United States. Many of these parents, however, want their children to know the Samoan language and to continue to use it at home (Maga/1964).

The Samoan language remains in use in Samoan households. Shu and Satele found (1977, p. 39) that 86 percent of respondents spoke Sa-

TABLE 9.8

Language Spoken at Home for Persons 5 Years and Over for Pacific Islanders: 1980

Language Spoken at Home	United States (in 000's)	Total Pacific Islander	Hawaiian	Samoan	Tongan	Guamanian	Other Micronesian
IN HOUSEHOLDS	210,247	223,974	151,046	32,508	5,171	26,465	3,757
Speak only English at home	187,187	159,537	136,152	7,538	645	13,313	755
Percent	89.0	71.2	90.1	23.2	12.5	50.3	20.1
Speak a language other than English at home	23,060	64,437	14,894	24,970	4,526	13,152	3,002
Speak Asian/Pacific Islander language	(NA)	55,647	12,057	24,055	3,580	10,183	2,422
Percent	(NA)	86.4	81.0	96.3	79.1	77.4	80.7
Speak other language	(NA)	8,790	2,837	915	946	2,969	580

SOURCE: U.S. Bureau of the Census, PC80-1-C1, Table 99, PC80-2-1E.

NA: Not available.

TABLE 9.9

Ability to Speak English for Persons 18 Years and Over for Pacific Islanders: 1980

Ability to Speak English	Total Pacific Islander	Hawaiian	Samoan	Tongan	Guamanian	Other Micronesian
ersons 18 + years	41,646	10,178	15,707	2,294	8,958	1,990
Percent	100.0	100.0	100.0	100.0	100.0	100.0
Speak English:						
Very well	60.6	71.4	53.9	36.4	71.7	45.8
Well	29.3	23.5	32.6	37.2	24.1	44.7
Not well	8.7	4.9	11.5	22.1	3.7	8.3
Not at all	1.4	0.2	2.1	4.3	0.4	1.2

DURCE: U.S. Bureau of the Census, PC80-1-C1, Table 99, PC80-2-1E.

moan in their homes. About the same proportion considered Samoan to be their first language. Only 8 percent of this sample reported that they were unable to speak English at all. The authors concluded that about half of the respondents either were not fluent in English or could not speak it. However, 43 percent of the sample householders would consider using an interpreter to help explain medical problems to an English-speaking doctor (Shu and Satele 1977, p. 40).

Micronesians also have difficulties with the language transition. At two Oregon colleges, for example, the "students tend to be shy and embarrassed by their perceived inability to communicate well in English which inhibits the students' abilities to make friends quickly and deters the students from participating in class" (Leinwald 1981, p. vi).

Micronesians by nature do not talk much with strangers or other outsiders in authority (Levin and Naich, manuscript). Frequently Micronesians do not even communicate well among themselves. The problem is less linguistic than cultural—respect for authority requires listening, not speaking. Micronesians offer the classic case of being seen but not heard.

Language data from the language item on the sample show that 67,720 persons spoke a Pacific Islander language at home in 1980 (Table 9.10). Of these, 48,917 (72 percent) spoke Polynesian languages, 17,089 (25 percent spoke Micronesian languages, and 1,174 (3 percent) spoke Melanesian languages. The 27,475 persons speaking Samoan formed the largest Pacific Islander group speaking a specific language. The 13,694 Hawaiian speakers and 12,063 Chamorro speakers were second and third largest groups. Also, 4,857 persons spoke Tongan.

Immigration for Education and Employment: Many Pacific Islanders must work part-time or full-time since financial aid for education is

TABLE 9.10

Pacific Islander Language Spoken at Home: 1980

Language Spoken at Home	Number	Percent	Percent of Group
TOTAL	67,720	(x)	—
Percent	(x)	100.0	—
Polynesian	48,917	72.2	100.0
Samoan	27,475	40.6	56.2
Tongan	4,857	7.2	9.9
Hawaiian	13,694	20.2	28.0
Other Polynesian	2,981	4.4	6.1
Micronesian	17,089	25.2	100.0
Chamorro	12,063	17.8	70.6
Chuukese	508	0.8	3.0
Kosraean	1,239	1.8	7.3
Marshallese	511	0.8	3.0
Palauan	1,027	1.5	6.0
Yapese and Ulithian	687	1.0	4.0
Other Micronesian	1,054	1.6	6.2
Melanesian	1,714	2.5	100.0
Fiji	1,033	1.5	60.3
Other Melanesian	681	1.0	39.7

SOURCE: U.S. Bureau of the Census unpublished data.

rarely enough to cover their expenses. As time passes and the Pacific Islanders work but do not remain in or reenter colleges, a kind of *de facto* immigration occurs. Since skills are lacking, English language ability deficient, and because many Pacific Islanders settle in small cities without adequate transportation, most take jobs at and remain in entry-level positions.

Return migration *is* problematic. For American Samoans, for example, a pattern of circular mobility has developed between Hawaii and Samoa, and between the United States mainland and Samoa, particularly for those who adapt less well to American society (Franco 1978; Lyons 1980). Lyons found, for example, "over 40 percent (176 out of 393) [of his sample] had visited some place outside the Samoan Islands and 41 percent (158 out of 384) indicated they had visited Hawaii or the United States mainland" (1980, p. 68). Also, Lyons (1980, p. 72) noted "the relationship between return visiting and migration to American Samoa is an important dimension of the migration streams," with many short visits occurring in his study.

Micronesians have a more difficult time practicing this type of mobility because of the distances and costs (air transportation between Hawaii and Samoa charged at domestic rates, between Micronesia and Hawaii at international rates). Also, the minimum wage in American Samoa is less than in the United States. Rates in Micronesia are even lower, so families are hard pressed to help when Micronesian graduates are ready to return to Micronesia. Many cannot get home, even if they want to go, because they cannot afford a ticket. Finally, as Levin and Naich (manuscript) note, many who want to return have not been thoroughly "redeemed," and therefore cannot easily return to "face the music."

As Pacific Islanders have trouble adjusting to labor force participation in the United States, many also have difficulty adjusting to the different circumstances in their home areas if they return. Serious psychological and financial risks exist for Pacific Islanders who try to adjust to the island life-style, particularly abandonment of the more material aspects of the West—MTV and movies and tape recorders. In fact, ". . . return migrants, despite or more probably because of the status (in the modern and nontraditional sense) they have gained from migration, are a 'source of dissatisfaction with village life and the predominantly subsistence economy' (Meleisea and Meleisea 1980, p. 37), introduce new discontents, values and aspirations, do not settle long themselves and induce others to follow their lead" (Connell 1984, p. 24). Naich (personal communication), however, notes that "returnees who are not part of the *status quo* or the Establishment tend to bark like some restless mad dog. They tend to move to the left (hence, viewed as troublemakers). But they shut their mouths up once they're absorbed into the system, or once they create their own 'Establishment'."

Also, as the Pacific Islanders find limited economic opportunities in the United States, many of the problems with potential return have to do with a different kind of limited employment opportunities. Some Micronesians on Pohnpei, for example, do not engage in subsistence activities, but desire only "continued and increased access to the goods and prestige provided by employment" (Petersen 1979, p. 37). In a study of Palauans in Hawaii, Vitarelli found that "if and when the subjects return to Palau, the overwhelming majority want to work in upper level white-collar jobs . . . Unfortunately, however, it seems likely that there won't be enough jobs for all who return to Palau looking for them" (1981, p. 18). Very few jobs are available in Micronesia, for example. Many of the available jobs are filled in recent years by those persons having only limited education. These people will not be retiring for many years, leaving the increasing numbers of educated young people with few job prospects.

Thompson summarizes the increased expectations of Micronesians:". . . an army of agriculture graduates will do nothing for agricultural production if they are only content to work as government extension agents but are unwilling to farm" (1981, p. 4). Thompson also notes that if returning students have impossibly high expectations, "returnees become more, not less, dependent on the government for their livelihood" (1981, p. 4).

Employment

Pacific Islanders seek jobs, not careers: Those Pacific Islander immigrants who do stay must adapt to the marketplace to compete. Pacific Islander immigrants, partly because they lack a commitment to immigration and want to maintain cultural ties with their sending islands, find themselves in a dilemma. Labor force participation in American society centers on the market economy. The socioeconomic position occupied by most of the population reflects an ability to compete in labor markets as well as fluctuations in the market demand for labor. Most Pacific Islanders try to enter labor markets containing large numbers of other immigrants (particularly Asians and Mexicans) with similar aspirations and abilities. Obviously, markets are highly competitive for the few Western-oriented skills that many Pacific Islander immigrants have. Furthermore, these markets have probably become more competitive in recent years as the American economy has moved through various recessions. The assessment of the socioeconomic position of Pacific Islanders must therefore consider the structural and institutional factors influencing how they find work.

Different Pacific Islander groups participate in the labor market in different ways, depending partly on the migration flow and partly on cultural circumstances. Micronesians, for example, arrive mostly as single individuals and do not have to worry about supporting families. Sometimes an extended family of sorts develops when students or former students force other Micronesians to support them. Some of these dropouts (or "drop-ins") have worked, "but others—unable to continue school and unwilling to return home—spent their time living off other students: borrowing money, and living and eating in student apartments without paying rent" (Tun and Sigrah 1975, p. 25).

Tongan immigrants, like Samoan and Chamorro immigrants, come as family units. In her study of Tongan immigrants to Salt Lake City, Chapman found that all households communally redistributed incomes, continuing the extended family structure found in Tonga (1972, p. vii). Samoans in Hawaii were more like the Tongan example than Samoans in California, closer to the U.S. average (Hayes and Levin 1984a).

Labor Force Participation: In 1980, 62 percent of the persons 16

300

years and older in the United States were in the labor force. All the Pacific Islander groups except Micronesians had close to or greater proportions in the labor force. About 71 percent of Tongans, for example, were in the labor force, followed closely by 70 percent of Guamanians. Hawaiians and Samoans had percentages similar to those of the United States population with 65 percent and 60 percent, respectively.

Major differences existed in male and female labor force participation, but these paralleled the differences for the total United States. For males, in fact, the percentage of Pacific Islander males in the labor force was slightly greater than for the total United States (76 percent compared to 75 percent). Fully 86 percent of all adult Tongan males were in the labor force, as were 81 percent of Guamanian males. On the other hand, only 69 percent of "other" Micronesian males were in the labor force. More than half of all Pacific Islander females in 1980 were in the labor force. Guamanians had the largest proportion at 58 percent, and "other" Micronesians the lowest at 39 percent. The proportion of females in the labor force was smaller than for males for all groups. Although the patterns for males did not vary very much, significant differences existed for females. Micronesian and Samoan females 16 years and over had the lowest proportions in the labor force, while Guamanians and Tongans had higher proportions in the labor force.

The unemployment rates for 1980 are only of historical interest now. Although a slightly higher percentage of Pacific Islander males were unemployed (7.5 percent) than for the United States (6.5 percent), more than 9 percent of the Tongan, Samoan, and "other" Micronesian males were unemployed. Although the percentage unemployed was the same for both sexes in the United States, Pacific Islander females were less likely to be unemployed than males. Samoan females, for example, were more likely than males to be unemployed. For most of the other groups, males had higher unemployment. The rates for Tongans were widest— 9.3 percent of the males, but only 4.3 percent of the females being unemployed.

All Pacific Islander groups except Tongan and Micronesian females had unemployment rates higher than the U.S. average in the 1980 census. As the impact of the Compacts of Free Association begins, more Micronesian immigrants will probably come for schooling. Micronesians will also come to work since they can flow freely into and out of the United States. Labor force participation rates and unemployment rates could increase.

Although the recorded rates were fairly low in 1980, for Samoans at least, studies describe unemployment as one of the major problems Samoans face in the United States. Part of the unemployment problem for Samoans occurs because of lack of prior training and language skills, and because of negative stereotyping. Also, many Samoans live in Honolulu, San Francisco, and southern California. These areas of high competition attract other immigrant groups seeking the same unskilled and semi-skilled jobs. Franco (1984), for example, has examined the relationship between low educational attainment of Samoans and high unemployment. He found that the U.S. school system, combined with problems with the English language, has not led to completely successful socialization.

Researchers site Samoan unemployment rates ranging from 29 percent (Shu and Satele 1977, p. 69–70) up to 65 percent (informant quoted by Maatz 1978). The Census Bureau defines labor force participation in a very specific way. The census does not include as part of the labor force persons who have stopped looking for work because they have become discouraged, become unpaid family baby sitters or household workers, or are working for a matai or other leader in the community without pay. Unemployment rates include them in neither the numerators nor denominators. These persons may be in the labor force but unemployed in the surveys taken by Shu and Satele and others. Since the labor force definition differs, comparisons with census rates are not always possible. The very high rates other researchers get at least show Samoan perceptions of high unemployment.

Sometimes "unemployment" is actually unpaid employment. For example, Ablon found that Samoans with young children make every effort to have overlapping jobs to watch the children. However, even then, they may need a baby sitter. They might recruit one of the relatives from home. "These young women share the economic fortunes of the family with whom they live. Most eventually go on to jobs outside of the household, frequently as nurses' aides in the same institutions where older women of their households work" (Ablon 1970, p. 79).

Several Pacific Islands' cultural factors contribute to this perceived high unemployment. Since Islanders pool and redistribute incomes, family members can become alienated, leading to youthful "unemployment, underemployment and undereducation" (Rolff 1978, p. 224). The repercussions of reducing job commitments and concomitant income are minor, and "sanctions are limited usually to scoldings and demands that they find work" (Rolff 1978, p. 220).

The dual factors of job sharing and job covering also affect unemployment rates. For example, if Pacific Islander employees take leave for a feast or a funeral, "others will willingly assume the extra tasks" (Lewthwaite et al. 1973, p. 151). Similarly, Pacific Islanders frequently move in and out of the work force for one reason or another, with other family members or other members of the Pacific Islander community replacing them.

Also, as Omari notes, "Low paying jobs . . . do not add to the prosperity and status of the household, nor do jobs where opportunities for advancement are limited . . . Consequently, the Samoans are under criticism by the community for having thirty percent of their people on welfare and an unemployment rate of 36.3 percent" (Omari 1972, p. 10).

Class of Worker: Pacific Islander groups had proportions of private wage and salary workers that did not differ much from the 76 percent for the United States in 1980. On the other hand, Hawaiians (7 percent), Samoans (8 percent), and especially Guamanians (16 percent) were employed as federal workers in far greater proportions than the 4 percent for the total United States. Nearly 5 percent of all workers in the United States worked for state government, compared to 9 percent of all Hawaiians. Also, 16 percent of Micronesians worked for state government (the latter being notable, since the 291 Micronesians in this category were probably non-citizens in 1980).

Occupation and Industry: Table 9.11 shows occupations by sex. For both sexes combined, for the managerial and professional occupations, all Pacific Islander groups except Hawaiian (17 percent) were far below the 23 percent for the total United States. Although 30 percent of the United States' population were employed in technical, sales, and administrative occupations, smaller proportions of Tongans (19 percent) and Micronesians (23 percent) and a larger percentage of Guamanians (34 percent) were employed in this category. On the other hand, 34 percent of all Micronesians, 26 percent of Tongans, and 22 percent of Hawaiians had service occupations, considerably above the 13 percent for the total United States. Also, although 18 percent of the United States' employed population were operators, fabricators, and laborers, 27 percent of the Samoans and 25 percent of the Tongans had these occupations.

At 18 percent, Pacific Islander males were twice as likely as U.S. males in general (9 percent) to be in service occupations in 1980. Pacific Islander males were more likely to be operators, fabricators, and laborers, but less likely to be managers and professionals or technicians. Pacific Islander females were even more likely to be in service occupations than the total U.S. population. More than 1 in every 4 Pacific Islander women had service occupations, compared to about 1 in 6 for the total population.

Again, there have been very few independent studies of Pacific Islander occupations. Most evidence suggests that Pacific Islanders remain at entry-level occupations. For example, the "employment of Tongans in Salt Lake (City) has not reached the point where it could be termed specialization. Most of the jobs can be learned rapidly by anyone; custodian, seamstress, laundress, landscaper" (Chapman 1972, p. 92).

TABLE 9.11

Occupation for Pacific Islanders: 1980

Occupation	United States (in 000's)	Total Pacific Islander	Hawaiian	Samoan	Tongan	Guamanian	Other Micronesian
EMPLOYED MALES							
16 years +	56,005	54,029	37,201	6,476	1,470	6,435	1,119
Percent	100.0	100.0	100.0	100.0	100.0	100.0	100.0
Manag. and prof. specialties	23.6	15.1	16.0	11.8	10.7	13.6	13.6
Tech, sales, and admin.	19.0	15.9	15.2	16.4	11.9	20.7	14.8
Service occupations	9.2	17.6	17.1	17.3	22.4	16.3	35.0
Farm, forestry, fish	4.3	4.7	5.2	2.9	10.2	2.6	5.0
Precision production, craft and repair occupations	20.7	19.5	19.7	17.6	16.8	22.5	13.0
Operators, fabricators and laborers	23.2	27.2	26.8	34.0	28.0	24.2	18.6
EMPLOYED FEMALES							
16 years +	41,634	43,789	31,198	4,622	811	5,531	538
Percent	100.0	100.0	100.0	100.0	100.0	100.0	100.0
Manag. and prof. specialties	21.5	16.1	17.3	13.3	10.9	13.6	13.4
Tech, sales, and admin.	45.6	43.7	43.9	40.4	32.6	50.4	40.5
Service occupations	17.9	26.1	27.1	23.2	32.2	20.6	27.5
Farm, forest, fish	1.0	1.0	1.1	0.3	0.6	0.3	3.7
Precision production, craft and repair occupations	2.3	2.6	1.9	5.3	3.5	3.5	4.1
Operators, fabricators, and laborers	11.7	10.5	8.7	17.4	20.3	11.5	10.8

SOURCE: U.S. Bureau of the Census, PC80-1-C1, Table 104, PC80-2-1E.

Also, Pacific Islanders seek jobs that are people-oriented, rather than machine-oriented. If one or a set of relatives starts working for a particular corporation or agency, however, others will frequently follow. The families, and community in general, work as employment agencies. For example, "The gravitation of Samoan men into ship-building, metal-jobbing and construction work and of women into nursing thus reflects more than chance or even prior experience at Pago Pago or Pearl Harbor, and these strong patterns of family and community guidance are also evinced in the characteristic clusterings of Samoan employment" (Lewthwaite et al. 1973, p. 151).

Rolff (1978, pp. 177–178) has compared military and civilian employment, and the relationship between the two. She notes Samoans like service industries and occupations because they "ensure residential adaptability" and "wages appear to be high in comparison to those in the Armed Forces" (1978, pp. 177–178). Rolff also notes that these jobs are less secure than the military since the former sometimes involve layoffs and lack fringe benefits. Rolff concludes, "the employment shift had thus contributed to the increased marginalization of Samoans in the American economy."

In 1980, the largest proportion (22 percent) of the employed population in the United States 16 years and over was working in manufacturing industries. The largest proportions of Guamanians (24 percent), Samoans (23 percent), and Tongans (20 percent) were also in these industries. The largest proportions of Hawaiians, however, were in retail trade and professional and related services (health, education, and other professional services). About 38 percent of employed Micronesians were in professional and related services compared to 20 percent of the total U.S. employed population. Also, 29 percent of the total Micronesian population were working in education compared to 9 percent for the total U.S. population. Of course, many of these employed persons may have been students, and were working on or near their college campuses. Other large proportions of Micronesians were also working in retail trade (18 percent) and manufacturing industries (17 percent).

In general, the distribution of the Pacific Islander work force differed considerably from the work force of the total United States in 1980. For example, although 14 percent of the employed in the United States were in the manufacturing of durable goods, 18 percent of Guamanians worked in these industries (although only 6 percent of the Hawaiians were making durable goods). Hawaii, where most Hawaiians work, has few durable goods manufacturers. Also, while 4 percent of the U.S. population was in personal, entertainment, and recreational industries, 6 percent of the Guamanians worked in these industries. On the other hand, other Pacific Islander populations—Micronesians (9 percent), Samoans (9 percent), Hawaiians (10 percent), and Tongans (16 percent)—were in these industries in more than double the proportions of the total U.S. population. Also, 5 percent of the United States population was employed in public administration, compared to 10 percent of the Hawaiians and 11 percent of the Guamanians.

Labor Force Participation in All of 1979: Until now, the discussion of labor force participation has focused on the week before enumeration (or April 1, 1980). The 1980 census also asked a series of questions on labor force participation during all of 1979. The use of a full year allowed analysis of movement into and out of the labor force over the year (using weeks worked and weeks of unemployment). Full- and part-time employment came from hours usually worked per week.

All Pacific Islander groups except Micronesians did full- and part-time work in about the same proportions as the rest of the country. For the United States, 98 percent of all persons 16 years and over in the labor force in 1979 actually worked at some time in 1979. Also, of the total persons, 59 percent worked 50 or more weeks, and 26 percent worked less than 40 weeks. Among the Micronesians, only 37 percent worked 50 or more weeks, while fully 48 percent worked less than 40 weeks. All Pacific Islander groups experienced more unemployment at some time during 1979 than the U.S. average of 19 percent of the work force. Also, all groups had higher proportions of workers unemployed for 15 or more weeks than the total U.S. population.

Only about 6 in 10 Pacific Islander males worked the whole year in 1979, compared to about 2 in 3 for the total U.S. population (Table 9.12). Fewer than 4 in 10 of the "other" Micronesian males worked the whole year (while more than 1 in 3 worked less than half the year). Many of these Micronesians were students so presumably could work for only part of the year. Pacific Islander males were also more likely to be unemployed at some time during the year than was the total U.S. male population.

About half of the Pacific Islander females worked the whole year, about the same proportion as the U.S. population in general. However, only about 3 in every 10 "other" Micronesian females worked the whole year. Also, the Pacific Islander females were more likely than the total U.S. population to be unemployed at some time during 1989.

About 1 in every 5 Pacific Islanders worked part-time (1 to 34 hours per week) in 1979. Only "other" Micronesians varied considerably from this average. About 2 in every 5 of them worked part-time.

About 4 in every 10 U.S. families in 1979 had 2 workers, and another one-third had 1 worker. These proportions were about the same for Pacific Islanders. On the other hand, a slightly smaller proportion of

TABLE 9.12

Labor Force Status in 1979 for Pacific Islanders: 1980

Labor Force Status in 1979	United States (in 000's)	Total Pacific Islander	Hawaiian	Samoan	Tongan	Guamanian	Other Micronesian
MALE, 16+ IN LABOR FORCE							
1979	65,770	68,116	45,521	8,894	1,666	9,117	1,432
Worked in 1979	64,868	66,476	44,500	8,554	1,630	8,939	1,407
Percent	100.0	100.0	100.0	100.0	100.0	100.0	100.0
50 to 52 weeks	66.5	60.8	62.1	60.0	61.3	59.9	38.5
27 to 49 weeks	19.4	21.6	21.1	21.7	21.1	22.4	25.5
1 to 26 weeks	14.1	17.6	16.8	18.3	17.5	17.7	36.0
With unemployment in 1979	11,758	14,627	9,343	2,121	443	1,921	405
Percent	17.9	21.5	20.5	23.8	26.6	21.1	28.3
FEMALE, 16+ IN LABOR FORCE							
1979	50,796	53,511	37,896	5,852	965	6,764	819
Worked in 1979	49,610	51,554	36,655	5,479	912	6,536	796
Percent	100.0	100.0	100.0	100.0	100.0	100.0	100.0
50 to 52 weeks	50.9	49.4	51.2	43.6	53.7	46.2	30.2
27 to 49 weeks	25.4	24.6	24.1	25.4	15.9	27.6	23.9
1 to 26 weeks	23.8	26.0	24.6	31.0	30.4	26.2	46.0
With unemployment in 1979	9,912	12,079	7,855	1,760	218	1,680	231
Percent	19.5	22.6	20.7	30.1	22.6	24.8	28.2

SOURCE: U.S. Bureau of the Census, PC80-1-C1, Table 106, PC80-2-1E.

Pacific Islanders had no family workers in 1979, and a slightly larger proportion had 3 or more workers.

More family members would still be welcome in the house even if the educational attainment and economic status of Pacific Islanders were not lower than for the total United States. Extended families are common among Pacific Islanders, causing both more workers and dependents per family. Shu and Satele note, "it may also be a matter of economic necessity that relatives find it more advantageous to live together rather than separately" (1977, p. 33). Finally, because of the extended family, and since some of the immigrants may not be able legally to get welfare benefits, fewer families would have no workers.

The Tongans—the group least likely to have legal status—had the lowest proportion of families with no workers (2 percent) and the largest percentages of families with 3 or more workers (20 percent). Less than 10 percent of the Guamanians and Micronesians had no family workers. All groups had proportions of families with 3 or more workers per family above the U.S. average, once again, probably because of the continuation of the extended family ethos.

Income and Poverty

Income: The 80.5 million households in the United States in 1980 had a 1979 median income of $16,800 and a mean income of $20,300 (Table 9.13). Hawaiians ($16,600), Tongans ($16,200), Guamanians ($16,900), all had median incomes above $16,000 in 1979. Samoans at $13,800 and Micronesians at $11,100, however, were significantly below the United States average. Similarly, although none of the Pacific Islander groups had mean incomes above the U.S. average, Samoans ($16,500) and Micronesians ($13,000) were considerably below the U.S. mean. Family income showed similar patterns. Tongan family income did not differ very much from Tongan household income since few Tongans lived alone or only with non-relatives. Tongan family income, then, was more than $3,000 below the median for the total United States.

None of the groups approached the United States' total per capita income of $7,300. The per capita income of Hawaiians was $5,700, that of Guamanians was $5,500, of Tongans was $3,700, of Samoans was $3,600, and of Micronesians was $3,000 (less than half the U.S. total).

As noted earlier in the section on work in 1979, Pacific Islanders tended to work fewer weeks and fewer hours per week than the total United States population. Therefore, their income levels were lower. Rolff (1978, p. 147) notes, for example, "Many of the employed . . . hold marginal positions in the American economy as they work in factory and

TABLE 9.13

Income in 1979 of Pacific Islanders: 1980

Income in 1979	United States (in 000's)	Total Pacific Islander	Hawaiian	Samoan	Tongan	Guamanian	Other Micronesian
FAMILIES	59,190	52,785	36,153	6,963	1,236	6,543	738
Percent	100.0	100.0	100.0	100.0	100.0	100.0	100.0
Less than $5,000	7.3	9.3	8.7	13.1	6.1	7.9	16.4
$5,000–$9,999	13.1	15.3	14.3	20.2	20.5	12.6	24.7
$10,000–$14,499	14.7	16.4	15.2	19.1	18.0	19.1	24.4
$15,000–$19,999	15.1	14.3	13.8	14.5	15.2	16.2	14.0
$20,000–$24,999	14.3	13.2	13.7	10.3	18.8	13.3	10.4
$25,000–$34,999	19.1	17.7	18.6	14.3	12.5	19.3	4.2
$35,000–$49,999	10.7	10.0	11.3	6.6	5.5	8.6	4.5
$50,000 or more	5.6	3.8	4.4	1.8	3.5	3.0	1.5
Median (dollars)	NA	17,984	19,196	14,242	16,717	18,218	(NA)
Mean (dollars)	NA	20,616	21,495	16,968	18,587	20,959	(NA)
Married-couple families	48,990	39,811	26,474	5,428	1,172	5,206	538
Median (dollars)	NA	20,847	22,242	16,276	16,793	19,847	(NA)
Mean (dollars)		23,123	24,478	18,801	18,698	22,905	(NA)
Female H/H, no husband present	8,205	10,225	7,701	1,267	46	960	124
Median (dollars)	NA	8,340	8,600	6,647	18,929	9,550	(NA)
Mean (dollars)	—	11,561	11,200	9,030	17,677	11,650	(NA)
Per capita income (dollars)	7,298	5,220	5,691	3,573	3,671	5,533	(NA)

SOURCE: U.S. Bureau of the Census, PC80-1-C1, Table 107, PC80-2-1E.

309

service jobs subject to frequent layoffs or high turnover rates. These people's incomes are therefore fluctuating and unreliable."

Also, Pacific Islanders have difficulty amassing any wealth because of societal demands. Lower household and family incomes, and much lower per capita rates reflect this income dispersion. The social impacts are less readily seen in the statistics, but are still there. Often, an individual must by custom give up material goods or income he may want for himself or his family to maintain cultural equilibrium.

Income levels, while low, are still higher than those found in the U.S. outlying areas (although the standard of living is also lower in most of the territories). In fact, increased financial opportunity is often the reason for immigration (Harbison 1986, p. 89).

Remittances: Many Pacific Islander migrants, like their Asian counterparts, send money back to their families in the home countries. These monies are remittances. The 1980 Census could not measure remittances directly since the census collected only income. In theory, data on Samoan remittances to American Samoa, at least, could come from that concurrent census. However, "remittances" was not a separate category on the American Samoa questionnaire in 1980 (although it will be in 1990). The category that was available, "income from other sources," showed households who received "other income" receiving an average of $4,300 during 1979 (Summary Tape File 3A, Tables 71 and 72). The 1980 census did not collect "remittances" data from the other U.S. territories, but the 1990 census collected the data.

The tradition of remittances among Pacific Islanders has been most prominent among the Samoans, whose strong family ties remain unbroken by separations due to military enlistment or migration for work or sub-family unification. A large part of the early nonmilitary Samoan migration was to New Zealand, and the decision to migrate was not always the individual's alone. For example, Graves et al. found that only about half of the men and 16 percent of the women immigrated on their own initiative. Families commonly sent their single daughters to New Zealand, since they were more likely than sons to send remittances home. Families paid more than 3 out of every 4 fares (Graves et al. 1983, p. 14). Ieremia (1971) and Lyons (1980, p. 144) have also discussed the encouragement of migration for remittances for the United States Samoan community. Further, Ala'ilima and Stover discuss a Samoan male who joined the military to escape an uncle's pressure to give up all his previous civilian income. "Of the $280 he earned the first month, he kept $80 and sent $200 to his parents [in American Samoa]" (1986, p. 125).

Remittances have monetary importance since they increase the lower incomes received in the territories (except Guam). They also have social value in reinforcing kinship and other social and economic ties. Again, most of the research in this area is on Samoans. Ala'ilima and Stover record, for example, that one Samoan sends money back to Samoa because "if she did not respond she would no longer 'feel like a Samoan.' It is important to her sense of identity to continue to be an active member of her family of origin even though she may never return" (1986, p. 142).

Poverty: Although 17.0 percent of all persons in the United States were below poverty level, and only 13.9 percent of Guamanians and 15.8 percent of Hawaiians, 21.8 percent of Tongans, 29.5 percent of Samoans, and 37.9 percent of Micronesians were below poverty in 1979 (Table 9.14).

The data for families in poverty were equally striking for some groups. About 13.4 percent of all families in the United States in 1979 were below poverty level, compared to 11.6 percent of the Guamanian families, 14.3 percent of Hawaiian, 18.0 percent of Tongans, 25.5 percent of Micronesian and 27.7 percent of Samoan families.

Conclusions

Pacific Islanders in the United States in 1980 made up about one-tenth of 1 percent of the total United States population. Hawaiians were the majority of this minuscule population, making the Pacific Islander immigrant population even tinier. Yet, the 1980 and 1990 censuses both included separate entries for Samoans and Guamanians, showing their importance to federal agencies. Tongans, Micronesians, and other Pacific Islander groups also received special attention.

Many Pacific Islander immigrants come to the United States as part of a "trip," a traditional transition to adulthood. Some of the Islanders join the military and end up settling in the United States permanently. Other Islanders migrate for schooling, and then marry, have children, and settle here. Others come as family units. Many of these families, like most immigrants, come poor, and "look" very poor in the census statistics.

Part of this perceived poverty exists because Pacific Islanders are younger and have larger households and families and higher fertility than the rest of the U.S. population. As noted earlier, traditional social structure and the physical structure of the housing units influence Pacific Islander households and families in the United States. Once again, Pacific Islander immigrant extended families remain strong and cohesive, with fluid household composition.

The continuum of labor force participation and general adaptability

TABLE 9.14

Income in 1979 below Poverty Level for Pacific Islanders: 1980

Poverty Status in 1979	United States (in 000's)	Total Pacific Islander	Hawaiian	Samoan	Tongan	Guamanian	Other Micronesian
PERSONS 15 YRS + FOR WHOM POVERTY DETERMINED	(NA)	28,304	17,059	5,751	622	2,836	1,245
Percent below poverty level	(NA)	16.4	14.4	25.5	17.5	13.9	37.9
Percent female	(NA)	59.6	64.1	54.7	48.4	56.1	NA
FAMILIES	7,919	8,479	5,174	1,917	223	761	193
Percent below poverty level	13.4	16.1	14.3	27.5	18.0	11.6	25.5

SOURCE: U.S. Bureau of the Census, PC80-1-C1, Table 108, PC80-2-1E.

among Pacific Islanders shows that the farther from the Pacific Islands in time, space, and orientation, the more integrated into American society. Because this chapter is already very long, data by U.S. targeted immigration area are not presented. In another paper (Levin, manuscript), data for Samoans in American Samoa, Hawaii, and California show the continuums of adaptation for time, space, and orientation.

The census data on Samoans in 1980, for example, show that although many Samoans in California were in the lower levels of employment, they were firmly in the labor force. In Hawaii much larger proportions were unemployed or, as yet, unemployable (Hayes and Levin 1984a). Since many Samoans and other Pacific Islanders in Hawaii have left their islands only physically, psychologically remaining at home, continuing extended family structure, they may not assimilate as much. Families so much larger than the U.S. average are almost certain to have different life-styles as well.

Pacific Islanders often stay in entry-level employment positions to balance traditional and Western cultural constraints. However, frequently the Western constraints far outweigh the traditional ones. Connell's statement about Pacific Islanders in general is probably true for the United States immigrants:

> Most migrants from the South Pacific, including some of those with skills, are in the 'secondary segment' of the labor force . . . where social, institutional and economic barriers prevent movement into the 'primary segment' so that they remain in unskilled jobs with low wages, unstable tenure, poor working conditions, few benefits, high unemployment and low unionisation (1984, p. 42).

That Pacific Islanders were disproportionately in poverty is clear from the 1980 census data. What is less clear is how to interpret income levels in cultural terms—both the Western and the Pacific Islander terms. Samoans in Samoa, at least, expect remittances. If these remittances were to show up in the income and poverty statistics, the economic situation of Samoans would look even worse. The financial loss, however, is often offset by the cultural gain.

Therefore, the Pacific Islander community continues to look inward for financial and social reinforcement:

> Though modified in different settings, the *faaSamoa* continues to be maintained in response to institutional racism, some individual prejudice, and the deprivation of economic and social rewards which result from these conditions. That Samoans in the United States once again adhere to the *faaSaoma* is not simply a matter of conservatism, but rather of poverty and lack of social recognition from non-Samoans. The

various Samoan social networks, ceremonial redistributions, and modified forms of traditional social inequality are all means of coping with such deprivation (Rolff 1978, p. 8).

Since the 1980 Census was the first to provide data for all groups except Hawaiians, the 1990 Census will be the first decennial census to permit tracing trends for Pacific Islander immigrants. In a few years, when these new data become available, we will be able to assess the statistical changes in the Pacific Islander community. That will be the time to start testing hypotheses. That will also be the time for Pacific Islanders to consider their place in American society, where they have been, and where they are. Pacific Islanders, both individually and collectively, will then have to assess if they want to be part of the traditional-Western continuum.

CLOSING THOUGHTS

ADVICE TO A YOUNGER BROTHER

. . . Listen, (our parents) left their country, the only country they ever knew, with three thousand years of family history and tradition left behind. And for what, the land of opportunity? Do you think their situation here is that great? Mom and Dad were some of the lucky ones. A doctor, at least, can still work as a doctor in this country. Some parents came, giving up Ph.D.s and very respected positions, knowing that all their life work would be rendered absolutely useless in this new "land of opportunity." They had to open grocery stores, laundromats, restaurants, working sixteen-hour days, always being treated as inferior because of their color and their accents, suffering the "humiliation of the immigrant." But they had their reasons. No amount of sacrifice was too much for their children. Nothing in their lives meant more to them than their legacy—us. Our lives are everything to them. . .

Paul Y. Hahn

Narrowing the Generation and Culture Gaps: A Letter to A Younger Brother[1]

THIS POIGNANT statement expresses perfectly the ambivalence many Asian and Pacific Islander immigrants and children of immigrants feel about their new home. The "land of opportunity" has sharp edges for newcomers. Yet, as we have seen, nearly all immigrants from Asia will remain, become American citizens, and find some niches in American society. Chances are, the longer they stay, the more like other Americans they will become, warts and all. But from what we have seen in the preceding pages, that does not imply a "melting away" into the great American pot. More important, the process of adapting to America will be different: relatively smooth for some (the writer of the

[1]From a talk given by Paul Y. Hahn at the 18th Annual Conference, Koreans and Korean Americans in the United States, Yale University, May 5, 1986. Quoted in *Korean and Korean American Studies Bulletin* 3:3 (Spring/Summer 1989).

above passage is a student in a prestigious medical school), and extremely difficult for others.

We began this investigation with a very simple question: How well are the new waves of Asian immigrants adapting to American society? The public image is certainly one of responsible adults with substantial earnings reflecting considerable attainments; of families that are stable and successful—unabashed models of what American families are supposed to be—and of children who work and study hard, do well, and succeed. This image is so compelling, in fact, that it has stirred anger and even violence in some quarters (United States Commission on Civil Rights, 88, 1988a).

We have found that the answer to our question is not that simple. Some Asian Americans certainly fit the "Model Minority" image, and then some. But Vietnamese did not, as of 1980; in fact, they displayed demographic and social characteristics more typical of the "castelike" minorities—blacks, American Indians, and Hispanics. From what we know, the same was true of other Southeast Asian refugees. It was not the case with many Japanese—they mirrored white characteristics in many respects. Asian Indians as a group were the super models, but only in the case of the newer immigrants, and only because their immigration was so selective.

Squeezed between these two extremes were the Chinese, Filipinos, and Koreans. Filipinos in the eastern United States appeared much like Asian Indians, but in the West, especially in Hawaii, their socioeconomic characteristics resembled those of Hispanics in many respects. Conversely, some Chinese, particularly in the West, might well have been the models for the new American elite, but in Eastern cities many reside in poverty-stricken, crime-ridden ghettos. Koreans seem almost perfectly bimodal, some resembling successful Chinese and Asian Indians, and others in much the same situation as Vietnamese refugees.

Some research has concluded that Asian Americans are healthier than other Americans, but we have found that this also depends upon which groups, and upon their migration histories. "Health" also depends upon whether we are talking about infant mortality, age-specific mortality, or causes of death.

Pacific Islanders have presented a different portrait altogether. In the first place, their immigration may be a relatively ephemeral and circular affair, at least subjectively. As is pointed out in Chapter 9, many Pacific Islanders see physical movement as a part of the maturation process. Consequently, the business of "settling down and making a new life" may not be taken too seriously. Whatever the reason, Pacific Islanders do not fit the image of a successful model minority in the continental United States. The situation of Hawaiians is different still, but they more resemble the "caste" minorities than successful Asians.

Have we made any sense of all this? To some extent, the answer is "Yes," at least to the extent that we know more than we did when we began. But the issues are complex. To begin with, we are dealing with at least six Asian American ethnic groups, not to mention the many groups of Pacific Islanders. Each of those groups varies enormously on every demographic and social dimension we have attempted to study. Furthermore, those dimensions overlap and interact. To illustrate: some Asian Americans are native-born in the United States; others are immigrants. Some immigrants have been in the United States for a short time; others, for 20 years or more. Some immigrants come to the United States with advanced educational degrees and years of technical expertise; others are nearly illiterate. Some speak English well; others speak only their native languages.

Asian Indians happen to be represented by mostly new immigrants with superior educations, who were recruited for professional occupations. English is often their second language. Japanese are mostly native-born Americans, with educational levels, occupations, and family characteristics similar to those of whites. Vietnamese are nearly all very recent immigrants (actually refugees), most of whom had very poor educations, marginal occupational skills, with no jobs waiting for them in the United States. Korean immigrants exhibit a marked gender imbalance, with a preponderance of females. Older Chinese and Filipino immigrants show a preponderance of males. And so it goes. We did find one commonality among Asian Americans: with the exception of a few remaining farm laborers in the West and a few Southeast Asian refugees, nearly all have settled down in urban places, most in large metropolitan areas.

What this is leading up to, in part, is an admission of reluctance on our part to repeat the complexities of our findings, all of which are summarized in the Conclusions or Summaries of each of the preceding chapters. What we will do here is to review what we think are the most general conclusions we have come to at this point.

Nativity and Migration

From what we have seen, nativity and migration histories are more important in affecting Asian Americans than their countries of origin or cultures. First, as of 1980, American-born Asians (natives) were much different from Asian-born people, even of the same ethnicity. The native-born were bimodal in age, in that they were either American-born children of recent immigrants, or longtime residents of second, third, or fourth generations. The older natives reflected a different migration history, in that they or their ancestors were brought to the United States as farm laborers. They faced discrimination, which shows in their incomes and educations. These were inferior to those of natives or of whites or Asian immigrants who had resided in the United States for only slightly more than 10 years. Most of the Asian immigrants to America before World War II were rural, relatively poor, and unprepared for urban, industrial life. Recent immigrants from Asia (excepting Indo-Chinese) were more likely from sophisticated urban backgrounds, many with excellent educations and technical skills.

Of immigrants, we have seen that length of residence in the United States is a very powerful predictor of demographic characteristics, geographical residence, family and household composition, occupational status, and income level. We suspect that length of residence may also affect education, but census data do not allow us to distinguish between education attained abroad or in the United States. In general, as far as we can see through some of the confounding factors, recent immigrants, especially those who migrated 5 years or less before the census was taken, showed characteristics more similar to those of their previous homelands. The longer immigrants had resided in the United States, the more they resembled white Americans socially. Or outdid white Americans. As of this writing, we really cannot generalize about Vietnamese, because most of them entered the United States after 1975. However, Chapter 6 suggests that children of Southeast-Asian refugees may be outperforming children of Japanese, Chinese, Korean, or Filipino immigrants.

Many other factors, discussed at length in Chapters 2, 3, and 8, confound the picture somewhat, but nativity and/or immigration histories really do seem to determine a great deal of what becomes of Asian immigrants. Given this, we can distinguish three different groupings of Asian Americans, who must be understood somewhat differently. Again, native-born Asians must be distinguished from immigrants. First, most Japanese-Americans are native-born, and they most resemble whites socially and demographically. Second, nearly all Vietnamese are recent immigrants. In addition, they were refugees, and for some time "wards" of the government. In all respects, they are *least* like whites. Conversely, they are *most* like blacks and Hispanics.[2] Third, Chinese, Fili-

---

[2]Which makes them especially important for studies of the 1990 Census. If they show the same patterns as other Asian Americans as they remain in the United States over time, they may provide support for some version of assimilation theory. If, however,

pinos, Asian Indians, and Koreans all have varying mixes of natives and migrants, with Chinese the fewest migrants, and Koreans the most. Each of these groups differs on other demographic and social-background dimensions also, so one should not be cavalier in lumping them together. For example, Asian Indians have the highest educational levels of all ethnic groups we have studied. Still, most of the people in these groups are immigrants.

All this might be seen as qualified support for the assimilationists' point of view, but things are not quite that simple.

Remaining Disparities and Differences

The remarkable educational levels of Asian Americans are often cited as a principal reason for their "successes," but this actually depends upon which groups we examine. Asian Indians, Chinese, Filipinos, and Koreans all appeared to be better educated than whites in 1980. Japanese educational levels were about the same as those of whites. Vietnamese educations were much inferior to those of whites, again resembling blacks and Hispanics. Native-born Asian Americans completed less education than immigrants. However, newer cohorts of immigrants (those who entered the United States between 1975 and 1980) appeared to have completed less education than the older cohorts. This is probably because newer immigrants were mostly relatives of earlier immigrants, many of whom had entered as students or professionals. Nevertheless, the 1989 Current Population Survey data showed overall high educational levels for Asians, suggesting that newer immigrants and children of older immigrants were achieving high levels of education in the United States. So, again, some Asian Americans are better educated than whites and most are better educated than blacks or Hispanics, but simple generalizations are misleading.

Some popular treatments of Asian Americans also suggest that they are overrepresented in the professions, hence producing their very high incomes. Again, this is an oversimplification. Overall, the occupational distributions of Asian Americans look very much like those of whites, except that only Japanese are as well represented as executives and managers. Asian Indians, Filipinos, and Chinese do have large representations in the professions, but Chinese and Filipinos, along with Koreans, are also very well represented in low-prestige occupations. Koreans *are*

they retain their similarities to blacks and Hispanics, we must begin to look at structural constraints, which, in turn, will lead to a thornier question: Why should they be different from other Asian Americans?

more likely to be petite entrepreneurs than are other groups, but aside from that, their overall occupational distribution is quite even. It is important to emphasize that, for immigrants, occupational prestige does not change greatly, the longer people stay in the United States. Their incomes do increase, which is also significant.

Personal incomes of most groups of Asian Americans, if not controlled for other factors, often appear higher than those of whites. This is especially true of Asian Indians. However, when we control for gender, occupation, education, migration history, and other relevant variables, only Japanese appear to have reached income parity with whites. Census data do not give us a complete answer as to why this should be so, but we note that the discrepancy between white and Asian American incomes appears very similar to the discrepancy between men and women: it is well known that women are paid less than men for occupations of similar prestige. It seems that the same is true of Asian Americans, particularly new immigrants. It is very tempting to suggest that some exploitation, intentional or institutional, is involved.

Some Adaptive Strategies

Although personal incomes of most Asian Americans are lower than those of whites, household incomes are often higher, especially for Filipinos. One of the chief determinants of household income is the number of household workers. Newer immigrants, especially, appear to cope with other disadvantages (underemployment, unemployment, and low wages) by aggregating incomes in expanded households. Asian Americans, again excepting Vietnamese, tend to have relatively stable households, which helps to overcome other disadvantages.

In stable households, children tend to remain in school longer, and personal support from other family members may help to lessen stress, leading to better health. Most Asian Americans also appear to reduce fertility, which of course helps economically. Then, of course, better incomes may produce better health, which reduces mortality rates. The delicate balance of forces here can be seen among Korean immigrants, who have an overabundance of women, more single householders, and less income.

Conclusions

Asian Americans do not represent a single block of persons about whom one can generalize easily. Japanese Americans are not much different from whites on most of the dimensions we have studied. On the other hand, Vietnamese appear more like blacks and Hispanics. Chinese, Filipinos, Asian Indians, and Koreans are alike in that they are made up mostly of immigrants, but they are different from each other in many respects. Pacific Islander Americans are different yet, in almost all respects.

What we make of this depends upon the comparisons we choose. As we pointed out in Chapter 8, many or most Asian Americans are disadvantaged compared to white Americans. But with the exception of Vietnamese, they are much better off than blacks or Hispanics on the demographic and social variables we have studied. Because most Asian Americans are new immigrants, this latter comparison leads to a fundamental question: Why have many Asian Americans been relatively successful in "making it" in America, while blacks, American Indians, native Hawaiians, and Hispanics in general have not?

The question is not simple, and census data do not allow us to answer it. Assimilation advocates point to education, adaptation, hard work, and so on as determinants. Structuralists, on the other hand, look at differential institutional blockages or, conversely, differential access to success. The answer may very well lie with both positions. Whatever the truth in this matter, we should like to close with the observation that the adaptation of peoples of Asian or Pacific Island descent to America is not complete. Tensions and racial discrimination have not disappeared, a lesson that Japanese Americans learned most painfully with the advent of World War II.

Bibliography

Ablon, Joan "Samoans in Stateside Nursing." *Nursing Outlook* 18 (1970):32–33.
——— "Bereavement in a Samoan Community." *British Journal of Medical Psychology* 44 (1971):329–337.

Aguirre, B. E., Rogelio Saenz, and Sean-Shong Hwang "A Test of the Assimilation and Ethnic Competition Perspectives." *Social Science Quarterly* 70:594–606.

Ahlburg, Dennis and Michael Levin *The Northeast Passage: A Study of Pacific Islander Migration to American Samoa and the United States.* Canberra: National Centre for Development Studies Research School of Pacific Studies. The Australia National University, 1990.

Ala'ilima, Fay, ed. "Education: Challenge and Change." Samoan Heritage Series Proceedings. Manuscript, May 26–27, 1972.

Ala'ilima, Fay and Mary Liana Stover "Life Histories." In Paul T. Baker, Joel M. Hanna, and Thelma S. Baker, eds. *The Changing Samoans: Behavior and Health in Transition.* New York: Oxford University Press, 1986.

Allen, James Paul "Recent Immigration from the Philippines and Filipino Communities in the United States." *Geographic Review* 67 (1977):195–208.

Allen, James Paul, and Eugene James Turner *We the People: An Atlas of America's Ethnic Diversity.* New York: Macmillan Publishing Company, 1988.

Almaguer, Thomas, et al. *The Diversity Project: An Interim Report to the Chancellor.* Berkeley: University of California, Institute for the Study of Social Change, 1990.

Anonymous "Profile of Tomorrow's New U.S." *U.S. News and World Report,* 1986.
———"Census Forms Anger Asian Americans." *Honolulu Advertiser,* 1987.
———"Lung Cancer Without Smoke." *Asianweek* 70 (1989).
——— "Racial Diversity Likely Cause of Low Cancer Rate." *Honolulu Star-Bulletin* (1989):A-5.
——— "A State Bill Seeks Census Changes." *Honolulu Advertiser,* 1987.

Arnold, Fred, and James T. Fawcett *The Value of Children. Vol. 3, Hawaii.* Honolulu, HI: East-West Population Institute, 1975.

Arnold, Fred, Urmil Minocha, and James T. Fawcett "The Changing Face of Asian Immigration to the United States." In J. T. Fawcett and B. V. Carino, eds. *Pacific Bridges: The New Immigration from Asia and the Pacific Islands.* Staten Island, NY: Center for Migration Studies, 1987.

Asian and Pacific American Federal Employee Council "A Brief History of Asians in America." Washington, DC.: APAFEC, 1984.

Asian Pacific American Legal Center of Southern California "Asian Pacifics and U.S. Immigration Policy: IRCA legalization, phase I." San Diego, CA: Asian Pacific American Legal Center of Southern California, 1988.

Baker, Paul T. Preliminary report: "The Samoan Migrant Project." Pennsylvania State University, Human Biology Program, 1976.

Baker, S. P., B. O'Neill, and R. S. Karpf *The Injury Fact Book.* New York: Heath and Company, 1984.

Balboni, Jennifer, and Nguyen Qui Duc "The Pressure of Being a Model Minority." *Rice* 1 (1988):34–35, 52.

Ballendorf, Dirk "Education in Micronesia: Is There a Braindrain Coming?" *Micronesian Perspective* 1 (1977):4–8.

Barringer, Herbert R., and Gene Kassebaum "Asian Indians as a Minority in the United States: The Effect of Education, Occupations and Gender on Income." *Sociological Perspectives* 32 (1989):501–520.

Barringer, Herbert R., David T. Takeuchi, and Peter Xenos "Education, Occupational Prestige, and Income of Asian Americans." *Sociology of Education* 63 (1990):27–43.

Barringer, Herbert R., and Sung-nam Cho *Koreans in the United States: A Fact Book.* Paper No. 15. University of Hawaii, Center for Korean Studies, 1990.

Bartel, Ann P. "Where do the New U.S. Immigrants Live?" *Journal of Labor Economics* 7 (1989):371–391.

Bartlett, Larry *Dixie* Cited in *Filipinos in Louisiana,* by Marina E. Espina. New Orleans: A. F. Laborde and Sons, 1988.

Bean, Frank D., and John P. Marcum "Differential Fertility and the Minority Group Status Hypothesis: An Assessment and Review." In Frank D. Bean and W. Parker Frisbie, eds. *The Demography of Racial and Ethnic Groups.* New York: Academic Press, 1978.

Bean, Frank D., and W. Parker Frisbie *The Demography of Racial and Ethnic Groups.* New York: Academic Press, 1978.

Bean, Frank D., and M. Tienda *The Hispanic Population of the United States.* New York: Russell Sage, 1987.

Beaujot, R. P., K. J. Krotki, and P. Krishnan "The Effects of Assimilation on Ethnic Fertility Differentials." Paper presented at the annual meeting of the Population Association of America, 1977.

Bell, David A. "The Triumph of Asian-Americans." *The New Republic* (1985):24–31.

Bellah, R. *Tokugawa Japan.* New York: Free Press, 1957.

Berg, I. *Education and Jobs: The Great Training Robbery.* New York: Praeger, 1969.

Berkman, L. F., and S. L. Syme "Social Networks, Host Resistance, and Mortality; A 9-Year Follow-up Study of Alameda County Residents." *American Journal of Epidemiology* 109 (1979):186–204.

Bernard, William S. "A History of United States Immigration Policy." In R. A. Easterlin, David Ward, W. S. Bernard, and Reed Ueda, eds. *Immigration.* Cambridge: The Belknap Press of Harvard University (1982):75–105.

Bidwell, C. E., and N. A. Friedkin "The Sociology of Education." In N. Smelser, ed. *Handbook of Sociology.* Beverly Hills: Sage, 1988.

Blau, Peter M., and Otis Dudley Duncan *The American Occupational Structure.* New York: John Wiley, 1967.

Bonacich, Edna "A Theory of Ethnic Antagonism: The Split Labor Market." *American Sociological Review* 37 (1972):547–559.

——— "A Theory of Middlemen Minorities." *American Sociological Review* 38 (1973):583–594.

——— "Asian Labor in the Development of California and Hawaii." In Lucie Cheng and Edna Bonacich, eds. *Labor Immigration under Capitalism: Asian*

Workers in the United States Before World War II. Berkeley: University of California Press, 1984.

—— "The Limited Social Philosophy of Affirmative Action." *The Insurgent Sociologist* 14, 1 (1987):99–116.

Bonacich, Edna, and Lucie Cheng, eds. "Introduction: A Theoretical Orientation to International Labor Migration." *Labor Migration under Capitalism: Asian Workers in the United States Before World War II.* Berkeley: University of California Press (1984):1–56.

Bonacich, Edna, and T. H. Jung "A Portrait of Korean Small Business in Los Angeles." In E. Y. Yu, E. H. Phillips, and E. S. Yang, eds. *Koreans in Los Angeles: Prospects and Promises.* Los Angeles: California State University, Center for Korean-American and Korean Studies, 1982.

Bonacich, Edna, and Ivan Light *Immigrant Entrepreneurs: Koreans in Los Angeles, 1965–1982.* Berkeley: University of California Press, 1988.

Bonacich, Edna, Ivan Light, and C. Wong "Small Business among Koreans in Los Angeles." In E. Gee, ed. *Counterpoint: Perspectives on Asian America.* Los Angeles: University of California, Asian American Studies Center, 1976.

Bonacich, Edna, and J. Modell *The Economic Basis of Ethnic Solidarity: Small Business in the Japanese-American Community.* Berkeley: University of California Press, 1980.

Bouvier, Leon F. "U.S. Immigration: Effects on Population Growth and Structure." In Mary Kritz, ed. *United States Immigration and Refugee Policy.* Lexington, MA: D. C. Heath and Co. (1983): 193–210.

Bouvier, Leon F., and Anthony J. Agresta "The Fastest Growing Minority." *American Demographics,* 1985.

—— "The Future Asian Population of the United States." In James T. Fawcett and Benjamin V. Cariño, eds. *Pacific Bridges.* Staten Island, NY: Center for Migration Studies, 1987.

Bouvier, Leon F., and Robert W. Gardner "Immigration to the U.S.: The Unfinished Story." *Population Bulletin* 41, 1986.

Bouvier, Leon F., and Philip Martin *Population Change and California's Future.* Washington, DC: Population Reference Bureau, 1985.

Bowles, S., and H. Gintes *Schooling in Capitalist America: Education Reform and the Contradictions of Economic Life.* New York: Basic Books, 1976.

Brand, David "The New Whiz Kids." *Time* 31 (1987):42–46, 49, 51.

Breslow, L., and B. Klein "Health and Race in California." *American Journal of Public Health* 61 (1971):763–775.

Bromley, Mary Ann "Identity as a Central Adjustment Issue for the Southeast Asian Unaccompanied Refugee Minor." 1988.

Buell, Philip, and John E. Dunn, Jr. "Cancer Mortality among Japanese Issei and Nisei of California." *Cancer* 18 (1965):656–664.

Bulletin of Statistics Statistics Department, Trust Territory of the Pacific Islands. Saipan: 1977.

Bunzel, J. M., and J. K. D. Au "Diversity or Discrimination? Asian Americans in College." *The Public Interest,* Spring 1987.

Burch, T. K. "Comment on 'Minority Status and Family Size: A Comparison of Explanations' by R. Jiobu and M. Marshall." *Population Studies* 33 (1979):375–376.

Burch, Thomas A. "Racial Differences Between Linked Births and Infant Deaths Records in Hawaii." *Research & Statistics Report* No. 44. Honolulu: Hawaii State Department of Health, 1983.

Burki, S. J., and S. Swamy "South Asian Migration." *Economic and Social Weekly* 22 (1987):513–517.

Butterfield, Fox "Why Asians Are Going to the Head of the Class." *New York Times,* August 3, 1986.

Cabezas, Amado, Larry Hjime Shinagawa, and Gary Kawaguchi *Evidence for a Structural Origin of Income Inequality for Asian Americans in the San Francisco Bay Area and Los Angeles in 1980.* Berkeley, CA: University of California, Ethnic Studies Department, Asian American Studies Program, 1980.

Caces, M. Fe "Personal Networks and the Material Adaptation of Recent Immigrants: A Study of Filipinos in Hawaii." Ph.D. dissertation, University of Hawaii, May 1985.

Cafferty, Pastora San Juan, Barry R. Chiswick, Andrew M. Greeley, and Teresa A. Sullivan *The Dilemma of American Immigration: Beyond the Golden Door.* New Brunswick, NJ: Transaction Books, 1983.

California Post Secondary Education Commission "Eligibility of California's 1986 High School Graduates to Its Public Universities." *Sacrament,* March 1988.

Caplan, Nathan, John K. Whitmore, and Quang L. Bui *Southeast Asian Refugee Self-Sufficiency Study: Final Report.* Prepared for the Office of Refugee Resettlement, Department of Health and Human Services. Ann Arbor: University of Michigan, Institute for Social Research, 1985.

Cater, John, and Trevor Jones "Asian Ethnicity, Home-ownership and Social Reproduction." In Peter Jackson, ed. *Race and Racism: Essays in Social Geography.* New York: Allen Unwin, 1987.

Chamnivickorn, Suchithra "Fertility, Labor Supply and Investment in Child Quality among Asian American Immigrant Women." *P/AAMHRC Research Review* 6 (1988):28–29.

Chang, Pao-Min *Continuity and Change: A Profile of Chinese Americans.* New York: Vantage Press, 1983.

Chapman, Barbara Anne "Adaptation and Maintenance in the Extended Family of Tongan Immigrants." Master's thesis, University of Utah, Salt Lake City, 1972.

Chataway, C. J., and J. W. Berry "Acculturation Experiences—Appraisal, Coping, and Adoption: A Comparison of Hong Kong Chinese, French, and English Students in Canada." *Canadian Journal of Behavioral Science* 21, 1989.

Chau-Eoan, Howard G. "Strangers in Paradise." *Time Magazine,* March 5, 1990.

—— "A Promised Land?" *Time Magazine,* April 9, 1990.

Cheng, Lucie "The New Asian Immigrants in California." Paper presented at the Conference on Asian-Pacific Immigration to the United States. Honolulu: East-West Population Institute, East-West Center, 1984.

Cheng, Lucie, and Edna Bonacich, eds. *Labor Immigration under Capitalism.* Berkeley: University of California Press, 1984.

Chiswick, Barry R. "An Analysis of the Earnings and Employment of Asian-American Men." *Journal of Labor Economics* 1 (1983):197–214.

—— "Differences in Education and Earnings among Racial and Ethnic Groups: Testing Alternative Hypothesis." Working paper no. 39. Chicago: University of Chicago, Center for the Study of the Economy and the State, 1986.

——, ed. *The Gateway: U.S. Immigration Issues and Policies.* Washington, DC.: American Enterprise Institute, 1982.

Cho, Lee-Jay, Robert D. Retherford, and Minja Kim Choe *The Own-children Method of Fertility Estimation.* Honolulu: The East-West Population Institute, 1986.

Choi, B. M. "Korean Small Businessmen: An Empirical Test of the Middleman

Minority Hypothesis." Unpublished Research Paper. Honolulu: University of Hawaii, Department of Sociology, 1988.

Chung, Tom Lun-Nap "Job Expectations and Opportunities of Asian American Clients." Boston: Chinatown/South Cove Neighborhood Council, 1987.

Cobas, José A. "On the Study of Ethnic Enterprise: Unresolved Issues." *Sociological Perspectives* 30 (1987):467–472.

Cohen, Gary B. "Ethnic Persistence and Change: Concepts and Models for Historical Change." *Social Science Quarterly* 65 (1984):1029–1042.

Collins, R. "Functional and Conflict Theories of Educational Stratification." *American Sociological Review* 36 (1971):1002–1019.

Connell, John "Paradise Polynesia Voyagers in the Modern World." Paper presented for the Conference on Asia-Pacific Immigration of the United States. Honolulu, HI: East-West Population Institute, 1984.

Cook, John M. "Samoan Patterns in Seeking Health Services, Hawaii, 1979–1981." *Hawaii Medical Journal* 42 (1983):138–142.

Crystal, David "Asian Americans and the Myth of the Model Minority." *Social Caseworker* September (1989):405–413.

Davis, Cary, Carl Haub, and JoAnne Willette "U.S. Hispanics: Changing the Face of America." *Population Bulletin* 38. Washington, DC: Population Reference Bureau, 1983.

Dearman, M. "Structure and Function of Religion in the Los Angeles Korean Community." In E. Y. Yu, E. H. Phillips, and E. S. Yang, eds. *Koreans in Los Angeles: Prospects and Promises.* Los Angeles: California State University, Center for Korean-American and Korean Studies, 1982.

De Jong, Gordon F., and James T. Fawcett "Motivations for Migration: An Assessment and a Value-Expectancy Research Model." In Gordon F. De Jong and Robert W. Gardner, eds. *Migration Decision Making. Multidisciplinary Approaches to Microlevel Studies in Developed and Developing Countries.* New York: Pergamon Press (1981):13–58.

Denton, Nancy A., and Douglas S. Massey "Residential Segregation of Blacks, Hispanics, and Asians by Socioeconomic Status and Generation." *Social Science Quarterly* 69 (1988):797–817.

Desbarats, Jacqueline "Indochinese Settlement Patterns in Orange County." *Amerasia Journal* 19 (1983):12–46.

——— "Ethnic Differences in Adaptation: Sino-Vietnamese Refugees in the United States." *International Migration Review* 20 (1986):405–427.

Desbarats, Jacqueline, and L. Holland "Indochinese Resettlement in the United States." *Annals of the American Association of Geographers* 75 (1985):522–538.

Divoky, Diane "The Model Minority Goes to School." *Phi Delta Kappa* 70 (1988):219–222.

Doerner, William R. "Asians to America with Skills, Special Immigrants Issue." *Time,* July 8, 1985:48.

Doi, Mary L., Chien Lin, and Indu Vohra-Sahu, eds. *Pacific-Asian American Research: An Annotated Bibliography.* Bibliography Series No. 1. Chicago: Pacific/Asian American Mental Health Research Center, 1981.

Duke University Center for Demographic Studies "Life Tables for 1979–1981 by Ethnicity." Unpublished report submitted to the DH&LS Task Force on Minority Health, 1984.

Dunn, William "Census to Split Asian Count." *USA Today,* January 16, 1989.

Enesa, Devon S. "The Aging Samoan in Hawaii." Master's thesis, University of Hawaii, 1977.

Epenshade, Thomas "Marriage Trends in America: Estimates, Implications and Underlying Causes." *Population and Development Review* 11 (1983):193–245.

——— "Black-White Differences in Marriage, Separation, Divorce and Remarriage." Paper presented at the annual meeting of the Population Association of America, Pittsburgh, 1985.

Erickson, Ken C. "Vietnamese Household Organization in Garden City, Kansas: Southeast Asians in a Packing House Town." *Plains Anthropologist* 33 (1988):27–36.

Espina, Marina E. *Filipinos in Louisiana.* New Orleans: A. F. Laborde and Sons, 1988.

Farley, Reynolds "An Investigation of the Quality of Ancestry Data in the United States Census." Paper presented at the annual meeting of the Population Association of America, Toronto, Canada, 1990.

Fawcett, James T., and Benjamin V. Cariño, eds. *Pacific Bridges: The New Immigration from Asia and the Pacific Islands.* Staten Island, NY: Center for Migration Studies, 1987.

Feagin, Joe *Racial and Ethnic Relations.* Englewood Cliffs, NJ: Prentice Hall, Inc., 1984.

Featherstone, Donald L., and R. M. Hauser *Opportunity and Change.* New York: Academic Press, 1978.

Fine, Mary Jane "Asians Find Success in New World." *NY-DIO Buffalo News,* November 30, 1986.

Flies, Kenneth H., Myron P. Gutmann, and John Vetter "The Creation of Mexican-American Reproductive Patterns: Mexicans and Mexican-Americans in Rural Texas, 1880–1910." Paper presented at the annual meeting of the Population Association of America, Toronto, Canada, 1990.

Forbes, Susan S. "Residence Patterns and Secondary Migration of Refugees." *Migration News* 1 (1985):3–18.

Forster, John "Aspects of Family Organization among Samoan Immigrants to Hawaii." *Proceedings of the Minnesota Institute of Sciences* 25–26 (1956):289–298.

Franco, Robert "Samoans in California: the Aiga Adapts." In Cluny Macpherson, Bradd Shore, and Robert Franco, eds. *New Neighbors: Islanders in Adaptation.* Santa Cruz: Center for South Pacific Studies, 1978.

——— "A Demographic Assessment of the Samoan Employment Situation in Hawaii." Final report on Contract No. 10315 Between the East–West Population Institute and the Commission on Population and the Hawaiian Future. Honolulu: Hawaii State Department of Planning and Economic Development Manuscript, 1984.

——— "Samoan Perception of Work: Moving Up and Moving Around." Ph.D. dissertation, anthropology, University of Hawaii at Manoa, 1985.

Frost, Floyd, and Kirkwood K. Shy "Racial Differences Between Linked Birth and Infant Death Records in Washington State." *American Journal of Public Health* 70 (1980):974–976.

Fujii, Ann "Japanese Americans: High Rate of Diabetes Discovered." *International Examiner* (Seattle), December 7, 1988, 3.

Fung, Kam Pui, Tze Wai Wong, and Sum Ping Lau "Ethnic Determinants of Perinatal Statistics of Chinese: Demography of China, Hong Kong and Singapore." *International Journal of Epidemiology* 18 (1989):127–131.

Gabriel, Paul E., and Susanne Schmitz "The Relative Earnings of Native Immigrant Males in the United States." *Quarterly Review of Economics and Business* 27 (1987):91–101.

Gardner, Robert W. "Life Tables by Ethnic Group for Hawaii, 1980." *Research and Statistics Reports* no. 43. Honolulu: Hawaii State Department of Health, 1984.

——— "Asian Immigration: The View from the United States." *Asian and Pacific Migration Journal* 1 (1992): 64–99.

——— "Mortality." In Nolan Zane and David Takeuchi, eds. *Asian and Pacific American Health Issues.* San Francisco: Asian American Health Forum, forthcoming.

Gardner, Robert W., and Robert C. Smith "Ninety-Seven Years of Mortality in Hawaii." *Hawaii Medical Journal* 37 (1978):297–302.

Gardner, Robert W., Bryant Robey, and Peter C. Smith "Asian Americans: Growth, Change and Diversity." *Population Bulletin* 40 (1985):1–44.

Gerber, Linda M. "The Influence of Environmental Factors on Mortality from Coronary Heart Disease among Filipinos in Hawaii." *Human Biology* 52 (1980):269–278.

Glazer, Nathan, ed. *Clamor at the Gates.* San Francisco: Institute for Contemporary Studies Press, 1985.

Glick, C. *Sojourners and Settlers: Chinese Migrants in Hawaii.* Honolulu: University of Hawaii Press, 1980.

Glick, Paul "Marriage, Divorce and Living Arrangements." *Journal of Family Issues* 5 (1984):7–26.

Goldscheider, Calvin, and Peter R. Uhlenberg "Minority Group Status and Fertility." *American Journal of Sociology* 74 (1969):361–372.

Gong, Yooshik "Asian Suburbanization in Chicago, 1980: Segregation or Integration?" Paper presented at the annual meeting of the Population Association of America, Baltimore, 1989.

Goode, William J. *Principles of Sociology.* New York: McGraw-Hill, 1977.

Gordon, Linda W. "New Data on the Fertility of Southeast Asian Refugees in the United States." Washington: Department of Health and Human Services, Office of Refugees Resettlement, 1982.

——— "Migration of Refugees Within the United States: New Data Sources and Findings." Paper presented at the annual meeting of the Population Association of Geographers, 1984.

——— "The Missing Children: Mortality and Fertility in a Southeast Asian Refugee Population." Paper presented at the annual meeting of the Population Association of America, Chicago, 1987.

——— "Southeast Asian Refugee Migration to the United States." In James T. Fawcett and Benjamin V. Cariño, eds. *Pacific Bridges.* New York: Center for Migration Studies, 1987.

Gordon, Milton M. *Assimilation in American Life: The Role of Race, Religion, and National Origin.* New York: Oxford University Press, 1964.

——— *Human Nature, Class and Ethnicity.* New York: Oxford University Press, 1978.

Gordon, T. "Mortality Experience among the Japanese in the United States, Hawaii, and Japan." *Public Health Reports* 72 (1957):543–553.

——— "Further Mortality Experience among Japanese Americans." *Public Health Reports* 82 (1967):973–984.

Gould, Ketayun H. "Asian and Pacific Islanders: Myth and Reality." *Social Work* 33 (1988):142–147.

Graves, T. D., N. B. Graves, V. N. Semu, and I. Ah Sam "The Price of Ethnic Identity: Maintaining Kin Ties among Pacific Immigrants to New Zealand." Paper presented at the 15th Pacific Science Congress, Dunedin, New Zealand, 1983.

Gurak, Douglas T. "Sources of Ethnic Fertility Differences: An Examination of Five Minority Groups." *Social Science Quarterly* 2 (1978):295–310.

——— "Assimilation and Fertility: A Comparison of Mexican American and Japanese American Women." *Hispanic Journal of Behavioral Sciences* 2 (1980):219–239.

Gutierrez, Felix "Ad Campaigns Target U.S. Asians." *Honolulu Star Bulletin*, May 21, 1988, A-4.

Hackenberg, R. A., L. Gerber, and B. Hackenberg "Cardiovascular Disease Mortality among Filipinos in Hawaii: Rates, Trends, and Associated Factors." (unpublished, no date).

Haenszel, William, and Minoru Kurihara "Studies of Japanese Migrants: I. Mortality from Cancer and Other Diseases among Japanese in the United States." *Journal of the National Cancer Institute* 40 (1968):43–68.

Halli, S. S. "Toward a Re-Conceptualization of Minority Group Status and Fertility Hypothesis: The Case of Orientals in Canada." *Journal of Comparative Family Studies* 20 (1989):21–45.

Harbison, Sarah F. "The Demography of Samoan Populations." In Paul T. Baker, Joel M. Hanna, and Tyhelma S. Baker, eds. *The Changing Samoans: Behavior and Health in Transition.* New York: Oxford University Press, 1986.

Harbison, Sarah F., and Marjorie E. Weishaar "Samoan Migrant Fertility: Adaptation and Selection." *Human Organization* 40 (1981):268–273.

Harlen, Douglas "The College of Micronesia." The President's Report to Congress. Manuscript, 1977.

Hauser, Robert M., and P. A. Mossel "Fraternal Resemblance in Educational Attainment and Occupational Status." *American Journal of Sociology* 91 (1985):650–673.

Hawaii Commission on Manpower and Employment *Samoan Task Force Survey Report on the Samoans on Oahu.* (1971):35–43.

Hawaii State Department of Health *Hawaii State Department of Health Annual Statistical Report,* 1988.

Hayes, Geoffrey, and Michael J. Levin *A Statistical Profile of Samoans in the United States.* Manuscript, 1984a.

——— "How Many Samoans? An Evaluation of the 1980 Census Count of Samoans in the United States." *Asian and Pacific Census Forum* 10 (1984b):1–16.

Hechter, H. H., and N. O. Bohrani "Longevity in Racial Groups Differs." *California's Health* 22 (1965):121–122.

Hellmich, Nanci "Chinese Diet Most Healthy, New Study Says." *Honolulu Star Bulletin,* June 7, 1990, A-15.

Henry, William A., III "Beyond the Melting Pot." *Time Magazine,* April 9, 1990.

Herman, Masako, ed. *The Japanese in America, 1843–1973.* Dobbs Ferry, New York: Oceana Publications, Inc., 1974.

Hezel, Francis X. "The Education Explosion in Truk." *Micronesian Reporter* 26 (1978):24–33.

Hirschman, Charles "America's Melting Pot Reconsidered." *Annual Review of Sociology* 9 (1983):397–423.

—— "Minorities in the Labor Market: Cyclical Patterns and Secular Trends in Joblessness." In Gary D. Sandefur and Marta Tienda, eds. *Divided Opportunities: Minorities, Poverty and Social Policy.* New York: Plenum, 1988.

Hirschman, Charles, and Ellen P. Kraly "Racial and Ethnic Inequality and Labor Markets in the United States, 1940 and 1950." Paper presented at the annual meeting of the Population Association of America, San Francisco, 1986.

Hirschman, Charles, and Morrison G. Wong "Trends in Socioeconomic Achievement among Immigrant and Native-Born Asian-Americans, 1960–1976." *Sociological Quarterly* 22 (1981):495–514.

—— "Socioeconomic Gains of Asian-Americans, Blacks, and Hispanics: 1960–1976." *American Journal of Sociology* 90 (1984):584–607.

—— "The Extraordinary Educational Attainment of Asian Americans." A Search for Historical Evidence and Explanations. *Social Forces* 65 (1986):1–27.

Ho, J. J. "Some Epidemiologic Observations on Cancer in Hong Kong." *National Cancer Institute Monograph* 53. Second Symposium on Epidemiology and Cancer Registries in the Pacific Basin. Washington, DC: National Institute of Health Publication no. 79-1864 (1979):35–47.

Hofstetter, Richard R., ed. *United States Immigration Policy.* Durham: Duke University Press, 1984.

Hsia, Jayjia "Asian Americans Fight the Myth of the Super Student." *Educational Record* 68 (1987–1988):94–97.

—— "Limits to Affirmative Action. Asian American Access to Higher Education." *Educational Policy* 2 (1988):117–136.

Hu, Jane H., and Jack E. White "Cancer Incidence in the Western United States: Ethnic Differences." *Journal of the National Medical Association* 71 (1979):345–348.

Huber, Joan, and Glenna Spitze "Considering Divorce." *American Journal of Sociology* 86 (1980):75–89.

Hune, Shirley *Pacific Migration to the United States: Trends and Themes in Historical and Sociological Literature.* RIIES Bibliographic Studies no. 2. Washington, DC: Smithsonian Institution Research Institute on Immigration and Ethnic Studies. (A shorter version is found as an introductory essay in Kim, 1989).

—— "The 'Success' Image of Asian Americans: Its Validity, Practical and Theoretical Implications." Paper presented at the annual meeting of the American Sociological Association, New York, 1986.

——"Uprooting and Adjustments: A Sociological Study of Migration and Mental Health." Final Report for the National Institute for Mental Health. Macomb, IL: Western Illinois University, 1988.

——"Religious Participation of Korean Immigrants in the United States." *Journal for the Scientific Study of Religion* 29 (1990):19–34.

Hurh, Won Moo, and Kwang Chung Kim "Adhesive Sociocultural Adaptation of Korean Immigrants in the U.S.: An Alternative Strategy with Minority Adaptation." *International Migration Review.* Forthcoming.

Hwang, Sean-Shong, and Rogelio Saenz "The Impact of Recent Asian Immigration on the Marriage Markets of Asian Men and Women." Paper presented at the annual meeting of the Population Association of America, New Orleans, 1988.

Ichihashi, Yamato *Japanese in the United States: A Critical Study of the Prob-*

lems of the Japanese Immigrants and Their Children. Stanford: Stanford University Press, 1932. Reprint. New York: Arno Press, 1969.

Ieremia, Eliu Personal Interview, cited in Robin Lyons: "Emigration from American Samoa: A Study in Migration, Cultural Assimilation and Economic Development." Ph.D. dissertation, geography, University of Hawaii, 1971.

Janes, C. R. "Migration and Hypertension: An Ethnography of Disease Risk in an Urban Samoan Community." Ph.D. dissertation, University of California, San Francisco and Berkeley, 1984.

Jenks, C. "A Reassessment of the Effect of Family and Schooling in America." *Inequality.* New York: Harper and Row, 1972.

Jiobu, Robert M. *Ethnicity and Assimilation: Blacks, Chinese, Filipinos, Japanese, Koreans, Mexicans, Vietnamese, and Whites.* Albany: State University of New York Press, 1988.

———— "Ethnic Hegemony and the Japanese of California." *American Sociological Review* 53 (1988):353–367.

Jiobu, R. and M. Marshall "Minority Status and Family Size: A Comparison of Explanations." *Population Studies* (1977):509–518.

Johnson, D. L., M. J. Levin, and E. L. Paisano *We the Asian and Pacific Islanders.* Washington, DC: Department of Commerce, Bureau of the Census, 1988.

Johnson, Nan E., and Linda M. Burton "Religion and Reproduction in Philippine Society: A New Text of the Minority Group Status Hypothesis." *Sociological Analysis* 48 (1987):217–233.

Johnson, Nan E., and Suewen Lean "Relative Income, Race, and Fertility." *Population Studies* 39 (1985):99–112.

Johnson, Nan E., and Ryoko Nishida "Minority-Group Status and Fertility: A Study of Japanese and Chinese in Hawaii and California." Paper presented of the annual meeting of the Population Association of America, East Lansing, Michigan, State University Department of Sociology, 1980.

Kagan, A., B. R. Harris, W. Winkelstein, et al. "Epidemiologic Studies of Coronary Heart Disease and Stroke in Japanese Men Living in Japan, Hawaii, and California: Demographic, Physical, Dietary, and Biochemical Characteristics." *Journal of Chronic Diseases* 27 (1974):345–364.

Kahn, Joan R. "Immigrant Selectivity and Fertility Adaptation in the United States." *Social Forces* 67 (1988):108–128.

Kan, S., and W. Lin "The Educational Status of Asian Americans: An Update from the 1980 Census." In N. Tsuchiya, ed. *Issues in Asian and Pacific American Education,* 1–12. Minneapolis, MN: Asian/Pacific American Learning Resource Center, 1986.

Kantrowitz, Nathan *Ethnic and Racial Segregation in the New York Metropolis.* New York: Praeger, 1973.

Kasindorf, Martin, et al. "Asian-Americans: A 'Model Minority'." *Newsweek,* December 6, 1982, 39–42, 51.

Kee, Norman Lau "Testimony Before the Subcommittee of Immigration, Refugee, and International Law." Mimeo, 1986.

Keely, Charles B. "Effects of the Immigration Act of 1965 on Selected Population Characteristics of Immigrants to the United States." *Demography* 8 (1971):157–169.

Kennedy, R. E., Jr. "Minority Group Status and Fertility: The Irish." *American Sociological Review* 38 (1973):85–96.

Kern, Richard "The Asian Market: Too Good to Be True?" *Demographics* (1988):39–40, 42.

Kim, Hyung-Chan, ed. *The Korean Diaspora: Historical and Sociological Studies of Korean Immigration and Assimilation in North America.* Santa Barbara, CA: ABC-Clio Press, 1977.

———— "Korean Community Organizations in America: Their Characteristics and Problems." *The Korean Diaspora: Historical and Sociological Studies of Korean Immigration and Assimilation in North America.* Santa Barbara, CA: ABC Clio Press, 1977.

———— *Asian American Studies: An Annotated Bibliography and Research Guide.* New York: Greenwood Press, 1989.

Kim, Illsoo "Korea and East Asia: Premigration Factors and U.S. Immigration Policy." In J. T. Fawcett and B. V. Cariño, eds. *Pacific Bridges: The New Immigration from Asia and the Pacific Islands.* Staten Island: Center for Migration Studies, 1987.

———— *New Urban Immigrants: The Korean Community in New York.* Princeton, NJ: Princeton University Press, 1981.

Kim, Kwang Chung, and Won Moo Hurh "Korean Americans and the 'Success' Image: A Critique." *Amerasia Journal* 10 (1983):3–21.

Kim, Kwang Chung, Won Moo Hurh, and Marilyn Fernandez "An Exploratory Analysis of Business Participation of Three Asian Immigrant Groups." *P/AMITR Research Review* 6 (1988):19–22.

King, Haitung, and William Haenszel "Cancer Mortality among Foreign-Born and Native-Born Chinese in the United States." *Journal of Chronic Diseases* 26 (1973):623–646.

King, Haitung, and Frances B. Locke "Health Effects of Migration: U.S. Chinese in and Outside the Chinatown." *International Migration Review* 21 (1987):555–575.

Kitagawa, Evelyn M., and Philip M. Hauser *Differential Mortality in the United States: A Study in Socioeconomic Epidemiology.* Cambridge, MA: Harvard University Press, 1973.

Kitano, Harry H. L. *Japanese Americans: The Evolution of a Subculture.* Englewood Cliffs, NJ: Prentice-Hall, 1976.

Kitano, Harry H. L., and R. Daniels *Asian Americans: Emerging Minorities.* Englewood Cliffs, NJ: Prentice-Hall, 1988.

Kitano, Harry H. L., and Stanley Sue "The Model Minorities." *The Journal of Social Issues* 29 (1973):1–9.

Kleinman, Joel C., and Samuel S. Kessel "Racial Differences in Low Birth Weight." *New England Journal of Medicine* 317 (1987):749–753.

Knoll, Tricia *Becoming Americans.* Portland, Oregon: Coast to Coast Books, 1982.

Koo, Hagen, and E. Y. Yu "Korean Immigration to the United States: Its Demographic and Social Implications for Both Societies." Honolulu, Hawaii: East-West Population Institute, population paper no. 74, 1981.

Kotchek, Lydia D. "Ethnic Visibility and Adaptive Strategies: Samoans in the Seattle Area." *Journal of Ethnic Studies* 4 (1977):29–38.

———— "Migrant Samoan Churches: Adaptation, Preservation, and Division." In Cluny Macpherson, Bradd Shore, and Robert Franco, eds. *New Neighbors: Islanders in Adaptation.* Santa Cruz: Center for South Pacific Studies, 1978.

Kraley, Ellen Percy, and Sharon Mengchee Lee "A Comparative Perspective on the Asian Sojournes: Chinese and Japanese Migration to the United States, 1860–1940." Paper presented at the annual meeting of the Population Association of America, San Francisco, 1986.

Kramarow, Ellen, Philip Morgan, and Susan Cotts Watkins "Fertility among Ethnic Groups in the United States in 1910." Paper presented at the annual meeting of the Population Association of America, New Orleans, April 20–23, 1988.

Kritz, Mary M., ed. *United States Immigration and Refugee Policy.* Lexington. MA: D.C. Heath and Co., 1983.

Kuo, Wen "Theories of Migration and Mental Health: An Empirical Testing on Chinese-Americans." *Social Science and Medicine* 10 (1976):297–306.

—— "Assimiliation among Chinese-Americans in Washington, D.C." *Sociological Quarterly* 18 (1977):340–352.

Kurzeja, Paul L., Soon D. Koh, Tong-He Koh, and William T. Liu "Ethnic Attitudes of Asian American Elderly: The Korean Immigrants and Japanese Niseis." *Research on Aging* 8 (1986):110–127.

Kwitko, Ludmilla "Selected Housing Characteristics of Asian American Households in 1980." Unpublished research paper. Honolulu, Hawaii: University of Hawaii, Department of Sociology, 1986.

Langberg, Mark Lawrence *Residential Segregation and the Assimilation Process: The Case of Asian Americans in 1980.* Ph.D. dissertation, University of Michigan, 1986.

Langberg, Mark Lawrence, and Reynolds Farley "Residential Segregation of Asian Americans in 1980." *Sociology and Social Research* 70 (1985):71–75.

Larson, Robert Bruce *Between Two Cultures: Tukese College Students in the United States.* Master's thesis, University of Iowa, 1979.

Lee, H. S. "Korean-American Voluntary Associations in Los Angeles." In E. Y. Yu, E. H. Phillips, and E. S. Yang, eds. *Koreans in Los Angeles: Prospects and Promises.* Los Angeles: California State University, Center for Korean-American and Korean Studies, 1982.

Lee, J. T. "Economic Development and Industrial Order in South Korea: Interaction Between the State and Labor in the Process of Export-oriented Industrialization." Ph.D. dissertation, University of Hawaii, 1987.

Lee, Rose Hum *The Chinese in the United States of America.* Hong Kong: Hong Kong University Press, 1957.

Lee, Sharon M., and Keiko Yamasake "Intermarriage in the Asian American Population." Xeroxed papers, n.d.

Leinwald, Adrienne Sue "The Relationship Between Micronesian Education and Culture and the Adjustment of Micronesian Students at an American College." Dissertation: University of Oregon, 1981.

LeMay, Michael C. *From Open Door to Dutch Door: An Analysis of U.S. Immigration Policy since 1820.* New York: Praeger, 1987.

Levin, Michael J. "Eauripik Population." Dissertation: University of Michigan, 1976.

—— "Pressure Cooking on Eauripik, Micronesia." Paper presented at American Anthropological Association Convention, December 1982.

—— "Samoans in the United States." Manuscript, no date.

Levin, Michael J., and Reynolds Farley "Historical Comparability of Ethnic Designations in the United States." *Proceedings of the American Statistical Association,* Social Statistics Section. Washington, DC., 1982.

Levin, Michael J., and James Naich "Micronesian Migration and Redemption." Manuscript, no date.

Levin, Michael J., and Robert D. Retherford "Own Children Estimates of Recent Fertility Trends in the Pacific Islands." Honolulu: East-West Population Institute, 1986.

Levine, Daniel B., Kenneth Hill, and Robert Warren, eds. *Immigration Statistics: A Story of Neglect.* Washington, DC: National Academy Press, 1985.

Lewthwaite, Gordon R., Christine Mainzer, and Patrick J. Holland "From Polynesia to California: Samoan Migration and Its Sequel." *Journal of Pacific History* 8 (1973):133–137.

Lieberson, Stanley *A Piece of the Pie: Black and White Immigrants since 1880.* Berkeley: University of California Press, 1980.

Lieberson, Stanley, and Lawrence Santi "The Use of Nativity Data to Estimate Ethnic Characteristics and Patterns." Mimeo, 1983.

Light, Ivan *Ethnic Enterprise in America.* Berkeley, Los Angeles: University of California Press, 1972.

Light, Ivan and Edna Bonacich Immigrant Entrepreneurs: Koreans in Los Angeles; 1965–1982. Berkely, Los Angeles: University of California Press, 1988.

Light, Ivan, Im Jung Kwuon, and Den Zhong *Korean Rotating Credit Associations in Los Angeles.* Los Angeles: University of California, Department of Sociology, 1988.

Lind, Andrew W. *Hawaii's People.* Honolulu: University of Hawaii Press, 1967.

Lindsey, Robert "The New Asian Immigrants." *The New York Times Magazine,* May 9, 1982, 22–42.

Lin-Fu, Jane S. "Population Characteristics and Health Care Needs of Asian Pacific Americans." *Public Health Reports,* January–February 1988, 18–27.

Liu, William T. "Health Services for the Asian Elderly." *Research on Aging* 8 (1986):156–175.

Lockwood, Charles, and Christopher B. Leinberger "Los Angeles Comes of Age." *The Atlantic Monthly,* January 1988:31–56.

Lyman, Stanford M. *The Asians in North America.* Santa Barbara: ABC-Clio, Inc., 1977.

Lyons, Robin "Emigration from American Samoa: A Study in Migration, Cultural Assimilation and Economic Development." Dissertation, University of Hawaii, 1980.

Maatz, Larry "The Samoans—Contradictions and Contrasts." *San Francisco Examiner,* October 11, 1978, F-2.

McBee, Susanna "Asian-Americans: Are They Making the Grade." *U.S. News and World Report,* April 2, 1984, 41.

—————— "Asian Merchants Find Ghettos Full of Peril." *U.S. News and World Report,* November 24, 1986, 30–31.

McKenney, Nampeo R., Arthur R. Cresce, and Patricia A. Johnson "Development of the Race and Ethnic Items for the 1990 Census." Paper presented at the annual meeting of the Population Association of America, New Orleans, 1988.

McKeown, Thomas, and R. G. Brown "Reasons for the Decline of Mortality in England and Wales During the Nineteenth Century." *Population Studies* 16 (1962):94–122.

McLeod, Beverly "The Oriental Express." *Psychology Today* (July 1986):48–52.

Madhaven, M. C. "Indian Immigrants: Numbers, Characteristics and Economic Impact." *Population and Development Review.* September 1985.

Maga, Tu'ulima "Talofa Means Aloha: The Story of a Samoan Family in Waianae." Honolulu: Technical Assistance Center, 1964.

Malin, Andrea "Asian Women in Corporate America." *Rice* 1 (1988):38–41.

Manning, Wendy, and William O'Hare "The Best Metros for Asian-American Businesses." *American Demographics* (1988):35–37, 59.

Mare, Robert D., and Christopher Winship "Ethnic and Racial Patterns of Educational Attainment and School Enrollments." In Gary D. Sandefur and Marta Tienda, eds. *Divided Opportunities: Minorities, Poverty and Social Policy.* New York: Plenum, 1988.

Marmot, Michael G., and S. Leonard Syme "Acculturation and Coronary Heart Disease in Japanese Americans." *American Journal of Epidemiology* 104 (1976):225–247.

Marmot, M. G., S. L. Syme, and A. Kagan, et al. "Epidemiologic Studies of Coronary Heart Disease and Stroke in Japanese Men Living in Japan, Hawaii, and California: Prevalence of Coronary and Hypertensive Heart Disease and Associated Risk Factors." *American Journal of Epidemiology* 102 (1975):514–525.

Marshall, F. Ray, and Leon F.Bouvier *Population Change and the Future of Texas.* Washington, DC: Population Reference Bureau, 1986.

Marshall, H. H., and R. M. Jiobu "An Alternate Test of the Minority Status and Fertility Relation." *Pacific Sociological Review* 21, (April 1978):221–236.

Marshall, Mac "Education and Depopulation on a Micronesian Atoll." *Micronesia* 15 (1979):1–11.

Martinelli, Phyllis C., and Richard Nagasawa "A Further Test of the Model Minority Thesis: Japanese Americans in a Sunbelt State." *Sociological Perspectives* 30 (1987):266–288.

Massey, Douglas S., and Nancy A. Denton "Trends in the Residential Segregation of Blacks, Hispanics, and Asians: 1970–1980." *American Sociological Review* 52 (1987):802–825.

——— "Suburbanization and Segregation in U.S. Metropolitan Areas." *American Journal of Sociology* 94 (1988a):592–626.

——— "The Dimensions of Residential Segregation." *Social Forces* 67, 2 (1988b):281–315.

Massey, Douglas S., and B. P. Mullen "Processes of Hispanic and Black Spatial Assimilation." *American Journal of Sociology* 89 (1984):836–873.

Massey, Douglas S., Gretchen A. Condran, and Nancy A. Denton "The Effect of Residential Segregation on Black Social and Economic Well-being." University of Pennsylvania, Population Studies Center, 1986.

Mayes, S. S. "The Increasing Stratification of Higher Education: Ideology and Consequence." *The Journal of Educational Thought* 11 (1977):16–27.

Meleisea, M., and P. Meleisea "The Best Kept Secret: Tourism in Western Samoa." In F. Rajotte and R. Crocombe, eds. *Pacific Tourism: As Islanders See It.* (1980):35–46.

Melendy, Howard Brett *Asians in America: Filipinos, Koreans, and East Indians.* New York: Twayne, 1977.

——— *Chinese and Japanese Americans.* New York: Twayne, 1984.

Miike, Lamy "Summary of Mortality Data on Native Hawaiians." Draft. Mimeo, 1986.

Miller, K. A., M. L. Kohn, and C. Schooler "Educational Self-Direction and Personality." *American Sociological Review* 51 (1986):372–390.

Model, Suzanne "The Economic Progress of Europeans and East Asians." *American Sociological Review* 53 (1988):363–380.

Momeni, Jamshid A. *Demography of Racial and Ethnic Minorities in the United States.* Westport, CT: Greenwood Press, 1984.

Montero, Darrel "The Japanese Americans: Changing Patterns of Assimilation over Three Generations." *American Sociological Review* 46 (1981):829–839.

Montero, Darrel, and Ronald Tsukashima "The Case of the Second Generation Japanese-American." *The Sociological Quarterly* 18 (1977):490–503.

Morganthau, Tom, Noelle Gaffney, Sue Hutchison, Bob Cohn, and Paul Keating "The Jittery 'Other Illegals'." *Newsweek,* October 5, 1987, 35–36.

Morris, John W., and Patrick C. L. Heaven "Attitudes and Behavioral Intentions Toward Vietnamese in Australia." *The Journal of Social Psychology* 126 (1986):513–520.

Nagi, S., and E. Haavio-Mannila "Migration, Health Status and Utilization of Health Services." *Sociology of Health and Illness* 2 (1980):174–193.

Nagoshi, Craig T., Ronald C. Johnson, and Frank M. Ahern "Phenotypic Assortative Mating vs. Social Homogamy among Japanese and Chinese Parents in the Hawaii Family Study of Cognition." *Behavior Genetics* 17 (1987):477–485.

Naich, James Personal communication.

National Cancer Institute *Cancer among Blacks and Other Minorities: Statistical Profiles.* Pub. 491-313/44712. Washington, DC: U.S. Government Printing Office, 1986.

National Center for Health Statistics "Vital And Health Statistics." Supplements to the Monthly Statistics Report. National Center for Health Statistics. *Vital Health Statistics* 24, 1989.

———— "Advance Report of Final Marriage Statistics 1982." *Monthly Vital Statistics Report.* Hyattesville, MD, Public Health Service 34 (1985):3.

Nee, Victor, and J. Sanders "Limits of Ethnic Solidarity in the Enclave Economy." *American Sociological Review* 52 (1987):745–773.

Nee, Victor, and Jimy Sanders "The Road to Parity: Determinants of the Socioeconomic Achievement of Asian Americans." 1985

Nee, Victor, and Herbert Y. Wong "Asian American Socioeconomic Achievement: The Strength of the Family Bond." University of Michigan. *Sociological Perspectives* 28, 3 (1985):281–306.

Nelson, Gloria Luz M. *Assimilation in the United States: Occupational Attainment of Asian Americans, 1980.* Population Studies and Training Center Working Paper Series 88-103. Providence, RI, Brown University, 1988.

Nordyke, Eleanor C., and Richard K. C. Lee "The Chinese in Hawaii: A Historical and Demographic Perspective." *The Hawaiian Journal of History,* 1989.

Norris, Frank D., and Paul W. Shipley "A Closer Look at Race Differentials in California's Infant Mortality, 1965–1967." *HSMHA Health Reports* 86 (1971):810–814.

Office of Refugee Resettlement "Refugee Resettlement Program: Report to the Congress." Washington, DC: Office of Refugee Resettlement, 1985.

Ogbu, J. *Minority Education and Caste: The American System in Cross Cultural Perspective.* New York: Academic Press, 1978.

Omari, Gary K. *The Samoans: Culture in Conflict.* Manuscript, 1972.

Osako, Masako M. "Aging and Family among Japanese Americans: The Role of Ethnic Tradition in the Adjustments to Old Age, 1979."

Pacific Islands Monthly "Students Survey Alarms Samoans." *Pacific Islands Monthly* 45 (1974):9.

Park, Robert E. *Race and Culture.* Glencoe, IL: Free Press, 1950.

Park, Siyoung "Korean Residential Concentrations in Chicago." *Bulletin of the Illinois Geographical Society* 30 (1988):12–22.

Parsons, T. "The Social Class as a Social System: Some of Its Functions in American Society." *Harvard Educational Review* 1 (Reprint Series) (1968):69–90.

Passel, Jeffrey, and David L. Ward "Problems in Analyzing Race and Hispanic Origin Data from the 1990 Census: Solutions Based on Constructing Consistent Populations from Micro-level Data." Paper presented at the annual meeting of the Population Association of America, Chicago, April–May, 1987.

Patterson, W. "The First Attempt to Obtain Korean Laborers for Hawaii, 1896–1897." In H. C. Kim, ed. *The Korean Diaspora: Historical and Sociological Studies of Korean Immigration and Assimilation in North America.* Santa Barbara, CA: ABC Clio Press, 1977.

Petersen, Glenn "External Politics, Internal Economics, and Ponapean Social Formation." *American Ethnologist* 6 (1979):25–40.

Petersen, William *Japanese-Americans: Oppression and Success.* New York: Random House, 1971.

——— "Chinese Americans and Japanese Americans." In Thomas Sowell, ed. *Essays and Data on American Ethnic Groups.* Washington, DC: Urban Institute, (1978):65–106.

Pomerantz, L. "The Background of Korean Emigration." In L. Cheng and E. Bonacich, eds. *Labor Immigration under Capitalism: Asian Workers in the United States Before World War II.* Berkeley: University of California Press, 1984.

Population Reference Bureau *World Population Data Sheet.* Washington, DC, 1980.

Portes, Alejandro "One Field, Many Views: Competing Theories of International Migration." In J. T. Fawcett and B. V. Carino, eds. *Pacific Bridges: The New Immigration from Asia and the Pacific Islands.* Staten Island, NY: Center for Migration Studies, 1987.

Portes, Alejandro, and Robert L. Bach *Latin Journey.* Berkeley, Los Angeles, London: University of California Press, 1985.

Portes, Alejandro, and Robert D. Manning "The Immigrant Enclave: Theory and Empirical Examples." In Susan Olzek and Joane Nagel, eds. *Competitive Ethnic Relations.* Orlando: Academic Press, 1986.

Portes, Alejandro, and A. Stepick "Unwelcome Immigrants: The Labor Market Experiences of 1980 (Mariel) Cuban and Haitian Refugees in South Florida." *American Sociological Review* 50 (1985):493–514.

Portes, Alejandro, and Cynthia Truelove "Making Sense out of Diversity: Recent Research on Hispanic Minorities in the United States." *Annual Review of Sociology* 13 (1987):359–385.

Poston, Dudley L., Jr., David Alvirez, and Marta Tienda "Earnings Differences Between Anglo and Mexican American Male Workers in 1960 and 1970: Changes in the 'Cost' of Being Mexican American." *Social Science Quarterly* 57 (1976):618–631.

Poston Dudley L., Jr., and Jia Zhongke "The Economic Attainment Patterns of Foreign-Born Workers in the United States." Population and Development Program, Working Paper Series 1.01. Providence, RI: Brown University, 1989.

Ramirez, Anthony "America's Super Minority." *Fortune* 114 (1986):148–162.

Reid, Alexander "New Asian Immigrants, New Garment Center." *New York Times*, May 10, 1986.

Reimers, David M. "Recent Immigration Policy—An Analysis." In Barry R. Chiswick, ed. *The Gateway: U.S. Immigration Issues and Policies.* Washington, DC: American Enterprise Institute, 1982.

Retherford, Robert D., and Lee-Jay Cho "Age-Parity-Specific Birth Rates and Birth Probabilities from Census or Survey Data on Own Children." *Population Studies* 32 (1978):567–581.

Retherford, Robert D., and Michael J. Levin "Is the Fertility of Asian and Pacific Islander Americans Converging to the U.S. Norm?" *Asian and Pacific Population Forum* 3 (1989):21–26, 35.

Rindfuss, Ronald R., and James A. Sweet *Postwar Fertility Trends and Differentials in the United States.* New York: Academic Press, 1977.

Roberts, R. E., and E. S. Lee "Health Practices among Mexican Americans: Further Evidence from Human Population Laboratory Studies." *Preventive Medicine* 9 (1980):675–688.

Rogers, Richard C. "Ethnic Differences in Infant Mortality: Fact or Artifact?" *Social Science Quarterly* 70 (September 1989):642–649.

Rolff, Karla "Fa'Asamoa: Tradition in Transition." Dissertation, University of California at Santa Barbara, 1978.

Rumbaut, Rubén G., and K. Ima *The Adaptation of Southeast Asian Refugee Youth: A Comparative Study.* San Diego, CA: San Diego Office of Refugee Resettlement, Final Report, September, 1987.

Rumbaut, Rubén G., and John R. Weeks "Fertility and Adaptation: Indochinese Refugees in the United States." *International Migration Review* 20 (1986):428–465.

——— "Infant Health Among Indochinese Refugees: Patterns of Infant Mortality, Birthweight and Prenatal Care in Comparative Perspective." *Research in the Sociology of Health Care* 8 (1989): 137–196.

Sandefur, Gary D., and Jiwon Jeon "Migration, Race, and Ethnicity." University of Wisconsin, 1988. Photocopy.

Sandefur, Gary D., and Anup Pahari "Racial and Ethnic Inequality in Earnings and Educational Attainment." *Social Service Review* 63 (1989):199–221.

Schaefer, Richard T. *Racial and Ethnic Groups.* 2d ed. Boston: Little, Brown and Company, 1984.

Schmidt, Robert "Differential Mortality—Honolulu Before 1900." *Hawaii Medical Journal* 26 (1967):537–541.

Schultz, Wendy L. "Demographics in Transition: The Changing Ethnic Mix in Hawaii and Throughout the U.S." Draft. Honolulu, Hawaii: Social Science Research Institute, 1990.

Schwartz, John, George Raine, and Kate Robins "A 'Superminority' Tops Out." *Newsweek*, May 11, 1987, 48–49.

Schwartz, John, Dorothy Wang, and Nancy Matsumoto "Topping into a Blossoming Asian Market." *Newsweek*, September 7, 1987, 47–48.

Scimecca, J. A. *Education and Society.* New York: Holt Rinehart and Winston, 1980.

Sewell, W. H., R. M. Hauser, and W. C. Wolfe "Causes and Consequences of Higher Education: Models of the Status Attainment Process." In W. H. Sewell, R. M. Hauser, and W. C. Wolfe, eds. *Schooling and Achievement in American Society,* 9–27. New York: Academic Press, 1976.

Shin, Eui Hang "Interracially Married Korean Women in the United States: An Analysis based on Hypergamy Exchange Theory." In E. Y. Yu and E. H. Phillips, eds. *Korean Women in Transition: At Home and Abroad.* Los Angeles: California State University, Center for Korean-American and Korean Studies, 1987.

Shu, Ramsey, and Adele Satele "The Samoan Community in Southern California: Conditions and Needs." Occasional paper number 2. Chicago: Asian American Mental Health Research Center, 1977.

Siegel, Paul M. "On the Cost of Being Negro." *Sociological Inquiry* 35 (1965): 41–57.

Sklare, M. *America's Jews.* New York: Random House, 1971.

Smith, Peter C. "Asians in the United States: A Mid-1980s Profile." Paper presented at the Conference on the United States a Decade after the Vietnam War. At the Institute of American Culture (Academia Sinica), Taipei, Taiwan, RDC, June 6–8, 1986.

Sowell, Thomas *Essays and Data on American Ethnic Groups.* Washington, DC: Urban Institute, 1978.

—— *Ethnic America: A History.* New York: Basic Books, 1981.

Staples, Robert, and Alfredo Mirande "Racial and Cultural Variations among American Families: A Decennial Review." *Journal of Marriage and the Family* 42 (1985):887–904.

State of California, Department of Finance, Population Research Unit "Estimates of Refugees in California Counties and the State: 1986." Department of Finance, Population Research Unit, Report SR 86-1, 1987.

—— "Projected Total Population for California by Race/Ethnicity." Department of Finance, Population Research Unit, Report 88 p-4, 1988.

Stavig, Gordon R., Amnon Igra, and Alvin R. Leonard "Hypertension and Related Health Issues among Asians and Pacific Islanders in California." *Public Health Reports* 103 (1988):28–37.

Steinberg, Stephen *The Ethnic Myth: Race, Ethnicity, and Class in America.* New York: Atheneum, 1981.

Stephen, Cookie White, and Walter G. Stephan "After Intermarriage: Ethnic Identity among Mixed-heritage Japanese-Americans and Hispanics." *Journal of Marriage and the Family* 51 (May 1989):507–519.

Stevens, G., and J. H. Cho "Socioeconomic Index and the New 1980 Census Occupational Scheme." *Social Science Research* 14 (1985):142–168.

Sullivan, Teresa A. "Documenting Immigration: A Comparison of Research on Asian and Hispanic Immigrants." In J. T. Fawcett and B. V. Cariño, eds. *Pacific Bridges: The New Immigration from Asia and the Pacific Islands.* Staten Island, NY: Center for Migration Studies, 1987.

Sung, Betty Lee *The Story of the Chinese in America.* New York: Macmillan, 1967.

Survey Marketing Services "Office of Economic Opportunity Update Survey, Honolulu, HI, 1978.

Suzuki, Bob H. "Education and Socialization of Asian Americans: A Revisionist Analysis of the 'Model Minority' Thesis." *Amerasia* 4 (1977):23–51.

Taffel, Selma "Characteristics of Asian Births: United States, 1980." *Monthly Vital Statistics Report* 32 (supplement), 1984.

Tainer, Eveline M. "English Language Proficiency and the Determination of Earnings among Foreign-born Men." Paper presented at the annual meeting of the Population Association of America, San Francisco, April 3–5, 1986.

Takaki, Ronald "They Also Came: Chinese Women and the Migration to Hawaii." Paper presented at the Conference "Lucky Come Hawaii: The Chinese in Hawaii." Honolulu: East-West Center, 1988.

Tan, Chee-Beng "Acculturation, Ethnicity and the People of Chinese Descent." Paper presented at the Conference "Lucky Come Hawaii. The Chinese in Hawaii." Honolulu: East-West Center, 1988.

Temme, V. Lloyd *Occupational Meaning and Measures.* Washington, DC: Bureau of Social Science Research, 1975.

Thernstrom, Stephan "Counting Heads: New Data on the Ethnic Composition of the American Population." *Journal of Interdisciplinary History* 22 (1989):107–116.

———, ed. *Harvard Encyclopedia of American Ethnic Groups.* Cambridge: Belknap Press of Harvard University, 1980.

Thompson, David M. *The Social Adjustment of Overseas-educated Micronesians.* Master's thesis, University of Hawaii, 1981.

Thompson, Mark "An Asian-American Politician has Arrived." *Far Eastern Economic Review,* October 16, 1986, 50–51.

——— "The Elusive Promise." *Far Eastern Economic Review,* October 16, 1986, 46–47.

Thompson, Stephen I. "Assimilation and Nonassimilation of Asian-Americans and Asian Peruvians." *Comparative Studies in Society and History* 21 (1979):572–588.

Thornton, Michael C., and Robert J. Taylor "Intergroup Attitudes: Black American Perceptives of Asian Americans." *Ethnic and Racial Studies* 11 (1988):474–488.

Tienda, Marta, and D. T. Lii "Minority Concentrations and Earnings Inequality: Blacks, Hispanics and Asians Compared." *American Journal of Sociology* 93 (1987):141–165.

Tolbert, Charles, P. M. Horan, and E. M. Beck "The Structure of Economic Segmentation: A Dual Economy Approach." *American Journal of Sociology* 85 (1979): 1095–1116.

Tran, Thanh V. "Sex Differences in English Language Acculturation and Learning Strategies among Vietnamese Adults Aged 40 and over in the United States." *Sex Roles* 19 (1988):747–758.

Treiman, Donald J., Vivian Lew, Hye-Kyung Lee, and Thad A. Brown "Occupational Status Attainment among Ethnic Groups in Los Angeles." Paper presented at the annual meeting of the Population Association of America, San Francisco, 1986.

Treiman, Donald J., and Hye-Kyung Lee "Income Differences among 28 Ethnic Groups in Los Angeles." Paper presented at the annual meeting of the Population Association of America, New Orleans, April 21–23, 1988.

Trueba, Henry T. "Culturally Based Explanations of Minority Students' Academic Achievements." *Anthropology and Education Quarterly* 19 (1988):270–287.

Trust Territory of the Pacific Islands *Bulletin of Statistics.* Manuscript, 1977.

Tsuang, Grace W. "Assuring Equal Access of Asian Americans to Highly Selective Universities." *Yale Law Journal* 98 (1989):659–678.

Tun, Petrus and Joah Sigrah *A Report to the Sixth Congress of Micronesia Concerning Certain Aspects of Education.* Manuscript, 1975.

Ueda, Reed "False Modesty: The Curse of Asian American Success." *The New Republic* July 3, 1989, 16–17.

United States Bureau of the Census "Part 1: United States Summary." *1970 Census of Population.* Vol. 1, *Characteristics of the Population.* Washington, DC: U.S. Government Printing Office, 1973a.

——— "Japanese, Chinese, and Filipinos in the United States." *1970 Census of Population, Subject Reports.* Washington, DC: U.S. Government Printing Office, 1973b.

——— *Historical Statistics of the United States. Colonial Times to 1970.* Part 1. Washington, DC: U.S. Government Printing Office, 1975.

—— "Asian and Pacific Islander Population in the United States: 1980." *1980 Census of Population*. Vol. 2, *Subject Reports*, PC80-2-1E. Washington, DC: U.S. Government Printing Office, 1980.

——"Race of the Population by States: 1980." *1980 Census of Population, Supplementary Report*, PC80-S1-3. Washington, DC: U.S. Government Printing Office, 1981.

—— "Ancestry of the Population by States: 1980." *1980 Census of Population, Supplementary Report*, PC80-S1-10. Washington, DC: U.S. Government Printing Office, 1983a.

—— *1980 Census of Population, General Social and Economic Characteristics, United States Summary*, PC80-1-C1. Washington, DC: U.S. Government Printing Office, 1983b.

—— "Asian and Pacific Islander Population by States: 1980." *1980 Census of Population, Supplementary Report*, PC80-S1-12. Washington, DC: U.S. Government Printing Office, 1983c.

—— "Part 1: United States Summary." *1980 Census of Population*. Vol. 1, *Characteristics of the Population*. Chapter B, *General Population Characteristics*. Washington, DC: U.S. Government Printing Office, 1983d.

—— "Part 1: United States Summary." *1980 Census of Population*, Vol. 1: *Characteristics of the Population*. Chapter C, *General Social and Economic Characteristics*. Washington, DC: U.S. Government Printing Office, 1983e.

—— "Part 2: State Volumes." *1980 Census of Population*. Vol. 1, *Characteristics of the Population*. Chapter C, *General Social and Economic Characteristics*. Washington, DC: U.S. Government Printing Office, 1983f.

—— "Part 1: United States Summary. Section A: United States." *1980 Census of Population*. Vol. 1, *Characteristics of the Population*. Chapter D, *Detailed Population Characteristics*. Washington, DC: U.S. Government Printing Office, 1984a.

—— "Part 1: United States Summary. Section B: Regions." *1980 Census of Population*. Vol. 1, *Characteristics of the Population*. Chapter D, *Detailed Population Characteristics*. Washington, DC: U.S. Government Printing Office, 1984b.

—— "Marital Characteristics." *1980 Census of Population: Subject Reports*, PC80-(2)-4C. Washington, DC: U.S. Government Printing Office 1985.

—— *We, the Asian and Pacific Islander Americans*. Washington, DC: U.S. Government Printing Office, 1988.

—— "Census Bureau Announces Final Proposal for 1990 Census Race Question." *U.S. Department of Commerce News*. CB88-90.4, 1988.

—— "United States Population Estimates, by Age, Sex, Race, and Hispanic Origin: 1980 to 1988." *Current Population Reports, Population Estimates and Projections*, Series P-25, no. 1045, January 1990.

United States Commission on Civil Rights "Social Indicators of Equality for Minorities and Women." *A Report of the United States Commission on Civil Rights*. Washington, DC, August 1978.

—— *Recent Activities Against Citizens and Residents of Asian Descent*. Washington, DC: U.S. Commission on Civil Rights, Clearinghouse Publication 88, 1987.

—— *The Economic Status of Americans of Asian Descent: An Explanatory Instigation*. Washington, DC: U.S. Commission on Civil Rights, Clearinghouse Publication 95, 1988.

United States Department of Health and Human Services *Report of the Secre-*

tary's Task Force on Black and Minority Health. Vol. 1, *Executive Summary.* Washington, DC: Publication no. 491-313/44706, 1985.

—— "Health, United States, 1988." Hyattsville, MD: U.S. Department of Health and Human Services, 1988.

United States Immigration and Naturalization Service *Annual Report.* Washington, DC: U.S. Government Printing Office, 1943–1978.

—— *Statistical Yearbook.* Washington, DC: U.S. Government Printing Office, 1979–1989.

—— *Statistical Yearbook of the Immigration and Naturalization Service.* Washington, DC: U.S. Government Printing Office, annual.

United States National Center for Health Statistics "Health, United States, 1979." DHEW publication no. (DHS) 80-1232, Hyattsville, MD, 1980.

—— **(a)** *Vital Statistics of the United States.* Vol. 1, Natality. Hyattsville, MD: National Center for Health Statistics, Centers for Disease Control, Public Health Service, Department of Health and Human Services, annual.

—— **(b)** *Vital Statistics of the United States.* Vol. 2, Part A, Mortality. Hyattsville, MD: National Center for Health Statistics, Centers for Disease Control, Public Health Service, Department of Health and Human Services, annual.

—— *Vital Statistics of the United States.* Vol. 2, Part A, Mortality, Table 2.4. Hyattsville, MD: National Center for Health Statistics, Centers for Disease Control, Public Health Service, Department of Health and Human Services, 1984.

—— "Advance Report of the Final Natality Statistics, 1982." *Monthly Vital Statistics Report* 33 (Supplement), 1984.

—— "Advance Report of the Final Natality Statistics, 1983." *Monthly Vital Statistics Report* 34 (Supplement), 1985.

United States Office of Disease Prevention and Health Promotion *ODPHP's Prevention Fact Book: Life Expectancy in the United States.* Washington, DC: Office of Disease Prevention and Health Promotion, Public Health Service, U.S. Department of Health and Human Services, 1987.

United States Senate "Amending the Immigration and Nationality Act to Deter Immigration-Related Marriage Fraud and Other Immigration Fraud." *Senate Report* (1986):99-461.

U.S. News & World Report "Asian Merchants Find Ghettos Full of Peril", November 24, 1986, 30–31.

Ventura, Stephanie J. "Births of Hispanic Parentage, 1985." National Center for Health Statistics. *Monthly Vital Statistics Report* 30 (Supplement), 1988.

Vitarelli, Margo "A Pacific Island Migration Study: Palauans in Hawaii." Manuscript, 1981.

Viviano, Frank "The Biggest Bucks—but the Fewest Votes." *Far Eastern Economic Review,* October 16, 1986, 49–51.

—— "From the Asian Hills to a U.S. Valley." *Far Eastern Economic Review,* October 16, 1986, 47–49.

Vohra-Sahu, Indu *The Pacific Asian Americans: A Selected and Annotated Bibliography of Recent Materials.* Bibliography Series, no. 4. Chicago: Pacific Asian American Mental Health Research Center, 1983.

Walker, Robert and Michael Hannan "Dynamic Settlement Processes: The Case of U.S. Immigration." *The Professional Geographer* 41 (1989):172–183.

Wang, J. "Korean Assimilation in the Multi-ethnic Setting of Hawaii: An Examination of Milton Gordon's Theory of Assimilation." Unpublished Ph.D dissertation, University of Hawaii, 1981.

Warren, Robert, and Ellen Percy Kraly "The Elusive Exodus: Emigration from the United States." *Population Trends and Public Policy,* No. 8. Washington, DC: Population Reference Bureau, 1985.

Waters, Mary C. "Ethnic Heterogeneity Within Racial Groups: Census Data on Blacks." Paper prepared for the annual meeting of the Population Association of America, New Orleans, April 21–23, 1988.

Weber, M. *The Protestant Ethic and the Spirit of Capitalism.* New York: Scribners, 1958.

Weeks, John R., and Ruben G. Rumbaut "Infant Mortality among Indochinese Refugees in San Diego County." Paper submitted for presentation at the annual meeting of the Population Association of America. San Diego: San Diego State University International Population Center and Department of Sociology, 1988.

Westoff, Charles F. "Fertility Decline in the West: Causes and Prospects." *Population and Development Review* 9 (1983):99–104.

White, Clay "Residential Segregation among Asians in Long Beach." *Sociology and Social Research* 70 (1986):266–267.

White, Michael J., and Peter R. Mueser "Race and Residential Natality in the U.S., 1940–1980." Paper presented at the annual meeting of the Population Association of America, April 1988.

Whittemore, Alice S., Anna H. Wu-Williams, Marion Lee, Zheng Shu, Richard P. Gallagher, Jiao Deng-ao, Zhou Lun, Wang Xianghui, Chen Kun, Dexter Jung, Chong-Ze Teh, Ling Chengde, Xu Jing Yao, Ralph S. Paffenbarger, Jr., and Brian E. Henderson "Diet, Physical Activity, and Colorectal Cancer among Chinese in North America and China." *Journal of the National Cancer Institute* 82 (1990):915–926.

Wickberg, Edgar "Contemporary Overseas Chinese: Ethnicity in the Pacific Region." Paper presented at the Conference "Lucky Come Hawaii: The Chinese in Hawaii." Honolulu: East-West Center, July 18–21, 1988.

Wilson, Reginald, and Manuel J. Justiz "Minorities in Higher Education: Confronting a Time Bomb." *Educational Record* 68 (1988):9–14.

Wilson, Robert A., and Bill Hosokawa *East to America: A History of the Japanese in the United States.* New York: William Morrow and Company, Inc., 1980.

Winslow, C. E. A., and K. W. Hoh "The Mortality of the Chinese in the United States, Hawaii, and the Philippines." *Journal of Hygiene* 4 (1924):330–355.

Wong, E. "Asian American Middleman Minority Theory: The Framework of an American Myth." *The Journal of Ethnic Studies* 13 (1985):52–88.

Wong, Morrison G. "Changes in Socioeconomic Status of the Chinese Male Population in the United States from 1960 to 1970." *International Migration Review* 14 (1980):511–524.

———— "The Cost of Being Chinese, Japanese, and Filipino in the United States: 1960, 1970, 1979." *Pacific Sociological Review* 25 (1982):59–78.

Wong, Morrison G., and Charles Hirschman "Labor Force Participation and Socioeconomic Attainment of Asian-American Women." *Sociological Perspectives* 26 (1983):423–446.

Woo, D. "The Socioeconomic Status of Asian Women in the Labor Force: An Alternative View." *Sociological Perspectives* 27 (1985):307–338.

Workman, Randy, et al. "Island Voyagers in New Quests: An Assessment of Degree Completion among Micronesian College Students." Agana, Guam: Micronesian Area Research Center, 1981.

Worth, Robert M., George Rhodes, and A. Kagan, et al. "Epidemiologic Studies of Coronary Heart Disease and Stroke in Japanese Men Living in Japan, Hawaii, and California: Mortality." *American Journal of Epidemiology* 102 (1975):481–490.

Xenos, Peter, S., Robert W. Gardner, Herbert R. Barringer, and Michael J. Levin "Asian Americans: Growth and Change in the 1970s." In J. T. Fawcett and B. V. Carino, eds. *Pacific Bridges: The New Immigration from Asia and the Pacific Islands.* Staten Island, NY: Center for Migration Studies, 1987.

Xenos, Peter, Herbert R. Barringer, and Michael J. Levin "Asian Indians in the United States: A 1980 Census Profile." Paper of the East-West Population Institute, no. 111, July 1989.

Yang, Wen Shan, and W. Parker Frisbie "Racial/Ethnic Trends in Divorce, Separation, and Remarriage." *Texas Population Research Center Papers* no. 11.02, 1989.

Yao, Esther Lee "A Comparison of Family Characteristics of Asian American and Anglo American High Achievers." *International Journal of Comparative Sociology* 26 (1985):198–208.

Ye, Wen Zhen "The Fertility Behavior of the Chinese in the United States: An Exploratory Analysis." Paper presented at the Overseas Chinese Conference, Hilo, Hawaii, July 24–29, 1989.

Yim, S. B. "The Social Structure of Korean Communities in California, 1903–1920." In L. Cheng and E. Bonacich, eds. *Labor Immigration under Capitalism: Asian Workers in the United States Before World War II.* Berkeley: University of California Press, 1984.

Yu, C. "The Correlation of Cultural Assimilation of the Korean Immigrants in the United States." In H. Kim, ed. *The Korean Diaspora: Historical and Sociological Studies of Korean Immigration and Assimilation in North America.* Santa Barbara, CA: ABC-Clio, (1977):167–176.

Yu, Elena "The Low Mortality Rates of Chinese Infants: Some Plausible Explanatory Facts." *Social Science and Medicine* 16 (1982):253–265.

Yu, Elena S. H., Ching-Fu Chang, William T. Liu, and Stephen H. Kan "Asian-White Mortality Differentials: Is There Excess Deaths." Bethesda, MD. A special report submitted to the NIH Task Force on Black and Minority Health. Chicago: Pacific Asian American Mental Health Research Center, University of Illinois, 1984.

Yu, Eui-Young "Koreans in Los Angeles: Size, Distribution, and Composition." In E. Y. Yu, E. H. Phillips, and E. S. Yang, eds. *Koreans in Los Angeles: Prospects and Promises.* Los Angeles: California State University, Center for Korean American and Korean Studies, 1982a.

———— "Occupations and Work Patterns of Korean Immigrants in Los Angeles." In E. Y. Yu, E. H. Phillips, and E. S. Yang, eds. *Koreans in Los Angeles: Prospects and Promises.* Los Angeles: California State University, Center for Korean American and Korean Studies, 1982b.

———— "Korean Communities in America: Past, Present, and Future." *Amerasia Journal* 10 (1983):23–52.

Yu, Eui-Young, and E. H. Phillips, eds. *Korean Women in Transition: At Home and Abroad.* Los Angeles: California State University, Center for Korean American and Korean Studies, 1987.

Yu, Eui-Young, E. H. Phillips, and E. S. Yang, eds. *Koreans in Los Angeles: Prospects and Promises.* Los Angeles: California State University, Center for Korean American and Korean Studies, 1982.

344

Name Index

Subject Index

Boldface numbers refer to figures and tables

A

accidents: as a leading cause of death, 76, **78**

adaptation: and education of immigrants, 166–167

administrative support occupations: and education, **212**; ethnic distribution of, **198–199, 206, 207**; and gender, **198–199, 230**; income of, **244–245**; occupational prestige of, **214**; *see also* white collar occupations

Afghanistan: as part of Asiatic Barred Zone, 30*n*

Africa, 2

Africans: naturalization law affecting, 20; naturalization rate of, 46

age, 19, 90–93, **94, 95,** 96, 100; and education, 174, **180**; and fertility of, 54, 56*n*; and household income, **262**; at immigration and fertility of, 57; and income, 249, **250, 253,** 255; and mortality of, 82; and occupational prestige, **229**; of Pacific Islanders, 277, **278**; -sex composition of, **94–95**; and sex ratios, 99

age-sex composition, of Asian Indians, **95**; of Chinese, **94**; of Filipinos, **94**; of Japanese, **94**; of Koreans, **94**; of Vietnamese, 95

age structures of immigrant groups, 92–93, **94, 95,** 100–101, 103, 104

agriculture: ethnicity of workers in, **209**; occupational prestige of, 213; shift away from employment in, 205; *see also* farming, fishing, forestry

alcohol consumption: and mortality, 87

alien land laws, 27–28

aliens: marrying U.S. citizens fraudulently, 35

aliens ineligible for citizenship, 27–28; barred from immigration, 28; category abolished, 30

American Indians, 9, 18*n*, **31,** 316; causes of death 76, **77**; educational performance of, 166; fertility of, 59, **61**; income of, 59; nativity of, **61**; population growth rates, **40–41**; sex ratios, 97, **102**

American Samoa, 268, 269–270, 285; administration of, 270; as birthplace of U.S. immigrants, **286**; emigration from, 287; high school graduates in, 290; as a migration point, 270, 271, 287

ancestry: census data collected on, 3, 5, **6,** 7; Chamorro, 272; Guamanian, 272; Hawaiian, 271–272; multiple, 5, **6,** 7, 272, **273**; of Pacific Islanders, **273**; and race, 5*n*; Samoan, 272

annexation: of Hawaii, 37; of Korea, 27*n*; of the Philippines, 28, 29

Arabia: as part of Asiatic Barred Zone, 30*n*

armed forces: and gender, **230**; *see also* United States armed forces

Asia, 2; immigration from, 15–16, **23–26,** 28, **29,** 31, **32, 33**

Asian American aged: potential care needs, 103–104

Asian Americans, 1, 2–3, 5, 10, 17–18, 37–38, **39, 45,** 49, 107, 108; citizenship of, 20, 46, **47,** 48; comparisons to white, black, and Hispanic Americans, 17; emigration of, **29**; fertility of, 53, 54, **55,** 56, 60, **61**; fertility projections for, 64–65; foreign-born, 43, **45, 47, 117, 119**; geographic distribution of, **110–113**; heterogeneity of, 17; home ownership by, 158, **159,** 162; immigration of, 8, **29,** 31, 120–

East Asia, 2

East India: part of Asiatic Barred Zone, 30n

Eastern Europe: immigration from, 28

economic "dependency", 96

economic security: as a route to social mobility, 12

education, 16, 283–284, 290–292, 318; achievements of Asian Americans in, 164; and adaptation of immigrants, 166–167; and age, 174, **180;** blockage from, 16; and culture, 167; emigration for, 284; and employment, 297–299; and English-speaking ability, **184;** and family, 168; and fertility, 58–59, 64; and gender, 170, 173, **174–175, 176, 177;** of household heads, 188, **190–191;** and household income, **264;** of immigrants, 319; and income, 237, 239–240, 242, 243–244, **254,** 255, 266; income for additional, 239–240, **241;** income by class of worker and, **247;** Japanese in, 201; of Koreans, 319; in Micronesia, 271; and nativity, 175; and occupational prestige, 216, 217, **219,** 224, 226–227, **229;** and period of immigration, 175, 189; return on, 233; as a route to social mobility, 11–12; in Samoa, 285; and socioeconomic status, 165; and status, 164; structural critiques of role of, 166; and success, 195; of Vietnamese, 19; whites in, 201

educational requirements: for employment, 210

elites, 32

elderly: Pacific Islanders, 277

emigration, 19, 20, 28n, **29,** 107n; for education, 284; from Korea, 271; from Philippines, 271; records kept by United States, 28n

employers: American, 193

employment, 16, 220, **221,** 222, 224; and culture, 300, 302; demographic differentials and, 194; discrimination in, 197; and education, 297–299; opportunities limited in Pacific Islands, 299; resources and, 194; *see also* underemployment, unemployment

employment-based immigrants, **36**

employment-creating immigrants, **36**

employment expectations: of Pacific Islanders, 292, 299–300

engineers: ethnic distribution of, **203**

English language ability, 182, 184, **184–185,** 185, 194, 295, 297, **297,** 317; and period of immigration, **191;** and school completion rates, **184–185**

entertainment and recreation: ethnicity of workers, **209**

ethnic groups, 3; listed separately in 1980 Census as "race" items, 5

ethnic pluralism, 12

ethnic violence: Asian Americans as targets of, 196

ethnicity, 3n, 5n; conventions and definitions for defining, 53; and sex ratios, **98**

exercise: and mortality, 87

exploitation, 197

extended family, 134, 135, 136, **148,** 149, 151; among Pacific Islanders, 308

F

family, 134, 144–145; American, 135; census definition of, 136; composition, 16, **146;** and educational achievement, 168; and employment, 305; of Pacific Islanders, 279–280, 302–303; *see also* primary family

family-based immigrants, 35, **36**

family households, 135, 147, **148,** 149, **150,** 151; children in, 149

family reunification: as preference category, 30–31

family size, **146,** 147, 197; preferences in, 56–57

family-sponsored immigrants, **36**

family workers, 197, 208, **210–211;** income of, **246**

farm labor: by Japanese immigrants, 22; immigration of, 8

farming, forests, fishery occupations: and education, **212;** ethnic distribution of workers in, 198–199, 204, 205, **206, 207;** and gender, **198–199, 230;** income of, **244–245, 253, 264;** Japanese in, 200; occupational prestige of, **214;** Pacific Islanders in, **304;** shift away from employment in, 205; *see also* agriculture

federal government workers, 208, **210–211;** Guamanians as, 303; Hawaiians as, 303; income of, 243, **246**

Federated States of Micronesia, 269; as birthplace of U.S. immigrants, **286;** com-

N

naturalization requirements for, 48*n*; of
U.S. servicemen admitted, 30
women: as administrative assistants, 205,
206; Asian American in blue-collar occupations, 233; Asian American in service occupations, 233; Asian in professional occupations, 242; in education,
201; effect of nativity on income, 237,
238; employment of, 220, **221;** as family
workers, 208, **210–211;** Filipino as professionals and managers, 199, 200; in
government employment, 208; hours of
labor, 222, 224; income by industrial
sector, 245, **248;** income by occupational
category, 242, **244–245;** income differentials, 232, 235, 242, 255, 266; income of,
235, **235;** as managers, 198, 200, 205,
206; occupational distribution of, **198–
199,** 200, **202, 208;** occupational prestige
and income, 249; occupational prestige

of, 220; as operators, assemblers, and inspectors, 200; overrepresented in service
industries, 200; in the peripheral economy, 216, **218;** private sector employment, **210–211;** public sector employment, **210–211;** self-employment, **210–
211;** underrepresented in precision production occupations, 200; unemployment, 220, **221,** 222–223; white in professional occupations, 233, 242; *see also*
gender, sex
workers per household, *see* household
workers

Y

Yapese: spoken at home, **298**
years of education, **178**
"yellow peril", 1